"From the beginning Margaret M̲ͤ Augustine, and a perh̲ writ̲ earliest feminist thinkers to enga̲ always been surprisingly charitable and po̲ of essays—on Augustine, Augustine's antec̲den̲ and several of Augustine's more prominent conceptual inheritors—deepens and nuances her view of Augustine's thought and age, revealing an even more shaded and subtle assessment than before. This collection of essays underscores Miles's gifts as an interpreter and confirms her place as one of the best and most mature thinkers in the contemporary academy engaging with Augustine's thought."

—*Charles Mathewes, University of Virginia*

"Reading Miles reading Augustine is a delight and a window on the development of modern critical theory applied to historical theology. Miles is simply brilliant and her Augustine shines with a brilliance borne of Miles's careful and close reading, important new theories, and her love of Augustine that brings the ancient theologian to life. This is a significant collection of essays that no serious historian of theology should miss."

—*Richard Valantasis, Candler School of Theology, Emory University*

"This book does what few academic books attempt—a real engagement and conversation with an ancient author, letting our thoughts and views interact with his. As Miles touches on diverse topics of interest to any modern person, others are also brought into the conversation—not just Augustine, but also Plato, Aristotle, Calvin, and Luther. Whether one wishes to discredit or to appropriate Augustine's views, one will find here much material that challenges and leads to further discussion."

—*Kim Paffenroth, Iona College*

REREADING HISTORICAL THEOLOGY

REREADING HISTORICAL THEOLOGY

Before, During,
and After Augustine

MARGARET R. MILES

CASCADE *Books* · Eugene, Oregon

REREADING HISTORICAL THEOLOGY
Before, During, and After Augustine

Cascade Books
A Division of Wipf and Stock Publishers
199 W. 8th Ave., Suite 3
Eugene, OR 97401

ISBN: 978-1-55635-216-4

Cataloging-in-Publication data:

Miles, Margaret Ruth.

Rereading historical theology : before, during, and after Augustine / Margaret R. Miles.

xviii + 308 p. ; 23 cm.

Includes bibliography

ISBN: 978-1-55635-216-4

1. Augustine, Saint, Bishop of Hippo. 2. Theology, Doctrinal—History—Early church, ca. 30–600. 3. Theology, Doctrinal—History—Middle Ages, 600–1500. 4. Theology, Doctrinal—History—Modern period, 1500–. 5. Porete, Marguerite, ca 1250–1310. 6. Eckhart, Meister, d. 1327. 7. Luther, Martin, 1483–1546. 8. Calvin, Jean, 1509–1564. I. Title.

BR65.A9 M55 2008

Manufactured in the U.S.A.

For Owen.

Contents

PART III Augustine's Successors

Acknowledgments

Chapters of this book appeared in an earlier form in various journals and books. The author and publisher gratefully acknowledge permission to reprint from these publications:

1. "'*Facie ad Faciem*': Visuality, Desire, and the Discourse of the Other" was originally published in *Journal of Religion* 87 (2007) 43–58.
3. "Happiness in Motion: Desire and Delight" was originally published in *In Pursuit of Happiness*, edited by Leroy S. Rouner, 38–56. Boston University Studies in Philosophy and Religion 16. Notre Dame: University of Notre Dame Press, 1995.
4. "Patriarchy as Political Theology: The Establishment of North African Christianity" was originally published in *Civil Religion and Political Theology*, edited by Leroy S. Rouner, 169–86. Boston University Studies in Philosophy and Religion 8. Notre Dame: University of Notre Dame Press, 1986.
5. "Roman North African Christian Spiritualities" was originally published as "North African Christianity in the Roman Period." In *African Spirituality: Forms, Meanings, and Expressions*, edited by Jacob K. Olupona, 350–71. World Spirituality 3. New York: Crossroad, 2000.
6. "The Body and Human Values in Augustine of Hippo" was originally published in *Grace, Politics, and Desire: Essays on Augustine*, edited by H. A. Meynell, 55–70. Calgary: University of Calgary Press, 1990.
7. "Infancy, Parenting, and Nourishment in Augustine's *Confessions*" was originally published in *Journal of the American Academy of Religion* 50 (1982) 349–64.

8. "Not Nameless but Unnamed: The Woman Torn from Augustine's Side" was originally publisihed in *Feminist Interpretations of Augustine,* edited by Judith Stark. Rereading the Canon. University Park: Pennsylvania State University Press, 2007.

9. "'*Jesus patibilis*': Augustine's Debate with the Manichaeans" was originally published in *Faithful Imagining: Essays in Honor of Richard R. Niebuhr,* edited by Sang Lee, Wayne Proudfoot, and Albert Blackwell. Scholars Press Homage Series 19. Atlanta: Scholars, 1995.

10. "Sex and the City (of God): Is Sex Forfeited or Fulfilled in Augustine's Resurrection of Body?" was originally published in *Journal of the American Academy of Religion* 73 (2005) 307–27.

11. "Santa Maria Maggiore's Fifth-Century Mosaics: Triumphal Christianity and the Jews" was originally published in *Harvard Theological Review* 86 (1993) 155–75.

12. "Vision: The Eye of the Body and the Eye of the Mind in Augustine's *De trinitate* and *Confessions*" was originally published in *Journal of Religion* 63 (1983) 125–42.

13. "A Sea of Love: Marguerite Porete's *A Mirror for Simple Souls*" was originally published in *Christian Century* 110, no. 4 (February 1993). ©The Christian Century, 1993. Subscriptions $49/yr. from P.O. Box 378, Mt. Morris, IL 61054. 1-800-208-4097.

14. "The Mystical Method of Meister Eckhart," was originally published in *Studia Mystica* 4, no. 4 (1981) 57–69.

15. "'The Rope Breaks When It Is Tightest': Luther on Body, Consciousness, and the Word" was originally published in *Harvard Theological Review* 77 (1984) 239–58.

16. "Theology, Anthropology, and the Human Body in Calvin's *Institutes of the Christian Religion*" was originally published in *Harvard Theological Review* 74 (1981) 303–23.

Introduction

> "All the genuine deep delight in life is in showing people
> the mudpies you have made: and life is at its best when
> we confidingly recommend our mudpies to each other's
> sympathetic consideration." (J. M. THORNBURN)

Scholars, as you may know, tend to take themselves very seriously. Yet most of us became scholars because, as children, we liked to read. Scholarship is a luxury and a privilege. For this reason I have treasured the above quotation for many years.[1] To get a quick sense of this, imagine a society that had to choose between maintaining its scholars or its garbage collectors. I believe that it is necessary—and sufficient—to be faithful to the "genuine deep delight in life." Augustine, the historical author from whom I have learned for forty years put it this way: "Delight is, as it were, the weight of the soul. For delight orders the soul. . . . Where the soul's delight is, there is its treasure."[2]

Because scholarship is a luxury and a privilege, it should be engaged in with delight and responsibility. I have admired and endeavored to imitate scholarship that can inform and enhance life, my life, and others' lives. Thus, as an historical theologian, I have wanted to understand as much as I can about how people of the past constructed religious orientations that held them in the exigencies of life and death. Present attention to diversities of race, ethnicity, gender, sexual orientation, and religion—to name only the most obvious—has prompted my interest in diversities in the communities and societies of the past. I seek a more inclusive history than the ideas, be-

---

1. The eminent twentieth-century philosopher Susanne Langer quotes this at the end of the preface of her profoundly serious book, *Philosophy in a New Key*.

2. Augustine *De musica* 6.11.29.

liefs, and institutions that have dominated Western societies. Along with, and informed by, many other scholars I search for the history of women, of slaves, and of so-called heretics—people who in fact had distinctive and rich religious sensibilities and convictions for which they were willing to suffer. I am interested in bodies and practices, in what people looked at and sang as well as the words they heard in church. What made them laugh?[3] What did they fear?

My lifelong love affair with an ancient author began when I first read Augustine in a graduate seminar at San Francisco State University. The essays in this volume were written over a twenty-six-year period in which my interest in Augustine's life and thought, and his influence in the history of Christianity, was sustained and grew. So did my questions. I was trained, in the 1970s, to read texts "in the best possible light," attentive above all to the author's intentions. Early in my teaching career, a student in my "History of Christian Thought" course at Harvard Divinity School commented that the course should be renamed "Mistakes before Augustine, Augustine, and Mistakes after Augustine." Apparently, my fascination with the richness of Augustine's beautiful Latin and the profundity of his thought *showed* much more than did my questions. As the field of historical theology changed, my interest in Augustine reflected those changes, expanding to more critical approaches. The essays in this volume reflect not only certain themes that have drawn my attention in Augustine's writings, but also the methods of reading and writing history that developed in the last quarter of the twentieth century.

Since my graduate studies, new questions proposed by critical historiographers have greatly enlivened the practice of historical study: How was an authorial voice authorized, in a particular society at a particular time? A number of new approaches contributed to making possible "thick" historical description. Social and institutional history, intellectual and political history, the history of epidemics and medicine—any or all of these, and more, might be critical to understanding an event or an historical text. Gender socialization, religious beliefs and practices . . . the list of potentially relevant approaches could go on and on. Today historical theologians are reading old texts with new eyes, at least as interested in tracing the effects of ideas and

3. In *The Great Cat Massacre and Other Episodes in French Cultural History* Robert Darnton argues that historical people's humor, frequently puzzling to historians, provides a strong sense of the cultural *differences* that make history both interesting and very challenging, revealing profound differences between historians' assumptions and those of the societies we study.

doctrines as in their authors' intentions. They also recognize the value of artworks and material evidence for reconstructions of the past.

No author is an island. The traditional model of the scholar, working alone at his desk, finally appearing (in print or at a podium) to pour his ideas and arguments over the heads of passive readers/listeners is not an adequate picture of authorship. Authors receive tools for thought (consisting of ideas, assumptions, and preoccupations) from the authors we read and from the people with whom we talk. Fortunately, few of us have friends like Socrates' conversation partners, who seem to have consistently responded, "Quite right, Socrates," to his proposals. The most valuable conversation partners are critical friends who prompt us to think with, reject, or refine the tools we receive. In turn, we pass them on, in altered form, to other readers.

This is as true of Augustine's authorship as it is of mine. His predecessors helped Augustine to recognize what is serious in human life—for example, beauty, happiness, and bodies—and his writings pointed his successors to these themes. Overwhelmed and compelled by his experience of "beauty so old and so new," Augustine carried forward both Plato's description of beauty as philosophical method[4] and Plotinus's sense of the universe as made and sustained by the "great beauty" who does not "give and pass, but gives on forever."[5]

Augustine recognized in desire an irreplaceable human treasure, an energy that can, with God's help, be liberated from fascination with ephemeral delights and aimed at the one true and secure delight. Augustine had two definitions of the source and goal of happiness. Commenting on 1 John 4:16, "God is love," he said that one needn't know anything more about God than that "God is love."[6] In *De trinitate*, he amplified: "Neither should we let this other question disturb us, how much love we ought to spend upon our brother, how much upon God. . . . We love God and our neighbor from one and the same love."[7] Augustine's second definition for God appears in *De doctrina Christiana*: "Only they can think of him without absurdity who think of him as life itself."[8] Thinking of God as life and love makes it pos-

---

4. Plato *Symposium* 210–11.

5. Plotinus *Ennead* 6.9.9.

6. Augustine *Sermo* 7.6.

7. Augustine *De trinitate* 8.8.12.

8. Augustine *De doctrina christiana* 1.8: "et quoniam omnes qui de Deo cogitant, vivum aliquid cogitant, illi soli possunt non absurda et indigna existimare de Deo, qui vitam ipsam cogitant."

sible to seek God within human experience. Indeed, Augustine sought to understand God by noticing the structure of human being, made in God's image. He undertook this exercise in *De trinitate*, finding in the human functions of knowledge, memory, and will a reflection of the triune God. He was fascinated, not only with experience of God, but also with experience that spins a person away from happiness.

In his *Confessions,* he described in detail and with vivid metaphors the construction of desire and the power of habit. He did not have the modern term "addiction," but he would have found it useful. To grasp his respect for the stability and durability of habits woven into a body by numberless repetitions *("consuetudine carnalis")*, we must dramatically strengthen the meaning of "habit." In modern usage, "habit" implies that a destructive pattern can be broken, and more fruitful behavior substituted, by an *act of will.* Nothing could be further from Augustine's idea of the *force* of habit, supported by custom. Augustine's *Confessions* is a book-length illustration of the intractability of habits, a concept much more consonant with the modern idea of "addiction," which implies helplessness in the face of a "disease." Indeed, the point of the *Confessions* is that, in his own life, Augustine found that change was possible only through God's powerful intervention. His image of God's action was dramatic. God grasped his head and gently turned it ("fovere caput").[9] He found that fundamental change is not the result of trying harder, but of letting go. "Cessavi de me paululum," he wrote, "I relaxed a little from myself."[10]

The essays in Part I of this volume seek to identify Augustine's toolbox, the preoccupations of his predecessors that focused his attention and contributed to his projects.[11] Interest in a particular topic is contagious; one catches it from someone who has it. Catching an interest works best with warm bodies in a room, but it can also result from attentive reading. Like his predecessors, Plato, Aristotle, and Plotinus, Augustine considered happiness a primary goal of human life.[12] Like them, he puzzled over the role of bodies in the elusive construction of human happiness. As a Christian, working with

---

9. Augustine *Confessiones* 7.20–21; a "distinctly maternal image" discussed by O'Connell, *Augustine's Early Theory of Man*, 66–70.

10. Augustine *Confessiones* 7.14.

11. Michel Foucault argued against the academic truism that one must understand and accept a thinker's whole agenda if one is to work with her/his ideas. Foucault offered his ideas as a toolbox, to be used as they are useful.

12. See Augustine *Confessiones* 10.20.

beliefs in creation, the Incarnation of Jesus Christ, and the resurrection of bodies, he gave the concept of happiness a complexity and richness not found in his predecessors.

Part II examines some of the features of Augustine's culture, institutional environment, and social location that interacted with his thinking. These factors are not presented as "context" for his thought, as if text and context are separate entities that subsequently "relate" to one other. Rather, texts represent one voice in a complex cultural conversation, discourse, or debate that can be understood adequately only when we do our best to reconstruct the wider conversation. Who were Augustine's "opponents?" What were they saying that prompted Augustine's rejoinders? How did different intellectual values, persuasions, and perspectives position the interlocutors? Only by exploring Roman North African society can we begin to understand the creativity and energy with which Augustine sought to accept, resist, and shape his world. Part II discusses the North African Christian values and institutions Augustine inherited, the gender assumptions of his society, his attitudes toward sex, and his debates with fellow Christians—Donatists and Manichaeans—who proposed beliefs and values alternative to those he had learned in his sojourns in Italy.

The essays in Part III visit several of Augustine's successors chosen from myriad authors who might have been included solely on the basis of my interest as I taught and wrote. Perhaps the most fundamental characteristic the authors in this section share with Augustine was the passion with which they thought and wrote about "God and the soul," Augustine's self-described consuming and exclusive interest.[13] But despite his proclamation at the beginning of his authorship that he cared about nothing but God and the soul, he narrated his conversion in book eight of the *Confessions* as a physical, as well as an emotional and intellectual, experience. Porete, Eckhart, Luther, and Calvin were similarly fascinated by the body's role in intense religious experience. In each of these successors, bodies are central to theological knowledge.

Second, the authors discussed in Part III shared Augustine's impatience with theology that specifies what must be done but does not suggest effective methods for achieving it. How are the physical senses not only metaphors for, but participants in, an experience of God? *Which* senses give the most trustworthy evidence of God's presence in the world? Augustine proposed that vision, that touches its object, played this role most adequately. Approximately two centuries before Luther insisted that the ear is "the only

13. Augustine *Soliloquiorum* 1.1: "Deum et animam scire cupio."

organ of a Christian," Eckhart placed hearing above seeing. He argued that "we shall all be blessed more . . . by our power to hear than by our power to see," for hearing is passive; hearing allows God to act.[14] In short, Augustine and his successors were preoccupied with the attempt to articulate essentially ineffable experiences of God. Augustine said that although it is impossible to talk about God with any accuracy or precision, it is better to *try* than not to try.

Claims for the "objectivity" of historical knowledge were largely abandoned in the last decades of the twentieth century. The historian's perspective inevitably permeates the story she tells, from the evidence she selects as relevant, to her interpretation of that evidence. Recognizing this, an historian can be attentive to the fact that her work reveals aspects of her perspective of which she may not have been consciously aware. History is good for self-knowledge. The exercise that has taught me this most strongly is my practice of rereading Augustine's *Confessions* every few years. It has been astonishing to me that rereading the *same text* with different experience and questions has made a *different* text pop into my eyes. Each time I've reread this admittedly fertile text, I have noticed different themes, attitudes, and allegiances. These differences, I realized, had more to do with my life experiences than with Augustine's text. A book—not just any book, perhaps, but a book similar to the *Confessions* in richness—can become a palimpsest that maps the reader's interests and stages of understanding.

The essays in this volume are arranged roughly according to the historical chronology of their themes, not according to the chronology of their writing. But the date of each essay's first publication reveals the topics I needed to explore at that particular moment in my life and career as a scholar. Like Augustine, I write in order to know what I think and, like Augustine, I found the work to be difficult and rewarding in equal parts.[15] I hope that the amazing privilege of endeavoring to understand the passionate mind of Augustine is evident in these essays.

Margaret R. Miles
Berkeley, California
March 2007

14. Eckhart, "This is another sermon," 108.

15. Augustine *Confessiones* 10.16: "For me, Lord, certainly this is hard labor, hard labor inside myself, and I have become to myself a piece of difficult ground, not to be worked over without much sweat."

PART I

Augustine *and the* Classical Tradition

CHAPTER I

Facie ad Faciem: Visuality, Desire, and the Discourse of the Other[1]

"We are what we look upon and what we desire."

(PLOTINUS *ENNEAD* 4.3.8)

Many people who have a nodding acquaintance with the Platonic tradition think that its most fundamental teaching is that of a line that divides the intelligible from the sensible worlds and establishes the inestimably greater beauty and reality of the world of ideas.[2] When the dividing line is understood as a metaphysical picture of reality, it seems to advocate that the human good lies in dissociating from, or transcending, the sensible in order to identify with the intelligible. Proof texts from Plato to Augustine and beyond can be cited in support of this interpretation. Indisputably present in the texts, it is, however, a partial and reductive understanding of a complex tradition that received its originary articulation, development, and refinement over at least a thousand-year period.

According to the Platonic account, one's approach to the intelligible is energized by desire. But desire itself is morally neutral. A bad *eros* makes idols of the self and the neighbor. But there is also a good *eros* (*concupiscentia* for the good, as Augustine put it).[3] Recently, for example, René Girard described mimetic desire as characteristic of human beings from earliest childhood. He developed the concept of mimetic desire as an explanation of the origin

1. An earlier version of this article was given as a plenary lecture at the International Colloquium on Violence and Religion in Koblenz, Germany, July 2005.

2. Plato *Republic* 6.509d.

3. Price, "Plato, Zeno, and the Object of Love," 183–84.

and ubiquity of violence. He writes: "We don't each have our own desire . . . we borrow desires . . . our neighbor is the model for our desires."[4] If the goods that my neighbor and I desire are in short supply, my efforts to possess these goods generate chaos, conflict, and ultimately, violence. Desire, Girard says, can prompt either imitation of God's "detached generosity," or Satan's covetous idolatry.

Why do we imitate others? Why, as an aspect of this mimesis, do many of us seek the wisdom of a philosophical or religious tradition? Consider the poignant human situation that underlies mimetic desire: A single human life is simply not long enough to figure out "from scratch" how to address the pressing question, How should we live? We recognize that we do not know what is generously responsible in the particular situations in which we find ourselves. We see with clarity only our own intentions. We do not *know* the good; we pursue the human good without assurances of its realization. Because of the difficulty of living in and with such ambiguity, we seek suggestions, even directives from others who have responded to this question. We find or design principles to provide us with guidance that we hope will limit the damages of our actions. Because we recognize that we all, always, must somehow act with conviction in the dark, in uncertainty, we seek reassurance that our choices will actually make the good come into being for us. But finally, whether we recognize it or not, we live by faith.

How is desire generated and stimulated? The role of physical vision in the scenario of desire is critical. In brief, in the Platonic tradition, physical vision informs and supports not one but *two* epistemologies. The epistemology for which the tradition is famous seems to begin by rejecting or transcending the sensible world of bodies and objects. But there is another, less noticed, epistemology that originates in focused attentiveness to sensible objects. In what follows I seek to demonstrate that physical vision is central to both. I trace the activity of vision in the construction of desire from Plato to Plotinus, and on to the Christian Platonist, Augustine. After sketching this thick terrain, I consider two frequently-heard criticisms of the Platonic tradition, namely, that (1) because of an intellectualist bias, bodies are absent and (2) the Other is missing. In concluding, I explore the implications of a desire that is generated and energized by perception of sensible beauty.

---

4. Girard, *I See Satan Fall Like Lightning*, 10. The concept of desire as mimetic challenges Freud's reduction of desire to sexual desire and his identification of the essence of humans as sexuality.

Plato

In Plato's *Symposium*, the male banqueters offer three accounts of the origin of desire (ἐπιθυμεῖν). First, Aristophanes describes the original human beings as round creatures composed of one of three sexes—male, female, or hermaphrodite. These creatures, having four arms and four legs, navigated by turning cartwheels, a rapid and effortless mode of travel. Their arrogance, however, prompted Zeus to split them in half. Henceforth, Aristophanes said, we seek our other half: Individuals split from an original hermaphrodite seek an opposite sex lover; women split from an original female creature seek another woman to love; men split from a male creature seek a male lover. The happiness of each is to be found, he says, in "the healing of our dissevered nature" by the consummation of love.[5]

Agathon proposes a similar, but less graphic, account of desire. Desire, he says, is generated by lack: "everything longs for what it lacks" (ἐνδεια).[6] Thus far, consensus at the banquet seems to be building that desire is founded on need, lack, poverty. But these accounts merely set the stage for Socrates' exploration of the matter. When called upon, Socrates proclaims himself unable to contribute anything at all to the "flood of eloquence" already unleashed on the assembled company, but he requests permission to ask "a few simple questions."[7] His questions, of course, quickly lead to an impasse that Socrates proposes to address by describing lessons in the nature of desire given him by Diotima, a Mantinean teacher.

Socrates' account of Diotima's teaching begins by extending and refining the earlier analyses.[8] Love's parents, Diotima says (according to Socrates), are Resource and Need, Plenty and Poverty; thus, love always includes a component of need.[9] Combining his mother's poverty and his father's wealth, Love is "at once desirous and full of wisdom, a lifelong seeker after truth." Possessed by a passion for immortality, lovers want "the beautiful to come into being for us."[10] Desire is the medium by which mortal lovers create immortality:

5. Plato *Symposium* 193c.

6. Ibid., 200a.

7. Ibid., 198b, 199c.

8. Socrates' Diotima rejects the view that "lovers are people who are looking for their other halves"; Plato *Symposium* 205e.

9. Ibid., 203b.

10. Andrea Nye's translation of γενέσθαι ἁυτω, literally, "to come to be for someone." See Nye, "Irigaray and Diotima," 200.

> This is how every mortal creature perpetuates itself. It cannot, like
> the divine, be still the same throughout eternity; it can only leave
> behind new life to fill the vacancy that is left in its species by obso-
> lescence. This . . . is how the body and everything else that is tem-
> poral partakes of the eternal; there is no other way. . . . the whole
> creation is inspired by this love, this passion for immortality.[11]

This analysis of human longing assumes and requires the fundamental consanguinity of mortality and immortality, time and eternity.[12] Immortality is
created within time. But, unlike the blessed immortals who banquet at their
ease on Mount Olympus, mortals exist in a constant state of flux. According
to Diotima's account, our deepest longing is to create immortality from the
stuff of our mortal moments, "the silken weavings of our afternoons," as the
poet Wallace Stevens wrote.[13] If this is the case, it becomes highly important
to know how this transfiguration can be facilitated, an issue to which I will
return.

But Diotima's "final revelation" focuses on a quite different analysis of
desire. Rather than build on images of desire as need, she proposes that desire
begins with a vivid, overpowering and transforming vision of beauty. In the
former accounts of desire as need-based, vision plays no role; for Diotima's
revelation, it is central. Vision is the foundation, ground, impetus, and energy of desire. Diotima tells Socrates that he must "strain every nerve" to
understand *this* analysis of desire.[14]

Beginning with "the beauties of the body," "[the lover] will fall in love
with the beauty of one body." Attentive to that beauty, she then notices that
"the beauty of each and every body is the same."[15] So she becomes "the lover
of every beautiful body." Next, she notices that "the beauties of the body are
as nothing to the beauties of the soul." "From this perception, she will be
led to contemplate the beauty of laws and institutions [and] the sciences,
[finally] turning her eyes toward the open sea of beauty," to "that wondrous
vision which is the very soul of the beauty she has toiled for so long, . . . an

11. Plato *Symposium* 208b.

12. See Manchester, "'As long as that song could be heard'."

13. Stevens, "Sunday Morning," 69.

14. Plato *Symposium* 210a. Plato's only treatise on beauty, the *Greater Hippias*, inquires
into "what is beauty itself," concluding: "the beautiful things are difficult" (304c). See also
Plato *Republic* 4.435c, 6.497d: "τα καλα . . . χαλεπά."

15. Plato says that all bodies are beautiful (*Symposium* 210b), as does Plotinus (*Ennead*
1.3.2).

eternal oneness [of which] every lovely thing partakes." Diotima reiterates the process: "Starting from individual beauties, the quest for the universal beauty must find him ever mounting . . . from bodily beauty to the beauty of institutions, from institutions to learning in general to the special lore that pertains to nothing but the beautiful itself—until at last he comes to know what beauty is."[16]

The lover is never required to renounce "lower" forms as she "mounts" toward "beauty itself." Rather, Diotima describes an ever increasing and more inclusive ability to perceive beauty, along with a widening of the benefits of perceiving objects *as* beautiful.[17] Plato's attention is on the uprights of the ladder that hold the whole together, not on valuing one rung more than another.[18] Access to beauty is not gained by turning away from beautiful objects, but on penetrating more deeply into their surface beauty. The whole route begins with "one beautiful body." And this body is never to be scorned in favor of more worthy objects of desire.

Plato emphasizes the *physical* effects of perceiving beauty through sight, "the keenest mode of perception vouchsafed us through the body." Again, I summarize:

> First there comes upon him a shuddering. . . . Next, with the passing of the shudder, a strange sweating and fever seizes him. For *by reason of the stream of beauty entering in through his eyes* there comes a warmth, and with that warmth the roots of the soul's wings are melted . . . [The soul] is feverish and is uncomfortable and itches. . . . When the soul gazes upon the beloved] she receives a flood of particles streaming therefrom.[19]

Clearly, the lover has not observed the beloved and made an aesthetic judgment. Rather, he has *perceived* the beloved *as* beautiful. The perception of beauty is informed by a concept of beauty he has *gathered* in the process that began with one beautiful body. Perception of beauty is an act with physical symptoms: it is not an intellectual judgment. Heat and desire pass through the eyes to the soul. Long before such experience was analyzed by modern physiology, Plato understood that intense visual experience registers on the

---

16. Plato *Symposium* 210a–211c.

17. Nye, "Irigaray and Diotima," 201.

18. Plato *Symposium* 211c.

19. Plato *Phaedrus* 251a–e. Emphasis added.

skin (sweating, itching), while its signification registers in modulations of heartbeat and breathing (fever, discomfort).

Plato thought of vision as a kind of touch.[20] He described the physiology of the desiring eye:

> So much of fire as would not burn, but gave a gentle light, [the gods] formed into a substance akin to the light of everyday life, and the pure fire which is within us and related thereto they made to flow through the eyes in a stream smooth and dense, compressing the whole eye and especially the center part, so that it kept out everything of a coarser nature and allowed to pass only this pure element. When the light of day surrounds the stream of vision, then like falls upon like, and they coalesce, and one body is formed by natural affinity in the line of vision, wherever the light that falls from within meets an external object. And the whole stream of vision, being similarly affected in virtue of similarity, diffuses the motions of what it touches or what touches it over the whole body, until they reach the soul, causing that perception which we call sight.[21]

In other words, Plato's theory of vision pictured a quasi-physical ray of light projecting from the eyes to *touch* its object. Vision *connects* viewer and object, establishing a two-way street on which, as the viewer gazes, the object travels back along the visual ray to imprint itself on the memory, affecting one's character. "Do you think it possible not to imitate the things to which anyone attaches himself with admiration?" Plato asked in *Republic* VI.[22] Plato's visual ray theory has long been superseded by more accurate accounts of vision yet, *as an account of the experience of vision,* it has validity. For, as philosopher Maxine Sheets-Johnstone wrote, "The natural power of optics is not strictly a visual lure; whatever attracts us visually or whatever we long to see is not purely a visual datum but something that encompasses or spills over into other sense modalities, most specifically, touch."[23]

For Plato, physical vision was the medium of both intimate and cosmic orientation. "Vision," Plato continues, "is the cause of the greatest benefit

20. Greek and Latin authors (like Achilles Tatius) extended Plato's idea of vision as touch to vision as a kind of copulation with the object, calling the act of looking "almost a *mixis* [intercourse]," and also an "συμπλοχή [embrace]"; see Goldhill, "Erotic Experience of Looking," 378–79.

21. Plato *Timaeus* 45b–46c.

22. Plato *Republic* 6.500c.

23. Sheets-Johnstone, *Roots of Power*, 28.

to us," for observation of the universe prompts research into its nature and thus gives birth to philosophy.[24] Images are the medium in which philosophy must be conducted. "I strain after images," he said.[25] Images enable thought, linking the abstract to the concrete. This is possible because, in reality, the visible and the intelligible are one, as his discussion of the perception of beauty and its effects demonstrates. In fact, the "divided line" is one of Plato's most misunderstood images. He made it clear that distinguishing sensible and intelligible into "two entities" is an arbitrary and purely *conceptual* act.

Plotinus

Plotinus did not consider himself a "Neoplatonist," but rather a faithful interpreter of Plato. He both used and modified Plato's description of the role of vision in desire. Like Plato, Plotinus noticed the physical effects of seeing beauty, namely, "wonder and a shock of delight, and longing and passion and a happy excitement," a "wild exultation" that is its most intense when a beautiful soul is revealed "in yourself or in someone else."[26]

Plotinus's only polemical treatise, *Ennead* 2.9, made explicit his admiration and esteem for sensible beauty:

> There are such beauties in things perceived by the senses that one admires their maker and believes that they come from a higher world, and *judging from them* says that the beauty there is overwhelming; one does not cling to them, but goes on from them to the beauties of the higher world, but without insulting these beauties here.[27]

What is the status of the object of vision? As everyone who has read *about* Plotinus knows, matter *opposes* Intellect. Yes, as the "opposable" thumb opposes the fingers of the hand, both thumb and fingers are necessary for effective use of the hand. That is precisely how matter opposes Intellect, as its necessary and essential colleague.[28] It is unproblematic, then, for Plotinus to say that the sensible world is an *image* (εἴκον) of the great beauty that forms and informs the universe. To see the visible world *as* icon is to apprehend its reality, to *imagine the real*.

24. Plato *Timaeus* 47b–c.
25. Plato *Republic* 6.488a: "ως γλίσχρως εικαζω."
26. Plotinus *Ennead* 1.6.4, 1.6.5.
27. Ibid., 2.9.17; emphasis added.
28. Ibid., 3.3.6.

The Plotinian terms for describing the relationship of visible to invisible have generated a great deal of misunderstanding, leading to characterizations of "Neoplatonism" as "dualistic." Translations have not helped at this point: When Plotinus says that the visible is a "reflection" of the invisible, even his best translator, A. H. Armstrong (for Loeb Classical Library), adds the word "only"—"only a reflection."[29] But Plotinus made it clear that "perfect" would more accurately modify "reflection":

> What other fairer image of the intelligible world could there be? For what other fire could be a better image of the intelligible than the fire here? Or what other earth could be better than this, after the intelligible earth? And what sphere could be more exact or more dignified or better ordered in its circuit after the self-enclosed circle there of the intelligible universe? And what other sun could there be which ranked after the intelligible sun and before this visible sun here?[30]

> [The visible world is] coherent, and clear and great and everywhere life, manifesting infinite wisdom, how should one not call it a clear and noble image of the intelligible gods? If, being an image, it is not that intelligible world, this is precisely what is natural to it; if it was the intelligible world, it would not be an image of it. But it is false to say that the image is unlike the original; for nothing has been left out which it was possible for a fine natural image to have.[31]

Of course the problem, for any philosopher who distinguishes intellectual and physical experience, is to exhibit also their interconnection. Lacking distinctions, the universe would be, in Plato's memorable phrase, a "miserable mass of unmixed messiness"—in a word, chaos.[32] Plato had several proposals for demonstrating the unity of the universe. Mathematics, he said, participates in both intellectual and sensible.[33] Moreover, as we have seen, vision crosses the divided line, producing both strong physical and mental effects. Like Plato, Plotinus distinguished only for the purpose of showing the order-

---

29. Ibid., 2.4.5.

30. Ibid., 2.9.4.

31. Ibid., 2.9.8, and also 5.8.6: "What could be more beautiful than this visible universe?"

32. Plato *Philebus* 64e.

33. Plato described mathematics as beautiful; *Greater Hippias* 303c.

liness of the universe. But his primary interest was always on seeing the one thing, the "One thing."[34] He taught that visible objects themselves, endowed with "a beauty that is not visual but becomes visible," link the intelligible and sensible worlds.[35] Beauty is the most direct and vivid evidence of the visible world's status as icon of the great beauty.

Because the concept of image (εἴκον), trace (ἴχνος), reflection, or shadow (σκιά), is so crucial to his metaphysics, Plotinus specified carefully what he meant by it. Image, as represented by paintings, he said, is not the "strict and proper sense" of "image." Paintings do not require for their existence the presence of the original; indeed, paintings are often done to remind viewers of the original in its absence.[36] But images that appear in mirrors, pools of water, or shadows *depend on the presence* of the original. When the original vanishes, so does the image. In fact, the existence of *each* depends on the other, for the original *must*, by its very nature, generate a reflection: "for it is utterly impermissible (θεμιτόν) that there should be no beautiful image of beauty and reality."[37] *This* kind of image would no longer exist "if cut off from that from which it is," for "the image has its existence in the strict and proper sense from the prior original, and comes to be from it, and it is not possible for what has come to be to exist cut off from it."[38] This description values "image" very differently than as inferior to "the real thing."

However, Plotinus's primary interest has moved from Plato's interest in the inspiring/inspiriting beauty of objects to the *perceiver's* activity in seeing the great beauty in objects in the sensible world.[39] For Plotinus, beauty is not perceived by the sluggish eye, the eye that waits passively to be caught by the enchanting object as Plato's "beautiful body" "caught the eye." Rather, the ability to see *as* beauty is the result of a strenuous and patient effort, a spiritual *discipline*. Plotinus modified the Platonic account of vision and desire:

34. "If the truest life is life by thought, and is the same thing as the truest thought, then the truest thought lives, and contemplation, and the object of contemplation at this level, is living and life, and the two together are one. . . ." *Ennead* 3.8.8. See also *Ennead* 5.9.8: "Being and Intellect are therefore one nature . . . one thing. . . . But they are thought of by us as one before the other *because they are divided by our thinking*."

35. Price, "Plato, Zeno, and the Object of Love," 184.

36. Plotinus *Ennead* 6.4.10.

37. Ibid., 5.8.12. Armstrong translates the term as "unlawful."

38. Ibid., 6.4.10; see also 5.8.12: "Every natural image exists as long as its archetype is there . . . as long as that higher reality gives its light, the rest of things can never fail; they are there as long as it is there; but it always was and will be."

39. μέγα κάλλος; see Plotinus *Ennead* 1.6.9.

How then can you see the sort of beauty a good soul has? Go back into yourself and look; and if you do not yet see yourself beautiful, then, just as someone polishing a statue which has to be beautiful cuts away here and polishes there and makes one part smooth and clears another until he has given his statue a beautiful face, so you too must cut away excess and straighten the crooked and clear the dark and make it bright and never stop working on your statue until the divine glory of virtue shines out in you, till you see your self-mastery enthroned upon its holy seat.

If you have become this, and see it, and are at home with yourself in purity, with nothing hindering you from becoming in this way one, with no inward mixture of anything else, but wholly yourself, nothing but true light . . . when you see that you have become this, then you have become sight; you can trust yourself then; you have already ascended and need no one to show you; concentrate your gaze and see. . . . This alone is the eye that sees the great beauty. . . . For one must come to the sight with a seeing power made akin and like to what is seen. No eye ever saw the sun without becoming sun-like, nor can a soul see beauty without becoming beautiful. You must first become all god-like and all beautiful if you expect to see god and beauty.[40]

In short, Plotinus asked himself: If desire is generated and directed by vision, how is desire for the *in*visible generated? And he answered: by seeing *as* beauty.[41] I return to this point.

Augustine

Augustine's account of desire builds on that of Plato and Plotinus, with some interesting and important differences. Augustine adopted Plato's theory of the visual ray that *touches* its object as a perfect model for his description

---

40. Ibid.

41. Miles, *Plotinus on Body and Beauty*, 45–46. Plotinus, in his own time as in ours, has frequently been accused of denigrating visible objects. He explained that he did so reluctantly, and only for teaching purposes: "One must therefore speak in two ways to people who are in this state of mind [utter ignorance of God] if one is going to turn them around . . . and to lead them up to what is highest, one, and first. What . . . are these two ways? One shows how contemptible are the things now honored by the soul; . . . the other teaches and reminds the soul how high its birth and value are, and this is prior to the other one and when it is clarified will also make the other obvious." *Ennead* 5.1.1 (see also 5.8.12). Plotinus says in this passage that he will develop the first method "elsewhere," but he never did. His sustained interest lay, not in denigrating body and the visible world, but in the second method, that is, displaying soul's origin and value.

of both the potential danger of desire and for his account of positive desire resulting in the vision of God. Augustine, always interested in *the way things work,* gave a detailed description of the mechanics of desire:

> The force of love is so great that the mind draws in with itself *those things upon which it has long reflected with love,* and to which it has become attached through its devoted care [*curae glutino inhaeserit*], even when it returns in some way to think of itself. And because they are bodies which it has loved outside of itself through the senses of the body, and with which it has become entangled by a kind of daily familiarity, it cannot bring them into itself as though into a country of incorporeal nature, and, therefore, it fastens together their images, which it has made out of itself, and forces them into itself. For in forming them it gives them something of its own essence. . . . But the mind errs when it binds itself to these images with a love so strong as even to regard itself as something of this kind.[42]

Like Plato and Plotinus, Augustine described two epistemologies; whether he invoked one or the other depends upon whether he exhorts readers to notice something *other* than sensible objects, or whether he seeks to specify their metaphysical value.[43] In these different contexts, a sensible object can be *either* a distraction or an indispensable starting point. Nothing about the object determines whether it will act as one or the other. Two passages, written twenty-five years apart, in *Confessions* and *The Trinity* address Augustine's method that begins with sensible objects. Refusing to take their existence as given, Augustine questions sensible objects vigorously:

> And what is this God? I asked the earth and it answered: "I am not he," and all things that are on the earth confessed the same. I asked the sea . . . the creeping things . . . the blowing breezes, the heaven, the sun, the moon, the stars. . . . And I said to all those things that

---

42. Augustine *De trinitate* 10.5–6; emphasis added.

43. Jean-Luc Marion's distinction between the idol and the icon is helpful. The idol absorbs the gaze, dazzling it and saturating it with the visible, ravishing it. "The icon, on the other hand, summons the gaze to surpass itself by never freezing on a visible, since the visible only presents itself here in view of the invisible. . . . The icon opens to the gaze, enabling sight to go back "infinitely from the visible to the invisible by the grace of the visible itself. . . . The icon opens in a face, where man's sight envisages nothing, but goes back infinitely from the visible to the invisible by the grace of the visible itself. . . . The icon opens in a face that gazes at our gazes in order to summon them to its depth." Marion, *God Without Being,* 19.

stand about the gates of my senses: "Tell me about my God. Tell me something about him." And they cried out in a loud voice: "He made us." My question was in my contemplation of them, and their answer was in their beauty.[44]

The open secret of the created universe is revealed to the one who asks the question that elicits its beauty: "He made us." For Augustine, the *significance* of the beauty of sensible objects is that they were created by the great beauty, "Beauty so ancient and so new."[45]

Similarly, in *De trinitate* Augustine seeks the "goodness of every good" by noticing the goodness of sensory objects. I summarize a long passage:

the earth, its lofty mountains, its gentle hills, its level plains, the beauteous and fertile land, the well-built house, bodies of living things, pleasant and healthful food, health, and the human face, poems, and profound thought. . . . This is good and that is good. . . . Take away "this" and "that," and look, if you can, upon good itself. Then you will see God, the goodness of every good, . . . the good Good."[46]

Augustine's method is abstraction. But the pejorative connotations of modern usage of the word "abstraction" conceal Augustine's intent. Augustine abstracted "the good Good" from the many good objects he gathered, not by jettisoning those objects, but by looking more deeply *into* them. Their surface beauty and goodness urgently invites the attentive observer to consider them "in the life," that is, in their structure, their essence, and the source of their existence.

Thus far, Augustine has elucidated and Christianized his Platonic mentors. But he did not enjoy their self-confidence about the possibility of accurate judgment. He was acutely aware of the fragility and fallibility of discernment. For, as Herbert Fingarette has remarked, "The easiest person to deceive is oneself."[47] In *The Spirit and the Letter,* Augustine analyses why self-deception is an inevitable and pervasive feature of human life:

Perfect righteousness . . . would come about if there were brought to bear the will sufficient for such an achievement; and that might be, if all the requirements . . . were known to us, *and* if they in-

---

44. Augustine *Confessiones* 10.6.

45. Ibid., 10.29.

46. Augustine *De trinitate* 8.4.3.

47. Fingarette, *Self Deception,* 2; quoting Edward Bulwer-Lytton.

spired in the soul such delight as to overcome the obstacle set by any other pleasure or pain. . . . For we are well aware that the extent of a person's knowledge is not in his own power, and that he will not follow what he knows to be worth pursuing unless he delight in it no less than it deserves his love. . . . We often go wrong in the belief that what we do is pleasing or not pleasing to God. . . . "For we see now through a glass darkly, but then face to face."[48]

Augustine invoked the scriptural text to which he referred more frequently than any other throughout his authorship, 1 Cor 13:12.[49] Two major, and fundamentally insurmountable, obstacles, he said, prevent the attainment of perfect love of God, inadequate knowledge and insufficient attraction. *In the face of these obstacles*, the best strategy is to work with the very desire that had become glued to certain objects, reorienting that desire. From the "footballs, nuts, and pet sparrows" of childish attachment and the "gold, estates, and slaves" of adult acquisitive desires, to "my weight is my love; by it I am carried wherever I am carried."[50] But how is this to be done, if we cannot choose what delights us and we do not have the knowledge we need to make accurate and realistic choices? Recall Augustine's epistemology that begins by questioning sensible objects and ends in the revelation of their beauty. Augustine valued beauty because beauty generates love, and it is love that supplies the energy and momentum necessary for seeing the great beauty, for "unless we already love him, we shall never see him."[51]

Two Critiques of the Platonic Tradition

Plato, Plotinus, and Augustine all urged that the self be intentionally constructed by imitation of "the one thing." I now consider briefly the most articulate proponents of two very widespread current criticisms of the Platonic tradition. Usually, these criticisms are based on proof texts and selective readings of Platonic authors in translation, but the two authors I consider have carefully articulated criticisms that are worth our attention. The French feminist, Luce Irigaray, criticizes Western fascination with "the one thing" and its failure to account for otherness. And the philosopher Maxine Sheets-

---

48. Augustine *De spiritu et littera* 63.

49. "Videmus nunc per speculum in aenigmate; tunc autem facie ad faciem."

50. Augustine *Confessiones* 1.19; see also 13.9: "Pondeus meum amor meus; eo feror quaecumquae feror"; and *De trinitate* 14.17.23.

51. Augustine *De trinitate* 8.6.4.

Johnstone criticizes the Western philosophical tradition's erasure of body, the result of its attention to language as "the only location of meaning."[52]

First, Irigaray: Advocacy of mimetic desire for the "one thing," she says, precludes committed attention to diversity, multiplicity, and difference—in short, to otherness. It does not foster "recognizing the other *as* an other who is different from me: neither me nor mine, nor *alter ego*, nor the same, nor like me."[53] She criticizes "monosexuate discourse," calling for attention to "the important role gender plays in defining subjectivity, rationality, [and] truth."[54] The "one thing" model, often existing at the level of unexamined assumption, she says, legislates and invokes "the neuter in an artificial and violent way."[55] Moreover, the "one thing" model assumes a closed energy system in which attention can *either* be directed to sensory objects *or* to intelligible objects. "We have decided that what we touch with our hands is never as real, good, or beautiful as what we produce with our intellect."[56] According to this model, "sublimating my sensible immediacy seems to be a condition of my authority to speak of truth."[57]

Sheets-Johnstone articulates a related concern. Speaking from a sociobiology perspective, her attention to the primacy of animate form leads to questioning language-based cultural critics. She finds intercorporeality the foundation of relationship. For example, our concept of power, she writes, arises from an "intercorporeal semantics," not from language, with its identification of an "abstract intersubjectivity."[58] "By absenting ourselves as bodies," she says, "we erase ourselves as subjects."[59] The *visible body* is the location of an "optics of power." It is "not a *tabula rasa* on which power makes its marks: the body is already inscribed and potent."[60]

In the Platonic authors we have surveyed, we noticed their descriptions of an intentional, incremental, cumulative activity of discerning a beauty that the socialized eye is unprepared to notice. *This* epistemology's starting point is bodies. Yet it must be conceded that an inevitable and irreducible ambiguity

---

52. Sheets-Johnstone, *Roots of Power*, 11.

53. Irigaray, *To Be Two*, 107.

54. Ibid., 103–4.

55. Ibid., 105.

56. Ibid., 99.

57. Ibid., 104.

58. Sheets-Johnstone, *Roots of Power*, 57.

59. Ibid., 11.

60. Ibid., 16.

remains. Bodies are the condition and the stimulus for generating desire and energizing it for pursuit of the beautiful. But they are also stepping stone, or bottom rung of the ladder, leading to the beautiful. In sum, we can respond to criticism of the intellectualist bias perceived in Platonic texts in two ways: On the one hand, closer attention can be paid to the alternative epistemology I have sketched. Having done so, however, it must be acknowledged that the Platonic tradition exhibits a fundamental and irreducible ambivalence about the status of the sensible world and the significance of its beauty.

Is it possible to discover in Platonic tradition the absent body and the missing Other? I think it is. I suggest that our inattention to the role of physical vision has distorted our interpretations of Plato, Plotinus, and Augustine. We can now, in conclusion, reprise the role of physical vision in generating and energizing a spiritual vision that recognizes and values bodies and others.

First, in the regime of the visual, self and the other configure in the same activity, the activity of looking.[61] As Sheets-Johnstone remarks: "To see is to see Others. We cannot, in fact, readily escape seeing Others; we can only readily escape acknowledging them . . . the simple act of looking has the power to . . . structure the nature and dynamics of what is a virtually inescapable intercorporeality."[62] All living bodies are beautiful, complex, coordinated collections of precision skills that together create our sense of the *person*. When we do not see the beauty of a particular body, when we miss noticing the person's *life* represented by that body, it is because we are accustomed to seeing only certain bodies as beautiful. We are also taught as children not to "stare" at anyone, that is, not to look at people attentively enough to discern their lives as revealed by their bodies.

Let us be more precise: recall Augustine's favorite verse, "We see *now* through a glass darkly, *then* however, face to face" (1 Cor 13:12). Emmanuel Levinas, has described the "face-to-face" encounter as "the primordial production of being."[63] He ignores Augustine's primary focus, the antitheses, "*nunc . . . tunc.*" In Levinas's interpretation, the verse that explained *so much* to Augustine about the frustrations and imperfections of present experience becomes simply a description of a moment in which my recognition of the specific and particular beauty of a face simultaneously illuminates my under-

---

61. This is Simon Goldhill's phrase; see his "Erotic Experience of Looking," 394.

62. Sheets-Johnstone, *Roots of Power*, 32.

63. Levinas, *Totality and Infinity*, 305.

standing of myself and of the person I see. The face is "the way in which the other presents himself, exceeding *the idea of the other in me*, . . . an encounter of unique beings that represents both separation and proximity; it is a breach of totality in which "thought finds itself faced with an other refractory to categories."[64]

The ancient theory of the visual ray explained to its adherents why vision generates desire for physical objects. Vision touches its object, which then moves back along the visual ray, stamping its imprint on the psyche. But if physical vision informs and directs desire for visible objects, how is desire for the *invisible* Good, the One, or God generated? It is at this point that the Platonic tradition became ambivalent. Physical vision is problematic when it stops short at the surface of objects, making them idols. Yet physical vision is still the key. For *to perceive the beauty of people and objects is to discern* Plotinus's "great beauty," Augustine's "beauty so old and so new." The great informing beauty gives *significance* to beautiful objects.[65] The "opposing" entities of sensible and intelligible generate a cyclical oscillation in which each energizes and escalates the other. Spiritual vision relies on physical vision: The traces, images, and shadows of the great beauty in the visible world are the *first clues,* the necessary information, prompting the lover of beauty to practice the spiritual discipline of seeing *as beauty.* Moreover, Augustine claimed that the accurate "seeing" of physical objects irreducibly involves the exercise of spiritual vision; to see accurately is to see lovingly, to participate in the very substance of the God-who-is-love.

Furthermore, desire based on the perception of beauty suggests a different mimesis. Specifically, the role of "the other" is altered. Beauty is not scarce; thus, desire instigated by beauty is neither competitive nor conflictual. Rather, mutual others encourage, model, and urge each other on to ever more expansive and inclusive perceptions of beauty. The other is not an opponent, but a friend who helps me to notice beauty that my experience and visual habits had not prepared me to see.[66]

I have directed attention to a feature of the Platonic tradition that has received much less sustained attention than Platonism's celebrated emphasis on "transcending" bodies, with all their terrifying instability. Transcendence,

64. Ibid., 40.

65. Augustine wrote in *De doctrina christiana* 1.22, "Whatever else appeals to the mind as being lovable should be directed into that channel into which the whole torrent of love flows."

66. Plato *Symposium* 209c.

useful as it is in painful situations, is dangerous as a daily habit. Beyond the goal of a more accurate representation of Platonic tradition, my interpretation has practical implications. It is impossible to state with precision to what extent the influence of assumptions about, and interpretations of, Platonic tradition have perpetuated detachment from the world's problems. It is likely, however, that despite loud academic protests against "Platonic dualism," some influence can be hypothesized. Thus it is important to examine and correct reductive interpretations. "What we misapprehend, we cannot use," Thomas Traherne said in the seventeenth century.

Recognizing the role of physical vision in *both* Platonic epistemologies challenges spiritualities that encourage escape from the twenty-first-century world's pressing problems of hunger, injustice in its myriad forms, and ecological disaster. When the capacity to *see as beauty* is understood to be fundamental to spiritual vision, enjoyment of the created world can energize work to preserve and sustain it. Platonic tradition's articulation and emphasis on enjoyment of beauty can correct an escapist transcendence. For, within this tradition, it is precisely the beauty of bodied others that makes pop into the eye what Augustine called the "beauty of all things beautiful."[67]

---

67. Augustine *Confessiones* 3.6: "puchritudo pulchrorum omnium."

CHAPTER 2

Who Are We *Really*?
A Platonist's Contribution to Christianity

The core of any religion is its teaching on human being. The third-century philosopher Plotinus proposed a distinctive answer to my title's question. Through the Platonist Christian, Augustine, Plotinus's answer had a long and rich history within Christianity. Plotinus was a wonderfully quirky philosopher. This essay has two foci: First, I explore an ancient philosopher as an historian, rather than as a philosopher, placing Plotinus's philosophy in the context of several of the most prominent features of his historical situation.[1] The second focus requires more explanation. Through the Platonist Christian, St. Augustine, Plotinus's mystical philosophy was Christianized; it influenced a long line of Christian philosophers and theologians. What does it mean to say that an author is "influential?" The usual meaning is that we can find traces of his thought in later authors. But we seldom consider that, in fact, "influence" also moves backwards, as later authors reinterpret an earlier author according to the later author's perspectives and predilections. As Western Christians, we understand Plotinus through Augustine's eyes, even though there are dramatic differences between them. It seems, then, a useful exercise to endeavor to consider Plotinus's philosophy for itself, subsequently comparing Plotinus's thought with Augustine's adoption and adaptation.

Ironically, after Augustine (and with some notable exceptions), Plotinus became the villain of Christian authors. He was—and is today—blamed for such theological villains as dualism, hatred of bodies, and disdain for the natural world. Curiously, his thought has been simultaneously absorbed into Christian philosophy and accused of subverting Christianity's incarnational message. In short, Plotinus is frequently used as a foil for Christians' religious or philosophical positions. Plotinus did not found a church or a religion, so he left no followers to insist that his thought be carefully and accurately interpreted. That is what I will try to do in this essay. Finally, I will also sug-

---

1. This essay is based on my book, *Plotinus on Body and Beauty*.

gest that Plotinus's thought can be directly useful and usable for twenty-first century people.

Here is the problematic: Contemporary philosophers who interpret historical philosophers tend to ignore the historical circumstances in which they wrote or spoke. Historians, on the other hand, tend to focus on the uniqueness of the historical situations they study, uninterested in commonalities across societies. "Universal" ideas are presently in disrepute; historians seek the particular, and rightly so, since the particular has too often been ignored. Thus, historians are usually very reluctant to draw any suggestions for the present from ancient authors.

Yet there *are* some perennial human questions, questions that cross the artificial boundaries erected by the academic disciplines between philosophy and religion. There are questions that every person must answer, if not by creating a comprehensive philosophical system, at least in actions and lifestyle. Such as: How should we live? How shall we find a satisfactory orientation to a bewildering and dazzling universe? How can we create a lifestyle that effectively embodies that orientation? There are also more personal questions: How can I accept this constantly changing and vulnerable body and adjust gracefully to its needs and capacities? Why do human beings suffer and die? The questions seem to be timeless, even though the answers are not. For many people who do not find religious answers to these questions persuasive, a third-century philosopher who thought about them intentionally and rigorously has some suggestions worth considering. Plotinus, who lived in the middle of the third century (d. 270 C.E.), provides a generous and inclusive worldview without invoking supernatural explanations.

It is sometimes assumed that philosophy is relevant because it is timeless. But if one studies a philosopher in the concrete social and personal circumstances in which he wrote it becomes clear that he intended to speak quite directly and pointedly to his own time, to his own conversation partners, and not to some impossible-to-imagine distant time. But an ancient philosophy can be useful precisely because it is not abstract—"timeless." It can be useful *because* it emerged from particular conversations with critical friends in a particular society, and responded to particular conditions. To understand a philosopher's proposals "in the life," then, we need to know something about those conditions. Only then can we consider his proposals within our own very particular lives and society.

Plotinus was, according to reports, one of the most eccentric and thoughtful people of his—or perhaps any—time. His student, friend, and biographer, Porphyry, gives a wonderfully odd, impressionistic, and personal account of his teacher. I summarize Porphyry's report. Plotinus was born in Lycopolis, Egypt:

- he nursed at the breast until he was eight years old and someone teased him about it, whereupon he gave up his nurse's breast;

- he came to Rome to teach when he was forty years old; when he was fifty he began his only written work, the *Enneads*;

- he never bathed, but had himself massaged every day at home;

- he had a disease of the bowels, but would not submit to enemas, saying (in effect) that enemas were beneath his dignity;

- he would not sit for a portrait painter, so his friends smuggled a famous portrait painter into the school to observe him as he taught and to paint his portrait later;

- he had poor eyesight, so he did not review or revise his manuscripts;

- he practiced vegetarianism;

- he rejected astrology;

- he had both male and female students and taught several physicians, senators, and a rhetorician who later became a philosopher;

- he was able to reverse magical attacks against him;

- he took orphaned children into his home, taught them, and took care of whatever resources they had until they came of age; and

- he died in 270 C.E. at the age of 66 of a disease so obnoxious that toward the end his friends, to a man, abandoned him.

According to Porphyry, Plotinus was a marvelous teacher. Porphyry writes:

> There was always a charm about his appearance, but [when he was teaching] he was still more attractive to look at: he sweated gently, and kindliness shone out from him, and in answering questions he made clear both his benevolence to the questioner and his intellectual vigor. (*Life* 13)[2]

---

2. Unless otherwise noted, translations are from A. H. Armstrong. See Plotinus, *Enneads*. Porphyry's *Life of Plotinus* is included in volume 1 of this Loeb Classical Library edition of the works of Plotinus.

Moreover, anyone would envy Plotinus's remarkable ability to concentrate; he was able, Porphyry reported, "to be present at once to himself and to others."

> Even if he was talking to someone, engaged in continuous conversation, he kept to his train of thought. He could take his necessary part in the conversation to the full, and at the same time keep his mind fixed without a break on what he was considering. When the person he had been talking to was gone. . .he went straight on with what he had been thinking, keeping the connection, just as if there had been no interval of conversation between. (*Life* 8)

Despite these observations of his beloved teacher, Porphyry's interpretation of Plotinus's philosophy cannot be accepted without question, especially at points at which Porphyry's own much more dualistic philosophy conflicts with Plotinus's. For example, one of the most often-quoted lines in Porphyry's *Life* claims that Plotinus was "ashamed of being in a body." But this statement directly contradicts Plotinus's own discussion of embodied life. Before considering his thoughts about bodies, however, it is necessary to sketch Plotinus's worldview.

Beauty

Plotinus taught that no one can understand the world who has not been startled and instructed by its beauty. Beauty's message, he said, is the unity of life, gift of the impersonal source he called the "great beauty." A person can recognize beauty by her kinship with it, for her life is one with universal life. Recognizing beauty is a transformative experience. Augustine was especially attracted to this Plotinian idea. He wrote:

> Late have I loved thee, Beauty so old and so new; late have I loved thee! And look, you were within me and I was outside, and there I sought you and in my ugliness I plunged into the beauties that you have made. You were with me and I was not with you. . . . You called, you cried out, you shattered my deafness: you flashed, you shone, you scattered my blindness; you breathed perfume, and I drew in my breath and I pant for you: I tasted, and I am hungry and thirsty: you touched me and I burned for your peace. (*Confessiones* 10.27)

Yet even here, in the midst of a very Plotinian ecstasy, Augustine "adjusts" Plotinus. Augustine's personal God, who addresses him intimately and forcefully *through his senses,* has no parallel in Plotinus. As Philip Cary has recently shown, Augustine learned to cultivate an *interior* life, a subjectivity, from Plotinus.[3] But, seeking reality, Augustine went *in* and then *up,* while Plotinus, as we will see, pictured a direct connection from his own center to all living beings and to the impersonal center of the universe. Plotinus, writing about beauty, said:

> There must be those who see this beauty. . .and when they see it they must be delighted and overwhelmed and excited. . . . These experiences must occur whenever there is contact with any sort of beautiful thing, wonder, and a shock of delight and longing and passion and a happy excitement . . . you feel like this when you see, in yourself or in someone else, greatness of soul, a righteous life, a pure morality, courage . . . he who sees them cannot say anything except that they are what really exists. What does "really exist" mean? That they exist as beauties. (*Ennead* 1.6.4)

Yet beauty was not, for Plotinus, what we might think of as an aesthetic category. To notice beauty is not to make a judgment about a quality of a particular object. Rather, to perceive beauty is to see an object *in its life,* that is, to grasp the interconnections that give it existence. Plotinus said that those who do not see this beauty are clueless. But no one is born with a natural capacity for perceiving beauty; it is not inherited in the genes, or automatically acquired in the process of socialization. The perception of beauty is not even what we might think of as a gratuitous mystical experience. Rather, it can and must, be trained by the practice of contemplation, a practice that Plotinus describes in some detail. In short, what you (can) see is what you get—either broken shards, scattered randomly, or the unity of "richly varied" (his term) life.

Plotinus described an intricate and complex universe in which life circulates from a source he usually called "the One." The name doesn't matter though, because it doesn't define but only points to an impersonal energy that Plotinus also called the great beauty, the Father, the self-sufficient, the good, or even on occasion, God. He alternated between impersonal and personal terms for the source of life, but he insisted that the One has no attributes and no intentions. *Life* is the fundamental element of the universe, intimately

3. Cary, *Augustine's Invention of the Inner Self,* chapter 5.

connecting all who share it. And he thought of "life" very inclusively; even rocks and soil have life. Rocks, he said, if left in their native soil, grow, but very slowly so that their growth cannot be measured in a human lifetime.

In the context of this conceptual scheme, Plotinus made some practical suggestions. His proposals respond to the following questions in a direct and still usable way: How can we think of our bodies most fruitfully? Is it more accurate and fruitful to think of one's body as friend, as enemy, or simply as tool or instrument? Or do we inevitably think of body differently at different times and in the midst of different experiences?[4] Does suffering have any meaning? Why should we take responsibility for the care of the earth and its living beings? Bodies are central to each question.

Ordinarily, philosophers do not work on a concept until the lack of an adequate conceptualization becomes a problem. Several factors provoked Plotinus to give serious philosophical consideration to body: he had friends who died in the plague of the mid-third-century, and he himself suffered from painful and distressing diseases. The colosseum culture of his society in which bodies were spectacles also motivated his thought. And he had heated conversations with other philosophers who disagreed with him about the value of bodies.

Like Plotinus, twenty-first century Americans have urgent interests in body. We are concerned about what we can do to live long and disease-free lives. We, as a society, are also concerned—perhaps more than any previous society—about whether we "look good." These interests can be easily demonstrated by statistics on cosmetic surgery, exercise, eating disorders, addictions, disease, diet, and exercise, to name only a few of our society's epidemic obsessions. Threatened ecological resources also concern many North Americans, and should concern all.

Unlike modern philosophers who largely neglect body, Plotinus treated body as a subject that deserved sustained reflection, focusing on it in several treatises. It is not an exaggeration to say that he was preoccupied with body. He was especially struck by the simultaneous fragility and preciousness of body.

---

4. Please notice that I do not refer to "the body," because the phrase implies a generic human body that no one has ever seen or touched. "Bodyness," the condition of being body is a universal human trait, but bodies are always gendered. They are also young or old; they have a social location, race, and ethnicity; they are healthy or ill, along with many other factors that loudly and intimately affect the experience of body. In short, "the body" does not exist. But bodies do.

Body as Spectacle

Plotinus's society, like our own, featured entertainment in which bodies were publicly torn, mauled by wild beasts, sliced, stabbed, and killed. In Roman society, however, the sights, sounds, and smells of the colosseum were real, not simulated screen violence. In the mid-third century while Plotinus was teaching in Rome, one of the largest spectacles of the Roman world took place—the thousandth anniversary of the founding of Rome. We cannot know if Plotinus attended these so-called "games," but he could not have been unaware of them any more than a twenty-first century person can be unaware of movies and television.

The Roman empire was the first entertainment culture, the first society to use entertainment to stimulate, reward, and pacify. The shows were free, and the Roman colosseum, built in the first century C.E., seated fifty thousand people, evidence that the gladiatorial and animal shows were indeed popular events. A mid-third century calendar reserves 176 days of the year for spectacles, of which ten were specifically for gladiatorial and wild beast shows.[5]

In her book *Blood in the Arena*, Alison Futrell emphasizes the centrality of Roman entertainment to the political agenda of the empire.[6] Emperors displayed power and gained popularity through lavish spending on shows featuring hundreds of gladiators, rare and exotic animals, and inventive stage sets. In the morning of a commemoration of an emperor's birthday, for example, wild beast "hunts" occurred, involving the slaughter of animals brought from all parts of the empire at tremendous expense. At noon, most spectators took a lunch break while criminals and prisoners were unceremoniously executed. In the afternoon, gladiators fought, often to death. Latin literature occasionally indicates that colosseum crowds empathized with wounded animals, but it is never mentioned that they experienced a similar sympathy with suffering humans.

Why did Roman crowds enjoy these bloody spectacles? Historians offer several possible reasons: the crowd context minimized individual feelings of responsibility for victims' suffering; the class stratifications of Roman society identified "humanity" with the upper classes, while people of the lower

---

5. Wiedemann, *Emperors and Gladiators*, 12.

6. Futrell, *Blood in the Arena*, 10: "The amphitheater must be viewed in association with Roman Imperialism as a conscious means of persuasion of the legitimacy, supremacy, and potential for violence of the Roman State."

classes were considered worthless, their bodies fair game for violent spectacle. But perhaps most importantly, the murderous games of the colosseum were thought of as sports.[7] Their violence was not the point. The point was the gladiators' skill, style, and his mastery of himself and his body. According to historian J. P. Toner, a colosseum crowd was "not a bloodthirsty mob but the most urbane sophisticates in the world."[8] They recognized, appreciated, and rewarded courage and skill, not merely brute strength.

Gladiators were simultaneously considered subhuman and admired, even idolized. They were the rock stars of late antiquity. Gladiators' pictures were painted on posters and buildings; murals and mosaics—-some of very high quality—also depicted gladiators and exotic animals on the walls of wealthy Roman homes. Pliny, a first-century Roman, said that "the portraiture of gladiators has been the highest interest in art for many generations now."[9]

American society exhibits some interesting parallels. Our society, like that of ancient Rome, depends on its entertainment media. Spectator sports are a huge part of our entertainment. But the state no longer sponsors free events; citizens support them at the expense of billions of dollars annually. Sports heroes appear on our billboards, newspapers, and magazines; their faces are at least as familiar to us as Roman gladiators' faces were to Romans. For North Americans also, bodies are spectacle.

Philosophical Opponents

Plotinus's second stimulus for working on ideas of body related to an important religious and philosophical school of the Roman Empire that thought of bodies as biodegradable and worthless. Plotinus wrote his only polemical tract against "Gnostics," or knowers, who believed that the world of the senses is the evil creation of an evil demiurge. They pictured a world in which the souls of all living beings were painfully trapped in bodies, but could be redeemed through knowledge of their true home in the kingdom of light, and through ritual and ascetic practices. Scornful of bodies and claiming to be eager to be disencumbered of them, Gnostics cited the pesky and painful things in the world—mosquitos, snakes, mice, and disease—as evidence for their belief that the world is a hostile environment for living beings. Plotinus

---

7. Hopkins, "Murderous Games."

8. Toner, *Leisure and Ancient Rome*, 39.

9. Quoted by Toner, *Leisure*, 45.

disagreed; he used the strongest language of his entire *corpus* in arguing against Gnostics.

Against Gnostics' denigration of bodies Plotinus argued that as long as we do not expect bodies to be flawless and permanent, they are *wonderful*. He condensed his argument into a parable: Gnostics' hatred of body, he said, is

> like two people living in the same fine house, one of whom reviles the structure and the builder, but stays there none the less, while the other does not revile, but says the builder has built it with the utmost skill, and waits for the time to come in which he will go away, when he will not need a house any longer: the first might think he was wiser and readier to depart because he knows how to say that the walls are built of soulless stones and timber and are far inferior to the true dwelling place. . . . While we have bodies we must stay in our houses, which have been built for us by a good sister soul which has great power to work without any toil or trouble. (*Ennead* 2.9.17)

Body and Self

But perennially it is not philosophical ideas but one's own body that supplies the strongest incentive for thinking about bodies. The knowledge that one must die is the most evident of pressures. Centuries after Plotinus lived, Samuel Johnson remarked that "nothing concentrates the mind like knowing one is going to be hanged in a fortnight." Constant vulnerability to disease and accident, especially in a time before antibiotics and anesthetics, also prompted serious thought about bodies. In Plotinus's time (the mid-third century), a severe and exceedingly contagious plague, probably bubonic plague, came to the Roman world. The ancient historian Dio Cassius reported 2,000 deaths a day in Rome alone (figures that are not, of course, entirely trustworthy, but that do indicate that contemporaries experienced the deaths as catastrophic). Although Plotinus did not catch the plague, he lost friends to it as I have mentioned. His own diseases gave him ample reason to think about body.

Yet Plotinus's philosophical statements about bodies have confused generations of scholars. In the context of addressing different audiences and interests he talked about body differently, sometimes praising bodies—human, animal, plant, and celestial bodies, the stars—as perfectly and beautifully *what they are*. Sometimes, however, in the context of urging his students to pay attention to the cultivation of their souls, he spoke quite disparagingly of bodies and the world of the senses. And in his last treatises, suffering from the disease he would die from, he understandably thought of death—release from body—as a great good.

If one expects a philosophy to be systematic, then such contradictory statements are confusing. But when the subject is as variable as bodies, statements that seem wildly dissimilar may accurately match the inconsistency of their subject. Bodies are the source of both the greatest pleasure and the greatest pains of human life. When we dance, lie in the sun, or listen to music, we are immensely grateful for our bodies. In the hospital with an undiagnosed and painful disease, during dental surgery, or struggling to walk on crutches—in these (and similar) circumstances we might be inclined to feel that body is not an unmitigated boon.

We can probably agree that bodies have limitations; they are continuously vulnerable, and they eventually and inevitably die. Plotinus instructed his students not to make the mistake of identifying self with body. Contemplative exercises demonstrate, he said, that there is more to human beings than body. To be sure, soul's first duty is animation of, and care for, body. But in contemplation, Plotinus said, we can "lift ourselves up by the part that is not submerged in body and by this join ourselves at our own centers to something like the center of all things" (*Ennead* 6.9.8).

Since it is through soul that life is given, and life is one, Plotinus taught that "if my soul and your soul come from the soul of the All, and that soul is one, these souls must also be one, allowing us to feel one another's feelings."

> We do share each other's experiences when we suffer with others from seeing their pain and feel happy and relaxed [with others] and are naturally drawn to love them: for without a sharing of experience there could not be love. (*Ennead* 4.9.3)

Contemplation also reveals the bond between living beings. Although bodies are separate, Plotinus believed that all human beings share the same soul. This is shown by the fact that we cannot feel one another's physical pain as we *can* (with generosity) feel one another's emotional pain. Strengthening one's identity with soul, the bearer of life, results in intensified identification with universal life. The good news and the bad news about body—its goodness *and* its limitations—supplies the basis for Plotinus's teachings on suffering and his sense of responsibility for all living beings.

Suffering

If anything is universal, it is suffering; in the words of a Bob Dylan song, "I know you've suffered much, but in this you are not so unique." Moreover, we can't see why one person suffers and another seems to enjoy a carefree life. We try to explain this to ourselves: Does an all-seeing deity know what each person can bear and assign just that precise amount of suffering? Or shall we blame the victim, hypothesizing that the suffering person has done something that "asks for" her suffering? Plotinus's answer is that pain is inevitable in a universe in which living beings struggle to grip and hold life. Both joys and pains circulate without plan or design. And each person, gracefully or gracelessly (the choice is ours), inherits pain and death when life goes on to other bodies, other forms. As Plato, Plotinus's mentor, said, why should it be surprising that mortals die?

Some of the circumstances we might assign to fate or providence, however, are actually the result of choices we make. In fact, even when chance intervenes in a person's life—people "must fall sick if they have bodies," Plotinus said that the choice of how one will confront the circumstance still exists. Human life supplies a rich and complex mixture of choice and chance. Through laziness one can think of oneself as constantly at the mercy of whatever happens. Or, on every occasion, one can exercise maximal choice within the parameters of chance situations. Human freedom consists of choosing how one will respond and act. We can accept the universe's exuberant provisions and create, with this haphazard mixture of benefit and suffering, a good life. By contrast, Plotinus said, "in the bad, life limps" (*Ennead* 1.7.3).

Is it possible to align ourselves with the universe's gifts in a way that maximizes benefit and minimizes pain? Yes, to some extent, Plotinus said. He gave an example:

> [It is] as if when a great company of dancers was moving in order a tortoise was caught in the middle of its advance and trampled because it was not able to get out of the way of the ordered movement of the dancers: yet if it had ranged itself with that movement, even it would have taken no harm from them. (*Ennead* 2.9.7)

Even though we can dance for awhile, eventually, inevitably, life will lift off from a used-up body and go on to animate other forms. When a person dies, the life she had is not destroyed; "it is simply no longer *there*" (*Ennead* 4.5.7). Plotinus's account of suffering and death differs greatly from Christian interpretations. It can readily be seen that in the rushing circulation of life through living bodies of all sorts he described, there is little room for last judgments and eternal destinies for individuals.

Plotinus insisted that there *is* providential care. But it is addressed to the *whole* universe, not to individuals; "the universe lies in safety" (*Ennead* 3.4.4; 6.4.5). Individuals are parts of the whole. This means that a person can enjoy the safety of the universe only if s/he accepts utterly and to the core, even while she is enjoying its gifts, that these gifts, including the gift of life, will sooner or later pass on to other forms of life. But, Plotinus said, isn't this what there *is*? So why not acknowledge and accept it? Why all this special pleading, why all this me, me, me? Why not recognize that I am not singled out for special treatment no matter what I believe or how virtuously I act, or—for that matter—how carefully I eat or exercise. If we understand the nature of the universe we will enjoy and/or bear what is provided uncomplainingly. We should not take personally a very broad range of the things that occur, for "the life of the universe does not serve the purposes of each individual but of the whole" (*Ennead* 4.4.39; 45; 3). To the whining query, Why me, Lord?, Plotinus responded, Why not me? Why should I not have a share in the pains that circulate among living beings? If my choices have not determined my sufferings, I suffer by chance. But even then, I can choose how to respond to whatever happens. The "provision" is ambiguous—evil and good, pain and gift. One can, however, cultivate a perspective from which the universe is seen as dazzling and trustworthy beauty, as "perfect safety."

Plotinus advocated prayer, but Plotinian prayer is not petition but contemplation that redirects a person's attention from personal concerns toward the whole. Plotinus gives instructions in the practice of contemplation by which a person *imagines the real,* the whole that we seldom recognize due to our fascination with our own bit part.

Community of Living Beings

No third-century person could have predicted twenty-first century concern over polluted air and water, endangered species, vanishing rain forests, and a threatened ozone layer. On this topic, Plotinus's suggestions did not respond to a perceived threat, but resulted from his vision of the universe as an intimately interconnected whole. Until the second half of the twentieth century, it was impossible to identify and map with scientific precision the effects living beings have on one another even across long distances. Plotinus's description of an interdependent web of living beings was intuited rather than demonstrated.

Throughout the history of western philosophy there have been authors with similar intuitions, but they have been labeled romantic, "soft," or nature worshippers by "hard-headed" philosophers. Presently, however, scientists can measure and prove the tangible effects of environmental crises such as the disappearance of rain forests, extinction of animal species, and pollution of air, water, and food. This information is no longer intuited or romantic, but concrete and well-documented, a fact of life in the twenty-first century. Plotinus said it first:

> The All is a single living being which encompasses all the living beings within it. . . . This one universe is all bound together in shared experience and is like one living creature, and that which is far is really near. . . . And since it is one living thing and all belongs to a unity nothing is so distant in space that it is not close enough to the one living thing to share experience. (*Ennead* 4.4.32)

This worldview, once Plotinus's mystical vision, now has obvious implications for practices that damage the natural world and kill people. Plotinus's worldview can inspire action based on the awareness that the community of human responsibility is not limited to humans, but extends to all living beings. In her novel, *China Men*, Maxine Hong Kingston put it this way: "Men build bridges and streets when there is already an amazing gold electric ring connecting every living being as surely as if we held hands, flippers, and paws, feelers and wings."[10]

I suggest that Augustine's direction of attention—*in, then up*, as Cary puts it—has contributed to the present ecological crisis. Plotinus's teaching that there is a direct connection from one's own center to all other living beings—to life itself—seems to allow more attention, concern, and care for the beings with whom we share the world. Of course, more robust Christian doctrines of creation, incarnation, and the resurrection of body could achieve a similar incentive to care for the life that populates "our island home." Why haven't these doctrines, presumably so central to Christian faith, *not* been more fully developed, emphasized, and advocated? I think we must acknowledge that Augustine's finger, insistently pointing in, then *up*, has been *one* of the encouragements to Western Christians to neglect the needy world.

10. Kingston, *China Men*, 92.

Augustine's model of spirituality, withdrawal and centering, should not be the only model for exercising a spirituality attentive to the world's needs. Plotinus's idea of our *connection* to the center of the universe and all living beings through a shared life can found a model that features concern and action on behalf of our interdependent world.

Who Are We Really?

Body's exigencies concentrate the mind, making time real and creating a longing to "have it all now." For although life itself is trustworthy, utterly safe, the particular configuration that comes into focus as *my* life will eventually lose focus and slide into the ocean of life. I do not have the luxury of banqueting at ease on Olympus with the "blessed immortals." To wish, to imagine, or to act as if one does, Plotinus said, to be shocked when confronted by old age or death—whichever comes first—is to miss the greatest opportunity we have, the opportunity of realizing our connection to the all, of training ourselves through contemplation to see the great beauty, the beauty of the whole circulation of life. Plotinus described an ethic in which the perception of beauty—the beauty of the connectedness of the All—funds responsibility for the well-being of all living beings.

Who are we really? A human being, Plotinus said, is double; on the one hand, we are what you see. Bodies-R-us. Bodies capture and contain the life circulated by the One source of all life, but bodies are not all of what it means to be "us." We also exist simultaneously "there," at the heart of the universe. And this is most essentially who we are. In our self-imposed isolation, senses fatigue, boredom dulls vision; we constantly long for some wonderful new stimulus to freshen our lives. We fall in love; we seek entertainment; we forget to look at one another, and above all we forget ourselves—our real selves and the amazing glory of the life we share with the company of living beings. Plotinus urged his readers to do the daily, disciplined and rewarding work of remembering who we are.

CHAPTER 3

Happiness in Motion: Desire and Delight

"Delight orders the soul; where the soul's delight is, there is its treasure."
(AUGUSTINE *DE MUSICA* 6.11.29)

Plato, Aristotle, Plotinus, and Augustine had ideas of human happiness that have influenced Western philosophy and theology to our own time, ideas that inform our concepts of happiness and the human good. I will first describe Plato's, Aristotle's, and Plotinus's distinctive proposals about the nature of human happiness and how it is to be achieved. I will then examine Augustine's revisions of the classical ideas he inherited. Throughout I will highlight one of the issues most central to discussions of happiness, namely the role of the body and sensuous life in happiness. Can "real" happiness be achieved and maintained, as some have suggested, only by excluding the vulnerability necessarily entailed in enjoyment of sense, sexuality, and relationship? Or are these familiar joys so integral that they must be a part of any happy life? Anyone asked to reflect on happiness can be expected to have a rather personal interest in the topic. And I do, so it would be an evasion of the assignment if I did not endeavor to construct for you my own idea of happiness and to analyze its constituent supports. The last part of my essay will do this, not because I suppose that I can think about the issue more clearly and competently than the giants of the past, but because, although I am heavily indebted to their thought, I am differently positioned in human history. For myriad reasons, my proposal of what constitutes happiness will necessarily be somewhat different from theirs, even though owing a great deal to their proposals.

I

For the Greeks, the happy, deeply satisfying life is the good life. Agreeing on that, they diverged in identifying its components, its requirements, and its characteristic activity. Recently Martha Nussbaum's intriguing book, *The Fragility of Goodness*, has discussed Greek philosophers' "central preoccupation" with the human good. Underlying and motivating this preoccupation, she writes, was "a raw sense of the passivity of human beings and their humanity in a world of nature, [together with] a response of both horror and anger at that passivity."[1] Human life needs redemption from this vulnerability to luck (*tyche*) or fate, to "what just *happens* to a person, as opposed to what [a person] does or makes." In the face of terrifying vulnerability, Nussbaum writes, Greek thinkers held the belief that reason's activity could make one safe, and thereby save the person "from living at the mercy of luck."[2]

For example, Plato's resolution of the Greek problem was to posit the possibility of a "self-sufficient and purely rational" human life.[3] The classical example of such a life of developed and concentrated rationality was that a person ought to be perfectly happy while being roasted alive in that ancient instrument of the cruelest torture, the bull of Phalaris. In the person with fully developed rationality, no amount of pain, loss, or terror could damage one's equanimity or loosen one's grip on a rational process that remained untouched by the inevitable incursions of fate. In short, Plato's solution to the problem of human vulnerability was transcendence based on a thoroughgoing recognition and acceptance of the limitations of physical life in the world of nature, and on self-identification with immortal Reason.

Thus far, however, we have gotten no further than our received picture of Plato's "disdain for the body." There is, however, more complexity to Plato's thought than this. He was not unaware that identification with rationality did rather neglect some of what Nussbaum calls our most "familiar and prized activities and allegiances," those organized by "our bodily and sensuous nature, our passions, our sexuality." And, of course, all of these are "powerful links to the world of risk [instability] and mutability."[4] How is that enormous range of things that are both necessary and pleasurable—from nourishment to sexuality—to be distributed in relation to the human good?

1. Nussbaum, *Fragility*, 78.

2. Ibid., 2–3.

3. Ibid., 5.

4. Ibid., 7.

As Nussbaum puts it, "We would like to find a way to retain our identity as desiring and moving beings, and yet to make ourselves self-sufficient."[5] Plato's answer to this dilemma, described most pointedly in the *Symposium*, is not a concept or an ideal but a method. It is worth listening again to his account of the redemption of human life from contingency and vulnerability:

> [The one] who would proceed aright . . . should begin in youth to visit beautiful forms: and first, if he be guided by his instructor aright, to love one such form only . . . and soon he will of himself perceive that the beauty of one form is akin to the beauty of another; and then, if beauty of form in general is his pursuit, how foolish would he be not to recognize that the beauty in every form is one and the same! And when he perceives this he will abate his violent love of the one . . . and will become a lover of all beautiful forms: in the next stage he will perceive that the beauty of the mind is more honorable than the beauty of the outward form. [He will then move on] to contemplate the beauty of institutions and laws and to understand that the beauty of them all is of one family; . . . and after laws and institutions he will go on to sciences, that he may see their beauty. . . .[6]

"Ascending under the influence of love," *collecting*, not discarding, particulars from the world of the senses, the student will come at last to a vision of "beauty absolute, separate, simple and everlasting." The method outlined here is to "begin from the beauties of earth and mount upwards . . . until [the lover of beauty] arrives at the notion of absolute beauty and at last knows what the essence of beauty is."[7] "True beauty," Plato says, is "not clogged with the pollutions of mortality and all the colors and illusions of human life." Thus, moved by the energy of enthralled love from "one beautiful body" to beautiful forms, beautiful practices, and beautiful ideas, one gradually isolates the element common to all of these disparate entities: the reality of beauty. Modern people would call this a process of abstraction, a process by which particularity, "color," and the perennial ambiguities of human experience vanish in—or are caught up in—"beauty absolute, separate, and everlasting." Beauty "pure and unalloyed" is a vision of beauty accessible only to the trained eye, the eye trained by disciplined recognition of myriad beauties.[8] The most careful

5. Ibid., 176.
6. Plato *Symposium* 211 (Jowett).
7. Ibid.
8. Ibid.

exposition of Plato's thought must reflect, rather than resolve, the irreducible ambiguity of his attitude toward "the silken weavings of our afternoons."[9]

Plato has made two proposals in this passage about how to enjoy sensual pleasures without placing oneself in a slavish and vulnerable position. First, what one loves in "one beautiful body" is not its uniqueness but its beauty, which is, after all, a repeatable and replaceable entity, a quality, in fact, shared by all beautiful bodies. If the "one beautiful body" is lost, it can be replaced by another. Secondly, and even more dramatically, one *kind* of beauty is *the same as* another: contemplation of beautiful bodies, or beautiful ideas, or beautiful ways of life gives roughly the same pleasure. What one irreducibly *has*, in the generosity of the universe, is what Plato calls a "sea of beauty." One can, then—and must—relax one's intransigent requirement that gratification must come from the one person one loves, and adjust one's love to beauty itself, in whatever form, wherever it is found. And it is found everywhere, Plato says; it is continuously adjacent to senses and intellect. Having recognized beauty in its collected and concentrated form, it pops into the eye everywhere.

This is the happy life. Plato, like Aristotle after him, will not scruple to call the possessor of such a life "divine" because she is not at the mercy of "whatever happens" but has become adept at focusing the vision of beauty-which-*is*-happiness. Thus the happy life is invulnerable, relying not at all on circumstances. The happy life is also individual. This is necessary to its invulnerability. It needs neither other people, nor society; indeed, it may be practiced in a more concentrated and focused way in isolation, though it is pleasant to confer with others occasionally; it is pleasant to whet one's mental powers by detecting and exposing their clumsy misunderstandings. It helps to have friends like those of Socrates, if one can find them—gentle people who do not interrupt one's train of thought with rude rebuttals. Rather they sit—or stroll—about saying, "Quite right, Socrates," to everything one says. Facetiousness aside, for Plato, friends are useful in the philosophic life; friends egg one another on in virtue and vision.

Aristotle's proposal for the happy life revised Plato's ideal of self-sufficiency and invulnerability. Aristotle acknowledged the possibility that determined and practiced self-identification with rationality might not be enough to make human life good, and therefore happy. He admitted that certain calamities—debilitating illness, severe financial reverses, or the loss of

---

9. Stevens, "Sunday Morning," 69.

those most dear—can, and regularly do, substantially alter a person, damaging personality and morality. For Aristotle, the good life is irreducibly and necessarily vulnerable, dependent on luck, external goods, health, and unimpeded voluntary action. In fact, the happier a person is, and the more she possesses, the more at risk she is of losing the resources and circumstances that have contributed to her happiness. For this reason Aristotle cautioned: "Call no one happy until he is dead." The possibility of dramatic reversals of fortune lasts as long as a human life. Yet Aristotle did not advise renunciation of those goods and pleasures that make one most vulnerable to loss—love of other human beings, material possessions, the pleasures of the senses. Rather, in Nussbaum's words:

> the goal of the Aristotelian is not so much happiness in the sense of contentment as it is fullness of life and richness of value; it is not a solution to omit a value for happiness's sake, to reduce your demands on the world in order to get pleasing answers from the world. The Aristotelian will simply take on the world and see what can be done with it.[10]

Aristotle begins his discussion of happiness in Book Ten of the *Nicomachean Ethics* by stipulating that happiness must be an activity rather than a state. But what kind of an activity? One that is desirable for its own sake and, preferably, one that needs few external circumstances or resources. Obviously, pleasant amusements do not qualify. They "need" too much: health, a relaxed mind, and the price of the ticket, to name only a few. Virtuous actions, then? Yes, but not the sort of virtuous actions that depend on the existence of a preexisting need and a recipient. Rather, Aristotle says, the most virtuous activities are those that flow directly and spontaneously from one's nature. It is not a long step from here to his agreement with Plato that since reason is the "best part" of human beings, virtue, and with it happiness, will lie in the exercise, the *activity*, of *this* part. Contemplation is this activity, and, perhaps predictably, since a philosopher is describing it, the philosopher has the happiest life. Happiness will come, not from pleasures, but from the good life itself. In Aristotle's metaphor: "The life of the actively good is inherently pleasant. So their life does not need to have pleasure fastened about it as a necklace, but possesses it as part of itself."[11]

---

10. Nussbaum, *Fragility*, 369.

11. Aristotle *Nicomachean Ethics* 1.8 (Thomson).

The life of contemplation, Aristotle said, is "too high" for a human being as such. It is possible only because "something divine" is present in the person. He concludes, "The life according to reason is best and pleasantest, since reason more than anything else is human. This life therefore is also the happiest."[12] The life of contemplation, he adds, "seems to need external equipment but little." Oh, *some* "external prosperity" will be needed; human beings do have a body that needs nourishment and "other attention," but "many things or great things" will not be needed for contemplation; "even with moderate advantages [Aristotle said], one can act virtuously."[13]

Thus, though Plato and Aristotle agreed that the life of contemplation and reason enjoyed by the philosopher is the best life, Aristotle contributed the requirement that happiness is active, the exercise of a human being's most essential and defining characteristic. And he admitted both that some material conditions were essential to happiness and that happiness could be damaged or destroyed by the intervention of cruel circumstances. Happiness, for Aristotle, is necessarily more vulnerable than it is for Plato; it is still—as for Plato—a highly individual achievement.

Plotinus, it is well to remember, did not see himself as a "Neoplatonist," but simply as a faithful interpreter of Plato. He inherited several fundamental problems noticed in Plato's teachings by philosophers like Aristotle, and addressed himself to exploring and explaining those problems. He also worked and thought in a different world than that of his predecessors. By Plotinus's time, Christianity, in its many forms, competed with the philosophical schools to provide the most cogent account of human existence and fulfillment. Plotinus's only polemical treatise is *Enneads* 2.9, "Against the Gnostics." He criticized Gnostics for alleging that the created world of bodies and material substances was the evil creation of an evil Creator. He acknowledged that some of their ideas came from certain Platonic suggestions, but he accused them of ignoring and misunderstanding Plato on some crucial points. The logical conclusion of Gnostic teaching, he wrote, is to desire to be put to death so that one can enjoy the life of the mind without physical encumbrances.[14] He tells a parable:

> Two people inhabit the same stately house; one of them declaims against its plan and its architect, but none the less maintains his

12. Aristotle *Nichomachean Ethics* 10.7 (W. D. Ross).

13. Ibid., 10.8.

14. Plotinus *Ennead* 2.9.17 (Armstrong).

residence in it; the other makes no complaint, asserts the entire competency of the architect and waits cheerfully for the day when he may leave it, having no further need of a house: the malcontent imagines himself to be the wiser and to be the readier to leave because he has learned to repeat that the walls are of soulless stone and timber and that the place falls far short of a true home.[15]

Plotinus suggests somewhat snidely that the Gnostics' complaints assume, and serve to mask, a "secret admiration" for those very "stones."[16] He concludes, "As long as we have bodies we must inhabit the dwellings prepared for us by our good sister the Soul in her vast power of laborless creation."[17] Because the Gnostics carried Plato's disregard for body and material world to its metaphysical conclusion, Plotinus was able to see that such views needed to be explicitly modified. This he set out to do.

Plotinus's own proposal for the happy life is that happiness comes from the recognition of beauty. But this sounds deceptively simple; Plotinus will derive from his definition of the happy life a metaphysics, an ethics, and what we might call a "spirituality." Far from being a simple aesthetic appreciation, the recognition of beauty is a complex emotion/intellection, requiring commitment and discipline.

There must be those who see this beauty by that with which the soul sees things of this sort, and when they see it they must be delighted and overwhelmed and excited much more than by those beauties we spoke of before [i.e., earthly beauties], since now it is true beauty they are grasping. These experiences must occur whenever there is contact with any sort of beautiful thing, amazement, and a shock of delight and wonder and passion and a happy excitement. . . . You feel like this when you see, in yourself or in someone else, greatness of soul, a righteous life, a pure morality, courage . . . the one who sees them cannot say anything except that they are

15. Ibid.

16. "But perhaps they may say that they are not moved, and do not look any differently at ugly or beautiful bodies; but if this is so, they do not look any differently at ugly or beautiful ways of life, or beautiful subjects of study; they have no contemplation, then, and hence no God. For the beauties here exist because of those first beauties. If, then, these here do not exist, neither do those. . . . But one should notice that they should not give themselves airs if they despised something ugly; they do so because they despise something which they begin by calling beautiful: and what sort of a way of managing is that?" (ibid.).

17. Ibid.

what really exists. What does "really exist" mean? That they exist as beauties.[18]

Since recognition of the beautiful is the primary activity that creates human happiness, Plotinus said, "all our toil and trouble is for this, not to be left without a share in the best of visions. The one who attains this is blessed . . . the one who fails to attain it has failed utterly."[19] Plato had similarly identified the goal of rational exercise as a vision of the beautiful. For Plotinus, as for Plato, identifying the beautiful was difficult and elusive. In Plato's treatise on beauty, the *Greater Hippias*, he set out to find, "not what seems to the many to be beautiful, but what is so." Yet at the end of the treatise he is forced to admit, as the only fruit of his search: "So Hippias, . . . I seem to myself to know what the proverb means that says, 'The beautiful things are difficult.'"[20]

Because the perception of beauty defines human happiness, misjudgments about what is the beautiful are the greatest human danger. Because "we are what we desire and what we look upon," the formative effects of contemplation of beauty are crucial to human happiness. Thus, Plotinus endeavored to elucidate a *method* for achieving the vision of beauty that revises Plato's method:

> And what does this inner sight see? When it is just awakened it is not at all able to look at the brilliance before it. So that the soul must be trained first of all to look at beautiful ways of life: then at beautiful works, not those which the arts produce, but the works of those who have a name for goodness: then look at the souls of the people who produce the beautiful works. How, then, can you see the sort of beauty that a good soul has? *Go back into yourself* and look; and if you do not yet see yourself beautiful, then, just as someone making a statue which has to be beautiful cuts away here and polishes there till he has given his statue a beautiful face, so you must cut away the excess and straighten the crooked and clear the dark and make it bright, and never stop working on your statue until the divine glory of virtue shines out on you. . . . If you have become like this, and see it, and are at home with yourself in purity, with nothing hindering you from becoming in this way one, with no inward mixture of anything else, but wholly yourself, nothing but true light: when you see that you have become this,

18. Plotinus *Ennead* 1.6.4 (Armstrong).

19. Ibid., 1.6.7.

20. Plato *Greater Hippias* 304e (Pangle 339). See also *Republic* 435c, 497; *Cratylus* 348a–b; *Protagoras* 339ff.

then you have become sight; you can trust yourself then: you have already ascended and need no one to show you: concentrate your gaze and see. This alone is the eye that sees the great beauty. . . . For one must come to the sight with a seeing power made akin to what is seen. You must first become all godlike and all beautiful if you expect to see God and beauty.[21]

While Plato's method consisted of abstracting the quality of beauty from the many objects and practices that exhibit it, Plotinus's method entailed a systematic movement from attention to external things to work on an inner life of subjectivity.

It is important to note that, for Plotinus, the primary effects of recognized beauty are *ethical*, not aesthetic: "beautiful works" are "not those produced by the arts," but "the works of those who have a name for goodness." Moreover, the one who has "become sight" understands intimately the *connectedness* of sentient beings, the basis of ethical feeling and activity:

It must, no doubt, seem strange that my soul and that of any and everybody else should be one thing only: it might mean my feelings being felt by someone else, my goodness another's too, my desire her desire, all our experience shared with each other and with the one universe, so that the very universe itself would feel whatever I feel. We are in sympathetic relation to one another, suffering, overcome at the sight of pain, naturally drawn to forming attachments; and all this can be due only to some unity among us.[22]

Plotinus himself did not write about how he translated this ethical vision into concrete practices. But Porphyry, his biographer, reports that Plotinus was a vegetarian, that he took into his home numerous orphans, conducted business of his own, and taught while maintaining a virtually invulnerable inner recollectedness.[23]

---

21. Plotinus *Ennead* 1.6.9.

22. Ibid., 4.9.3.

23. "He used to work out his design mentally from first to last; when he came to set down his ideas he wrote out at one spurt all he had stored in mind as though he were copying from a book. Interrupted, perhaps, by someone entering on business, he never lost hold of his plan; he was able to meet all the demands of the conversation and still keep his own train of thought clearly before him; . . . he never looked over what he had previously written, but he linked on what was to follow as if no distraction had occurred.

"Thus he was able to live at once within himself and for others; he never relaxed from his interior attention unless in sleep, and even his sleep was kept light by an abstemiousness that often prevented him from taking as much as a piece of bread, and by this unbroken

In Plotinus the direct apprehension of the connectedness of the universe is the quintessential human activity, *the* knowledge it would be tragic to miss. The *experience*, through contemplation, of the concrete organic unity of the world requires the integration of intelligence and feeling; it is participation in Beauty:

> But if someone is able to turn around . . . he will see God and himself and the All; at first he will not see *as* the All but then, when he has nowhere to set himself and determine how far he himself goes, he will stop marking himself off from all being and will come to the All without going out anywhere, but remaining there where the All is set firm.[24]

The Great Beauty "makes its lovers beautiful and lovable."[25] Moreover, bodies are not excluded from Plotinus's vision of beauty; rather, "the beauty of beautiful bodies is by participation in the Great Beauty."[26]

II

I have given a rather extended description of Greek thinkers on human happiness partly because I, like many Christian authors who have studied them, find them striking and beautiful. Also, mystical spirituality, although never a prominent feature of biblical Christianity, was so very influential within the history of Christianity. We will consider next one of the most influential of the Christian authors who adopted and adapted Greek versions of human happiness, Augustine, bishop of Hippo in Roman North Africa at the beginning of the fifth century. Like his classical predecessors, Augustine was preoccupied with the *beata vita*, the "happy life" (the title of his first treatise as a Christian). The theme weaves throughout his long career as author and preacher. He once said in a sermon:

> Everyone, whatever his condition, desires to be happy. There is no one who does not desire this, and each one desires it with such earnestness that it is preferred to all other things; whoever, in fact, desires other things, desires them for this end alone . . . in what-

---

concentration upon his highest nature." *Porphyry*, Life 8 (Armstrong).

24. Plotinus *Ennead* 6.5.7.

25. Ibid., 1.6.7.

26. Ibid., 1.15.

ever life one chooses . . . there is no one who does not wish to be happy.[27]

Augustine reworked the ideas of happiness that he received from Greek thought in two dramatic and decisive ways. First, he described happiness as fundamentally unattainable in this life, postponing its actualization to another time and space, outside present human experience. He identified the fulfillment of human happiness as the integration of person that would occur in the promised resurrection of the body. Until then, under the fragile and flawed conditions of human existence, nothing but momentary "glimpses" of happiness would be available. His insistence that happiness is not complete until the human body is fully integrated is a reworking of Greek authors' worry about the extent of vulnerability that can be incorporated in a happy life. Yet it also asserts the centrality of body to human being. No Greek thinker was willing to bear the expense of this intransigent proposal: postponing human happiness to an afterlife in which the body would be invulnerable to accident, disease, suffering, and death. Augustine was the first expositor of happiness to insist that it has something crucial to do with the body, that the realization of happiness cannot occur until body is rescued from mortality and vulnerability.

Augustine's second revision of classical ideas of human happiness was to describe present experiences of happiness as perpetually and irreducibly in motion, oscillating between poles of desire and delight. For Augustine, desire was a matter of survival, the act of self-identification of the hungry heart. For the soul, he said, is informed and shaped by the objects of its habitual attention and affection, by its desire and delight. He pictured a human self as plastic, composed and articulated by what it loves, stretches toward, and identifies with. To love the fragile fleeting objects and people in the world as if they could provide a total stimulus, a reason for being, then, is to make (quite literally) a deadening choice. When the objects vanish into thin air, so does the soul identified with, and defined by, them.[28] It is, then, a matter

---

27. Augustine *Sermo* 306.3

28. Augustine's idea of soul/self could be expressed in a twentieth-century language of the psyche: "The ego is the cumulative effect of its formative identifications. . . . Identifications not only *precede* the ego, but the identificatory relation to the image establishes the ego. . . . As a result the ego is not a self-identical substance, but a sedimented history of relations which locate the center of the ego outside itself, in the externalized imago which confers and produces bodily contours." Butler, "Lesbian Phallus," 148.

of survival for the soul to attach itself with desire and delight to a totally trustworthy object, an object that cannot die.

If "real" happiness is not to be found in this life, how can it even be sought? For Augustine believed that the happy life can be neither imagined nor experienced vicariously. It must somehow be identified in one's own experience if one is to find the energy to move in its direction. In short, an idea of the happy life must be collected from memories of individual personal joy. *Any joys will do*, "base joys and disgraceful things," as well as "good and worthy joys."[29] Once one has gathered composite memories of happiness and constructed from this collection a cumulative memory of what happiness is, then one has something both personal and concrete to *desire*, to long toward. Ultimately, of course, though one must perforce begin with memories of any old joys, it is joy in truth that energizes the happy life: "Certainly the happy life is joy in you, who are truth," he wrote, addressing God.[30]

For Augustine, happiness was not, in this life, a stable possession but a dynamic and a *process*. Its intensity—its delicate beauty—is predicated on its instability, its preciousness linked to its fragility. Yet Augustine also deeply distrusted happiness *now*. At least when he spoke as a theologian, he preferred suffering because one could learn from it. Present happiness is deceptive; it cannot last forever. And permanence was one of Augustine's requirements for true happiness—not merely the lifelong happiness Aristotle required for happiness worthy of the name, but *eternal happiness*.

Augustine's heady notion of eternal happiness has had its effects in the history of Christianity. His requirement that happiness worthy of the name is necessarily permanent eventuated in centuries of Christians who neither anticipated nor valued happiness now. They expected work and suffering; that is what they recognized as validating their Christianity. Too often in the history of Christianity, happiness was devalued to the point described by Thomas à Kempis in his fifteenth-century best-selling devotional manual, *The Imitation of Christ*. Human happiness, for Thomas, was limited to the security of being well prepared for death:

> A man is not only happy but wise also, if he is trying, during his
> lifetime, to be the sort of man he wants to be found at his death.
> We can be sure of dying happily if our lives show an utter disre-
> gard for the world, a fervent desire for progress in virtue, a love of

29. Augustine *Confessiones* 10.21 (Warner).

30. Ibid., 10.23.

discipline, the practice of penitence, denial of self, and acceptance of any adversity for the love of Christ.[31]

Curiously Augustine's overvaluation of happiness, his demand that it be a permanent state, his investment in sheltering it from the vulnerability of human life, have denied the possibility of "enough happiness," a "working happiness," a humanly achievable happiness. Moreover, the voluntary relinquishment of happiness in "this life" did not inspire committed work for just societies, only for individual salvation.

III

I must now "deliver," as promised, my own reconstruction of inherited conceptualizations of human happiness. I confess initially that, of the authors I have described, I can work most fluently with Plotinus's description of happiness. I need, however, to correct its individualism and its lack of systematic attention to just social arrangements. I want to modify its intellectualism by proposing that vigorous, committed action in the world can equally be a method for recognizing and augmenting the Great Beauty. In addition, I am committed to Aristotle's willingness to accept the condition of vulnerability in caring for people and objects that can—indeed *will*—eventually be lost. There are also features of Augustine's theory of happiness—its dynamism, its sensitivity to human suffering, for example—that I cannot jettison.

I will begin by asking what values, or "worths,"[32] are placed centrally in a particular theory of happiness. I assume that each theory of happiness endeavors to include and arrange all humanly desirable goods, to show how each "fits" in relation to others. Even Plato included bodily beauty as the *starting point* of his method of ascent to the vision of "beauty itself." Furthermore, each theory of happiness must show how human "goods" should be ordered in notoriously short and unstable human lives, lives that do not have the luxury of the gods who banquet in unthreatened leisure on Olympus.

We can agree immediately, I hope, that the activity of rationality has not been ignored in classical accounts of the happy life. Indeed, reason has been rather thoroughly defended as the core human happiness. In Augustine, of course, rationality was displaced by affectivity or the will as it leans out in self-defining love, either toward God or toward the "city" of this world. This alone would make Augustine a theologian rather than a philosopher. But

31. Thomas à Kempis, *Imitation of Christ*, 73.

32. My colleague, Richard R. Niebuhr, prefers this term.

even Augustine did not "dethrone" reason to the extent claimed by some of his commentators. He still considered rationality the "highest" single capacity of human beings, and he placed it above concern for human society or care for one's own and others' bodies. In short, in all the theories we have considered, two human "goods" are consistently marginalized; they are not articulated in thrilling prose but hastily gathered as afterthoughts. These entities are living bodies and a just society.

As we have seen, Augustine gave human bodies such importance that he refused to imagine a human happiness without invulnerable and permanent bodies, but the cost of this was to exclude the possibility of real happiness now. And when the philosophers and theologian we have considered sought to envision humanly good societies they either described utopias (like Plato's *Republic*), or a frankly nonexperiential heavenly city (like Augustine's).

Greek philosophers, like Augustine after them, understood human nature as thoroughly social; but they declined to envision happiness as social, as dependent on equality and mutuality in social arrangements, and on just institutions. Augustine could—and did, in great detail—imagine a glorious time of fulfillment and perfection for humanity in the resurrection of the body.[33] Yet even in heaven, he said, rewards will be unevenly distributed. The only difference Augustine envisioned from the heavily stratified city of this world will be that people with less reward will, in the heavenly city, be content. In fact, when I examine Augustine's model of permanent happiness, I see how utterly and transparently dependent it is on the "foretastes" or "glimpses" of happiness he knew. Because he had neither envisioned nor worked toward just social arrangements, he could not imagine with any concreteness the society of the heavenly city where, as he acknowledged, "all injustice will disappear and God will be all in all."[34]

Something like Plotinus's description of the connectedness of living things in a vast—and beautiful—universe of interdependence is needed to challenge the individualistic and futuristic salvation of Christian tradition. As Plotinus put it, "there is no place to draw a limit, to say, 'this and no further is I.'" The primary self-identity of a person must be with the universe seen as beauty, as a finely textured relationship of parts to whole in which none of the parts could be without the whole. Moreover, something like Aristotle's notion that happiness is an *activity,* *the* activity most characteristic of human

---

33. Augustine *De civitate Dei* 22 (Bettenson).
34. Ibid., 19.15.

beings, is necessary in order to overcome the potential quietism of contemplation of the beautiful. What if participation in the Great Beauty were to be understood as activity in the world of bodies and society rather than as a self-isolating activity of spiritual exercise?

Until the second half of the twentieth century, people have not been able to identify and to map with scientific precision the interconnectedness of living beings. Plotinus's notion of an interdependent web of sentient and non-sentient entities has been intuited rather than demonstrated, a romantic notion. The intuition has been represented by a long tradition of authors who have frequently been labeled "soft," or "nature worshippers," by a succession of "hardheaded" philosophers. But I suggest that a sea change for thought has occurred in our time, brought about by the scientific capacity to measure, and the technological capability to demonstrate, the tangible and intimate effects of such environmental crises as the disappearance of rain forests, the extinction of animal species, pollution of air, water, and food; the list could go on and on. We consider these situations with alarm, but what is needed to energize our committed work on behalf of bodies and the earth is that we recognize the import of all the news *together*. The universe is utterly interdependent. This knowledge is no longer intuited or romantic, but factual and concrete, *the* fundamental fact of life.

If the universe is irreversibly interconnected for damage, it is also interwoven through veins of energy and delight. Thus, what must be discovered if one is to be happy, now and here, is the broader generosity of the universe, the continuous, amazing circulation of gifts, of love, of light. And this discovery must become the centerpiece of one's identity so that one actually *feels* a part of this circulation of wealth. One's own family is seldom the perfect family to meet one's needs and wants; even chosen friends and lovers are not the right ones, at least for much of the time. And yet, there *is* in the world the very love, light, and plentitude one needs. It is there, circulating through living beings—vivid now in one, now in another. It is not gone from the world when it is gone from me. And knowing it is here, in motion, is enough. In a moment of overwhelming insight, the protagonist in Camus's *L'Etranger* says, "Je m'oeuvre pour le premier fois a la tendre indifference du monde" ("I opened myself for the first time to the gentle nonchalance of the world").

People know this on some level. It is the most evident open secret of the universe. There is music that can make one briefly, perfectly, happy. Many novels come to resolution when their characters discover that there is enough, and that they can find ways to participate in it, that they may finally abandon the effort to extract what they need from their lovers and families. This is also, I think, what Augustine meant when he said, "Cessavi de me paululum" ("I relaxed a little from myself"). The world contains enough, and the perception of this comes as an awareness of beauty, a relaxing. Poetry regularly marks it; Rainier Maria Rilke said:

> And we, who have always thought of happiness climbing, would
> feel the emotion that almost startles when happiness falls.[35]

In our own century, Alfred North Whitehead was one of the most articulate expositors of the interconnectedness of the universe: he refers in the concluding pages of *Adventures of Ideas* to

> a broadening of feeling due to the emergence of some deep metaphysical insight, unverbalized and yet momentous in its coordination of values. Its first effect is the removal of the stress of acquisitive feeling arising from the soul's preoccupation with itself. . . . It is primarily a trust in the efficacy of beauty. . . .[36]

Even fans of media stars know that the fame, beauty, and money the star has collected are—both symbolically and concretely—theirs. They take pleasure in participating in what the star crystallizes and displays for them. The star's social *function* is to demonstrate the existence of *so much*.[37]

What is finally required for happiness is faith in the immense generosity of the universe, experienced as beauty. There is "enough," enough for all, if we will only cease trying to stipulate and control the channels through which it may flow to us, if we will "await it with confidence, and accept it with gratitude."[38] This is not blind faith; it is grounded in vision and in the experience of many witnesses.

Interconnectedness, then, is a scientifically demonstrable fact as well as a feature of experience, but we seldom notice it. Yet there is something abundantly and compellingly energizing in those moments when we see the interconnectedness, what Plotinus calls the "unity," the interdependence of the universe. If, as I have claimed, happiness depends on intimate knowledge and experience of the consanguinity of living beings, then happiness is an art

---

35. Rilke, *Duino Elegies*, 10 (Leishman and Spender 85).

36. Whitehead, *Adventures of Ideas*, 283–84.

37. Interestingly, one of Madonna's recent commentators has claimed the social function of stars is to "fill the space of desire—this gap that constitutes the subject in desire for an object." Kaplan, "Madonna Politics," 152.

38. Dinesen, "Babette's Feast," in *Anecdotes of Destiny*, 60.

of perception, the vision of an eye that can, and must, be cultivated. Not a vision of the heavenly city; not that of an imagined utopia. But now. Here. Bodied and social. Happiness as desire and delight, delight and desire, in motion, *active* in the world.

We must, however, still ask, what is the relationship between happiness and social arrangements? If happiness is identical with seeing/participating in the Great Beauty, isn't activity antithetical to it? Twentieth-century people often assume that while one is absorbed in "seeing" one is not acting, not struggling to make the world and human society a better place to live for more human beings. Are contemplation of beauty and struggle for social change inevitably alternative postures toward the world? It is important to note that the metaphor of vision does not necessarily imply that the one seeing must be at a distance from the object seen, as some twentieth-century theorists of vision have claimed. Plato was the first to articulate a theory of physical vision that emphasized the viewer's activity and the connection of viewer and object. The visual ray theory states that a quasi-physical ray, created by the same fire that animates and warms the body, is at its most intense in the eyes. The act of vision occurs when the visual ray is directed to an object, *touches its object*, and the object travels back along the ray to imprint itself on the memory. Ancient and medieval folk beliefs about the evil eye, in which a malign look can cause physical and/or spiritual damage, rely on this model of vision as *touch*. The look, then, depends on the actualization of a connection between viewer and object, on the viewer's recognition of this connection and on her/his activity in establishing it. The visual ray theory did not emerge from an entertainment culture, a culture that thinks of seeing as passive; rather it assumes vigorous engagement with the object of vision.

Reliance on a vast unifying vision of beauty can be—and has been—dangerous in ways recently pointed out by twentieth-century philosophers and theologians. Liberation theologians and feminist philosophers and theologians have especially detected the capacity of beauty to blind people—even those who are themselves marginalized or oppressed—to social and institutional injustice. These theologians, righteously angry at unjust political and social arrangements, at oppressions based on race, class, and gender, have often sought to expose and jettison the beautiful texts, liturgies, ideas, and images that masked injustice. Clearly, articulations of beauty must be scrutinized and the ancient Grail question brought to them, "Whom does it serve?" Happiness, then, will require both an energizing and compelling vision of an intimately interconnected world as the site of the "real self," and continuous investigation and revision of the ways this vision is lived in "human, all too human societies."

If happiness, as Aristotle said, is an activity, and if it is, furthermore, an activity that flows spontaneously from our most fundamental gift, our aliveness, then participation in the Great Beauty cannot be confined to the intellectual vision of philosophers. And the life of the philosopher may not be the happiest human life, despite consensus on this among the masters of language.

Let us recall, in conclusion, the Greek anxiety over establishing a site for human happiness that is safe from threat—safe space. How vulnerable to contingencies—events, social arrangements, chance opportunities or the lack thereof—is human happiness? By *human* happiness I mean "enough" or "working" happiness as opposed to "ideal" or "fantasy" happiness. In Plotinus's generous vision, personal or individual vulnerability does not preclude the happiness that is inherent in seeing the great beauty. He did not, however, articulate quite so clearly that the important and irreducible vulnerability in an interconnected universe is transpersonal. But awareness of this kind of vulnerability can be put to work as energy for love and for work. Energized by "the eye that sees the great beauty," one recognizes simultaneously that the condition of vulnerability and the condition of the circulation of gifts are the same—interconnection, the Great Beauty.

Augustine

CHAPTER 4

Patriarchy as Political Theology:
The Establishment of North African Christianity

There are three stages in the orthodox resolution of the place of women in Christian churches in North Africa over the two-hundred-year period I am exploring. I want to show that the question about the place of women arose in relation to some of the most characteristic values and interests of the churches of North Africa, traceable in the earliest extant literature of African Christianity. To do so will help us understand the context of some of the arguments and resolutions that today we often take for granted as inevitable, and that some of us have been content to see as decisive.

Church historians agree that the real genius of early North African Christianity was ecclesiastical and practical rather than theological or dogmatic. Conflict within and among Christian groups and the "successful" resolution of this conflict was the particular focus of North African Christianity; the definition and handling of schism and the establishment of church order was the influential feat of catholic Christian groups in the third and fourth centuries. My intention is not to substitute an alternative to the "triumph of orthodoxy" ideology that underlies traditional church historiography, but to suggest that a description of the persistent serious conflict over the roles of women in early North African Christianity not only is legitimate but also provides an important piece of the history of our contemporary concern with issues of church order such as the ordination of women.

One side of the conflict over women's roles is preserved in the extant texts from the two hundred years of North African Christianity for which we have the most evidence. I do not understand this conflict as the gradual establishment of orthodox politics over schismatic politics, but as a conflict in which there were winners and losers. The difference is important; it is the difference between believing that orthodox ecclesiastical politics was scriptural, cosmically correct, and therefore inevitable; and seeing the conflict as caused by the existence of different perspectives and interests.

Moreover, I will not assume that the reasons given by losers in these conflicts were flimsy rationalizations of the wishes of these persons to live ideologically sloppy or sexually permissive Christian lives. Rather, I will try to identify, from the emphases and arguments of their opponents, principled reasons for dissent, legitimized, as we will see, by the earliest North African values and interests. It was these interests and values that gave the question about the place of women its high profile and its poignancy in the struggle over gender roles in North Africa.

We must first identify two intertwined and highly characteristic interests of North African Christianity: martyrdom and the activity of the Holy Spirit.

The beginnings of North African Christianity are shrouded in mystery. We do not know where or how Christianity originated here. The first document of Christianity in North Africa is an account of the trial and martyrdom of six Christians soon after the arrival of the new governor, Vigellius Saturninus, in Carthage.[1] The martyrs—three men and three women—bear native African names and probably came from rural areas surrounding Carthage. Their response to the verdict of condemnation, "Deo gratias," was to ring in the African air throughout the approximately five hundred years of African Christianity, on the lips of martyrs, Donatists, and Catholic bishops. The short *Acta* of the Scillitan martyrs reveals the high value of Christian martyrdom and the power of the martyr, both on earth and in heaven where martyrs are pictured as reigning with God.

Confessors—those who had been condemned to death as Christians— who by the third century were simply called martyrs, continued to be valued and powerful. The strenuous efforts of Cyprian, bishop of Carthage in the middle of the century, to limit and control their power to waive serious offenses of their petitioners demonstrate the prestige of the confessors. A century and a half later, at the beginning of the fifth century, Augustine describes the liturgical reading of their *Actae* on the anniversaries of local martyrs and the exuberance with which their birthdays into eternal life were popularly celebrated. Authority and martyrdom were very closely aligned indeed in North African churches.

1. See "Passio Sanctorum Scillitanorum," in Musurillo, ed., *Acts of the Christian Martyrs.*

The second highly valued interest of North African Christians was the continuing activity of the Holy Spirit in Christian communities. Again, the earliest Christian documents of North Africa present a strong picture of on-going inspiration, prophecy, and sustenance by the Spirit's leadership. The prologue of the *Acta of Saints Perpetua and Felicitas* repeats themes associated with the power of the Spirit. Perpetua, a twenty-two-year-old aristocratic Roman matron, and Felicitas, her slave woman, were martyred on March 7, 203 A.D., in the amphitheater at Carthage. The author of the *Acta*—perhaps Tertullian—far from restricting the activity of the Spirit to the earliest Christianity, writes:

> More recent events should be considered the greater, . . . a consequence of the extraordinary graces promised for the last stage in time. We hold in honor and acknowledge not only new prophecies but new visions as well.[2]

The Montanist movement did not originate in North Africa, but it had a special resonance there: it identified as essential the present work of the Holy Spirit in the churches, an ancient, scriptural, and intensely-felt value.

These two values of North African Christianity were not unconnected. The Holy Spirit was understood to provide both the training and the support for martyrdom. The authority of the martyr came directly from the Spirit's takeover of her or his personality. Confident of her participation in the power of the Spirit, Perpetua petitioned the release of her long-dead brother from afterlife suffering, a prayer whose success was shown her in a vision. She also dreamed vividly and informatively. Her fellow martyr Saturus also reported a vision that seems to reflect a conflict in the Christian community at Carthage; in it the bishop Optatus and the presbyter Aspasius, alienated and spatially distant from one another, pled with Saturus to make peace between them, "for you have gone away and left us thus." Interestingly, an angel in the vision urges the bishop to take a more authoritative role in his congregation: "You must scold your flock. They approach you as though they had come from the games, quarreling about the different teams."[3] This glimpse of internecine conflict allows us to see also the role of the Spirit-filled martyr in orchestrating the reconciliation of antagonists within the churches of North Africa. The martyrs had a great deal of personal and ecclesiastical power.

---

2. "Passio SS. Perpetua et Felicitas," in Musurillo, ed., *Acts of the Christian Martyrs.*

3. Ibid., 13.

The high value accorded to martyrdom and to the present leading of the Holy Spirit inevitably led to a sense of equality among North African Christians. Equal courage and commitment were required of women and men, and equal authority and power were bestowed on them; within the Christian community at Carthage, roles were based on personal charisma, insight, and courage. Perpetua, for example, takes a leadership initiative in many of the incidents narrated in the *Acta*. Women may have been attracted to the Christian movement by the opportunities for discovering and using their energy and talent without the restrictions of secular society. We learn from Tertullian's heavy censure of leadership roles for women that many of the attractive and successful Christian communities of North Africa were led by women, especially among the charismatic Montanists. Neither martyrdom nor inspiration by the Holy Spirit was restricted according to gender roles.

I

Tertullian is the only North African Christian leader who wrote pointedly against the leadership of women in Christian churches. In his time—the end of the second century and the beginning years of the third—his vitriolic invective against women leaders in Christian groups gives us a sense of the appeal of dissident groups, both for women, whose talents and personalities could be explored without restriction in these groups, and for men.[4] Moreover, the situation in which early Christians questioned and sometimes jettisoned their gender role conditioning was one in which they expected an imminent end of their world, either through the apocalyptic return of Christ or through their personal apocalypse in martyrdom.

Tertullian's writings reveal the presence of conflict over gender issues in the Christian community. Conversion to Christianity brought with it, for women as for men, a strong sense of liberation from the conventional patterns of late Roman corporate life. But gender role expectations were one of the least malleable because most inaccessible carryovers from a Christian's former life. "It is not permitted for a woman to speak in church," Tertullian

---

4. Schüssler Fiorenza, *In Memory of Her*, 54. "The acid polemics of the fathers against the ecclesiastical leadership of women and against their teaching and writing books indicate that the question of women's ecclesiastical office was still being debated in the second and third centuries C.E. It also demonstrates that the progressive patriarchalization of church office did not happen without opposition but had to overcome various early Christian values and praxis that acknowledged the leadership claims of women."

repeats, quoting Paul, "but neither is it permitted her to teach, nor to baptize, nor to offer, nor to claim to herself a lot in any manly function, not to say in any sacerdotal office."[5]

But women *were* speaking in churches, prophesying, even baptizing, Tertullian himself tells us. To be sure, these were "heretical" women, but we know too little about their doctrines to be able to say with assurance that their differences with the catholic Christians were primarily doctrinal. Tertullian also repeats Paul's idea of patriarchal order as Christian order against Carthaginian consecrated virgins who felt themselves exceptions to Paul's general injunction against women because of their total commitment to Christ, and the Christian community: "On the ground of her position, nothing in the way of public honor is permitted to a virgin."[6] In exegeting the Genesis text on the naming of woman by man (Gen 2) Tertullian says that woman is "a second human being made by God for man's assistance." Consecrated virgins must regard themselves as continuing to share this status: "If 'the man is head of the woman', of course he is head of the virgin too, from whom comes the woman who has married; unless the virgin is a third generic class, some monstrosity with a head of its own."[7]

For male ecclesiastical leaders, the enthusiastic participation of women in North African Christianity was a problem. In each of the three contexts in which we examine their responses to Christian women, we will see the acute discomfort of men culturally conditioned to expect docility and submissiveness from women. The issue of women's dress focused the ongoing conflict between male leaders and women who were feeling empowered to new energy and activity. Not until the end of the fourth century, when patriarchal order had been solidly established, did male ecclesiastical leaders stop trying to control women's dress. By Augustine's time dress was a matter of indifference. But Augustine's indifference, either to differentiating Christians from pagans or to protecting men from the distracting beauty of women, rests on the secure establishment and full theological rationalization of patriarchal order. The rantings of Tertullian come from a vastly different reality, one in which the "confusion" of gender roles threatened the power of a fragile male episcopate.

---

5. Tertullian *De virginibus velandis* 9. Herafter cited as *VV*.

6. Ibid., 9.

7. Ibid., 5.

The Carthaginian context of conflict over the roles of Christian women is crucial if we are to interpret accurately Tertullian's sarcastic attack on the women he addresses as "handmaidens of the Lord, fellow servants, sisters."[8] Although the two books of Tertullian *On Women's Dress* probably represent a minority opinion in the Carthaginian Christian community, we can, by examining these texts, recover information about the attitudes and practices against which he inveighs. Both books were written during Tertullian's catholic period, but they reflect his already strong discomfort with that Christian community. Although it is unlikely that he was ever a priest, he claims a Spirit-directed authority in order to tell Christian women what their attitude should be to clothing, finery, and cosmetics.

These texts reveal, first, a disagreement over the issue of acculturation versus separation. Some women were apparently arguing that a distinguishing drabness of dress was not called for in a Christian woman. The "salt of the earth" model, in which Christians flavored from *within* the secular world, espoused by Tertullian's opponents, is vehemently rejected in Tertullian's promotion of a separatist stance in relation to secular culture. In evaluating this conflict of interpretations on the role of the Christian in society, it is important to think of a rather wide area of late Roman culture as neither Christian nor pagan but simply secular, a common arena of economic, political, and social interaction. The confusion and disagreement evident in early Christian authors about what a Christian's appearance and behavior should be in this secular arena indicate that it was not at all easy to sort out which parts of life were directly relevant to the Christian life, requiring Christians to look and act differently from other people. Whether Christians should serve in the army, which professions Christians might follow, and how Christian women—men are not discussed—should look, as well as many other questions, are addressed very differently at different times and in different locations by Christian authors. It was not clear which areas of life required distinctive Christian behavior.

Second, Christian women felt restored to spiritual integrity so that appearances were no longer significant. Tertullian describes Christian women as saying: "To me it is not necessary to be approved by men; for I do not require the testimony of men: God is the inspector of the heart."[9] Freedom from the constant attention to reputation required of Roman women must have

---

8. Tertullian *De cultu feminarum* 2.1. Hereafter cited as *CF*.

9. Ibid., 2.13.

been one of the benefits for women of Christian faith. Tertullian snatches it away from them. No argument is too farfetched or involuted to support his insistence that consecrated virgins must be veiled, and other women should "remove all traces of natural grace by concealment and negligence."[10] Natural beauty, he writes with an uncharacteristic generosity, is not to be censured; it is, however, to be feared.[11] The word is revealing: by whom should women's beauty be feared? It is the salvation of males that Tertullian is protecting; men's salvation is at stake:[12]

> I beseech you, be you mother, sister, or virgin-daughter . . . veil your head: if a mother, for your sons' sakes; if a sister, for your brothers' sake; if a daughter, for your father's sake. All ages are imperiled in your person.[13]

Even more specifically, Tertullian himself had what his most recent biographer called a "natural sensitivity to feminine beauty."[14] Tertullian is more forthright than his biographer; he tells us in *The Resurrection of the Flesh* that in his youth he was an adulterer.[15] Tertullian, painfully aware of his "natural sensitivity," is concerned about his own salvation.

Tertullian's assumption that women care for their appearance only in order to please men is a familiar one. Moreover, he argues for the logical validity of projection; he can be confident, he says, that he recognizes a woman's motivation by the way he is affected by a woman's appearance. If a man is aroused by looking at a particular woman, that woman means to arouse him: "Seeing and being seen belong to the self-same lust."[16] Some of the Carthaginian consecrated virgins wore veils on the street but removed them in church since they felt themselves safe from intrusive gazes among the Christian community. This gesture of trust and Christian freedom Tertullian also rejects: "They fear strangers," he writes, "let them fear the brethren also."[17]

10. Ibid., 2.2.
11. Ibid.
12. Ibid.
13. Tertullian *VV* 16.
14. Barnes, *Tertullian*, 137.
15. Tertullian *De resurrectione carnis* 59.3.
16. Tertullian *VV* 2: "Eiusdem libidinis est videri et videre."
17. Ibid., 13.

Ironically, one of the authoritative values of Christian North Africa, guidance by the Holy Spirit, is invoked against women who have been empowered by their equal accessibility to the leading of the Spirit.[18] According to Tertullian, however, the special province of the Holy Spirit is "the direction of discipline,"[19] and predictably, "those who heed the present prophecy of the Spirit" agree with Tertullian. It is the Spirit's authority that guarantees the legitimacy of Tertullian's judgments on matters not mentioned in scripture. Quoting 2 Tim 3:16 from memory, Tertullian makes a telling error; instead of "all scripture is given by inspiration of God and is useful for . . . instruction," Tertullian writes, "all that is useful for edification is divinely inspired."[20]

A further methodological principle governs Tertullian's claim to authority. Not only are present prophetic utterances in matters of discipline decisive, but Tertullian claims the right to unlimited generalization from these inspired utterances:

> No enunciation of the Holy Spirit ought to be confined to the subject immediately in hand merely, and not applied and carried out with a view to every occasion to which its application is useful.[21]

The universalization of his personal point of view is painfully evident in Tertullian's identification of his own opinion with truth: his feeling that consecrated virgins should be veiled is, he writes, an observation prescribed by truth, which remains the same without influence of "space of times, influence of persons," or "privilege of regions."[22] Identification of truth with his own view gives Tertullian a heavy advantage; he can conclude: "Whatever savors of opposition to truth, this will be heresy."[23]

Although Tertullian was a dissident in the catholic Christian community and ultimately left this communion, on this issue his views have been highly influential. Indeed, too much has been made of a separation of Tertullian's "orthodox" period from his Montanist period. His harsher opinions of women cannot be comfortably cubbyholed to his Montanist period.[24]

18. Ibid., 17.

19. Ibid., 1.

20. Tertullian *CF* 1.3: "Et legimus omnem scripturam aedification habilem divinus inspirari."

21. Ibid., 2.

22. Ibid., 1.

23. Ibid., 13.

24. Tertullian *CF* 2 (A.D. 196–97); *CF* 1 (A.D. 205–6); *VV* (A.D. 208–9); only the last

Even though these opinions may have contributed to his departure from the catholic Christian community, they carried the perennial authority of skillful rhetoric and a male voice. Tertullian's opinions on matters as close to the bone as gender hierarchy are continuous through his church hoppings.

II

Approximately fifty years after Tertullian's treatises on women's dress, the "woman question" appears to be unresolved in North Africa. It is, however, demonstrably in process of resolution by the establishment of patriarchal order. Cyprian, bishop of Carthage in the mid-third century, no longer ranted against women taking leadership roles in the churches. Apparently by mid-third century a male ecclesiastical hierarchy can be taken for granted in African catholic communities; indeed, by now this feature of church order serves to distinguish catholic communities from schismatic Christian groups. Tertullian, threatened by the attraction to North African Christians of communities in which women were allowed to preach, celebrate, baptize, and teach, had heightened his rhetorical bombast. Cyprian called Tertullian "the master" and read his writings daily; he was indebted to Tertullian's opinions and arguments, but Cyprian no longer felt sufficiently threatened to denounce women leaders. Another aspect of the participation of women in the Christian community is more prominent in the writings of Cyprian.

Like Tertullian, Cyprian wrote a treatise on the dress of consecrated virgins. Cyprian's treatise is very informative about the attitudes and activities of mid-third-century consecrated virgins in the Carthaginian churches. We can glimpse, for example, why virginity was an attractive option for women. We can also see some familiar motifs, like male efforts to control the behavior and dress of women. The honored role of consecrated virgin carried the attractive potential of a much greater degree of personal autonomy and independence than did the secular possibilities for women in the late Roman world. In the secular world a young wife remained in the jurisdiction of her father until she reached the age of twenty-five; a woman who was not married by age twenty-five was placed under the formal supervision of a legal guardian.[25] Late Roman satirists repeatedly report the quaint Roman belief that an unsupervised woman was dangerous to herself and society.

---

of these writings falls firmly within Tertullian's Montanist period.

25. Schüssler Fiorenza, *In Memory of Her*, 314.

Until Constantine's legislation in the fourth century, the legal position and social relationships of consecrated virgins were ambiguous. As our contemporary, the late Joan Kelly, pointed out, it is in times of social ambiguity that women are able to create new roles and expand the range of old ones. Cyprian's treatise reinforces the impression of new roles and relationships within a community of Christian women. In the middle of the third century, vows of virginity consisted of private resolution without public ceremony or official ratification. There is no evidence that vows of poverty and obedience were included at this time. A consecrated virgin might continue to live at home, spending much of her time in prayer and charitable activities. Or she might live in a small community of similarly committed women associated with a local parish. We must keep in mind the highly informal nature of both vows and living arrangements. What we will examine in this context is a struggle between a bishop and some committed Christian women over the right to define their lifestyle and activities.

What picture of these women's lives do we get from Cyprian's writings? First, *virgines subintroductae*, consecrated virgins who lived with—but did not have sexual intercourse with—clerics are still in evidence. Women and men, living and working together in relationships that rejected the gender conditioning of their society, felt that the need to communicate and rapidly spread the gospel required new kinds of relationship. This practice, which originated in the excitement of the Christian missionary movement, is mentioned as early as the second-century *Shepherd of Hermas*. Repeatedly, and well into the fifth century, local and ecumenical councils condemned the practice, thereby attesting its continuation.

Cyprian's *Epistula 4* demands that these relationships be discontinued. In vain consecrated virgins volunteered to undergo medical examinations to prove their continued virginity;[26] Cyprian finds cohabitation too dangerous to be permissible. Speaking of women, he writes: "Not only is there the weakness of their sex (*sexus infirmus*), but they are still at a vulnerable age (*aetas adhuc lubrica*) and ought to be guided completely by our direction and control."[27] Cyprian's parable of God as jealous husband of the virgin living with another man is not subtle: "Christ is our Lord and our Judge: when he observes his own virgin who has been vowed to him and dedicated to his holy

---

26. Cyprian *Epistula* 4.3.1.
27. Ibid., 4.2.1.

estate lying with another man, imagine his rage and his fury and the punishments he threatens to exact for such unchaste associations."[28]

Apparently these relationships were often simultaneously loving, meaningful, and nonsexual, if we are thus to understand the willingness of some of the consecrated virgins to prove their virginity by medical examination. Cyprian, as a bishop, had, however, the power to demand that such relationships cease. Indeed, in his situation, in which his authority was frequently threatened, his control of the consecrated virgins of his diocese may have been a key to strengthening his authority.

It was not a threat to the salvation of these women that lies closest to Cyprian's heart; rather, "it is our duty to take pains to ensure by every possible means that every one of our brothers can escape his spiritual sword and the approaching day of his judgment."[29] Although, he says, the responsibility for these relationships is with his clerical brothers, the punishment he threatens is for the women who live with them. They are to be warned, Cyprian writes, that their "life and salvation"[30] will be "taken away" if they refuse "to obey their bishops and priests" in this matter.[31]

Second, another aspect of Cyprian's struggles with celibate women is revealed in *The Dress of Virgins*. Freedom from the authority of a husband or father seems to have been at least a part of the attraction of the celibate life. In a society in which women had few options for an independent autonomous lifestyle, the community of celibate women must have provided such an opportunity. Cyprian gives us a picture of the activities of celibate women in his objections to their behavior. Since they had neither renounced possessions nor vowed obedience they felt that their clothing, cosmetics, and grooming were a matter of personal taste. They liked a good party, too; Cyprian complains that their attendance at typical bawdy Carthaginian wedding parties might threaten their vow of virginity, which must be "guarded with anxious fear."[32] And since they felt no sense of shame, nor did they "look immodestly" at anyone, they saw no problem with bathing at the integrated public baths.

They acted, it must be surmised, somewhat more freely than did dutiful daughters and married women. Cyprian mentions "notorious and detest-

---

28. Ibid., 4.3.2.

29. Ibid., 4.3.3.

30. That their *Christian life* is what is meant here is clear from ibid., 4.4.3.

31. Ibid., 4.4.2.

32. Cyprian *De habitu virginum* 2.

able gossip" about them that caused the church "frequently to bewail her virgins."[33] But again, as with the women who were living as *subintroductae*, Cyprian's concern is not primarily for the women themselves. Rather he insists repetitively that their freedom is causing men problems. Berating consecrated virgins who used makeup with "causing another's ruin,"[34] Cyprian insists that the women will be accountable for those they have "ruined":

> Without perhaps losing your own soul, you nevertheless ruin others and offer yourself [as] a sword and a poison, as it were, to those who behold you; you cannot be excused on the ground that your mind is chaste and pure.[35]

He speaks sternly to virgins, Cyprian says, for their own good and because he cares for them so much. He explicitly compares himself to God in chastising in order to correct: "Now if God chastises whom he loves, and chastises that he may correct, brethren also, and priests particularly, do not hate but love those whom they chastise."[36] The figure of the Roman *paterfamilias* is the model Cyprian has in mind when he admonishes, "Listen, virgins, as to a father, . . . listen to one who is faithfully watching over your advantages and interests."[37] If one of the attractions of celibacy for women was freedom from a paterfamilias who held their practical destinies in his hand, denial of their ability for self-definition and the imposition of yet another paternal authority, that of the Christian bishop, cannot have pleased the women to whom it was addressed. We may surmise that Cyprian's command, "Be such as the hand of the Father has fashioned you,"[38] carried for them all the ambiguity that we can detect in it.

Cyprian's problem with Christian women is different from that of Tertullian. Women are no longer mentioned as occupying leadership roles in Christian groups. Yet the control of groups of celibate women associated with local churches has become a focus of the bishops' power. Cyprian's letters and treatises suggest that the fragile power of a mid-third-century bishop, in Cyprian's case a power already questioned by ecclesiastical rivals, could be

33. Ibid., 20.

34. Ibid., 13.

35. Ibid., 9.

36. Ibid., 1.

37. Ibid., 21.

38. Ibid.

strengthened and demonstrated by the successful assertion of the authority of a paterfamilias over celibate women.

III

The final situation in North African Christianity that we will explore is that of Augustine, bishop of Hippo Regius in the beginning of the fifth century. Augustine's situation and problems are different from either those of Tertullian, in early third-century Carthage, or Cyprian, in mid-third-century Carthage. Augustine's authority among the North African Catholic churches was secure. But the society was not. Following the unbelievable sack of *Roma eterna* in 410 C.E., the shock waves quickly spread to North Africa, itself the location of internal political upheaval and threatened barbarian invasion.

Augustine's philosophical and theological work from 410 on can be understood partly as a massive attempt to support and promote the stability of Roman culture under the Christian emperor. His answer to the perilous slipperiness of what he thought of simply as civilization was the theological rationalization of a pervasive hierarchical orderliness. Almost thirty years before he wrote *The City of God* he outlined, in his treatise *On Continence*, three hierarchical pairs: spirit and flesh, husband and wife, and Christ and the Church. In about 420 C.E., writing in the sober wake of the sack of Rome, he needs only to add to these paradigms "ruler and people" to have a comprehensive model of human life from individual to society. "Of these," he wrote in 395 C.E., "the former cares for the latter in each case, and the latter waits upon the former. All are good when among them, some, excellently as superiors, and others, fittingly as subjects, preserve the beauty of order."[39]

Augustine's model of human being as hierarchically structured—body controlled by soul, soul controlled by God—both reflected and, in turn, came to be reflected by Western Christian society. His idea of the proper relationship of husband and wife provides an example of what he saw as the necessarily hierarchical structure of society. The subordination of women is central to Augustine's attempt to prescribe for the social and political instability of his time. In late Roman culture, Augustine saw an extension of his anthropological model in a necessary and inevitable subordination of some people to others. In the slippery world of the newly sacked city of Rome, he specifically urged that this hierarchical model be accepted as the lesser of the social evils. Although in Book 19 of *The City of God* he describes social

---

39. Augustine *De continentia* 23.

inequality as part of the evidence that human beings exist in a fallen state, a state of punishment, Augustine does not criticize this order but counsels respect for dominance and subordination on every level of society, from families to kingdoms. Social inequality, Augustine says, is the result of the anxious craving of the few for dominance over the many. "God did not wish the rational being, made in God's own image, to have dominion over any but irrational creatures, not human over human, but human over the beasts." Nevertheless, the "ordered harmony" Augustine advocates for society begins in the mini-society of the home where "the husband gives orders to the wife, parents to children, and masters to servants."[40]

Conspicuously missing from Augustine's program for ordered harmony under the permanently unsettled and unsettling conditions of this human pilgrimage is any glorification of inequality; but neither could he envision social arrangements in which dominance and subordination would not be necessary for peace. His is the rationalization that has been used throughout the history of the Christian West to justify dominance and subordination: the one who gives orders, Augustine writes, must consider himself the "servant," caring for the needs of those to whom orders are given; he must act from "dutiful concern," not from "lust for domination."[41]

Augustine's model of society is human being, a complex organism in which orderliness is necessary for life on the physical level and the body's subordination in value and activity to the soul is never questioned, even—or especially—when he calls the body the spouse[42] of the soul. Likewise, in the family and in society, Augustine sees only the inevitability of dominance and subordination; his model of body and soul does not—as it certainly might—provide him with a model of interdependence.

In Augustine's writings we do not find anything faintly resembling the rantings of Tertullian against women leaders; no women leaders are in sight. Nor do we find Tertullian's and Cyprian's concern about women's dress and the control of potentially autonomous women. Consecrated virgins by Augustine's time took vows that stipulated their obedience as well as virginity. He still wrote treatises addressed to virgins and widows, but the questions he takes up are those of attitudes, not of behavior. The spiritual danger of pride, of being puffed up because of their special gift of virginity, does not

40. Augustine *De civitate Dei* 19.14.

41. Ibid., 19.15.

42. Ibid., 15.7.

seem to have had political dimensions with the consecrated virgins Augustine addresses. One still senses something of the anxiety provoked by women not directly in the jurisdiction of a male in his careful instructions to celibate women. And there is still the sense of unattached sexuality as simultaneously miraculous and dangerous, but the more extreme metaphors of Tertullian and Cyprian do not appear in Augustine's advice. He explicitly rejects Cyprian's metaphor of God as jealous husband: "He is not the kind to whom someone may lie about you and cause him to fly into a jealous rage."[43]

Augustine's horizons have widened from the relatively small embattled and persecuted Christian communities of the third century, and his treatment of the place of women reflects this altered context. It is women's place in the society and the world that occupies him, not primarily in the Christian churches. Yet women and their roles are still crucial to his prescription for the maintenance of society. Submission, docility, obedience—these are the virtues urged on wives, consecrated virgins, and widows alike. The humility of the virgin must parallel the submissiveness of the wife, "thinking how she may please her husband."[44]

It is striking that Augustine promotes these virtues on women so frequently and so insistently, while men's temptations to tyranny on every level of society do not receive anything like the constant injunctions addressed to women's attitudes and behavior. In the 401 C.E. treatise, *The Good of Marriage*, Augustine discusses the question of why the patriarchs of the Old Testament were permitted to take more than one wife. His discussion reveals rather than states his attitude that unexamined domination is less to be feared than insubordination:

> It was permitted for one husband to have several wives, [but] it was not permitted for one woman to have several husbands, even for the sake of offspring. . . . For, by a hidden law of nature things that rule love singularity; things that are ruled, indeed, are subjected not only each one to an individual master, but also, if natural or social conditions allow, many of them are not unfittingly subjected to one master . . . just as many souls are properly subjected to the one God.[45]

43. Augustine *De sancta virginitate* 55.56.

44. Augustine *De bono coniugali* 11.13.

45. Ibid., 17.20.

"Things that rule love singularity"; again the rationale demonstrates the implicit identification of the male with God: "just as many souls are properly subjected to the one God." Augustine has learned a great deal from his African forefathers; their attitudes appear again and again in the different social and textual context in which Augustine used them. In Augustine's writings, the "woman question" has been fully resolved, philosophically and theologically rationalized in a form that will remain for 1500 years of Western Christian history.

These three stages in the development of the Christian churches and society reveal that patriarchal order was not, as we may have come to think of it, inevitable, God-ordained, and scripturally based. It was the gradual implementation of women's subordination, in churches and in society, over women who understood Christian faith to render obsolete the gender stipulations of their culture, who experienced the freedom of Christ specifically as freedom for the cultivation of a lifestyle and spiritual life undefined by males.

We are today faced with the challenge of a reinterpretation of these early struggles over the involvement of Christian women in the Christian churches. We must question whether Christian churches can continue to confine and limit women's roles and participation. The world in which we live gives us a sense of peril and urgency similar to that created in the early churches by an expected imminent eschatological limit to human life and work. Like early Christians, we live in a time in which the churches and the world desperately need to engage to the fullest the talent and energy of each Christian person. We are challenged, as were the earliest Christian communities, to service based on talent, regardless of gender, and to the establishment of the equality and dignity of every person. We are challenged to envision and create communities of love and service that reject our individual and cultural gender conditioning in the interest of working as speedily as possible to prevent war, to promote political and economic justice, and to further global peace. Recognizing and acknowledging the extent to which the political essence of Christianity has been patriarchal order, we must reappropriate the struggle, begun so long ago, for gender equality and we must give this struggle a different outcome in our perilous world.

CHAPTER 5

Roman North African Christian Spiritualities

In the three-hundred-year period of Christianity's greatest strength in North Africa, between the late second century C.E. and the mid-fifth century, distinctive forms of Christian spirituality emerged. The geographical context was a relatively small area of Roman North Africa, including the provinces of Numidia, Mauretania, and Proconsular Africa. In Roman North Africa, Christianity showed both continuities of characteristic problems, attitudes, ideas, and practices, and changes as the social and political position of North African Christians changed.

Attention to this small geographical area over a limited time period exemplifies the inadequacy of generalizations about "the early church." In a time before public communication media, local configurations must be respected as carefully as temporal distances. Moreover, the particularities of Christian spiritualities on Roman North African soil come clearly into focus only when Christian ideas and practices are approached from a comparative perspective, that is, one in which the primary native religions of North Africa are understood both as informing and as competing with Christianity. An ecumenical perspective is also essential to recognizing the distinctiveness of North African Christianity.

Traditional histories of Christianity usually begin from the hindsight of a late-fourth-century triumphant church and proceed to reach behind that *fait accompli* to identify its development or emergence. This, however, puts the cart before the horse. Not only does it mask the continuous conflict in which dominant interpretations of Christian belief and practice emerged, but it also—and more seriously—ignores the committed intellectual and ethical commitments of the full spectrum of North African Christians. Interpretations of Christian belief and practice that later came to be understood as heretical or schismatic from an orthodox perspective, flourished in Roman North Africa as attractive explanations of Christian beliefs and values. I will, then, adopt both comparative and ecumenical perspectives in the following discussion. I will regard Christian groups that identified themselves as Christian as alternative interpretations of Christian belief and practice rather than as heretics, especially in the time periods before the ecclesiastical decisions that branded them as such were made.

Roman North Africa

Three racial strains converged to produce "native" North Africans: semi-nomadic Libyans or Berbers, an indigenous race with roots going back to the ninth millennium B.C.E.; Phoenicians, a seafaring people from the eastern Mediterranean who gradually established themselves in North Africa, founding the city of Carthage (now Tunis), according to tradition, in 1186 B.C.E.; and the Italians who recolonized North Africa after the Punic Wars. By the Christian era, it was language, not race, that distinguished Berbers, Phoenicians, and Latin-speaking Romans in contemporary literature.

Carthage, the "New City," was, by the Roman period, a great Mediterranean power based largely on its agriculture and shipping. Carthage was the breadbasket of the Mediterranean, a practical hegemony that was maintained until the fifth century C.E. Its ship-building industry created and maintained the Roman navy. Explorers from ancient Carthage may have sailed as far as England and Ireland. Moreover, it was an international center of education and artistic activity; for example, mosaics were invented in Carthage. Its power rivaled and threatened Rome, leading to three Punic Wars between 246 and 146 B.C.E., in which ancient Carthage was destroyed and subsequently recolonized. By the mid-third century C.E., Carthage was again equal in wealth and productivity to Alexandria, and second only to Rome in power. Carthage was also an important center of Christianity.

Christianity in Roman North Africa

The origins of North African Christianity are lost in obscurity. The two most plausible theories are that Christianity emerged from the large Jewish community in Carthage in the second century, or that traders and immigrants from the eastern Mediterranean carried Christianity to North Africa. Even the African Christian author Tertullian, writing at the end of the second century, did not know the origins of North African Christianity; he reports legends concerning its origins in his *Prescription against the Heretics*. All Christian liturgies and literature in North Africa—as elsewhere in the empire—were in Greek until the beginning of the third century, when Tertullian wrote several of his treatises in Latin. The first Latin versions of the New Testament came from North Africa, and the Latin liturgy also originated there.[1]

Christianity was a popular movement in Roman North Africa. About 150 names of bishops in Mauretania, Numidia, and Proconsular Africa are known from the period up to the mid-third century. Only one of these had a Punic name, while about a dozen more were non-Latin. By the beginning of the fifth century, about seven hundred bishops were listed, though it is important to note that bishops often existed in towns less than ten miles apart. Christianity flourished in North Africa until the seventh century, when it was replaced by Islam.

The first extant reference to North African Christianity is in the mid-second-century C.E. African secular author Apuleius, who remarks scornfully on Christians in his *Metamorphoses*. The first extant document of African Christianity is the *Acts of the Scillitan Martyrs*, which describes the trial, on 17 July 180, of seven men and five women who were accused of being Christians and were sentenced to death on the arrival in Carthage of a new governor, Vigillius Saturninus. One of the governor's first official acts was to condemn to death these twelve African Christians with native names from a small town near Carthage. As they were led to execution, it is recorded that they cried, "*Deo gratias!*" "Thanks be to God!"—a phrase that was to become a rallying cry of African Christianity for several centuries.[2]

Three powerful and influential authors are primarily responsible for forming the Roman North African Christianity that, by the beginning of the fifth century, was synonymous with Catholic Christianity. In different social and political circumstances, Tertullian (d. 220 C.E.), Cyprian (d. 258 C.E.), and Augustine (d. 430 C.E.), shaped the religious life of Christians in relation to secular society, to dissident Christians, and to the church. Each author dealt, on location and under pressure, with issues of church discipline, the establishment of an authoritative church hierarchy as the basis for a heavily advocated but slenderly achieved Christian unity, and the crafting of a stable relationship between church, society, and Roman government. These three authors' interpretations of Christian values, lifestyle, and institutions

---

1. Saxer, *Vie Liturgique*, 11–12.
2. Musurillo, *Acts*, 86–89.

came to be normative in North Africa, as well as influencing the development of the Catholic Church across the Roman empire. Although later authors revered the earlier—Cyprian called Tertullian "the Master," and Augustine acknowledged the great respect North African Christians felt for Cyprian, the martyr-bishop of a century and a half before—each rejected particular decisions made by their antecedents in their different social and institutional circumstances. What these North African Christian authors shared, then, was not unanimity in belief and practice but commitment and creativity in interpreting Christianity in relation to the needs and opportunities of their own time.

Two characteristic preoccupations of North African Christianity make it distinctive: preoccupation with martyrdom and interest in the activity of the Spirit in Christian communities. One might without exaggeration characterize North African Christian spirituality as passionate, often to the point of fanaticism, and uncompromising, sometimes to the point of violence. Frequently unhappy with a geographically distant and, by the fourth century, wealthy imperial church, many North Africans chose Christian groups in which they could pursue extra-scriptural knowledge (the Manichaeans), or worship in locally governed Christian groups (the Donatists) or in groups in which the Spirit was still believed to speak immediately and directly through prophets who were not necessarily ordained to professional Christian leadership (Montanists). These groups dissented from Catholic belief, organization, and/or practice, but this essay will endeavor to demonstrate that they insistently preserved characteristically North African religious interests and values.

Roman Religion in North Africa

Archaeological and literary evidence for the practice of the cult of Saturn in North Africa is fragmentary but fascinating. The Saturn cult was a Punic religion, adopted by the African Berbers and popular primarily among the lower classes in Roman North Africa. It is striking that the only two Christian authors to report accusations of child sacrifice against Christians were Africans—Tertullian and Minucius Felix.[3] Did Africans find such accusations plausible because the practice of infant sacrifice continued in indigenous religions in remote regions in secret, as Tertullian claimed (*Apology* 9.3), even in his own day?

3. Rousselle, *Porneia*, 109.

Archaeological discoveries in Carthage have revealed numerous troph-ets, or urns for human sacrifice. More than four hundred urns have been excavated, containing human and animal bones buried between 700 and 146 B.C.E.[4] Lawrence Stager estimates that between 400 and 200 B.C.E. alone, about twenty thousand urns were buried, each containing at least one human baby, an average of one hundred sacrifices a year.[5] Thirty percent of the bones analyzed from the early period were those of infants under four. Of urns containing a single child, 68 percent contained a child of one to three years; the rest were young infants. Thirty-two percent of the urns contained two or more children. The ancient writer Diodorus Siculus described these public sacrifices:

> The people were filled with dread because they believed that they had neglected the honor of the gods that had been established by their fathers. In their zeal to make amends for their omission they selected 200 of the noblest children and sacrificed them publicly; others who were under suspicion sacrificed themselves voluntarily, in number not less than 300. There was in their city a bronze image of Cronus, extending his hands, palms up and sloping toward the ground, so that each of the children when placed thereon rolled down and fell into a sort of gaping pit filled with fire.[6]

Child sacrifice seems to have functioned either as expiation for guilt, as described above, or as a bid for success. A third-century B.C.E. document, reports that "the Carthaginians, whenever they seek to obtain some great favor, vow one of their children, burning it as a sacrifice to the deity, especially if they are eager to gain success."[7]

As archaeological evidence demonstrates, the substitution of animal for human sacrifice began in the second century when the cult of Saturn was romanized. Depictions of Saturn from this period represent the god as a bearded Roman in a toga. Rather than understanding the cruelty and vio-lence of the Saturn cult as discontinuous with Roman culture, however, it needs to be placed in the context of a violent society. One form of violence was the brutal wars by which a fifth to a sixth of the then world's popula-tion was brought under Roman jurisdiction in the last two centuries B.C.E.

4. Charles-Picard, *Les religions.*
5. Stager, "Rite of Child Sacrifice."
6. Quoted in Stager, "Rite of Child Sacrifice," 11.
7. Ibid., 6.

Another was violent public entertainment in the cities of the Roman empire. An "atmosphere of violence, even in peace" was maintained by public execution of prisoners, fights to the death between hundreds of gladiators, and the "indiscriminate slaughter of domestic and wild animals."[8] The popularity of these bloodbaths is attested by the huge colosseums in cities of the empire. Public killings were a common spectacle of Roman life.

Were there continuities between human sacrifice and Christian martyrdom in North Africa? It is not a stretch of the imagination to interpret gladiatorial fights to the death, public punishment and execution of criminals, and martyrdom of Christians as replacements for the human sacrifice abolished by Tiberius. Spectacles of the colosseum incorporated symbolic reference to North African religions. The Carthaginian martyrs Perpetua and Felicity were ordered, when they entered the arena, to put on the robes of a priestess of Ceres, while their male companions were to don the robes of priests of Saturn. Moreover, like the victims of infant sacrifice, Christians condemned to death were given a feast the day before their execution. When Saturus was attacked by a leopard, the crowd's exclamation on seeing Saturus's blood was "*Saluum lotum! Saluum lotum*!" "Well washed; well washed!" which may have been a ritual exclamation during a sacrifice to Saturn.

A final parallel between human sacrifice and Christian martyrdom in North Africa is even more illuminating. Sacrificial ritual required that the victim die happily—or "appear" to die happily. In the case of infants, "the parents played with them so that they would die laughing for the salvation of themselves, the city, and their family."[9] In *Apology* 8.7, Tertullian describes the "ritual laughter or at least gaiety which was supposed to accompany human sacrifices to Saturn: 'You need a baby which is still tender and which does not know of death and laughs as you raise your knife.'" Like sacrificial victims in the Saturn cult, African Christian martyrs are consistently reported to have met their deaths joyfully, embracing martyrdom as the "baptism by blood" that was believed to anticipate the general eschaton and guarantee them instant reception into heaven. The association of joyful death with individual and communal salvation was an ancient one in North Africa.

8. Hopkins, "Murderous Games," 2.

9. Rousselle, *Porneia*, 119; see also Reinach, "Le rire rituel."

Martyrdom and North African *Acta*

In *Confessions* 6.11, Augustine, bishop of Hippo, near Carthage, describes the immense interest the spectacles of the colosseum held for fourth-century Romans. He narrates the addiction of his friend and fellow African Alypius to gladiatorial fights and other entertainments. A century before, Christians had themselves been part of the spectacle as they were thrown to wild beasts, burned, and stabbed. Christian martyrdom made a lasting impression on North African liturgy and spirituality. *Acta*, accounts of the trials, tortures, and death of the martyrs were read on the anniversary of the martyr's death in North African liturgies.[10] Moreover, martyrdom as a fact of church life through the second and third centuries set an intransigent and lasting standard for radical commitment to Christianity.

Martyrdom was not, of course, uniquely the experience of North African Christians, but by the third century a "developed cult of martyrdom" can be identified in North Africa.[11] The leaders of African Christianity wrote treatises encouraging Christians to aspire to martyrdom. Tertullian and Cyprian—himself a martyr and the first African bishop to be martyred—urged steadfastness in the face of imprisonment, torture, and execution. Confessors—those who awaited death after condemnation for their Christian witness—were so revered in North Africa that their perceived power to forgive sin and to adjudicate differences among Christians was sometimes feared and resisted by church leaders.

North African Christian *actae* consistently emphasize the happiness of martyrdom. Clearly, the laughing infants sacrificed to Saturn hover in the common cultural background of North Africans. One of the most poignant documents of Roman North African Christianity, the *Passio Sanctarum Perpetuae et Felicitatis*,[12] describes the trial, imprisonment, and martyrdom of Perpetua, an educated member of an upper-middle-class family, and her slavewoman, Felicity. Perpetua and Felicity were arrested early in 203 C.E. for confessing adherence to Christianity. The central sections of the *acta* are widely accepted as the prison journals of the twenty-three-year-old Perpetua. The *acta* narrates the events just before their martyrdom. On the occasion of the confessors' last meal, Perpetua and her companions spoke to the crowd of curious voyeurs, "stressing the joy (*felicitatem*) they would have in their

---

10. Saxer, *Morts, martyrs, reliques*, 157.

11. Ibid., 154.

12. Musurillo, *Acts*.

suffering." On the day of their martyrdom—the "day of their victory"—the editor of the *acta* writes:

> They marched from the prison to the amphitheatre joyfully ("hilares") . . . trembling, if at all, with joy ("gaudio") rather than fear. . . . Perpetua went along with shining countenance and calm steps, as the beloved of God, as a wife of Christ . . . they rejoiced at this that they had obtained a share in the Lord's sufferings.[13]

The Holy Spirit in North African Christianity

The second emphasis of North African Christianity—interest in the continuing activity of the Holy Spirit—is also associated with martyrdom. By Tertullian's time it was commonly believed that the Holy Spirit accompanied persecuted Christians from the time of their arrest, through their time in prison, and to the moment of their translation into heaven. The expected spiritual privilege of the confessor is evident as Perpetua relates that she received visions, prayed for—and was assured of—the healing of her long-dead brother, and experienced the immediate cessation of physical and mental distress when her nursing infant son was taken from her. The prologue of the *acta* describes North Africa's interest in the present activity of the Spirit:

> Let those then who would restrict the power of the one Spirit to times and seasons look to this: the more recent events should be considered the greater. . . . We hold in honor and acknowledge not only new prophecies but new visions as well. . . . Thus no one of weak or despairing faith may think that supernatural grace was present only among those of ancient times, either in the grace of martyrdom or in visions, for God is always working as he promised.

North African Montanists

Perpetua and Felicity's *acta* seems to have emerged from a group of Montanist Christians, judging from their lively interest in the present activity of the Holy Spirit. Montanism originated in Phrygia in Asia Minor, but its importance within the history of Christianity lies in its development in North Africa. In a treatise from his Montanist period, *De pudicitia*, Tertullian acknowledges Montanism as threatening ecclesiastical hierarchical authority: "The church

---

13. Ibid., 18.

is not a conclave of bishops but the spirit manifested through a spiritual person."[14] Despite this, Montanism almost gained ecclesiastical recognition, as Tertullian testifies. The evident attraction for North African Christians of a Spirit-directed church is apparent in the fact that Montanism was still acceptable in North Africa as late as 203 C.E., a decade after its rejection in Rome. If we place Montanist dissent in the context of pervasive North African Christian interest in the guidance of the Spirit, Montanists appear less as dissidents in relation to Catholic Christianity than as faithful to one of African Christianity's strongest values.

Frequently, dissenting Christian interpretations—and groups of earnest and committed people—can be reconstructed only from the writings of their victorious opponents. However, Tertullian himself became an adherent of the "New Prophecy," and it is primarily from the writings of his Montanist period that one can reconstruct the interests, values, and practices of Montanists. An ecumenical perspective reveals the North African Montanists as a group committed to maintaining what they legitimately considered the core of African Christianity.[15]

Was Montanism in North Africa a separate church? Was it a "holy club" within North African congregations? It was apparently neither a heresy nor a schism, but it does appear to have been an enthusiastic and intransigent group characterized by adherence to a stricter discipline as well as to ongoing revelation as part of the Spirit's present activity. According to his own testimony, Tertullian was attracted both by the discipline and by Montanists' attention to the present prophetic activity of the Holy Spirit. Women prophets were associated with Montanus; before she died in 179 C.E., the prophet Maximilla, speaking as the voice of the Spirit, said: "I am driven as a wolf from the sheep. I am not a wolf; I am word, spirit, and power." Montanism continued to be referred to in writings until the eighth century, but no development can be discerned past the third century C.E.

In discipline, Montanists insisted on stricter and more frequent fasts than were customary for Catholic Christians. In addition to more demanding fasts, Montanists were expected to practice the xerophagy, or dry fast, two weeks (five days each) a year. There may be a connection between Montanist food practices and their interest in ecstatic prophecy and visions, both of which can be stimulated by fasting. Moreover, Montanists protested an in-

---

14. Tertullian *De pudicitia* 21.17.

15. Ash, "Decline of Prophesy."

creasing institutionalization of prescribed fasts, insisting on the time-honored practice of tailoring ascetic practices both to individual ability and to the goal for which the fast was undertaken. Montanists preferred self-discipline to external discipline, or legislation of common—and therefore necessarily nondemanding—fasts for the whole church. Tertullian notes that Catholics compared Montanists' fasting practices to those of pagans in that they lacked the element of communal, externally imposed discipline.

Montanists also proscribed second marriages, even when one of the partners had died. Tertullian's treatise *De monogamia*, connects insistence on one marriage to belief in one God, claiming that, although not to be found in scripture, "the Paraclete has taught" the restriction of marriage to one partner. Finally, Montanists rejected the prerogative of flight in times of persecution, a much-debated issue in North Africa. Claiming that because persecution represents "the just judgment of the Lord," Tertullian said that Christians must not endeavor to escape it. He especially deplored "persons in authority" taking to flight. However, the widespread rejection of his interpretation of Christians' duties is suggested by the fact that, as far as we know, no African bishop was martyred before Cyprian suffered martyrdom in the Decian persecution of the 250s C.E. Cyprian himself fled in the first wave of persecution, understanding this action as nothing more or less than judicious and in the best interests of the church for which he was responsible. Yet the intransigent and heroic Christianity represented by Montanist belief and practice needs to be understood in the context of an indigenous church whose origins come to light in the account of the uncompromising and joyful Scillitan martyrs, who departed to their death saying, "Thanks be to God! Today we are martyrs in heaven!"

Donatists

Like Montanists, Donatists differed from North African Catholics not in theological doctrine but in values and ecclesiastical loyalties. Originating in the persecution of Diocletian at the beginning of the fourth century, the Donatist church was, by Augustine's time, the majority Christian church in North Africa. By the end of the fourth century, a long history of dispute, debate, and violence separated Catholics and Donatists.

Donatists alleged that a Catholic bishop, Caecilian, was ordained in 311 C.E. by Felix of Aptunga, who had become a *traditore* by surrendering the holy scriptures to authorities of the Roman state during the persecution. His ordination was condemned by eighty Numidian bishops, but recognized by a greater majority of North African bishops. Throughout the fourth century the schism widened as intermittent persecution by imperial forces polarized the division between a "persecuted church" and a "persecuting church." At the beginning of the fifth century when public debates by Catholics and Donatists conducted under imperial sponsorship failed to bring the desired "unity," imperial laws were enacted against Donatists. Donatist clergy and lay people were required to become Catholic; Catholics were given Donatist property; Catholic bishops were charged with identifying Donatists who declined to transfer their allegiance to the Catholic Church, and Donatist clergy and lay people of all classes were fined for refusing to join Catholics. Formally, this was the end of the Donatist church, but underground Donatism persisted in North Africa until the Christian church in Africa was destroyed in the seventh and eighth centuries.

Did Donatists, like Montanists, perpetuate some ancient and thoroughly African religious values and attitudes? Donatism was the majority interpretation of Christianity on North African soil. And Donatists apparently held to ideas of ritual purity and the danger of contamination that can be related directly to the constant threat, and frequent reality, of martyrdom in the time before Constantine extended legitimacy and support to Christianity in 312 C.E. As confessors had rejected the assimilation of Christianity to the Roman state, so Donatists refused to participate in a Catholic Church they believed to be tainted by apostasy and actively engaged in spreading contamination through its sacraments.

Donatists also valued a self-governing North African church, autonomous in relation to the Roman empire. They seem to have supported the campaigns of two Moorish counts—Firmus in 372–375 C.E., and Gildo in the 390s—to rule Africa. Augustine mocked the Donatists on grounds that reveal his awareness of their nationalism. He ridiculed their view that they alone—a tiny branch of Christianity in relation to a world church—could claim to be a "pure" church. Their appeal to a time before the empire and the church were partners in governing society exposes their unwillingness to reconcile the contradiction between a Catholic Church in partnership with the formerly persecuting Roman state and their self-identification with the local martyrs of the earlier North African church. The radical fringe of Donatism, the Circumcellians, who were especially active in the province of Numidia, dramatized this identification with African martyrs by their use of the Scillitan martyrs' cry, "Deo gratias." They sacked and whitewashed

Catholic churches, captured, tortured, and murdered Catholics, and even, in states of ecstatic frenzy, flung themselves to death over cliffs—martyrs, in their view, for Donatist Christianity.

Donatist spirituality and ritual practice were partly a protest against a Catholic Church that had become a venue for social upward mobility and privilege. Donatists criticized Augustine's acceptance of the church as a *corpus permixtus*, in which blatant sinners and "convalescent" Christians rubbed elbows. Augustine acknowledged:

> One who enters [the church] is bound to see drunkards, misers, tricksters, gamblers, adulterers, fornicators, people wearing amulets, clients of sorcerers, astrologers . . . the same crowds who press into the churches on Christian festivals also fill the theatres on pagan holidays.[16]

Augustine's favorite metaphor for the Christian church was the parable of the wheat and the tares lying together on the threshing-room floor until authoritatively separated on the day of judgment. By contrast, Donatists invoked scriptural metaphors that refer to the church as bride of Christ "without spot or wrinkle." Tyconius, a Donatist theologian, was the first to use a metaphor of the church in the world later made famous by Augustine: the two cities, radically separated by their loyalty either to this world or to God.

Donatists were well aware that their debates with Catholics did not occur in a situation in which political power was evenly distributed. Identifying the "true church" as the persecuted church, Donatists cited scripture to argue that Christ did not use force. Augustine reports the Donatist Petilian as saying: "'Blessed are they which are persecuted for righteousness' sake, for theirs is the kingdom of heaven.' You are not blessed, but you make us martyrs to be blessed."[17]

Repetitiously citing "unity" as a greater and more essential value than purity of sacraments, Augustine gave an elaborate rationale for coercion of Donatists. His *Epistle* 185 (417 C.E.) to Boniface, tribune and count in Africa, enumerates a sad list of rationales for coercion. Initially opposed to coercion, Augustine writes, he became convinced of its usefulness when Christians who had been forced to join the Catholics testified that they are grateful to have been shown the error of Donatism. Citing the forcible conversion of the apostle Paul, Augustine outlined a method for coercion: "As in the case of

---

16. Augustine *De catechizandis rudibus* 25.48.
17. Augustine *Contra litteras Petiliani* 72.

the Apostle Paul . . . let them acknowledge in him Christ first compelling and afterward teaching, first striking and afterward consoling."[18] In the face of the established Roman virtue of tolerance, Augustine argued that there are situations in which tolerance is nothing more than laziness and negligence. In fact, Augustine concluded,

> If you were to see the effects of the peace of Christ: the joyful throngs, their eagerness to hear and sing hymns and to receive the word of God, the well-attended, happy meetings; the sentiments of many among them, their great grief in recalling past error, their joy in contemplating the known truth . . . you would say that it would have been excessively cruel for all these to be abandoned to eternal loss and to the torments of everlasting fire. . . .[19]

Some of Augustine's rationalizations for coercion have had a very long history of use in situations far removed from that of the minority North African Catholic Church.

The theological consanguinity of Donatism and Catholic Christianity is evident in the fact that Donatist laypeople were admitted to the Catholic Church without rebaptism, and Donatist clergy retained their former ranks and offices within the Catholic Church after a brief period of repentance. Although theological differences between Donatists and Catholics were insignificant, the *religious* values and therefore the spirituality of Donatists and Catholics differed. A full picture of Donatist spirituality cannot be reconstructed from the "fragments that remain" of this vigorous movement. However, if one respects Donatists' intense attention to ritual purity, more can be detected in Donatism than the belligerent and obstinate self-isolation described by Augustine.

Moreover, the Donatists' fierce protection of Christian sacraments was directly in line with the martyr-bishop Cyprian's insistence that those who had been baptized in dissident Christian groups must be rebaptized upon joining the Catholic Church. Donatists rightfully claimed to be the faithful successors of Cyprian's views. Augustine was very aware that his claim that the sacraments belong to Christ and are not tainted by the imperfection of the minister was in conflict not only with Cyprian's insistence on rebaptism but also with Tertullian, who had been the first to declare non-Catholic baptism

18. Augustine *Epistula* 185.22.

19. Ibid., 185.32.

invalid. Tertullian had argued, in *De baptismo*, that because the Holy Spirit was not present in "heretical" baptism, it could not be effective.

Augustine's treatise *De baptismo* against the Donatists begins by acknowledging that Donatists are citing Cyprian's authority for their belief that the sacraments must be maintained in purity, but he argues: "The authority of Cyprian does not alarm me, because I am reassured by his humility." Cyprian, who died before there was a final resolution of issues surrounding rebaptism, was more concerned, Augustine insisted, about the unity of the church than about his own views on rebaptism. His final appeal, in *De baptismo*, dismissed a view of Christianity he had come to see as provincial, for that of a Catholic Church:

> how much more readily and constantly should we prefer, either to the authority of a single bishop, or to the council of a single province, the rule that has been established by the statutes of the universal church.

Manichaeans in North Africa

Mani, a Persian who called himself the "apostle of Jesus Christ," claimed to offer a revelation that superseded that of Christ's earthly teachings. He taught that the Holy Spirit, promised three centuries before, had finally descended in him. Mani was martyred by crucifixion in 276 C.E. at the instigation of Zoroastrian priests. Manichaeism was a missionary religion with claims to universality. Within Mani's lifetime it had spread beyond Mesopotamia to Iran and adjoining parts of the Roman empire. Advancing along commercial routes, Manichaean groups were also in Arabia, Armenia, Syria, Asia Minor, including Palestine, the Balkans, Italy, Spain, and Gaul. Manichaeism spread from Egypt to North Africa at an early date, nearly twenty years earlier than the first reference to Manichaeism in Rome.

Manichaeism was syncretistic, incorporating features of Buddhism, Zoroastrianism, Taoism, Confucianism, and Christianity. It was suspect in the Roman empire, however, not only for its ideas but even for its place of origin—Persia, the third-century "California" of new religious movements. And this most persecuted of heresies was not accepted by the religions with which it sought to affiliate, perhaps largely because Mani claimed to have the only true interpretation of each. Despite its claims to possess Truth, the virtual absence of polemical literature in Manichaeism is striking in comparison with the volume of anti-Manichaean literature.

Latin translations of Manichaean texts appeared at the end of the third century, less than a century after the first North African Christian writings in Latin. The aesthetic qualities of the great tomes that contained Mani's teachings were not the least of Manichaeism's attractions; they were inscribed with graceful calligraphy and lavishly illustrated. According to tradition, Mani himself was a skillful painter.

Only twenty years or so after Mani's death, sometime between 31 March 297 and the same date in 302, the emperor Diocletian dispatched the first prohibition of Manichaeism to Julianus, the proconsul of Africa. The rescript demanded that "Manichees and magicians and their sacred books" be burned. Yet, in the West, the fourth century was the time of the greatest numerical and geographical development—and the greatest persecution—of Manichaeism. Following Diocletian's edict of 297 outlawing Manichaeism, emperors throughout the fourth century reiterated and attempted to enforce the edict—Constantine in 326, Valentinian in 372, and Theodosius in 381. Yet Manichaeism survived both the Arian Vandal rulers of fifth-century North Africa, and Justinian's (sixth century) reconquest of North Africa, which brought renewed Catholic persecutions of Manichaeans. As late as 724, Pope Gregory II cautioned against the ordination of Africans who had fled to Italy from Islamic invaders because many of them had strong connections with Manichaeism. In North Africa, traces of Manichaeism can be identified until Christianity itself was extinguished by Islamic invasions.

At the time of Augustine's encounter with the Manichaeans, Manichaeism had been established in North Africa for almost a century. It flourished within Catholic congregations, claiming to be an intellectually sophisticated and rigorously ascetic version of Catholic Christianity, a Christianity of the inquiring mind. In his *Letter* 236, Augustine acknowledged that one of his subdeacons had been a Manichaean Hearer for years without being detected by the Catholic congregation to which he ministered. Differences between Catholics and Manichaeans seem to have been less evident on location than in retrospect. Both the popularity of Manichaeism and its compatibility with Catholic Christianity made it especially difficult to extirpate from North Africa.

Ironically, Augustine himself was repeatedly and throughout his life accused of Manichaeism. In his youth, he had been a Manichaean Hearer for nine years; his *Confessions* describe both his attraction to Manichaeism and his subsequent disenchantment. His ordination to Catholic priesthood was delayed while suspicions that he had not decisively broken with Manichaeism were investigated. Moreover, as a Catholic priest and bishop, his commitment to ascetic monasticism, and his teaching that marriage and sex are inevitably implicated in the transmission of original sin repeatedly sparked accusations that he had never completely departed from the religion of his youth. Perhaps his personal vendetta against Manichaeism was motivated at least in part by his eagerness to demonstrate his orthodoxy. His harshness toward the priest who simultaneously discharged his duties as a Catholic priest and participated in a Manichaean cell also witnesses to Augustine's need to demonstrate his lack of sympathy for the Manichaeans.

Manichaeans were dualists, positing a kingdom of light and a kingdom of darkness eternally at war with each other. Their primary appeal to the young Augustine lay in their clear and satisfying answer to the problem of the origin of evil. The kingdom of darkness, eternally at odds with the kingdom of light, was the cause of pain and evil; it was also the home of bodies and the natural world: However, Manichaeans' metaphysical dualism was tempered by their recognition that "in experience," the kingdom of darkness and the kingdom of light—the material and the spiritual worlds—were intertwined. This meant that all material things contain particles of spiritual light and thus are sacred. Manichaeans believed that these particles of light are sentient, suffering in their entrapment in the material world of bodies and objects, yearning to breathe free of their prisons and reunite with their spiritual homeland.

The suffering of all things did not, for the Manichaeans, remain an abstract notion; rather it was vivid and concrete. For example, the *Cologne Codex* relates that before Mani organized his own religion, while he was still a member of the Elchasaios sect, he was forced to do agricultural work. As he worked he found that "blood oozed from the places where the plants had been hurt by the blows of the sickle. They also cried out with a human voice because of the blows they received."[20]

Manichaean literature resounds with the poignant longing of the light particles to return to the Kingdom of Light, a longing believed to be at its most acute in human beings. "The drama . . . centers on the redemption of the Light Elements which have been swallowed by the archons of Darkness and have thus become mixed and sullied."[21] One Manichaean understanding of Jesus—an understanding documented only in North Africa—was that

---

20. Lieu, *Manichaeism*, 34.

21. Ibid., 14.

of "*Jesus patibilis*," Jesus as the prototypical and quintessential living soul (*viva anima*), perennially trapped and suffering in the world of the senses. Augustine quotes the Manichaean Faustus's description of the suffering Jesus: "The Holy Spirit, by his influence and spiritual infusion, makes the earth conceive and bring forth the mortal Jesus, who, as hanging from every tree, is the life and salvation of humanity."[22]

From Augustine's perspective, North African Manichees displayed a virtually neurasthenic sensitivity to all kinds of sufferings—human, animal, plant, and mineral.

Manichaeism was also a highly disciplined way of life. Augustine is the source of a rich store of information about Manichaean practices in North Africa. These must be described under two categories: those required of Hearers, and those expected only of the "Perfect" or Elect. Regulations for both were designed to avoid actions that might harm the light particles or further entrench them in matter. For Manichaeans, nothing short of the redemption of God was at stake: God is Light, trapped in the material world. The release of the light will actively serve to speed the "Future Moment" in which, the liberation of the Light nearly completed, the material world will be abandoned to its native evil and warfare. The faithful will be translated to the kingdom of light, there to participate in and enjoy this blissful reward—Hearers at the right hand of the triumphant Jesus, while the Elect are transformed into angels.

Hearers lived as fully functioning members of secular society. They were permitted to marry, but encouraged not to bear children. Their duties to the sect consisted primarily of a "soul service" in which they cared for the elect, providing and preparing their daily ritual meal. The *Kephalaia of the Teacher*, a fourth-century Egyptian document, describes the connection of food practices to the release of the light particles: "The alms which pass over to the Elect are made like many Icons, and they are purified, and they depart to the Country of the Living."[23] At their death, Hearers could expect to be reincarnated, and the body to which they were reassigned was contingent on the quality and faithfulness of their service to the elect.

The practices of the Elect were considerably more strenuous. They were contained in the "Three Seals" that Augustine described in *De moribus manichaeorum*: the Seal of the Mouth, the Seal of the Hands, and the Seal of the

---

22. Augustine *Epistula* 236 (20.22).
23. Wimbush, *Ascetic Behavior*, 205

Breast. What leaves the mouth as well as what enters is governed by the Seal of the Mouth: blasphemous speech was prohibited, as was the eating of meat and drinking of wine. Vegetarianism was prescribed because the bodies of animals contain fewer light particles than the plants. Animals ingest light by feeding on plants, but a portion of this light was believed to be obliterated in the transfer. Wine was forbidden because it induces intoxication and the forgetfulness of one's real self and home in the kingdom of light, a forgetfulness that Manichaean teachings, doctrines, hymns, and prayers resisted.

The Seal of the Hands stipulates that the faithful must not perform any task that might harm the particles of light. By this Seal, they were "forbidden to till the soil, or to pluck fruit, or to harvest any plant or to kill any animal, no matter how small."[24] Bathing was also forbidden: Manichees emphasized the pollution of the water by dirt from the body rather than the cleansing of the body. The Seal of the Breast forbids sexual intercourse in that its result is the propagation of more flesh in which light particles are painfully enslaved.

In the West, the ritual practices of Manichaeans were conducted in private homes. Once a day Hearers and Elect gathered, the Hearers to prepare and witness the meal—in North Africa it was called "eucharist"— consumed by the Elect. At this solemn ritual, the beautiful and haunting Manichaean hymn cycles and psalms were also sung. A weekly confession of sins—Hearers to Elect, and Elect to Elect—completed Manichaeans' ritual practice. Different religious sensibilities underlie Augustine's theology and that of the Manichaeans. In contrast to the Manichaeans' "emotional" view of the suffering universe, Augustine argued in his *Epistle of Manichaeus Called Fundamental* that the only "just judgment" results from a mind "composed," rational, and free of emotion. Augustine's idea of God's participation in the universe is interdependent with his view of suffering. Augustine's God is "present by the power of divinity, for administering and ruling all things, undefilably, inviolably, incorruptibly, 'without any connection with them.'" According to Augustine, the Manichaeans' God, by contrast, was "everywhere mixed up in heaven, in earth, in all bodies, dry and moist, in all sorts of flesh, in all seeds of trees, herbs, humans and animals . . . fettered, oppressed, polluted."[25] The Manichaeans' God was intimately and integrally engaged in the world and its processes, deeply interior to the universe.

---

24. Lieu, *Manichaeism*, 20.

25. Augustine *De natura boni* 46.44.

The continuity of Manichaeism with North African Christianity, and therefore the attractiveness of Manichaeism in North Africa, can be seen in its strict discipline and in its clear distinction of spiritual from physical. Manichaeism's claim to a revelation beyond scripture is also reminiscent of the Montanists' interest in the present prophetic activity of the Holy Spirit. Moreover, Manichaeism was a martyr church, the most persecuted of any Christian sect. Clearly, these strong connections with the earliest African Christianity contributed to its popularity in North Africa.

North African Catholics in the Roman Period

North Africa was the volatile location for the emergence of a constantly contested consensus on issues of ecclesiastical organization and order. Although the subject of this essay is not the practical matters of church authority and discipline that North African Christians struggled over, the spiritualities of these Christians cannot be treated in separation from these struggles. I have endeavored to demonstrate the continuity of these controversies with both the earliest Christianity and with indigenous religion in North Africa.

One group of Christians remains to be discussed: North African Catholics, especially as represented by their most prolific and influential bishop, Augustine of Hippo, pervasively affected the subsequent development of Christianity in the West to our own day. Augustine inherited North African Christian emphases and interests, but his sense of a broader world and a Catholic Church that could claim universality was the result of his sojourn as a successful young teacher of rhetoric in the imperial capital of Milan. Augustine revised characteristic North African Christian emphases and interests in the direction of bringing them into accord with a world Christianity and thus transmitted North African Christianity to the medieval West. Augustine was also the influential articulator of a model of Christian spirituality that has become the dominant model of Western Christianity.

Among Christian authors of the first centuries of the Christian era, Augustine is unique in his presentation of theological ideas in the context of his own life and experience. He was the first Christian author to demonstrate how his religious sensibilities were formed by people and events. His *Confessions* details the long and circuitous path by which his intellectual quest and his experience in relation to family, friends, and lovers brought him to understand God's activity in his life. Pursuing sex, professional success, and social position with all his energy, he came at the end of this exhausting agenda to understand his complete dependence on God's grace for salvation and nourishment. He named this agenda *concupiscentia*, a compulsive grasping at every object that crossed his path in the fear that something would be missed. Intellectual questions such as the origin of evil intermingled with personal unhappiness to lead him, at the age of thirty-two, to a more cosmopolitan version of the Catholic Church of his North African childhood.

The central moment in Augustine's autobiography, the moment for which the book is justly famous, is that of his conversion. Curiously, it was not a moment of intellectual insight; intellectual insight preceded and informed the moment of his conversion of the will, but it was not sufficient for this. Nor was it a moment of belief or religious ecstasy. Augustine narrates this experience quite explicitly as a conversion from compulsive sexual activity to continence.

Throughout the *Confessions*, prefiguring and mirroring his conversion account, Augustine described himself as alternatively distracted and dispersed among temporary pleasures or gathered and collected in a disciplined "return" to himself and to God. His model of the spiritual life as recollection has become the dominant model of Western Christian subjectivity and spirituality and has, in the twentieth century passed into secular culture in the form of numerous varieties of psychotherapy and secular spirituality. The model is one of centering, of arresting the hemorrhage of energy and attention that flows out of the self onto other human beings and objects of all sorts, and pulling that energy within—collecting, focusing, centering. Augustine's clearest definition of the model occurs in the *Confessions*:

> I have been spilled and scattered among times whose order I do not know; my thoughts, the innermost bowels of my soul, are torn apart with the crowding tumults of variety, and so it will be until all together I can flow into you [God], purified and molten by the fire of your love.[26]

Continence was the key to changing not only the course of Augustine's life but also the direction of his longing and passion. But continence was more than a resolution of his compulsive sexuality. It was also symbolic of a unified and unifying affection and attention. Thus, continence defined the form and dynamic of the spiritual life for Augustine and, as a result of the strength and beauty of his description, for Western Christianity.

26. Augustine *Confessiones* 11.29.

Augustine was ordained priest by congregational acclamation, and sub-sequently bishop, in the town of Hippo Regius as he and several companions were passing through the town on their return to North Africa. From this institutional base, he became a major figure in the translation of Christianity from a persecuted sect to the official religion of the Roman empire. Augustine's mature theology was formed in the heat of polemical struggle against the alternative interpretations of Christian faith that flourished in North Africa, especially Donatism, Manichaeism, and, later in his career, Pelagianism. Each of these controversies centered on conflicting interpretations of the human being and thus had, as we have seen in discussing Donatism and Manichaeism, implications for spirituality.

In Augustine's conflict with Pelagius, and later with Pelagius's younger advocate, Julian of Eclanum, Augustine articulated his sense of human beings as helpless infants, utterly dependent on God's grace for the accomplishment of every good act. Pelagius taught that the grace bestowed on each human being in her/his creation was a sufficient basis for accomplishing good. He advocated Christian adulthood, urging that people take responsibility for their actions and actively endeavor to perform the good. "Since righteous-ness is possible," he wrote to Demetrias, a prospective nun, "righteousness is obligatory."

Augustine saw in Pelagius's teaching a fatal temptation to Christians to depend on their own efforts rather than on God's grace. Augustine's develop-ment of the doctrine of original sin responded to Pelagius's optimistic view of the inherent goodness of human nature. Moreover, Augustine understood the inevitable undermining of human goodness and happiness not simply as a flaw, wound, or weakness as Tertullian had named it—*vitium*—but as *peccatum*, sin, a strand of sinfulness intimately woven into the character of each human being. In the last decade of his life, in his encounter with Julian of Eclanum, he identified the transmission of original sin as occurring at the moment of conception, an analysis that subsequently contributed to an institutionalized lack of esteem for human sexuality as a gift of God.

Augustine's own experience of sexuality as a "tyrant," in Plato's expres-sion, and his much later identification of original sin as transmitted by sexual activity is strangely dissonant with his lifelong committed effort to under-stand human bodies as integral and permanent to human persons. As he studied the scriptures and considered the doctrines of creation, incarnation, and resurrection of the body, he recognized that the classical philosophical description of human beings as hierarchically layered parts—that is, rational soul on top, then irrational soul, and body at the bottom—could not be integrated with those Christian doctrines that insisted on human bodies (both of male and female) as the good gift of a generous God.

Augustine's integration of body as essential to human beings and the condition of human salvation incorporated Tertullian's strong sense of the Christian sacraments as conjunctions of material and spiritual. In the context of conflict with Marcion, who believed that the body was accidental and incidental to human being and could not participate in the salvation of the soul, Tertullian had written:

> To such a degree is the flesh the pivot of salvation, that since by it the soul becomes linked with God, it is the flesh which makes possible the soul's election by God. For example, the flesh is washed that the soul may be made spotless; the flesh is anointed that the soul may be consecrated; the flesh is signed that the soul too may be protected; the flesh is overshadowed by the imposition of the hand that the soul may be illuminated by the Spirit; the flesh feeds on the body and blood of Christ so that the soul may become fat with God.[27]

Incorporating this strong view of the role of the body into the Christian faith, Augustine contributed the philosophical rationale for the body being an integral and permanent feature of the human being. This contribution further supported an enriched—and now institutionalized in the universal church—view of the Christian sacraments as a material vehicle of efficacious grace. Augustine described a complex theological system in which the union of body and soul in a single human being became the model and exemplar of the union of Christ and the Church as made present—localized—in the union of spiritual and material in the sacraments. He thus articulated—and his institutional authority stabilized—a strongly corporate spirituality practiced within the liturgy of the Catholic Church.

Augustine pictured all human beings as engaged in a long struggle toward the differing objects of each person's longing, desire, and delight. He distinguished the human race into two groups according to the objects of their desire. Those who belong to the "earthly City" pursue the powerfully attractive objects of sex, power, and possessions; and those of the "City of God" journey on pilgrimage toward the ultimate completion and fulfillment of human perfection in the resurrection of the body. Yearning for the moment

---

27. Tertullian *De carne Christi* 4.

beyond time and space when the resurrected body will be reunited with the redeemed soul, Christian pilgrims struggle across time toward a happiness and pleasure never fully present in the transitory world of present human existence. Briefly rewarded and nourished by glimpses of that future satisfaction, Christians journey in faith toward a moment when, Augustine wrote, the "eyes of the body" will somehow gaze on the incorporeal God.

Conclusion

This survey of Roman North African Christianity has endeavored to demonstrate the convergence of alternative interpretations of Christian belief and practice in the theology of Augustine of Hippo. Modified and philosophically examined in Augustine's writings, Augustine's interest in human bodies, in the activity of the Spirit symbolized in the sacraments, and in his acknowledged fanciful picture of the completion and fulfillment of the work of human salvation in the resurrection of the body form the characteristic interests of North African Christianity. It was Augustine who inherited, interpreted in the context of his own time, and transmitted these interests to Western Christianity. Both his model of individual spirituality as centering—returning to God through returning to self—and his construction of corporate spirituality as focused by the sacraments have become characteristic of Catholic Christianity. This mainstreaming of African spirituality was, however, not without loss, as lively dissident Christian groups were increasingly marginalized and gradually faded from the historical record. Ironically, it is because of this incorporation in "universal" Catholic belief and practice that the roots of Western spirituality in the characteristic interests and concerns of ancient North Africa have been forgotten. Western Christianity in all its modern branches owes a tremendous debt to the passionate spirituality of a Christianity defined by martyrdom and the ongoing activity of the Holy Spirit. North African Christian spirituality was redefined when martyrdom was no longer a threat. It was redefined to meet the demand of the corporate spiritual nourishment through the practice of sacraments and individual spirituality. It aimed at centering of attention and affection in longing and a delight that, as Augustine said, can be trusted to "order the soul,"[28] for "my weight is my love; by it I am carried wherever I am carried."[29]

28. Augustine *De musica* 6.11.29.
29. Augustine *Confessiones* 13.9.

CHAPTER 6

The Body and Human Values in Augustine of Hippo

Augustine, bishop of Hippo in the North African province of Numidia at the end of the fourth century, was the first Christian author to begin his thinking and writing with an analysis of human experience. In place of beginning as the pre-Socratic philosophers did, with speculation about the physical world, or as Plato did with a cosmological scheme, or yet with Aristotle's question about the behavior of people and things, Augustine began by examining the human condition, in particular his own human condition—the texture, the subjective color of the fabric of his life. In doing so, he was amazed that his starting point was so distant from the characteristic interests of most people:

> And people go abroad to wonder at the heights of mountains, the huge waves of the sea, the broad streams of rivers, the vastness of the ocean, the turnings of the stars—and they do not notice themselves.[1]

Augustine began, then, by noticing himself. "I came to understand," he wrote, "through my own experience."[2]

When you examine human nature as it is, Augustine said, the first thing you notice is that things are not as they should be: a puzzling and terrifying disjunction lies between every person's concerted efforts to be happy and the overwhelming pain human beings experience.

Everyone, whatever his condition, desires to be happy:

1. Augustine *Confessiones* 10.8 (Warner).
2. Ibid., 8.5.

94

> There is no one who does not desire this, and each one desires it
> with such earnestness that it is preferred to all other things; who-
> ever, in fact, desires other things, desires them for this end alone
> . . . in whatever life one chooses . . . there is no one who does not
> wish to be happy.[3]

Why, then, Augustine asked himself, looking around, did he see so little happiness in others and in himself? He recognized that part of the problematic
nature of human life lies in a vast amount of involuntary suffering, a constant
and lifelong vulnerability to an almost infinite supply of pains. In the *City
of God* he described the evidence he saw that there is too much pain in the
world, far more, that is, than one can learn from. He listed a long catalog
of woes that range from the discipline one must undergo as a child in order
to be socialized and educated to the "pains that trouble all humankind":
the human and non-human sources of pain, terror and death, the harshness
of weather—storms, tempests, floods, earthquakes—political upheavals, the
danger of being crushed by falling buildings, or of being attacked by animals:
"anyone walking anywhere is liable to sudden accidents, . . . the assaults of
demons, and diseases for which the treatments and medicine themselves are
instrument of torture."[4] The list goes on and on: restless dreams, fear itself,
. . . But it was not the involuntary pain experienced by human beings that
Augustine was most interested in, but the apparently voluntary way that human beings seemed to dismantle their own happiness as fast as they build it.
The *Confessions*, Augustine's own story, both illustrates this observation and
tries to explain it. To an extent unexampled in his predecessors, Augustine
insisted on setting his ideas in the context of his life and invited his readers
to do so also.

Augustine, newly elected bishop by congregational acclamation at the
age of forty, wrote a journal in order to understand his own experience. The
Confessions is therapy, not only in the modern sense of introspection and
reconstruction of one's personal past, but also in the much broader ancient
sense described by Plato when he called the practice of philosophical exploration *therapeia*—therapy, the attempt to locate and orient oneself not only
within the events of one's own life, but also within time and space, history
and the cosmos, the larger arena of human existence. Also, the *Confessions*

---

3. Augustine *Sermo* 306.3. See also my extended discussion of Augustine on happiness
in chapter 3 of this volume.

4. Augustine *De civitate Dei* 22.21 (Bettenson).

is a case history that Augustine shared with other interested people, not his private "journal." Part of Augustine's motivation in telling the story of his life was his reader's perennial interest and stimulation in hearing about someone else's "journey."

Augustine described the events and circumstances of his life as episodes in a frenzied struggle for happiness, accompanied by the cumulative disillusionment that eventually brought him to the burned-out condition in which he learned a new way of being and living. He wrote of his life as a prize-winning public speaker and popular teacher of rhetoric in Milan:

> I panted for honors, for money, for marriage. . . . I found bitterness and difficulty in following these desires. . . . How unhappy my soul was then! . . . I got no joy out of my learning. . . . I was eaten up by anxieties.[5]

Let us look at this subjective "tone" of Augustine's experience more closely. Augustine called his anxiety, his habitual grasping at every object that crossed his path in the fear that something would be missed, concupiscence. He saw it operating most nakedly, most undisguisedly, not in sex—contrary to his "press"—and not even in promiscuity. Rather his paradigm of concupiscence was the newborn infant. Taking his paradigm of concupiscence seriously helps to illuminate what Augustine meant by the often misinterpreted word "concupiscence." Augustine stripped off the rose-colored glasses through which adults romantically view babies and revealed the infant's behavior as anxious behavior. From the perspective of the infant's subjectivity, the world seemed at once very hard work and terrifying. The classical world, the world of Augustine's education, had seen old age as the time of human life that most deserved sympathy; Augustine wrote: "Who would not tremble and wish rather to die than to be an infant again if the choice were put before him?"[6] Compare the behavioral psychologist Jean Piaget's description of infant behavior in order to get a sense of what Augustine saw in the behavior of the infant:

> It is striking to observe . . . how the nursling, when its mother . . . is getting it ready for its meals, counts very little on her for obtaining the object of its desires; it makes a great fuss, becomes impatient, tries to grasp the breast or bottle . . . but is not at all content

---

5. Augustine *Confessiones* 6.6.
6. Augustine *De civitate Dei* 21.4.

to await the natural course of events. It all happens as though it depended only on itself to attain its goal?[7]

Moreover, Augustine saw in the behavior of the infant the form of all future concupiscence; as the infant grows up, his anxious grasping is not so much eradicated as extended, given different objects and wider scope. The anxiety of infancy gives way to the anxieties of childhood, adolescence and adulthood:

> For it is just these same sins which, as the years pass by, become re-lated no longer to tutors, school-masters, footballs, nuts, and pet sparrows, but to magistrates, kings, gold, estates, and slaves.[8]

What impressed Augustine was the continuity of the structuring role of anxious grasping, or compulsiveness.

Concupiscence pervades and organizes human life, from the first moment of the infant in which he grasps breath, to the adult's pursuit of sex, power and possessions. It is not, we must notice, a pleasant aspect of human experience. To interpret the element of concupiscence in human life as zestful and energizing, giving interest and motivation to life, is to misinterpret in the most fundamental way. To demonstrate this, Augustine gave his reader a long and sometimes excruciatingly detailed exposition of his experience—experience he consistently presents as painfully disoriented and joylessly compulsive. The conclusion at which he arrived was that the appropriate attitude toward concupiscence is sympathy. He marveled that "no one is sorry for the children; no one is sorry for the older people; no one is sorry for both of them."[9] Augustine called concupiscence "sin," but he did not use the word judgmentally to cast blame or to convoke personal guilt; rather, Augustine understood concupiscence as a sickness or wound, the result of an ancient fall which radically and disastrously debilitated human nature. No one, Augustine said, gives concupiscence the sympathy it deserves.

Augustine's account of the reinforcement of the habit pattern of concupiscence also insists on the unsatisfying nature of this compulsive behavior. From the perspective of the self-knowledge he had gained in his experience of conversion—the breaking of that ancient pattern—Augustine said that concupiscence is not, in fact, "nourished" by its objects, even in attaining

---

7. Piaget, *Construction of Reality*, 329.
8. Augustine *Confessiones* 1.1.
9. Ibid., 1.9.

them. The objects are, Augustine insisted, good in themselves; but they are nevertheless consistently unsatisfying to the person who pursues them concupiscently. Instead, the person, repetitiously following the grasping pattern of concupiscence, experiences an increasing lack of real nourishment: "For those who find their gratification in external things easily become empty and pour themselves out on things seen and temporal and, with starving minds, lick shadows."[10] The finite object's ultimate incapacity to provide infinite satisfaction, however, curiously only seems to prompt human beings to redouble their efforts to secure gratification, efforts that spin them deeper and deeper into the ruts of habitual behavior. Augustine summarized his cumulative experience of "enslavement" in his description: "From a disordered will came concupiscence, and serving concupiscence became a habit, and the unresisted habit became a necessity. These were the links—so I call them a chain—holding me in hard slavery."[11]

The pseudo-"nourishment" of the habit of concupiscence is the gratification of a repetition compulsion: in Augustine's vivid language, "scratching the itching scab of concupiscence"[12] rather than happy enjoyment of objects. Suffering from malnutrition, the psyche sinks into a state in which lethargy and anxiety are combined,[13] a state that assimilates the inertia of the sleepwalker with frenzied activity. The quality of relationships with other human beings in this mode is dramatically presented in Augustine's image of "eating one another up, as people do with their food."[14] The behavior of the infant at the mother's breast is disguised, but structurally unaltered in adult behavior. Augustine's real sympathy was not with the victim of this greedy use of another human being, but with the victimizer; Augustine knew by experience that the role of victimizer is at least as unpleasant—and perhaps more so—than that of the victim. "And no one is sorry for both of them. . . . "

Two questions emerge from Augustine's graphic, even lurid, description of human life as organized by the frantic pursuit of objects. First, what is the body's role in this pattern of anxious grasping? Is concupiscence really a happy enjoyment of bodily pleasures—at least until Augustine's guilt reinterpreted these pleasures as detrimental to the soul? The second question is, how

10. Ibid., 9.4.

11. Ibid., 8.5.

12. Ibid., 9.1.

13. Ibid., 9.13.

14. Ibid., 9.2.

has Augustine's account of human nature reached forward in time to affect twentieth-century people?

Let us consider first the relationship of concupiscence to the human body. Is Augustine responsible for the dualistic, body-denying ideas that have influenced the history of the West in both its most fundamental cultural and institutional forms and in the most private and intimate experience of the individual?

We began by speaking of Augustine's sharp, perhaps, to us, exaggerated, sense of the inevitable pain and suffering of human life; we need to recall Augustine's neuresthenic sense of the pervasiveness of human pain in order to understand the body's role as Augustine did. Beginning as he did with personal experience—not with received ideas, whether metaphysical or scriptural—Augustine interpreted human suffering as part of the evidence that the human race as a whole exists in a "state of punishment." Augustine found concupiscence and death the two clearest and most poignant pieces of evidence of such a state. Human life with its gratuitous suffering was unintelligible to Augustine without understanding suffering as a punishment: "What else is the message of all the evils of humanity?" This conclusion must be carefully and sensitively interpreted. Many twentieth-century people think it pessimistic to interpret human life as seriously and permanently damaged, weakened, and disoriented because of an ancient fault. A theory of original sin may, however, be a far gentler interpretation of concupiscence than personal responsibility.

Death was an even more conclusive evidence to Augustine than concupiscence that human life is a "state of punishment." In strong contrast to earlier Christian authors who urged their readers to "despise" or even happily to "embrace" death, Augustine had no such minimizing interpretation of this "greatest of human evils."[15] To his own question, "Is death, which separates soul and body, really a good thing for the good?" Augustine answered: "The death of the body, the separation of the soul from the body is not good for anyone . . . it is a harsh and unnatural experience."[16]

Like concupiscence, death's most obvious effect appears in the human body. Did this mean to Augustine that the body caused these evils? No, Augustine said; concupiscence is caused by the soul's insubordination from its creator, by the soul's unrealistic attempt to exist in isolation from

---

15. Augustine *De civitate Dei* 13.9.
16. Ibid., 13.6.

its source of being. The body is not responsible for concupiscence, nor for death, but is, rather, a "helpless victim" of the soul's—the psyche's—ruthless pursuit of objects. Unlike earlier Christian authors and classical authors who understood the body as insignificant, merely the "lowest" of the series of stacked components that compose human being,[17] Augustine recognized the permanent integrity of the human body in human being and attempted to describe a theological anthropology that highlighted this cornerstone of human nature. He objected to the late classical commonplace of referring to the body as a prison:

> You consider the flesh as fetters, but who loves his fetters? You consider the flesh a prison, but who loves his prison? No matter how great a master of the flesh you may be, and no matter how great may be the severity toward the flesh with which you are kindled, I am inclined to think that you will close your eye if any blow threatens it.[18]

Involuntary behavior contradicts flowery disclaimers of the value of the body, Augustine said. He also understood that the Christian doctrines of creation, the Incarnation of Christ, and the doctrine of the resurrection of the body all imply that the body has a high metaphysical status and is an integral and permanent part of human being.

In Augustine's painstaking rehabilitation of the body's public image, there are some curious and significant implications. We have seen that Augustine understood the pattern of concupiscence as resulting from the soul's presumptuous self-absorption with its own powers; as a result of this disorientation, the body, in turn, refuses to serve the soul. Augustine's primary example of the body's insubordination to the soul reveals his assumption that "the body" is male. Impotence, which reveals an embarrassing disconnection between the soul's desire and the body's ability to act on that desire, exemplified insubordination to Augustine. In spite of his rejection of philosophical anthropology in which the body was pictured as insignificant because of its position as the lowest aspect of human being, he still maintained a hierarchy of human being. The body is supposed to serve the soul—but sometimes does not—and the soul is supposed to serve its creator, and does not. The

17. Michel Foucault has recently demonstrated, however, that late classical "strategies of the cultivated self" involved attention to the physical practices by which a self alternative to the socially-constructed self was achieved: See Foucault, *Uses of Pleasure* and *Care of the Self*.

18. Augustine *De utilitate jejunii* 4.

resulting disorientation and disequilibrium pervade the whole human being and all his activities. What appear to be bodily desires, then, are in fact the soul's desires that use the body as a tool (*organon*) for the soul's agenda of self-promotion and deficit gratification.

This is Augustine's proposal for rehabilitating the body, for clearing its "good name," for affirming its goodness as created, and its permanence and integrity in human being. Did it work? It is time to go on to the second of our questions: What has Augustine to do with us? Why does his almost compulsive "confession" simultaneously so attract and repel us? Why does his philosophical and theological affirmation of the human body strike us as less compelling, less pungent, than his intense and colorful description of what he experienced—or at least what he recounted twenty years later—as vivid but unpleasurable erotic experience? These are questions that put us in touch with some problems that were not only Augustine's problems, but may also have reverberations in the twentieth century.

Concupiscence, in Augustine's description, is an agenda perpetrated on the body rather than instigated by the body. It includes all the debilitating forms of anxious grasping—whether it pursues the objects of power, possessions or sex. Yet there was still, for Augustine, a close association of concupiscence, the body and sexuality; sexuality defines a person; sexuality is a key to personality. For twentieth-century people as for Augustine, sexuality is important; for us, as for Augustine, there is often a bewildering sense of disjunction between different levels of the person, revealed most pointedly and poignantly in our sexual feelings and activities. It was probably Augustine, more than any other single person, who bequeathed to the West the notion that sexuality is, as Peter Brown has written, a uniquely resonant, because symbolically precise, clue to our personhood.[19] This does not immediately appear to signify anything but a recognition of the importance of sexuality, yet the implications of identifying sex as the key to who a person is has had some far-reaching, and often oppressive and repressive, repercussions in western individuals and societies. The "effective history," as Hans-Georg Gadamer calls the history of the influence of an idea, must be considered a central part of the significance of Augustine's ideas on sexuality. Augustine's description of the special status of sexuality has been more influential in the Christian West than his project of redefinition of the body's meaning and value.

19. Brown, "Augustine and Sexuality," 12.

Augustine spoke of sexuality from the perspective of his own experience, and his experience was unfortunate, not only for himself, but also for those who have inherited the effective history of his ideas of sex. While involved in sexual relationships, Augustine felt unfree, driven, compulsive. When a religious resolution occurred in his life, its first result was that it was a solution to his sexual compulsiveness—renunciation of all sexual activity, accompanied, he insisted, by feelings of relief and freedom. We can, of course, acknowledge and appreciate Augustine's unprecedented honesty and openness in recounting for us so much of his experience. But his more or less silent inference that, in fact, his experience is universal, mythically formulated in the story of Adam and Eve, and reenacted, to a point at least, by every human being, has led to a problematic effective history. The power of language to create the reality it claims merely to explain, if never before recognized, could be amply demonstrated by Augustine's example. Augustine's conversion was to continence, as he had known it would be. His famous prayer, "Give me chastity, but not yet," expresses both his recognition that sex was his special problem area, and his awareness that, for him an integrated sexuality was impossible. Augustine, I think, was keenly and humbly aware that one who is compulsive in a particular area may not be able to manage an integration of "goods" that someone who is not compulsive can enjoy with freedom and gratitude. There are persons for whom the only alternative to addiction is total abstinence.

It was not Augustine's universal recommendation of his resolution of sexual compulsiveness that was influential for centuries in which celibacy was valued as the highest form of Christian life in the West. Augustine did not urge his resolution on anyone else. But he did describe his experience of freedom and relief in such a vivid way that it was easy for his readers to forget hat he was talking about a personal resolution that emerged from—and responded to—his own particular experience, his own historically and geographically-located perspective. His ultimate rejection of sexuality appears to be contradictory to his lifelong and persistent effort to construct a new theological anthropology in which the body is affirmed.

What has Augustine to do with us? His identification of the unique religious significance of sexuality reaches to our time, to the way we imagine our lives, to the way we address questions of sexual preference, to the way we construe our responsibility to other human beings. This feature of Augustine's thought is not an entirely negative heritage; it is certainly, however, an ambiguous one. Perhaps no one can distinguish with clarity and precision the positive and negative effects of Augustine's construction of sexuality as significant, worthy of thought, responsibility and concern.

Secondly—and still asking, what has Augustine to do with us? How have his problems and resolutions become our problems and tools for interpreting and managing our lives? Augustine's model of human being as hierarchically structured—body controlled by soul, soul controlled by God—both reflected Roman society and, in turn, helped to produce western Christian society. Augustine extended his hierarchical anthropology so that it became his model for society. It was a model that featured the necessary and inevitable subordination of some people to others. In the slippery social world of the newly-sacked city of Rome, he specifically urged that a hierarchical model be accepted and reinforced as the lesser of the social evils. Social inequality, he wrote, is part of the evidence that human beings exist in a "state of punishment," the result of the anxious craving of a few for dominance over the many. But Augustine did not criticize this "order," but rather urged respect for dominance and subordination on every level of society, from kingdoms to families. Even though "God did not wish the rational being, made in God's image, to have dominion over any but irrational creatures, not human over human, but human over the beast," the "ordered harmony" that Augustine advocates begins in the household, where "the husband gives orders to the wife, parents to children, and masters to servants."[20]

Glorification of inequality is conspicuously missing from Augustine's program for "ordered harmony" under the permanently unsettled and unsettling conditions of this human pilgrimage. Yet Augustine could not envision social arrangements in which dominance and subordination would not be necessary for peace. Unknowingly, Augustine provided the rationalization that has been used throughout the history of the Christian West to justify dominance and subordination. The one who gives orders, Augustine said, must consider himself the "servant," caring for the needs of those to whom orders are given; he must act from "dutiful concern," not from "lust for domination."[21] Few medieval tyrants failed to appropriate Augustine's rhetoric of servanthood.

Society was, for Augustine, a macrocosm of the human being; both are complex organisms that require orderliness. In Augustine's anthropology, we have seen the body's lesser value in relation to the soul must result in its subor-

---

20. Augustine *De civitate Dei* 19.14.
21. Ibid., 19.15.

dination to the soul even—or especially—when Augustine calls the body the "spouse" (*sponsa*)[22] of the soul. Likewise, in society Augustine understood dominance and subordination as inevitable. His anthropology did not—as it certainly might—provide him with a model of interdependence. Rather, in society as in the body, slavery is inevitable; classicism and sexism is taken for granted.

Augustine, of course, had a very strong doctrine of original sin, a vivid sense of the dark undertow—not explainable by individual sin and guilt—of all human existence. If he had thought that people were basically good he might have been much more perplexed by his own experience and by what he saw about him in the last years of classical civilization. The story of his conversion in Book Eight of the *Confessions*, whether we take it as a literal or as a literary account of an event, illustrates Augustine's respect for the incremental, monumental weight of the habit of concupiscence, the result of an ancient and pervasive flaw in human nature. Conversion, for Augustine, was not simply the conscious reversal of intellectual decisions, but an overwhelming experience of coming—being led, he said, in retrospect—to the bitter end of his own agenda and resources. He was brought to the decisive experience in the garden at Milan that was to decide the whole future course of his life by following with all his energy the course in which he was most completely mistaken. Augustine never seemed to recognize, and never acknowledged, that the way—the journey—painful, damaging, and destructive as it was to himself and other human beings around him, was nevertheless, for him, a process of coming to what he described as a highly satisfying and productive synthesis in his life. Augustine is typical of many religious leaders who do not advise their readers to follow their path in order to come to understand what they have understood. Rather they express nothing but regret for and rejection of their experience as if it had nothing to do with their "seeing the light." They require their readers to learn from their "mistakes," to accept their conclusions, not their process.

But let us return, for a moment, to Augustine's conversion, the vivid emotional experience in which a new synthesis emerged. Augustine's respect for the inertial weight, the bottom-heaviness of the habit of relating to the world "concupiscently" is illustrated in his story. The moment of conversion occurred when Augustine realized that the objects he had so strenuously pursued and attempted to possess had instead, in effect, possessed him: and

22. Ibid., 15.7

"a slave can't enjoy that which keeps him enslaved."[23] The event Augustine described as his conversion—a conversion not of the mind but of the will—began with a painful but illuminating vision of himself:

> But you, Lord, were turning me around so that I could see myself;
> you took me from behind my own back, which was where I had
> put myself during the time when I did not want to be observed by
> myself, and you set me in front of my own face so that I could see
> how foul a sight I was—crooked, filthy, spotted, and ulcerous. I
> saw, and I was horrified, and I had nowhere to go to escape from
> myself.[24]

He recognizes this psychic "place"; from the perspective of "facing myself" he realizes that he has neither moved nor grown since his infant relation to the world, a relation characterized by anxious grasping—concupiscence. Then he became aware of a childish voice chanting, "Tolle, lege": take and read! His response was obedience, the trusting acceptance of the message as directed to him. It is this response that he must hereafter remember and reinforce; around this new and incredibly fragile response he must begin to organize a new relation to the world. The response of trust must replace the child's first instinct to grasp breath and life. Augustine's message to his readers was that real change is possible, although it is not easy, and, of course, real change occurs by the initiative of the grace of God. It was God who took him from behind his own back. The point of the *Confessions* is that change is possible; that is what Augustine's first readers were interested in hearing about.

What has happened to human values in Augustine's thought? We can now draw some observations by way of conclusion. First, as we have seen, the human body does well in Augustine's account. Sexuality, however, does not receive a similarly productive interpretation. The body—men's and women's bodies—can and will participate in Augustine's explicitly imaginary vision of the perfection and completion of human nature—the resurrection of the body. He described the resurrection of the body in the last book of the City of God and his vision is inclusive, sensual, and exuberant. We need to interpret Augustine's understanding of human life from the perspective afforded by this magnificent vision of the goal and fulfillment of human nature—what human nature is capable of—if we are to understand the problems he identifies in the present condition of human being.

23. Augustine *Confessiones* 8.5.
24. Ibid., 8.7.

Human bodies, sexually differentiated, "risen and glorious," will be the "ultimate fulfillment" of whole persons. But although there will be sexes in the resurrection, since sexes are not an "imperfection," there will not be sex. For Augustine, the absence of sex in the resurrection of the body is decisive. Although Augustine insisted on the presence of men and women in the resurrection, it was the male body he envisioned and described. His vision of the resurrected body preserves the male body intact and entire—nipples, beards, teeth, and sexual organs—in the interest of beauty, but not of use. Augustine did not fail to draw from the absence of sexual activity in his vision of physical perfection the inference that since present sexual activity cannot be understood as a foretaste of this reward, it must therefore be a part of the present "state of punishment" of humankind. In Augustine's thought, human actualization and fulfillment is postponed to another time and space, beyond human life and beyond the sensible world. To understand what Augustine valued, we must look at his fantasy of the resurrection of the body, based on, but not defined by, scripture, to see what appears. Equality among human beings appears; "all injustice disappears, and God is all in all."[25] Equality among all the aspects of human beings also appears; the body appears, all its senses raised to a heightened and intensified pleasure that even now may be "glimpsed" in brief, strong synesthetic experiences:

> There where the greatest peace will prevail, nothing will be unsightly, nothing inharmonious, nothing monstrous, nothing will offend the eyes, but in all things God will be praised. For it now, in such frailty of the flesh and in such weakened operation of our members, such great beauty of body appears that it entices the passionate and stimulates the learned and thoughtful to investigate it . . . how much more beautiful will the body be there . . . where there will be unending eternity, and beautiful truth, and the utmost happiness?[26]

The picture Augustine painted is enticing, but it is important to ask, not only about the intent of Augustine's description of the resurrection of the body, but also about the effects, observable in the Christian West to our own time, of the indefinite postponement of full human actualization. Augustine's vision, exuberant and provocative as it is, did not have the effect of compel-

25. Augustine *De civitate Dei* 22.15.

26. Augustine *Sermo* 243.8. See also my discussion of the resurrection of the body in chapter 10 below.

ling Christians to work toward just social arrangements in the present, the equality of women and men in present life, and affirmation of, and gratitude for, the beauty and goodness of sexuality. We have seen that Augustine's personal experience and his religious commitments provide some of the reasons for the nature of his vision of human "perfection." And a strain of body-denying, world-rejecting Augustinianism in the Christian West can be deplored without blaming Augustine himself for it.

Nevertheless, any attempt to understand a historical author in the context of his life and times enables us to see once again the complexity of human beings, and therefore, of historical interpretation. Our mutual attempt—author and reader—to understand both the intent and the effect of Augustine's thought and teaching on the body and sexuality permits us, in the final analysis, to find Augustine not so much a formidable and threatening authority of the history of Christian doctrine, but, as he asked and expected to be seen, in the context of his own struggles, our "fellow pilgrim."

CHAPTER 7

Infancy, Parenting, and Nourishment in Augustine's *Confessions*

The *Confessions* of St. Augustine, provocative to modern readers for its insistently contemporary flavor, yet difficult to translate into the language with which we explore the self, is the record of a fourth-century self-analysis. But the *Confessions* is not *only* recall and interpretation of Augustine's personal past, and his insights transcend the psychological. His "therapy" involves a process of orientation to a far more comprehensive universe than the conflicts within the self, the family, and the community that focus the interest of modern psychotherapy. His goals are more ambitious than those of contemporary psychology. Yet the events and crises to which Augustine draws attention, his understanding of the psyche as developing by a series of resolutions that emerge from and incorporate earlier stages, and his insistence that intellectual knowledge is not enough to effect change in settled patterns of behavior, all indicate the extent to which Augustine's preoccupations in the *Confessions* are cathartic and therapeutic.

The *Confessions* was written in about A.D. 400, when Augustine was in his early forties; the last thirty years of his life are not described in it. The years after the writing of the *Confessions* were marked, in many ways, by great productivity, but in them Augustine also saw the deterioration and destruction of much of the objective part of his life's work in the African church. In these years, Augustine's psyche became increasingly complex and weighted with pessimism regarding the fulfillment of human life in the present. It was in the *Confessions* that his understanding of human nature, so intimately tied to his understanding of his own process, began to be formulated. By the relentless examination of human nature nearest home, his own nature, Augustine attempted to describe and account for the mysterious complexity of the "weights" of human existence: "I came to understand . . . through my own experience."[1]

How does a person organize experience so that life does not appear to be a series of unrelated emotion-generating incidents? The intensity and immediacy with which a late-Roman man such as Augustine was permitted and conditioned to experience emotion must have provided both incentive to explore the emotional structure of his life and, simultaneously, made it difficult to achieve perspective on these emotions. And Augustine needed, in those last years of the fourth century, to collect and interpret his past in order to prepare himself for the demanding and hectic present life of a newly appointed bishop of the church of North Africa. Because the *Confessions* has become a classic, we tend to overlook this pressure for personal orientation; a classic, by definition, takes on a quality of timeless relevance for its readers.

Viewing the *Confessions* as therapy helps us to understand some of the difficulties of the book. The note of anxious introspection that often jars the first-time reader is to be expected in a therapeutic exploration. Also, the reader's frustration as Augustine over-describes some aspects of his life and omits to tell us items of basic interest in other aspects, may be partially alleviated by the recognition that Augustine is primarily interested in following the associations that seem most fruitful for his own task of clarification and integration. Perhaps Augustine was thinking of the *Confessions* when he wrote to Marcellinus a decade later: "I confess to be one of those who write because they have made some progress, and who, by means of writing, make further progress."[2] As an old man of seventy-four, Augustine testified to the value of the investment of time and energy in the *Confessions*; he wrote in the *Retractions*: "They still move me when I read them now, as they moved me when I first wrote them."[3]

The *Confessions* was catharsis for Augustine both in the sense of recall, reevaluation, and reinterpretation of old personal dramas—"past history as present meaning"—and in the sense of catharsis as "the vision of completion, the experience of unification and . . . transformation."[4] Books I–IX are largely re-collections of Augustine's past life; he describes his method in these books:

1. Augustine *Confessiones* 8.5.

2. Augustine *Epistula* 143.2.

3. Augustine *Retractationes* 2.32.

4. Miller, "Orestes," 33.

> I want to call back to mind my past impurities and the carnal cor-
> ruptions of my soul, not because I love them, but so that I may
> love you, my God . . . And gathering myself together from the
> scattered fragments into which I was broken and dissipated during
> all that time when, being turned away from you, the One, I lost
> myself in the distractions of the many.[5]

But even these recollections are constantly interwoven with moments of completion and transformation; Augustine's confession is not only of sin and faith, but also of praise. His reminiscences make sense to him only in the context of the experiences of unification that are the foundation of his understanding of himself, the world, and God. Books X–XIII are an extended description of the cosmic setting of the individual life unfolded in the earlier books.

Augustine does not simply construct a "case history"; the *Confessions* is primarily therapy in the Platonic sense of a methodical conversion from a "misidentification of reality," to recognition of the reality, the patterns of behavior, that has been implicit but unidentified within one's most intimate and pressing experience.[6] The *Confessions* is therapy in the modern sense of retracing of events with attention to the emotions and images that characterized those events; but it is *therapeia* in the ancient sense when Augustine gives this story of his life a cosmic setting and significance. The task of Platonic therapy is the construction of an articulated orientation to a final, authoritative, and implicit reality. It is only in the light of this reality—for Augustine, God—that he can see himself accurately: "You are the permanent light which I consulted about all these things, asking whether they are, what they are, and what weight they have."[7]

But it is not the "vision of completion," the cosmic setting of a human life as described in the later books of the *Confessions* that will occupy us here. Rather, we will trace a significant theme in Augustine's recounting of his early life to the time of that great transformation of the structure and dynamics of his psyche that we call the conversion experience. The thread we will draw from the colorful tapestry of Augustine's life for closer examination is a major organizing theme that not only holds together many other threads, but also indicates how the whole tapestry should be seen. Augustine's use of the lan-

5. Augustine *Confessiones* 2.1.

6. See Cushman, *Therapeia*.

7. Augustine *Confessiones* 10.40.

guage of infantile experience is, I will claim, not merely rhetorical metaphor, but accurate description of what actually occurred in his psyche in the garden of his rented home in Milan.

In our time, which has begun to rediscover the significance of infantile experience for the understanding of the adult psyche, it is both interesting and important to see that, despite major differences of assumptions and interpretation, a fourth-century person realized and articulated the necessity of examining the human psyche from the first months of its existence in order to understand its dynamics and to change its deficit patterns. Moreover, Augustine was not just any fourth-century person; his compelling insights, more than those of any other leader of the early centuries of the Christian church, have formulated the ideas of self and world, God and the church, that structure Western consciousness, whether our relation to this inherited worldview is one of acceptance or resistance. There is always, then, self-knowledge to be gained from a more accurate perception of Augustine's thought, and not only the delight of entering the conceptual world of any historical person. The *Confessions* "aim to present the texture of our experience, not just coherently, but with the patterns more visible and their significance more clearly displayed than before."[8]

Let us see, then, how Augustine made sense of his experience. No other late Roman person found it necessary to go back to earliest infancy—even to prenatal experience—in order to understand the meaning of experience. Yet Augustine found the roots of all experience in what is, properly speaking, pre-experience. His method, the observation of infants, assumes the universality of infantile experience and is his only access to the dynamics of his own infancy. What he observed and described was the anxiety of the infant; even though the reciprocity of the infant's need to suck and the mother's need to suckle virtually guarantee that the infant will be nourished, the infant apparently does not trust that nourishment will be forthcoming:

> I wanted to express my desires to those who would satisfy them; but this was impossible since my desires were in me and those to whom I wished to express them were outside and could not by any sense perception of their own enter into my spirit. And so I used to jerk my limbs about and make various noises by way of indicating what I wanted, using the limited forms of communication which were in my capacity, and which indeed were not very like the real thing. And when people did not do what I wanted, either because

8. Fingarette, *Self-Deception*, 7.

I could not make myself understood, or because what I wanted was bad for me, then I would become angry with my elders for not being subservient to me . . . and I would avenge myself on them by bursting into tears.[9]

Not only the need for necessary nourishment, but fantasies of power over the parents and possession of the nourishing breast[10] increase the child's frustration when the object of his desire is not immediately provided.[11] A "choice" has been made by the infant, motivated by anxiety, not to rely on the care that is volunteered but to grasp at objects without discrimination as to their beneficial effects.[12] Augustine called this anxious grasping at objects in the anxiety that something will he missed *concupiscentia*.[13] He saw it most nakedly and clearly in the anxiety of the newborn;[14] he also found in the behavior of the newborn infant the form of all future concupiscence. In future years the anxious grasping of the newborn will become the frenzied pursuit of sex, power, and possessions that Augustine illustrates with his own story. Concupiscence is merely given new objects and a wider scope; the adult learns to conceal and rationalize, rather than eradicate, the agenda of concupiscence: "For it is just these same sins which, as the years pass by, become related no longer to tutors, schoolmasters, footballs, nuts, and pet sparrows, but to magistrates and kings, gold, estates, and slaves."[15]

9. Augustine *Confessiones* 1.6.

10. Ibid., 1.7.

11. Compare Klein's description of the infant at the mother's breast: "The infant's desire for the ever-present, inexhaustible breast" makes for "unavoidable grievances." When the infant's feeling "that the mother is omnipotent and that it is up to her to prevent all pain and evils from internal and external sources" is not gratified, the resulting attitude of destructive rage, which Klein calls envy, "spoils and harms the good object which is the source of life. . . . The child feels recurrent anxiety that his greed and his destructive impulses will get the better of him." See Klein, "Study of Envy and Gratitude."

12. Compare Piaget: "It is striking to observe . . . how the nursling, when his mother is getting him ready for his meals, counts very little on her for obtaining the object of his desires; he makes a great fuss, becomes impatient, tries to grasp the bottle . . . but is not at all content to await the natural course of events. It all happens as though he depended only on himself to obtain his goal." See Piaget, *Construction of Reality*, 329.

13. Augustine also uses the words *libido* and *cupiditas* as synonymous with *concupiscentia*; see my discussion of *concupiscentia* in Augustine's works: Miles, *Augustine on the Body*, 67ff.

14. Augustine *Confessiones* 1.7.

15. Ibid., 1.19.

Concupiscence, then, pervades and organizes human life, from the anxiety-motivated response of the infant to the adult struggle for sex, power, and possessions. It is not, we must notice, a pleasant aspect of human experience. To interpret the element of concupiscence in human life as zestful and energetic, giving interest and motivation to life, is to misinterpret in the most fundamental way. Augustine walks his reader through a long and detailed exposition of his own experience with this deficit agenda, an experience he consistently presents as painful disorientation. Concupiscence, most apparent in infants and small children, should, Augustine says, be given the sympathy it deserves; and yet, "no one is sorry for the children; no one is sorry for the older people, no one is sorry for both of them."[16] Approximately twenty-five years after writing the *Confessions*, Augustine had not changed his mind about the appropriate attitude toward the inevitable admixture of concupiscence in human life. In contrast to the universal agreement in classical and late-classical literature that old age is the period of life most to be pitied and shunned, Augustine identifies infancy, the period of life in which concupiscence is most evident, as the primary locus of the miseries of life: "Who would not tremble and wish rather to die than to be an infant again if the choice were put before him?"[17]

The original adaptive response of the infant in gasping for breath—in grasping breath—is the response that will be articulated and become normative as the lifestyle of the individual. The grasping response of the newborn becomes the older child's motiveless theft. Basic to both is the anxiety that something will be missed. What fascinates Augustine in his recounting of the famous pear tree incident is the apparent gratuitousness of the theft; because the incident is trivial, it illustrates most accurately the agenda of concupiscence, the habitual indiscriminate grasping that has become automatic because of the constant repetition and reinforcement of this response. In a sense, the object does not matter; it is the irresistibility of habitual response that makes the pear tree incident a perfect paradigm of concupiscence: "Near our vineyard was a pear tree loaded with fruit, though the fruit was not particularly attractive either in color or taste. I and some other wretched youths conceived the idea of shaking the pears off this tree and carrying them away. We set out late at night . . . and stole all the fruit that we could carry. And this was not to feed ourselves; we may have tasted a few, but then we threw the

16. Ibid., 1.9.
17. Augustine *De civitate Dei* 21.4.

rest to the pigs. . . . I became evil for nothing, with no reason for wrongdoing except the wrongdoing itself."[18] Later, in young adulthood, even though he experienced what might have been a gratifying degree of success, Augustine describes his life as painful and unhappy: "I panted for honors, for money, for marriage. . . . I found bitterness and difficulty in following these desires. . . . How unhappy my soul was then! . . . I got no joy out of my learning . . . I was eaten up by anxieties."[19]

Along with his unfolding story of the anxiety-ridden agenda of his early years, Augustine gives a detailed description of the role of his parents in his development. Neither parent receives unambiguous appreciation from Augustine; rather, he emphasizes their role in directing and conditioning the styles of his pursuit of sex, power, and possessions. It was from his mother that he received both physical and spiritual birth, and Monica was consistently and compulsively anxious for the temporal and spiritual well-being of her son. In retrospect, Augustine interprets her warnings to him in adolescence as divine communication. Addressing God, he writes: "But though I did not know it, these warnings came from you. I thought you were silent and that it was my mother who was speaking, but you were not silent, you spoke to me through her, and in despising her, I was despising you."[20] But this is hindsight; at the time, Augustine found her overscrupulous, overbearing, and a nuisance. Her anxiety, her pressure on Augustine for professional success, and her "simple" faith, heavy with elements of superstition, were all quite difficult for Augustine to accept.[21]

His father, Patricius, who died when Augustine was seventeen, was a poor but ambitious man who sacrificed to send Augustine to school. Augustine interprets this as no more than self-interest on Patricius's part, and indeed, blames Patricius for supporting the "wanderings" by which Augustine reinforced his concupiscence. He repeatedly refers to his father as "fallen," and as affirming and encouraging Augustine's pursuit of sex.[22] Augustine describes

18. Augustine *Confessiones* 2.4.

19. Ibid., 6.6.

20. Ibid., 2.3.

21. O'Connell suggests that Monica's persistent badgering of Augustine in his early years may have been counterproductive: "Her prayers and her tears had much to do with his conversion, but one may be pardoned for wondering how long her possessive importunities did more to keep him away from the faith." O'Connell, *St. Augustine's Confessions*, 107.

22. Augustine *Confessiones* 2.3.

himself as deprived of adequate male models: "Considering the kind of men who were set up as models for me to imitate, it is no wonder that I was swept away into emptiness and that I went out of your presence, my God."[23]

Augustine thus presents both of his parents as training and rewarding different aspects of his youthful concupiscence. His conversion marks his rejection of the worldly ambitions entertained for him by both parents and introjected by Augustine himself at the same time that it compasses his rejection of the agenda of concupiscence:

> In these hopes (of professional success) both my parents indulged too much—my father, because he hardly thought of you at all, and only thought in the most superficial way [*inania*] of me; my mother, because in her view, these usual courses of learning would be, not only no hindrance, but an actual help to me in attaining you. So at least I conjecture when I recollect to the best of my ability what the characters of my parents were.[24]

We have thus far been following Augustine's description of infantile experience and its extrapolation in adult experience as unrelievedly negative. Before we look at another aspect of the infant's condition, we must pause to sketch the anthropological assumptions that inform Augustine's interpretation of the infant's anxious reactions.

Concupiscence, according to Augustine, is an adaptive response to the fact that the very essence of human nature is its intentionality. Human being does not contain "the good by which it is made happy."[25] A person is, then, defined and organized according to the selection of objects by which to be made happy. The center of personhood is this movement toward an object or objects. Corresponding to this energy of desire in the person, there is an intrinsic order in creation. Only by aligning oneself with this intrinsic order of being, reality, and value can a person be happy: "You have made us for yourself, and our hearts are restless until they rest in you."[26] This statement concentrates Augustine's idea of personhood as *constituted* by the object of attention and affection. To say that one is in relationship with the object of one's desire is to put it inaccurately and misleadingly. "Relationship" implies a distance to be overcome, a gulf to be bridged; the person is rather connected

23. Ibid., 1.18.

24. Ibid., 2.3.

25. Augustine *Epistula* 140.23.

26. Ibid., 1.1.

to what is desired, whether objects of the sensible world, other human beings, or God. If the wrong "choice" of an object is made, a choice that is hopelessly inconsistent with the intrinsic order of the created world, unhappiness is inevitable. And, as we have seen, the wrong choice is invariably made in the earliest infancy and reinforced throughout normal development.[27] This is Augustine's diagnosis of the human condition. His own story is the illustration and validation of this thesis.

But while he was "enslaved" to the agenda of concupiscence, Augustine was unable to analyze the pattern of his experience. It was only because of the change in his behavior that resulted from his conversion experience that he gained insight into his earlier operation. We will focus on Augustine's many-faceted insistence that it was only by returning to the psychic condition of infancy that a reversal of the original "choice" could be effective. The imagery with which he introduces the conversion experience is that of the child just learning to walk: "Throw yourself on him. Do not fear. He will not pull away and let you fail. Throw yourself without fear and he will receive you and heal you."[28] This strong imagery suggests, as do several other elements in the account, that what is necessary is a return to the earliest psychic condition of anxiety, a stripping of the cumulative object-orientation that, in adulthood, has become ingrained behavior: "The worse part of me was stronger from habit than the better part which was a novelty."[29]

Habit contains an inertial effect which Augustine calls "deadness"; "I hesitated to die to deadness and live to life." The affective aspect of the "strong force of habit" is described as simultaneously containing intense anxiety and "lethargy," "drowsiness," or "sleep."[30] Both the somnolence and the anxiety of

27. It is important to observe that in Augustine's description of concupiscence in the *Confessions* we do not have the strengthened version of original sin that evolved in the course of the controversy with Pelagius. Rather, his language is close to that of Pelagius in identifying the weakness and ignorance of the human condition as the result of habit: "The law of sin is the strong force of habit" (8.6). While it is tempting to interpret Augustine's description of his youthful pursuits as an illustration of the mechanics of original sin, this is unwarranted by the text. Augustine has already formulated in the *Confessions*, however, an argument against the future Pelagian description of how this "strong force of habit" can be overcome. The prescriptive aspect of Augustine's view of human nature is already in place in the *Confessions*, and will be discussed in the following section on his conversion experience. It will remain to him to formulate a diagnosis of human nature that can support his radical prescription.

28. Augustine *Confessiones* 8.1.

29. Ibid., 8.2.

30. Ibid., 8.5.

the newborn contribute to Augustine's condition at the time of his conversion. His "hesitation," actually less a hesitation than a paralyzing tension, was the condition in which he was enabled to reverse the "choice" made in infancy and rectify his disorientation by orienting himself to God, of whom he wrote elsewhere: "If anyone thinks of God as anything other than life itself, he has an absurd idea of God."[31] But the only place from which life can commence is the place at which it was initially arrested.

The overcoming of the inertia and deadness that was the cumulative result of long years of reinforcing the attitude and behavior patterns of concupiscence cannot be achieved by conscious choice. If both the mode of response and the object of one's orientation are to be altered, if, instead of grasping at objects, one is to become receptive—to trust—for the satisfaction of all desires, a new choice cannot simply be superimposed on the earlier "choice." Nothing less than returning to the terror and disorientation of the infant state in its full intensity and, from the same condition in which the original response was given, making a different response, will break the "violence of habit" in which Augustine was held as if in chains.[32] Augustine's psyche was so firmly invested in concupiscence that it was inaccessible to the usual methods of bribing or bullying by which human beings talk themselves into conscious choices.

Augustine pauses in his account of the conversion experience to describe at length the bodily state that accompanied his mental "storm." The picture we receive is that of the random flailing motions of the newborn infant:

> I made many movements with my body—the kind of movements which people sometimes want to make, but cannot make, either because they have not the limbs, or because their limbs are bound or weakened by illness. . . . I tore my hair, beat my forehead, locked my fingers together, clasped my knee. . . . Then a huge storm rose up within me bringing with it a huge downpour of tears . . . I flung myself down on the ground somehow under a fig tree and gave free rein to my tears; they streamed and flooded from my eyes.[33]

Even Augustine's physical behavior reinforces his narration of his return to a condition of infancy.

31. Augustine *De doctrina christiana* 1.8.

32. Augustine *Confessiones* 7.2.

33. Ibid., 8.8–12.

The moment of conversion occurs when Augustine realizes that the objects he had so strenuously pursued and attempted to possess had instead held and bound him in the paralysis in which he found himself. He suddenly saw himself, energetically following the course in which he was most completely mistaken, as *in fact* led unerringly to this moment: "In my own eyes I was stripped naked."[34] He saw that the meaning of his behavior and its motivation had been concealed primarily from himself: "The easiest person to deceive is one's own self."[35] Augustine's conversion begins with a painful, but accurate, sight of himself:

> But you, Lord, were turning me around so that I could see myself; you took me from behind my own back, which was where I had put myself during the time when I did not want to be observed by myself, and you set me in front of my own face so that I could see how foul a sight I was—crooked, filthy, spotted, and ulcerous. I saw and I was horrified, and I had nowhere to go to escape from myself.[36]

He now recognizes this psychic "place"; he has been there before, and it now seems to him that he has neither moved nor grown since the moment of that first response. In fact, he has not; he has learned nothing; he is still compulsively repeating his first response. His tears and bodily convulsions now lessen slightly and he becomes aware of a childish voice that says, "Tolle, lege!—take and read!" His response is obedience, the trusting appropriation of the message as for him. It is this response that he must hereafter remember and reinforce; it is around this incredibly fragile response that he must now begin to organize the operation of his psyche. But this reinforcement, by decision after decision to "throw yourself on him," can, unlike the original "choice," never become the unconscious agenda that the earlier choice had been. No unconscious pattern exists for the second choice, and so it must be consciously kept alive if it is not to fade and all traces of it to vanish from the psyche. The attitude and response of trust must replace the child's first response, but this time, *consciously*.

When we follow Augustine's analysis of the way in which concupiscence is perpetuated, some important insights emerge. From the perspective of the

---

34. Ibid., 8.4.

35. Fingarette, *Self-Deception*, 2.

36. Ibid., 8.7; see also Gay, "Against Wholeness," 549: "Freud argued that we would, if we saw clearly enough, wake up feeling morally corrupt and broken."

self-knowledge he has gained in the conversion experience, Augustine says that concupiscence is not, in fact, "nourished" and perpetuated by its objects. The objects that are, as Augustine repeatedly insists, good in themselves, are nevertheless consistently unsatisfying. The person, repetitiously following the grasping pattern of concupiscence, experiences an increasing lack of nourishment: "For those who find their gratification in external things easily become empty and pour themselves out on things seen and temporal and, with starving minds, lick at shadows. Oh that they would tire of their lack of nourishment and say, 'Who will show us good things?'"[37] The intrinsic incapacity of "things" to provide nourishment nevertheless prompts the person to redouble his efforts to secure gratification, efforts that spin him deeper and deeper into the ruts of habitual behavior. A short version of the saga of Augustine's experience of "enslavement" to the agenda of concupiscence is given in his description: "From a disordered will came concupiscence, and serving concupiscence became a habit, and the unresisted habit became a necessity. These were like links—so I call them a chain—holding me in a hard slavery."[38]

The "nourishment" of the habit of concupiscence, then, is in the gratification of a repetition compulsion; "scratching the itching scab of concupiscence,"[39] rather than enjoyment of the objects of concupiscence, led to a perpetuation of the habitual response. Nourished only by "deceiving words," the psyche sinks into lethargy and anxiety.[40] The quality of relationship with other human beings in this mode is dramatically presented in Augustine's image of "eating one another up, as people do with their food."[41] The behavior of the infant at the mother's breast is more or less adequately concealed, but remains unaltered in adult behavior. Augustine has told us enough about his attachments to other human beings in his early life to indicate the extent to which friendship inevitably and automatically became grasping longing to possess the other. The possessiveness and jealousy that Augustine described in one newborn is the paradigm of his own adult experience: "I myself have seen a baby who was envious; it could not yet speak, but it grew pale and

37. Augustine *Confessiones* 9.4.

38. Ibid., 8.5.

39. Ibid., 9.1.

40. Ibid., 9.13.

41. Ibid., 9.2.

looked bitterly at another baby sharing its milk."[42] Of his experience of being "in love" he writes: "I was fettered happily in bonds of misery so that I might be beaten with rods of red-hot iron—the rods of jealousy and suspicion, and fears and angers and quarrels."[43] In possessing, he was possessed; he was regularly unable to differentiate his own life from the life of the person he loved, whether it was his friend,[44] his mother,[45] or his beloved.[46]

The affective component of Augustine's reversal of the agenda of concupiscence, he tells us, was the healing of the capacity to love. A direct exchange occurs from the anxiety-ridden concupiscence which had ordered his existence to participation in the love of God:

> Now Scripture enjoins nothing except love and condemns nothing except concupiscence. . . . I mean by love that affection of the mind that aims at the enjoyment of God for his own sake and of oneself and one's neighbor for God's sake. By concupiscence I mean that affection of the mind which aims at the enjoyment of oneself and one's neighbor without reference to God. . . . *Now in proportion as the dominion of concupiscence is pulled down, in the same proportion that of love is built up.*[47]

In contrast to concupiscence, in which other human beings are used to reinforce and, temporarily, to alleviate the person's grasping anxiety—as the mother was used by the infant—"loving the other in God" frees both oneself and the other. One can now recognize and delight in the being and beauty of the other in a way that is impossible while one's method of operation is concupiscence. Anxiety is not a condition in which enjoyment is possible. The curious phenomenon, revealed in Augustine's conversion experience, of a person busily deceiving himself by thinking that he uses the other, while he is, in reality, *enslaved* to the gratification received from the other, is one of the pervasive themes of the *Confessions*.

There has been, Augustine tells us, an area of his life in which the agenda of concupiscence have been even more strongly directed than in other areas. He has felt most compulsive in the pursuit of sex. It is fashionable to

---

42. Ibid., 1.7.

43. Ibid., 3.1.

44. Ibid., 2.2, 4.4.

45. Ibid., 9.12.

46. Ibid., 6.15.

47. Augustine *De doctrina christiana* 3.10.

smile at Augustine's adolescent behavior as normal teenage behavior, but this is to ignore his own evaluation of sex as dominating, dictating, and ordering his life. Even if he had supplied us with many more concrete details of his sexual activity, we could not make a more accurate evaluation from the vantage point of our "objectivity" than the evaluation of Augustine himself, who found himself unfree in the pursuit of sex. Very simply, Augustine knew himself to be an addict, and the resolution of this addiction by the conversion to celibacy was not a solution that Augustine urged on anyone else who was not similarly addicted.[48]

We often neglect to notice, however, that Augustine's conversion was not *solely* from the sexual aspect of concupiscence, but also from the grasping pursuit of power and possessions. Sex, power, and possessions are inextricably interwoven in the agenda of concupiscence, and it was as a *whole* that the life organized by concupiscence was rejected by Augustine, just as it had been the *whole* agenda of concupiscence that had brought Augustine to the point of paralyzed anxiety: "I was tired out and wasted away with gnawing anxieties. . . . It was really a great burden to me and to help me bear such a heavy form of slavery I no longer had the impulse and encouragement of my old hopes and desires for positions and wealth."[49]

One further aspect of the conversion account that we must note is Augustine's reporting of his experience as one of complete helplessness and frustration in which the grace of God operated to heal and unify. Augustine had no sense of his own ability to reorder his psyche. Rather his experience was that of having his head "turned" *for* him.[50] Just as the infant's response can be said to be "chosen" only in the broadest sense of the word, so Augustine insists on the gratuitousness of his breakthrough.

For the sake of drawing and discussing one of the strongest threads in Augustine's account of his conversion, we have not paid attention to other important aspects. For example, the childlike naiveté of obeying the voice that said, "Tolle, lege," is balanced with the process of intellectual under-

48. Augustine did not consider his own "choice" of celibacy as normative, but as a gift, and he could imagine situations in which it would be counterproductive; he writes, in *Sermon* 354.9: "I dare to say that it is good for those who observe continence and are proud of it to fall, that they may be humbled in that very thing for which they praise themselves. For what benefit is it to anyone in whom is the virtue of continency if pride dominates him?"

49. Augustine *Confessiones* 8.1.

50. See O'Connell's extended discussion of the expression *fovere caput* in the *Confessions*. O'Connell, *St. Augustine's Early Theory*, 65ff.

standing with which he had been consciously occupied through his youthful years. The conversion experience was not, then, *only* the result of a process of breaking down and breaking through the habit patterns of thirty years, but also a process of gradual strengthening of his intellectual orientation. It was the convergence of both processes that prepared Augustine's conversion to the amazingly strong and resilient synthesis of his maturity. The strength of this synthesis is, I think, indicated in the resolution of his compulsive pursuit of sex. Describing his conversion to celibacy, Augustine calls it a "gift of God," not the result of a fierce and successful repression. He never tells us that it was hard to maintain his celibate state, but only that he found it tremendously freeing: "Now my mind was free of those gnawing cares that come from ambition and the desire for gain, and wallowing in filth and scratching the itching scab of concupiscence."[51] Although we may find the dramatic language of the converted addict overly dramatic when he describes what he has been converted from, we must honor Augustine's description as an accurate indication of the way he experienced and interpreted that experience.

All of Augustine's talk of growth in the Christian life, then, relies on the necessity of returning to the infancy condition and reversing the "choice" of a deficit pattern of behavior. Without this return to the place at which true growth—the opposite of repetitious extrapolation from an initial response—was arrested, talk of growth is too naive, too superficial, too optimistic. Augustine uses the language of the nourishment of the infant to describe the fragile progress of the Christian who must learn, just as the newborn learned by extrapolating the response of concupiscence, to progress in the life of trusting dependence on the new "parents" that emerge from the conversion experience, God and the Catholic Church as mother and father. The mothering activity of God is especially emphasized. A direct transfer of dependence and attachment from the training of the earthly parents to the parenting of God has been effected.

Augustine's last mention of his parents in the *Confessions* demonstrates that no longer are Monica and Patricius the "heavyweights" of Augustine's psyche that they have been throughout his early years and into young adulthood. He now sees them simply as "brethren," fellow pilgrims who, like him, suffer and struggle. New and loving regard for his parents resulted from his disengagement from the training of his early years so that now, although he can accurately evaluate this training, he is not resentful but finds that it was

---

51. Augustine *Confessiones* 9.7.

both inevitable *and* the particular route by which he was led to the moment of conversion. Augustine, in his last mention of his parents, urges that

> as many as shall read this may remember at your altar Monica, your servant, and Patricius, her husband, through whose flesh you brought me into this life, though how I do not know. May they with holy affection remember those two who were my parents in this transitory light, who are my brethren under you, Our Father, in our Catholic Mother, and my fellow citizens in the eternal Jerusalem for which your people in their pilgrimage sigh from the beginning of their journey until they return home.[52]

But the importance of the new parenting that emerged from Augustine's conversion experience can be stated much more strongly. Augustine's conversion was not, strictly speaking, to Christianity, but to the Catholic Church. As a Manichaean he had considered himself a Christian, and he had recognized more recently, but long before the experience in the garden in Milan, that he could not be content with any philosophy in which "the name of Christ was not there": "For this name, Lord, this name of my Savior, your son, had been *with my mother's milk* drunk in devoutly by my tender heart, where it remained deeply treasured. So I could not be swept away by anything, however learned or well written or true, which made no mention of this name."[53] Augustine's "conversion of the will" can be described with greater precision as his return to the infantile condition and selection of a different mother from whom to draw nourishment. Once the agenda to which his earthly parents had trained him was broken, Augustine was freed from his attachment to them that had been so stressfully characterized by the ambivalence of dependency and resentment. Augustine can now see Monica as she is, can describe her as a poor weak creature with her own life story rather than as the tyrant of his youthful experience. He can ask his readers to pray God's mercy for her sins, and he can acknowledge her role in bringing him to conversion.[54]

Just as his infant nourishment had come from Monica's breasts, the nourishment of his infancy in the Catholic Church is the food provided by "our Lord Jesus Christ [who] made himself milk for us":

> As then the mother, when she sees her child unfit for taking meat, gives him meat, but meat that has passed through her flesh, for the

52. Ibid., 9.13.
53. Ibid., 3.4.
54. Ibid., 9.13.

bread upon which the infant feeds is the same bread as that which the mother feeds on; but the infant is not ready for the table, he is only ready for the breast, and therefore bread is passed from the table through the mother's breast, that the same food may thus reach the little infant; thus our Lord Jesus Christ . . . the bread, made himself milk for us, being incarnate and appearing in mortal shape. . . . On this let us grow, by this milk let us be nourished. Let us not depart from our faith in the milk before we are strong enough to receive the Word.[55]

The church's training, paralleling that of the mother, is a carefully graded program of nourishment and expectation of growth. Although one must not demand solid food while still in earliest infancy and so run the risk of being "weaned before one's time," one must not want "to remain little" but must steadily advance from the milk of belief to the meat of understanding under the guidance of the "Catholic mother."[56]

The protection of the father is also an accurate image of God's watchful protection of the infant convert; "I am only a little child," Augustine writes, "but my father lives forever and my protector is sufficient for me. For he is the same who begot me and who watches over me."[57] But it is the nourishment imagery of the providing breast that Augustine finds most central to his description. God, Christ, and the Catholic Church are all described as providing this nourishment, and Augustine can find no more perfect image of his new condition of dependency and trust than that of the infant at the breast: "What am I, at my best, except an infant suckling the milk you give and feeding on you, the food that is incorruptible?"[58]

In contrast to the starvation rations yielded by concupiscence, the nourishment of God is the complete food of the psyche. Augustine is impatient with any description of what a person should do that does not provide the energy for doing it: "I found too that one is not only instructed so as to see you, who are the same forever, but also so as to grow strong enough to lay hold on you, and he who cannot see you for the distance, may yet walk along the road by which he will arrive and see you, and lay hold on you."[59] The

55. Augustine *Enarrationes in Psalmos* 130.9.11.

56. Augustine *Sermo* 23.3.

57. Augustine *Confessiones* 10.4.

58. Ibid., 4.1.

59. Ibid., 7.21.

difference between Augustine's earlier mystical experience,[60] and the conversion experience was that in the former Augustine "saw," but, since he had not stripped to the condition of psychic infancy, his life was not fundamentally reoriented in consequence of what he saw. The conversion experience met the additional condition that the whole energy of the psyche was freed from the "strong force" of its habits, and from the objects on which it was fastened, so that genuine growth could occur. Augustine's daily "nourishment" became no longer the anxious gobbling of objects, but the trustworthy nutrient that he received from God, "our mother who soothes and nourishes,"[61] by waiting with confidence and accepting with gratitude.

The complete and completely gratifying nourishment that supports and strengthens the infant Christian is never outgrown; the progress of the Christian is gain without corresponding loss. In contrast to the "development" of concupiscence, in which the content of earlier stages is continuously and restlessly changed even though the pattern remains the same, growth in the Christian life preserves and integrates every stage of growth. The earliest stage, belief, although it gradually becomes understanding, is not discarded:

> In passing over these stages and steps of your age you are not gradually unfolded, but abiding in the way you are renewed. For it is not that as the first dies the second follows, or that the rise of the third will be the destruction of the second, or that the fourth is now born that the third may die. . . . Though all these ages do not come at the same time, nevertheless in a soul that is pious and justified they persist on equal and harmonious terms.[62]

Trusting belief, and growth in the new response and orientation, is the constant condition of the Christian: "You set our feet on the way and speak kindly to us and say, 'Run, and I will hold you, and I will bring you through, and there also I will hold you.'" The same "sweet delight" that began to nourish Augustine at the time of his conversion continues to lead him to advance. Augustine describes the gratifying nourishment on which he is sustained in *Confessions* 10.6:

> But what do I love when I love you? Not the beauty of the body nor the glory of time, not the brightness of light shining so friendly to the eye, not the sweet and various melodies of singing, not the fra-

---

60. Ibid., 7.10.

61. Augustine *Enarrationes in Psalmos* 26.2.

62. Augustine *Sermo* 216.8.

grance of flowers and ointments and spices, not manna and honey, not limbs delightful to the embraces of the flesh: it is not these that I love when I love my God. And yet I do love a kind of light, melody, fragrance, food, embrace when I love my God; for he is the light, the melody, the fragrance, the food, the embrace of my inner being—there where is a brilliance that space cannot contain, a sound that time cannot carry away, a perfume that no breeze disperses, a taste undiminished by eating, a clinging together that no satiety will disrupt. This is what I love when I love my God.

CHAPTER 8

Not Nameless but Unnamed:
The Woman Torn from Augustine's Side

"Rather than re-establish those perceived as missing from the narrative
as fully present, it might be of interest to account for the fact that
the fragmented, erased, and ephemeral voices are nevertheless there,
miraculously clinging to the rock of historical narrative like so
many storm-battered mollusks." (IRIT ROGOFF, "TINY ANGUISHES:
REFLECTIONS ON NAGGING, SCHOLASTIC EMBARRASSMENT, AND
FEMINIST ART HISTORY")

"The woman with whom I was in the habit of sleeping was torn from my
side [*auulsa a latere meo*] on the grounds of being an impediment to my
marriage, and my heart, which clung to her, was broken and wounded
and dropping blood. She had returned to Africa after having made a vow
to [God] that she would never go to bed with another man, and she had
left with me the natural son I had had by her [*ex illa filio meo*]. . . . Nor
was the wound healed which had been made by the cutting off of my
[partner]. It burned, it hurt intensely, and then it festered and became
more chilling and desperate." (AUGUSTINE *CONFESSIONES* 6.15)

In his *Confessions*, Augustine famously grieved for a woman "torn
from his side" by what he describes as his mother's desire that he make
an advantageous marriage. She wanted him to marry an heiress, he wrote,
"so that expense would be no burden."[1] The notoriously desirous Augustine

---

1. Augustine *Confessiones* 6.11; translations of *Confessions* throughout are adjusted from
Rex Warner's translation.

represents himself as having no desire in the matter. Indeed, his mother and his partner seem, according to Augustine's narrative, to have engineered his desolation together. The passage seems to claim that his partner left him and her son voluntarily.

Revealed tantalizingly in a few brief passages in Augustine's *Confessions*, his partner of fifteen years and the mother of their son is an elusive figure.[2] She came to Milan from North Africa with Augustine. In the first year of their relationship, she bore their son, Adeodatus. She may have been a Christian, but the evidence is slender, largely consisting of the fact of her vow to remain celibate for the rest of her life. But she could also have been motivated to this choice by traditional Roman respect for a "*univira*," or one-man woman. There is no suggestion in the text that she and Augustine could or should have married. In the rigidly striated class structure of the later Roman Empire, a class difference meant that "formal marriage to her would have obliterated Augustine's social and vocational aspirations."[3] This summarizes what can be known about her from the only text in Augustine's voluminous writings in which she appears directly, the *Confessions*.

Problems, methods, and texts

A young woman who lived in late antiquity makes a brief appearance in a famous text. Her existence is not to be doubted. But her subjectivity, her passions and thoughts, are not represented. Indeed, the text's author, Augustine of Hippo, as well as numerous commentators across the centuries, present her briefly—if at all—as materializing specifically for the purpose of serving *his* passion: "In those years I lived with a woman who was not bound to me by lawful marriage; she was one who had come my way because of my wander-

2. The term I translate as "partner" is usually translated as "mistress" or "concubine." Kim Power rightly points out that Augustine's preferred term was simply "unam" (the one), which seems to me closer to the most ususal, twenty-first century term for persons in a committed relationship, "partners"; Power, *Veiled Desire*, 95.

3. Ibid., 97. While class, based on wealth (and somewhat on education, as in Augustine's case), played a large role in forming social expectations in North Africa, as elsewhere in the later Empire, apparently race did not. By late antiquity North African races—Punic, Berber, and "Ethiopian"—created a range of skin tones from very dark to light. Races were distinguished more by language than by color. The term "Berber," for example, "was a collective term for tribes whose distinctiveness in fact countervailed their implied homogeneity;" See "Berber" in *Late Antiquity*, 340.

ing desires (*uagus ardor*) and my lack of considered judgment; nevertheless I had only this one woman and I was faithful to her."[4]

For Augustine's purpose of demonstrating his youthful sinfulness, his partner is essential to the text, yet she is tantalizingly inaccessible. Readers of Augustine's *Confessions* can do no more than glimpse her, and we cannot with confidence identify her influence on her well-known partner. Without using far too much imagination, we cannot reconstruct a fully fleshed character. The *Confessions*, in which she makes brief appearances is, after all, Augustine's autobiography.

Augustine's partner creates for a feminist historian some interesting historiographical questions. Most historians' interest in this "nameless woman" is limited to understanding her in order to understand Augustine better. Is there enough evidence of her to permit us to reconstruct *her* historical presence?[5] My answer will be yes and no. I will not be able to reconstruct her as an individual with subjectivity. I will, however, suggest that a reconstitution of her social niche in Roman North Africa goes at least part of the way toward recovering a picture of her. I will first pose several methodological and theoretical questions that challenge features of contemporary feminist historiography. Using textual criticism and historical reconstruction, I will then explore what *can* be learned of a woman who was present but unnamed in a highly influential late fourth century male autobiography.

Let us begin by recognizing that Augustine's partner was not "nameless." Rather, Augustine did not reveal her name. Why? Cultural differences may be too profound and fundamental to warrant a guess. But there are more possible explanations than the few most frequently encountered. Feminist historians tend to think that Augustine withheld her name because of the misogyny they see in his later homosociality and commitment to celibacy.[6]

4. Augustine *Confessiones* 4.2. Centuries of scholars have accepted Augustine's self-presentation as a great sexual sinner. Presently, biographers tend to minimize his sexual experience. For example, Kim Power remarks, "Augustine's continence in a promiscuous world was remarkable," Power, *Veiled Desire*, 98. Similarly, Garry Wills: "[H]is sexual activity was not shocking by any standards but those of a saint," *Saint Augustine*, xvii. The decisive examination of Augustine's sexual behavior is Ramirez, "Demythologizing Augustine."

5. To my knowledge, only one article and one chapter in a book have sought to reconstruct Augustine's partner using historical evidence. These are Kim Power's "*Sed unam tamen*" and the same author's chapter, "Augustine the Lover," in *Veiled Desire*, 94–107.

6. Rousselle, *Porneia*, 182. Rousselle points out that no letters from women are included in Augustine's voluminous collected correspondence. He wrote fourteen letters to women, fewer than some of his contemporary celibate colleagues; John Chrysostom's correspondence includes fifty-three letters to women; Basil wrote thirteen letters to women;

Other historians usually interpret the fact in one of two ways. They say either that her name was withheld because the relationship was unimportant and insignificant, or they conjecture that Augustine sought to protect her. For example, Peter Brown finds historians' interest in Augustine's concubine "a very modern preoccupation," one that "Augustine and his cultivated friends would have found strange." For Brown, her primary role in Augustine's biography is that "this nameless woman bore Augustine's son, Adeodatus."[7] On the other hand, John Noonan writes, "With delicacy he never gives her name."[8] However, it is at least possible that, for Augustine, her name remained, after a decade, too resonant with the pain of their parting to mention. Perhaps Augustine also remembered all too well the pleasures and delights of intimate relationship, and these memories threatened his new life as a celibate priest and bishop.

Whatever Augustine's reasons for omitting her name, her "namelessness" signals the absence of her subjectivity from the text. It would be tempting to name her, selecting a name from known North African Christian women's names of the period: Afrania, Antonia, Apollonia, Crispina, Demetrias, Donatilla, Ecdicia, Faltonia, Felicitas, Januaria, Juliana, Lucilla, Manlia, Marcella, Maria, Maxima, Monnica, Ostoria, Perpetua, Pompeiana, Potamia, Proba, Quartilla, Restituta, Sabine, Secunda, Sextilia, Tertulla, Thecla, Thelica,

---

Jerome: thirty-four letters to women. Van der Meer, *Augustine the Bishop*, emphasizes that Augustine rejected women when he rejected sex. In *Soliloquiorum* 1.10 Augustine wrote: "Nothing is so powerful in drawing the spirit of a man downwards . . . as the caresses of a woman and that physical intercourse which is part of marriage." Van der Meer comments in a tone of grudging admiration: "These fierce words . . . came from the depths of his soul and he most strictly held to them He went even further. No woman might set foot over the threshold of his house. No woman might speak to him except in the presence of some other person. . . . He did not even make an exception for his own elder sister and his nieces, all three of them nuns" (215).

7. Brown, *Augustine of Hippo*, 50–51; also: "Augustine will lapse into a 'second class' marriage. . . . He will take a nameless woman as his concubine for the next fifteen years. . . . Whether he particularly enjoyed the experience is another matter" (27). Henry Chadwick, *Augustine*, calls Augustine's partner "his Cathaginian girlfriend . . . his common law wife" 15–16. As Rogoff remarks of another historical woman, Augustine's partner suffered from a "double betrayal": "Nor was her suffering and the indignity visited upon her by her deeply ambivalent and faithless lover any worse than that being visited upon her posthumously by . . . scholarship"; Rogoff, "Tiny Anguishes," 40.

8. Noonan, *Contraception*, 125. Wills, in *Saint Augustine*, finds it awkward not to have a name for Augustine's partner, and thus names her imaginatively: "To avoid clumsy titles, where *she has no name*, I shall call this woman Una [from *unam habebat*; my emphasis]," 16.

Verna, or Victoria. Rather than arbitrarily select a name for Augustine's partner, however, I must instead respect her "namelessness," acknowledging that her subjectivity is indeed lost to us, elided in Augustine's text, our only evidence of her existence. It would be presumptuous for an historian to attempt to reconstruct it. Too much imagination, projection, and speculation would be required.[9] Acknowledging this prompts me to reconsider two assumptions common to feminist reconstructions of historical women.

First, Irit Rogoff has suggested that when twenty-first century historians relate to historical women on the basis of current sympathies, sensitivities, and projections, it is "narcissistic and self-referential." Empathy should not be privileged "as the primary principle of historical analysis." Further, she suggests that when we write about "fragmented, erased, and ephemeral voices" we cannot and should not "robustly reconstitute them." What we can do instead, is to recognize that "without their vague and fragile presence at the margins, the stalwart presences at the center would lose much of their vitality."[10] We can then explore how this works in particular literary works.

Second, feminist historians tend to seek historical women who resisted victimization and found ways to achieve subjectivity and authorization for their work—individualists, in the context of their societies. In other words, we seek historical women characterized by those qualities that we—rightly or wrongly—believe ourselves to possess. Yet feminist historians, like historical women, are heavily inscribed by culture. In twenty-first century media culture, in fact, a technology for socialization replaces and improves upon the capacity for socialization of face-to-face societies of earlier times. Socialization addresses not only behavior but also subjectivity, the way a person thinks herself, her society, and her world and her feelings about these. Social psychologist Rom Harré has written, "To think, to perceive, to be rational and to experience emotions are cultural endowments not native achievements."[11]

> The fundamental human reality is conversation, effectively without beginning or end, to which, from time to time, individuals make contributions. All that is personal in our mental and emotional lives is individually appropriated from the conversation go-

9. Garry Wills makes this mistake in *Saint Augustine*. He reveals novelistic, as opposed to historical, interests by naming Augustine's partner and speculating on their meeting and courtship: "He was not merely persuading Una to live with him, but to make a break with her church (and, no doubt, her Catholic parents)" (17).

10. Rogoff, "Tiny Anquishes," 39–40.

11. Harré, *Personal Being*, 22.

ing on around us and perhaps idiosyncratically transformed. The structure of our thinking and feeling will reflect, in various ways, the form and content of that conversation. . . . A person is not a natural object, but a cultural artefact.[12]

According to Harré, within the strong influence of cultural matrices, two prerogatives for developing personhood are available. These are "the capacity to act intentionally, in contrast to one's behavior emerging from a nexus of causal chains, and autonomy, in the sense of the capacity to adopt one principle rather than some other in the management of action."[13] These, we may note, are precisely the capacities Augustine described himself as lacking in relation to sexual desire and activity.[14] They are, however, capacities that even Augustine's slender text reveals about his partner. Her choices become evident to the reader of the *Confessions* when she and Augustine part. As I will discuss below, by vowing future celibacy she exercised one of several options available to her. By framing her choice within her social and cultural situation, we will know all that can be known about Augustine's partner.

The Evidence

Scholars of Augustine often endeavor to understand his relationship with his partner on the basis of remarks made in his treatises on marriage, adultery, and virginity.[15] These treatises are invaluable for the occasional bits of information to be gleaned from them. But finally, what they give is Augustine's views, informed by his experience. If our primary interest is in his partner they do not get us much closer to her. Moreover, many suggestions about his relationship are woven into treatises in Augustine's corpus that do not deal primarily with sex or marriage. In fact, we find small clues about Augustine's partner throughout his prolific writings. For example, his most concentrated discourse on relationship occurs in *The Trinity*, and although he seeks to un-

---

12. Ibid., 20.

13. Ibid., 271.

14. But see Augustine *Confessiones* 4.2. In a text in which Augustine "confessed" to many large and small faults and "sins," it is striking (and not to be second-guessed), that he claims that he was faithful to his partner for the fifteen-year duration of their relationship. This was voluntary on his part; his culture and social niche would not have expected it. Augustine's faithfulness both undermines his claim to sexual addiction and his self-representation as a "great sinner." See Ramirez, "Demythologizing Augustine."

15. For an excellent example of this approach see E. Clark, "Adam's Only Companion."

derstand the triune God in this treatise, his knowledge of relationship was informed by his own most intimate relationship. From these and other writings, we can infer, with more or less confidence, something about *his* experience. Having done so, however, we do not know any more about his partner. In short, textual evidence is elusive; it allows us only suggestions, questions, and occasional small partial insights.

However, Augustine's assumptions about sex and heterosexual relationship can be recovered from his writings. For example, as the quotations above from the *Confessions* demonstrate, Augustine largely reduced his relationship with his partner to sex. Later, in his treatise *On the Good of Marriage*, he includes neither love nor marital friendship with the three goods of marriage that he identifies: offspring, fidelity, and the sacramental bond.[16] Why? To alleviate his despair at losing her? To feel less guilt about dismissing her in favor of a temporary mistress and an advantageous marriage? To emphasize the complete reversal brought about by conversion? So that he can feel no responsibility for someone who offered him her body and her life and, when dismissed, returned alone to her home in North Africa?

One of the striking features of the *Confessions* is Augustine's assumption that he can define and describe his relationship with his partner from his perspective alone. Yet relationships are, by definition, two-sided. To notice the absence of another perspective, another experience, is already to *miss* that perspective and experience. I would like to "unframe her from the constraints of victimhood," as Irit Rogoff wrote of another historical woman, to imagine her outside the terms of a powerful text that gives her "no place from which to speak."[17] I would like to do the same for Augustine's partner. She is too convenient a victim, framed within a narrative of the hero's journey to insight. Can she be seen in any other way than as a victim? The way to do this, I believe, is to place Augustine's partner in the social and cultural context in which she lived and within which her options were provided. Then her choices—albeit within a limited range—can be seen.[18]

In short, instead of seeking psychological explanations,[19] we must seek her niche in her society in her historical moment. We must ask, how did a newly powerful and upwardly mobile Christianity make use of gender to

16. Noonan, *Contraception,* 128.

17. Rogoff, "Tiny Anguishes," 43–44.

18. Wills probably overestimates her choices: "Can we say that he 'dismissed' her? She probably had some say in the matter." Wills, *Saint Augustine,* 41.

19. As, for example, Kim Power does, both in "*Sed unam tamen*" and in *Veiled Desire*.

identify and define its values and authorization procedures?[20] For Augustine's partner was not a woman with a "lone individual plight, a singular drama," but rather a woman who occupied a cultural subject position shared by many women.[21] Instead of seeking her subjectivity where it does not exist, i.e., in Augustine's text, I can use his text in two ways that Augustine almost surely did not intend. I can examine the social practices within which she made her choices, and I can compare her situation with that of the only other women the text allows us to glimpse: Monnica, Augustine's mother; the unnamed lover Augustine acquired after his partner returned to Africa; and the child heiress he intended to marry. How were these women differently positioned within nascent imperial Christian culture?

Women in Late Roman Society

First, the woman most fully represented within Augustine's *Confessions* was his mother. Augustine presented her as absorbed in securing for him social and professional advantages. He does not mention his siblings who, readers are expected to infer, did not occupy Monnica's interest to any significant extent. There are, however, several passages in which he narrates episodes from Monnica's life that give us an invaluable picture of female culture in North Africa and imperial Milan. I will mention only one.

The passage to which I will refer has been discussed repeatedly in Augustine scholarship. I will not repeat these discussions, except to highlight the information they give about women's social expectations in the later Roman Empire.[22] Augustine described his mother's marriage to a man his reader must somehow try to picture as simultaneously extremely kind (*beniuolentia praecipuus*) and repeatedly unfaithful, hot-tempered, and inclined to physical abuse. Monnica escaped the bruises regularly worn by her women friends by practicing the advice she gave her friends.

> [M]any wives with husbands much milder than hers . . . went about with their faces disfigured by the marks of blows, and when they got together to talk they would often complain of the way their husbands behaved. But my mother, speaking lightly, but giv-

20. Robin Lane Fox characterizes Augustine and his friends as "overachievers" in the Christian Empire in *Pagans and Christians*, 319 and *passim*. Peter Brown calls Augustine a "young man on the make." Brown, *Augustine of Hippo*, 51.

21. Rogoff, "Tiny Anguishes," 42.

22. See, for example, Power's discussion of Monnica in her chapter, "Augustine the Son," *Veiled Desire*, 71–93.

ing serious advice, used to say that the fault was in their tongues. They had all heard, she said, the marriage contract read out to them and from that day they ought to regard it as a legal instrument by which they were made servants; so they should remember their station and not set themselves up against their masters.[23]

Monnica further advised her friends not to contradict an angry husband, but to wait until he calmed down and then gently to explain the behavior that had aroused his anger. Blaming the victim and manipulation were Monnica's methods of avoiding marital conflict. The superior physical strength of most men, she believed, must be met by strategic accommodation. Domestic violence was apparently simply a fact of life for North African women. There is no evidence that Augustine's partner suffered from similar abuse; perhaps Monnica also taught her strategies for managing a man. But in a society in which intimate violence was to be taken for granted, no relationship could be free of its possibility and implicit threat.

The second woman who has a bit part in the *Confessions* was Augustine's second lover. Augustine wrote that after his partner's dismissal, "I had two years to wait before I could have the girl to whom I was engaged, and I could not bear the delay. So . . . I found another woman for myself—not, of course, as a wife."[24] This woman is the most mysterious of the women mentioned in the *Confessions*. Nothing is known of her but this one sentence. It was during or immediately after Augustine's less than two-year relationship with her that his conversion occurred. We do not know when, or under what circumstances their relationship ended. Augustine may have taken her also as a concubine—he does not say—so that he would not be in danger of being charged with *stuprum* or adultery.[25]

The third woman who appears in the *Confessions* is the young heiress to whom Augustine had proposed, and whose family had accepted him. Since the minimal age for marriage for Roman girls was twelve and the most common age was fourteen, the girl was probably between ten and twelve at the time she became engaged to marry Augustine.[26] To gain the advantages of marriage to a wealthy girl/woman, Augustine broke with his partner of

23. Augustine *Confessiones* 9.9.

24. Ibid., 6.15.

25. Rousselle says that "only by becoming spouses or concubines can a free and responsible man or woman avoid being accused of adultery." Rousselle, *Porneia*, 84.

26. "Marriage age varied according to class, region, and sex. Twelve was the minimum age for marriage for girls in Roman law." Bowersock, et al., *Late Antiquity*, 563.

fifteen years, the mother of his son.[27] We learn nothing about the religious commitments of the heiress and her family. All we know about her is that Augustine was interested only, or primarily, in her wealth.

The three women in sexual (or potentially sexual) relationships with Augustine were in very different social positions. The freedom with which Augustine was able to relate sexually to all of them serially must be seen as a context that significantly shaped the expectation each woman could hold. In a society in which women's circumstances were dictated by their relationship to a man, the flexibility of male sexual relationships meant that women's social positions were terrifyingly unstable. The only way for a woman to be in a strong position in the later Roman Empire was to own property, a relatively rare occurrence.[28] We cannot know whether Augustine's intended heiress might have eventually been in a position to compel his respect and to challenge his self-absorption, though arranged marriage at the age of twelve or fourteen would not seem conducive to developing a strong and independent spirit.

The success of a dominant male culture perhaps always requires a high degree of collaboration from women who are themselves excluded from the arenas in which social, political, and economic power is designed and administered. Michel Foucault defines "strong power" as power that attracts; "weak power" is forced to compel, having lost its attraction for a significant proportion of the population.[29] While male power is strong, many or most women concur with, work within, and support it. Contemporary feminists work hard to recognize historical women's creativity and energy in creating subcultures within which their needs and aspirations were more or less met. Yet there are all too many situations in which historical women's agency simply cannot be identified as anything but accommodation to the strictures of their social position.[30] Women's energetic initiative can be glimpsed, but women

27. Ramirez considers this action to be Augustine's most accurate claim to be a "great sinner." although he questions that the young Augustine's sexual practices constituted "great sin" by contextualizing them within accepted practices of his society, he initially finds Augustine's abandonment of his partner morally culpable. Yet, by insisting that "it is a matter that must be judged entirely by the social rules which prevail at the time," he ends by denying that even this can be considered blameworthy (72–73).

28. Rousselle, *Porneia*, 100.

29. Foucault, *Power/Knowledge*, 57.

30. It can be argued, of course, that no one has completely original agency, that everyone acts by bringing together in new combinations "provisions" found in her or his cultural repertoire. Yet it makes a great deal of difference whether one works with an enabling,

are often powerless to change dominant male assumptions and institutions. Often women's strategies can at best, like Monnica's, optimize women's positions on the margins of male culture.

The Christian Empire

Did the Christianization of Roman society offer women a new repertoire of choices? Did the instability of a historical moment in which the old values of empire were in conflict with new Christian values give women a wider range of opportunities? Christian asceticism and monasticism has been seen as offering women new and socially respected lifestyles.[31] Laws throughout the fourth century revised earlier restrictions on the length of time a woman could remain single after divorce or the death of her husband, allowing women to choose vowed celibacy rather than remarriage.[32] Ascetic women were free of the social expectation that they would marry and bear children, the primary role for women in late antiquity.[33] But what about women who married or became concubines, women such as those we meet in the *Confessions*?

The *Confessions* reveals a society in the making. Augustine converted to Christianity in the same decade—the 380s—in which Christianity was declared the official religion of the Roman Empire. He was part of a generation of young men who *formed* the Christian society whose values and institutions would survive the 410 C.E. fall of Rome. There was clearly a strong role for young men such as Augustine in the new Christian society. In the 390s they would elbow minority religions to the margins of society, rapidly removing Jews and adherents of Roman religions from public life.[34] "Multimedia" initiatives—laws, sermons, artworks, and mob violence—contributed to the

---

authorizing cultural repertoire, or whether one necessarily works against the cultural grain, against a social positioning that marginalizes and invalidates one's agency.

31. See Brown, *Body and Society*; Clark, *Ascetic Piety*; Cooper, *Virgin and the Bride*; Elm, *Virgins of God*; Miles, *Carnal Knowing*; Rousselle, *Porneia*; Ruether, "Misogynism and Virginal Feminism in the Fathers," in *Religion and Sexism*; Shaw, *Burden of the Flesh*; and essays in Wimbush and Valantasis, eds., *Asceticism*.

32. "The *lex Julia* (59 B.C.E.) [had] required a widow to remarry within ten months, and a divorced woman within six months. The *lex Papia* (65 B.C.E.) extended this period to a year." Rousselle, *Porneia*, 91.

33. For a discussion of the role of widows in the North African Church in the third century, see Brown, *Body and Society*, 148.

34. See my discussion of the treatment of Jews in the late fourth-century Roman Empire in chapter 11 below.

formation of a Christian society that would be firmly in place by about C.E. 450.

Moreover, despite many enormous changes, the values and institutions Augustine and his friends constructed would survive far into the future; some institutions, such as monasticism, survive to the present. In short, Augustine participated in, and narrated, the cultural excitements of the late fourth and early fifth centuries. He described vividly the intense emotions he experienced on hearing and reading of engaged couples who pledged celibacy and went to live in same-sex communities.[35] He repeatedly contrasted his own seriousness of purpose as a Christian with the social success epitomized and symbolized by a "good" marriage. Strong male friendships and excited plans for a male community free from worldly cares are a leitmotif throughout the *Confessions*.[36] Same-sex religious communities would quickly become stronger and more numerous, taking the place of imperial institutions in providing everything from social services to traversable roads in the medieval centuries.

Was there a new role for women in the Christian Roman Empire? Did Augustine's partner participate in the new excitements of the Christian empire? If she were indeed a Christian, the relinquishment of sex would have placed her at the center of the ascetic movement, setting an example Augustine was not immediately prepared to follow but which he admired greatly. Furthermore, her role in the *Confessions* is central. The figure of Augustine's partner does more than contribute narrative vividness to Augustine's story. Her decision to remain celibate for the rest of her life also supported Christian rhetoric concerning the impossibility of great progress without correspondingly great sacrifice. From Augustine's perspective—and we do not have hers—she is the required living sacrifice, at first, by her absence, exacerbating the discomfort that led to his conversion, and later providing the example of celibacy that would be referenced many times in his writings. Augustine admired and extolled her as exemplary.[37]

But she was Augustine's sacrifice, *his* martyrdom. Even though she outdid him by vowing to have sex with no man for the rest of her days, his text

35. Augustine *Confessiones* 8.6.

36. Ibid., 6.14.

37. Augustine *De fide et operibus* (*Of Faith and Works*) 19.35 (C.E. 413): "[I]n the case of a concubine, if she shall make profession that she will know no other man, even although she be put away by him unto whom she is in subjection, it is with reason doubted, whether she ought not to be admitted to baptism."

swallows her act. Significantly, the language of tearing, wounds, dripping blood, and brokenness with which Augustine narrates his separation from her is the language of martyrdom. Without sacrificing her, he could not have aspired to "the highest peak of human heroism."[38] In Augustine's time, martyrdom, no longer a literal act, was reinterpreted in the Christian Empire. In Athanasius's *Life of St. Antony*, Antony, the prototypical ascetic, is described as practicing the "daily martyrdom."[39] In valuing martyrdom above all other Christian acts, Augustine was very much a North African, sharing with his compatriots respect for the ultimate sacrifice for faith.[40] Augustine's conversion, then, began with a martyrdom, extreme pain caused by "the cutting off of my previous mistress. It burned, it hurt intensely, and then it festered, and if the pain became duller, it became more desperate."[41]

Augustine's partner converted to celibacy earlier than Augustine did, and at greater cost.[42] Hers was not simply a sacrifice of physical pleasure; it was also a critical social sacrifice in a society in which women's identity derived from their sexual arrangements. Augustine, by contrast, benefited socially from his vow of celibacy. He became a priest and a bishop at a time and in a place in which the Church was a route to status and authority. She was sent away, but she went on her own terms.[43] Why did she not take her son with her when she returned to Africa? Did she despair of being able to support him when she herself would lack male protection? Did she unselfishly leave him to the parent who was expected to marry an heiress and thus would be able to bring the boy up with every advantage?[44] I will address these

---

38. Brown, *Body and Society*, 397.

39. Athanasius *Vita Antonii* 47: Anthony was "daily martyr to his conscience, ever fighting the battles of the faith." See also Woodward and Mattingly, ed., *Barlaam and Joasaph*: "Monasticism arose from men's desire to become martyrs in will, that they might not miss the glory of them who were made perfect by blood."

40. See chapter 5 above, 71–93.

41. Augustine *Confessiones* 6.15.

42. We do not know how she lived after her return to North Africa. She may have returned to her family, or it is possible that she could have been regarded as a widow and cared for by the Christian community of her village or town. Lacking a man, she would have had to throw herself on the mercy of family or community.

43. Is there perhaps a touch of sexual pride in Augustine's boast that she will have no other man after him?

44. Capps speculates that leaving Adeodatus with Augustine indicates "her anger and disgust, the vow never again to get involved in such a no-win situation" ("Scourge of Shame," 89).

questions by exploring further Augustine's partner's situation and her options within it.

Sexual arrangements in Augustine's society

> I thought that I should be unbearably unhappy if I were deprived of the embraces of a woman. . . . I believed that continency was something that depended on one's own strength and I knew that I did not have enough strength for it.[45]

Two topics bear directly on the social world of Augustine's partner, concubinage and contraception. In "the Imperial period Roman marriage required no formal ceremony to be valid; cohabitation between eligible partners basically created marriage."[46] Beryl Rawson's investigation of the legal status of sexual arrangements in the later Roman Empire emphasizes that despite the ease of respected sexual arrangements, concubinage is not frequently attested for freeborn couples. Concubinage implied ineligibility for marriage, usually because of a class difference. The dissolution of such a relationship was similarly informal.[47] This informality, together with the severe penalty imposed by Augustus for adultery, namely death by sword, combined to make sexual arrangements anxiety provoking.[48]

Concubinage and Marriage

In *Porneia: On Desire and the Body in Antiquity*, Aline Rousselle discusses the difficulty of describing Roman concubinage practices with precision.[49] The evidence is fragmentary and sporadic. Historians are dependent for information on funerary inscriptions and "fragments of legal works written for the most part before the fourth century, and collected between 530 and 533 by a commission of jurists appointed by Justinian."[50] Also, changes occurred in the later empire, but it is difficult to know whether laws were enforced or whether local practices actually conformed to the laws. Gillian Clark has also

---

45. Augustine *Confessiones* 6.11.

46. Rawson, "Roman Concubinage," 279.

47. Rousselle writes of a "lack of formal acts to register the events of private life" (*Porneia*, 82).

48. Though never repealed, Rousselle notes that this penalty was "rarely applied, particularly to women, until the time of Constantine" (*Porneia*, 88 note 51).

49. See also Treggiari, "Concubinage."

50. Rousselle, *Porneia*, 80.

examined Roman law in relation to women, concluding that no generalizations can be made because of local variations, inconsistencies in enforcement of recorded laws, and class differences. She writes: "We can sometimes see fragments of a pattern, but no overall design."[51]

However, C. N. Cochrane notes that under Theodosius (in the later fourth century), "the most significant departure [from Roman family law] was the disintegration, under Christian influence, of classical conceptions of the family and of family right."[52] The all-powerful *paterfamilias* of earlier times was gradually replaced by families with legal rights and protections.[53] One of the effects of this change was the greater legal protection of concubines' rights. By the end of the fourth century, a concubine "even had the right to inherit a modest part of her partner's estate."[54]

Rousselle also sees concubinage in a positive light, arguing that concubinage was "a free union in which the partners renounced the right to prosecute one another for adultery and to ask the tribunal to impose a punishment."[55] Concubinage involved fidelity and cohabitation. It ended when one or the other partner (usually the man), repudiated the relationship.[56] Lacking both the security and some of the restrictions of marriage, concubinage "should be seen as representing progress towards the right to enjoy a less unequal relationship [than marriage]."[57] Augustine recognized the less binding nature of concubinage; he says in a sermon, "Marriage is an iron fetter; other fetters can be loosed by us here in the church, but not this one."[58] Children born of

51. Clark elaborates: "Every scrap of material should come labeled with date and place of origin, purpose and prejudices, social level." G. Clark, *Women in Late Antiquity*, 139.

52. Cochrane, *Christianity and Classical Culture*, 326.

53. However, Augustine still thought of fathers as "giving orders to" extended families consisting of family members and slaves. *De civitate Dei* 19.16.

54. Power, "*Sed unam tamen*," 63 note 20.

55. Rousselle, *Porneia*, 80.

56. "The fact that it was easier to bring a concubinage to an end and to show the legal dissolution of the relationship than it was to dissolve matrimonial ties did not make it any easier for those who were dependent to this degree on a man's decisions." Rousselle, *Porneia*, 97.

57. Rousselle, *Porneia*, 100. If a woman who had been a concubine lacked economic independence, however, it is difficult to see how concubinage represented progress toward more mutual relationships.

58. Augustine *Enarrationes in Psalmos* 149.15.

concubinage belonged to the mother and carried her name. They were not eligible to inherit the father's property or goods.[59]

By Augustine's time, concubinage was an "official and respected condition."[60] Even the Christian Church recognized it, though it favored legitimate marriage, forbade a man to have both a wife and a concubine at the same time, and "required a baptized woman not to have known more than one man."[61] As a bishop, however, Augustine was judgmental of his earlier sexual arrangements. Opposed to concubinage, he advocated two choices in relation to sexuality, Christian marriage and vowed virginity.[62] His view of "the good of marriage" lacks appreciation for anything but legitimate sex: "The crown of marriage is the chastity of procreation and faithfulness in rendering the carnal debt."[63] Only within marriage, and only for purposes of procreation could sex be seen as even a limited good. For the older Augustine, in defiance of an accepted social practice, concubinage was sin.

However, he respected relationships that were faithful over a period of years. Without referring to his own relationship, he acknowledged that faithfulness, at least by the male partner, was unusual when he commented in a sermon: "Women preserve chastity, which men will not preserve."[64] He repeatedly fulminated against the commonly accepted double standard:

59. Rousselle, *Porneia*, 91.

60. Ibid.

61. Ibid., 105.

62. Augustine describes his own earlier situation in *De bono coniugali* 5, acknowledging that a relationship of mutually vowed faithfulness in which there is no avoidance of conception might even be called marriage (*nuptiae*). Yet he is strongly judgmental of his own role in the relationship: "For if a man lives with a woman for a time, until he finds another worthy either of his high station in life or his wealth, whom he can marry as his equal, in his very soul he is an adulterer, and not with the one whom he desires to find but with her with whom he now lives in such a way as not to be married to her." His judgment is somewhat more lenient on his partner: "The same is true for the woman, who, knowing the situation and willing it, still has relations unchastely with him, with whom she has no compact as a wife. On the other hand, if she remains faithful to him and, after he has taken a wife, does not plan to marry and is prepared to refrain absolutely from such an act, surely I could not easily bring myself to call her an adulteress; yet who would say that she did not sin, when he knows that she had relations with a man though she was not his wife." In *Sermo* 312.2, he again refers to his earlier situation when he says: "If you have no wives, you may not have concubines, women you will later dismiss in order to marry a wife."

63. Augustine *De bono coniugali* 11. I disagree with Frederik van der Meer's assessment of Augustine's teachings on marriage, i.e., that "he is to be reckoned among the great eulogists of Christian marriage." See Meer, *Augustine the Bishop*, 186.

64. Augustine *Sermo* 82.2.

> I do not want Christian women to lie down under this. I solemnly
> warn you, I lay down this rule, I command you. I command you as
> your bishop; and it is Christ Who commands in me. God knows,
> in whose sight my heart burns. Yes, I say, I command you. . . .For
> so many years now we have baptized so many men to no effect, if
> there are none here who preserve the vows of chastity they took.[65]

Augustine's famous fantasies on the possibility of conception without
the urgency of sexual desire[66] and immortality without death[67] serve his argument, against Manichaeans, for marriage as a good.

> The bodies of the first marriage were both mortal at the first for-
> mation and yet would not have died, if they had not sinned. . . .
> Thus, even though through sexual intercourse generations of such
> bodies could have come into existence, which would have had in-
> crease up to a certain point and yet would not have inclined to old
> age, or they would have inclined as far as old age, and yet not to
> death.[68]

It is not marriage, he was careful to say, even with its inevitable entailment of
sex, that brought death into the world, but sin.

65. Augustine *Sermo* 392.4, 6; quoted by Peter Brown, *Augustine of Hippo*, 244.

66. Augustine *De civitate Dei* 14.26: Augustine's fantasy of conception without pleasure in *De civitate Dei* 14.23 imagines sex without lust: "[T]he sexual organs would have
been brought into activity by the same bidding of the will as controlled the other organs.
Then, without feeling the allurement of passion goading him on, the husband would have
relaxed on his wife's bosom in tranquility of mind . . . [the two] united for impregnation
and conception by an act of will, instead of by a lustful craving." In *De nuptiis et concupiscentia* 53 (written at approximately the same time), he has thought of an amusing analogy
for lustless conception: ejaculation could, like urination, be accomplished "at the bidding
of the will. . . ."

67. Augustine *De bono coniugali* 2.2. Woody Allen's "I don't want to be immortal
through my work; I want to be immortal by *not dying*. I don't want to live on in the
hearts and minds of my countrymen; I want to live on in my apartment," is a profoundly
Augustinian fantasy. Augustine writes in the passage cited: "For if God allowed the garments of the Israelites to remain undamaged for forty years, how much more could he
have allowed the bodies of those who obeyed him that most blessed halfway house of a
settled status until they were changed for the better—changed not by that human death
in which the body is forsaken by the soul, but by a blessed transformation from mortality
to immortality."

68. Ibid.

Contraception

> I learned by my own experience how great a difference there is
> between the self-restraint of the marriage covenant which is en-
> tered into for the sake of having children, and the mere pact made
> by two people whose love is lustful and who do not want to have
> children—even though, if children are born they compel us to love
> them.[69]

When discussing contraception in late antiquity, it is important to keep
in mind that contraceptive practices were not intended to improve women's
lives. Rather they "were essentially ways to avoid having to divide inheri-
tances.[70] Nevertheless, the contraceptive practices of their society defined
women's range of choices; they affected Augustine's partner as they affected
all heterosexually active women.

Late fourth-century Christian attitudes toward contraception developed at the intersection of several influences. The widespread existence of
contraceptive knowledge and methods was a fact of life in the later Roman
Empire. As John Noonan writes: "The existence of contraceptive methods
in the world from which the Christians came is established: by the [Hebrew
Bible], by the Talmud, by Aristotle, by Pliny, by the physicians, and by imperial law. . . . Contraception was a social phenomenon in the Roman empire
of which the Christians could not have been ignorant."[71]

However, Christians developed their attitudes toward contraception in
the midst of polemics against their rivals, the Manichaeans, whom they accused
of practicing sexual acts without procreative purpose. Writing sometime after
C.E. 363 in Asia Minor, the Catholic bishop Titus wrote a treatise *Against the
Manichaeans* in which he said, "[I]ndulging in pleasure more frequently, [the
Manichaeans] hate the fruit that necessarily comes from their acts; and they
command that bodies be joined beyond what is lawful and restrict and expel
what is conceived and do not await births at their proper time."[72] Noonan
comments, "Sexual intercourse without procreative purpose and abortion are
thus charged to the Manichees; *coitus interruptus* and anal intercourse may
also be ascribed to them by the phrase 'beyond what is lawful.'"[73]

---

69. Augustine *Confessiones* 4.2.

70. Rousselle, *Porneia*, 195.

71. Noonan, *Contraception*, 28–29.

72. Titus of Bostra *Against the Manichees* 2.33; quoted by Noonan, *Contraception*, 114.

73. Ibid.

Because Manichaeans thought of the created world as the evil production of an evil Demiurge, they sought to avoid perpetuating it by procreation. Read with a hermeneutic of generosity, Manichaeans' acute sensitivity to the suffering of all living beings led them to seek to prevent the possibility of further suffering by infanticide or exposure, and even by the long suffering of human existence. However, in the context of the Roman state's interest in replenishing its population, Manichaeans represent a radical critique of both the Creator and the state.[74]

Two other debates influenced Augustine's views on marriage, concubinage, sex, and contraception. Without discussing them in detail, we must note that in the last decade of the fourth century, the monk Jovinian reacted against the "wave of ascetic enthusiasm which [had] spread throughout the Church."[75] Jovinian taught that marriage and virginity were equally conditions in which spiritual growth was possible. Augustine wrote in his *Retractions* that he had written *The Good of Marriage* specifically to oppose the "monster," Jovinian, who had "equated the merit of consecrated virgins and conjugal continence."[76] Apparently, if I can be pardoned an anachronism, Jovinian's teaching became a feminist issue. Women found in his teachings a greater respect for women. From the male perspective, respect for women rose and fell with respect for marriage.[77]

In C.E. 401, when he wrote *The Good of Marriage*, Augustine sought to refute Jovinian; in 419 when he wrote *Marriage and Concupiscence*, it was Pelagius he argued against. Against Pelagius (and later, Julian of Eclanum), Augustine argued that although marriage is a good, the pleasures of lust (*concupiscentia*), even though it produces offspring, is not itself a "natural good," as Julian claimed. For Augustine, the pleasure of sex is only to be tolerated when it is *led*, and modified by, the intention of producing children.[78]

---

74. Peter Brown, in *Body and Society*, describes the life expectancy of citizens of the Roman Empire "at its height in the second century A.D" as less than twenty-five years. "For the population of the Roman Empire to remain even stationary, it appears that each young woman would have had to have produced an average of five children." In order to accomplish this replenishment of Roman citizens, women started young. "The median age of Roman girls at marriage may have been as low as fourteen" (6).

75. Hunter, "Resistance to the Virginal Ideal," 45.

76. Augustine *Retractationes* 2.48.

77. Jerome *Adversus Jovinianum* 2.47. I am simultaneously amused and offended by the many indexes in scholarly books that say "marriage, see women" (or "women, see marriage"), equating, as did Augustine and his contemporaries, marriage and women!

78. Augustine *De nuptiis et concupiscentia* 13.

Contraceptive Methods

Augustine and his partner were together for about fifteen years, from his sixteenth to his twenty-ninth year. Their son Adeodatus was born in the first year of their relationship (C.E. 373), and they had no further children. Interestingly, Augustine became a Manichaean in 373, the year of his son's birth, possibly attracted not only by the Manichaean solution to the problem of evil, but also by its preference for preventing conception. Since he had acknowledged that he did not want children, the possibility may even be advanced to a probability.[79] The timing is telling. It is highly probable that Augustine and his partner practiced contraception for the remaining years of their relationship.

Human beings seem perennially to exhibit more hostility toward practices they themselves engaged in than those known only by hearsay. Long after his relationship with his partner ended, arguing against Manachaeism in his treatise *Marriage and Concupiscence*, Augustine excoriated the full range of late Roman prophylactic practices: "[T]his lustful cruelty, or cruel lust, comes to this, that they even procure poisons of sterility [*sterilitatis venena*], and, if these do not work, extinguish and destroy the fetus in some way in the womb, preferring that their offspring die before it lives, or if it was already alive in the womb to kill it before it was born." Any of these practices effectively nullify a marriage, Augustine says. This is the only passage in Augustine's work that explicitly refers to artificial contraceptives.[80]

Augustine also refers to other contraceptive practices in his treatises on sex, virginity, and marriage. He claims to have heard at firsthand, during his time as a Manichaean, their teaching on the so-called "rhythm method" of contraception: "Is it not you who hold that begetting children is a greater sin than cohabitation? Is it not you who used to counsel us to observe as much as possible the time when a woman, after her purification, is most likely to

---

79. Augustine often refers to anal intercourse as a method of contraception. In *De bono coniugali* he writes, "But when the husband wishes to use the member of his wife that has not been given for this purpose, the wife is more shameful if she permits this to take place with herself rather than with another woman" (11). Augustine returns several times in this short treatises to "that use which is contrary to nature." The treatise is a fascinating mosaic of recognizable autobiography, advocacy for marriage, and condemnation of practices that prevent conception. Indeed, the reader is left wondering whether his repetitious injunctions against anal intercourse suggest that this might have been the young Augustine's preferred contraceptive method; see also *De nuptiis et concupiscentia* 35.

80. Augustine *De nuptiis et concupiscentia* 1.17.

conceive, and to abstain from cohabitation at that time, lest the soul should be entangled in flesh?"[81]

Conclusion

Desperately seeking Augustine's partner in a text that was not only uninterested in her, but actively presented her in a way that supported Augustine's present celibacy, has not been easy. At times I have lost the slender thread by which I hoped to pull her into view, and then, suddenly, it was all about Augustine, not about her. His flood of words tells us so much about himself, and so little about his lover of fifteen years. I have suggested that we can glimpse her through exploring the social arrangements that directed women's lives in the later fourth century. Her options, we saw, were not abundant, but she chose courageously when Augustine opted to end the relationship.

I have sketched her historical moment as a moment of social tension in which Christianity had become the official religion of state, and society was rapidly being organized according to new values. If my interest in her were primarily to better understand Augustine, it would be possible to examine the effects of their relationship on Augustine's theology. For example, I could suggest that Augustine may have learned what humility is—one of the central tenets of his theology—from his partner.[82] She apparently lived with Augustine without expectation, returning to North Africa without complaint when dismissed. This example of humility, seen at firsthand, could have been an even more vivid and immediate example of humility for Augustine than "the Word made flesh," which he says was initially so difficult for him to grasp.[83]

Or, if my interest were primarily in Augustine, it would also be possible to examine what we may consider Augustine's failures as the result of his inability to integrate sex into a loving and productive life.[84] I suggest that

81. Augustine *De moribus manichaeorum* 18.65. Perhaps this ancient teaching that a woman's most likely time to conceive is immediately after her menstrual period is the origin of the old joke, "What do they call people who use the rhythm method? Parents!"

82. He came, however, to rank humility very highly in the Christian life: "The way is firstly humility, secondly humility, and thirdly humility." Augustine *Epistula* 118.3.

83. Augustine *Confessiones* 7.19.

84. E. Clark, "Adam's Only Companion," 139. Clark argues that if Augustine had developed "unswervingly" the implications of his statement (in *De civitate Dei* 14.11) that Adam sinned because he "refused to be separated from his only companion, even if it involved sharing her guilt," he would have come to "a notion of marital friendship unique for his time and place."

we might also see Augustine's failure to integrate intimate relationship as connected to his inability to understand concern and care for the world as a form for spiritual growth and insight. He did not offer models other than that of withdrawal from the larger society and centering "within" as the ideal for the Christian life.[85]

• • •

She disappears from our view, as she has disappeared from this essay, without a trace. On the one hand, she can be seen as the victim of new economies of emotional, religious, and social desire. On the other, and precisely within the excitements of her time and place, she outdid Augustine, the representative and prototype of Christian desire, by her choice for celibacy. Whether or not she was a Christian—the evidence is, in my view, inconclusive—she exercised her agency within a limited palette of possibilities. She could certainly have gone on to either marriage or another concubinage relationship. But, even if she were not a Christian, to do so would have been to sacrifice Roman society's respect for the *univera*, or one-man woman. If she were Christian, entering a second concubinage under the strict requirements for women (only) for baptism and communion in the Christian Church would have sacrificed her good standing in the church.[86] We do not know whether she returned to North Africa to live in a religious community as Augustine did somewhat later. Let us conjecture that she did, for that is the only option offered by her society that would have permitted her to concentrate on the very aspect of her life that is most conspicuously missing in Augustine's *Confessions*, namely her subjectivity.

85. Miles, *Desire and Delight*, 98–99. See Cary, *Augustine's Invention*, 5. Cary argues that Augustine created the "inner self" as unshared space. Earlier philosophers, like Plotinus, had thought of the inner self as common space, the site of relationship to the universe. Augustine famously asks, "What do I seek? God and the soul. Nothing more? Nothing more." Augustine *Soliloquiorum* 1.1.

86. Augustine, by contrast, improved his moral standing in the eyes of the Church by sending his concubine away and planning marriage. Brown quotes Pope Leo I: "To abandon one's concubine in order to take a wife in legitimate matrimony was 'not bigamy, but a sign of moral improvement." Brown, *Augustine of Hippo*, 79. The older Augustine will urge other men to do the same. See Augustine *Sermo* 224.3.

CHAPTER 9

"Jesus patibilis":
Augustine's Debate with the Manichaeans

"It must, no doubt, seem strange that my soul and that of any and
everybody else should be one thing only: it might mean my feelings
being felt by someone else, my goodness another's too, my desire his
desire, all our experience shared with each other and with the one
universe, so that the very universe itself would feel what I feel. We are in
sympathetic relation to one another, suffering, overcome at the sight of
pain, naturally drawn to forming attachments; and all this can be due
only to some unity among us." (PLOTINUS ENNEAD 4.9.3)

Introduction

Historians are often troubled by the question of the relationship
of historical understanding to contemporary problems. We are likely to
be particularly uneasy when asked to speculate about the "lessons," valuable
to the present, taught by a historical situation. In spite of discomfort with
such questions, it also frequently seems unaffordably luxurious to study history for antiquarian interest alone. On the one side the Scylla of presentism
threatens; on the other, the Charybdis of irrelevance. How, then, to negotiate
the Straits of Messina between the two dangers? Can the sensitivities of the
present provide a critical perspective for the illumination of historical texts
and events? Can insight into contemporary issues be achieved from study of
the past?

This essay will attempt such a hazardous enterprise. Sensitized by present ecological crises to a problematic Western conceptualization of the natural world, I will explore the temporally and spatially distant historical moment in which the complex synthesis of beliefs, values, and loyalties that has supported the undisciplined use of natural resources and the abuse of animals was formulated and argued. Engaging the insights of the defeated position, I will suggest a concept of nature more supportive of careful and disciplined use of nature than the dominant Western view.

At the end of the fourth century of the Common Era, Augustine, bishop of Hippo, successfully argued for a particular understanding of human community and responsibility against the North African Manichaeans. The arena of human community, and therefore of human responsibility, Augustine said, is limited to the community of rational minds, that is, to human beings. As a result of his rhetorical skill and institutional power, Augustine's understanding became the dominant Western view.

Against Augustine's definition of "community," Manichaeans taught that humans participate irreducibly in a community of all living beings. They included animals, plants, and even soil and rocks in their idea of community, thereby positing a vastly enlarged province of human responsibility. In its own time, the Manichaean view of human community and responsibility was not a peculiar feature of their religious sensibility; this feature of Manichaeism was also shared by Stoics and by Neoplatonists.[1] Despite the widespread attraction of this view in late antiquity, it failed to enter the mainstream of Western assumptions and attitudes. Even so, remnants of empathy with all living beings are to be found in the later history of Christianity, especially in St. Francis's notion of the need for "mutual deference" between human beings and animals,[2] and in Anabaptists' "gospel of all creatures."[3]

The *effects* of Augustine's idea that humans can and should be indifferent to the suffering of any but rational beings and of his intense and detailed focus on human suffering cannot be enumerated here. They are, I suspect, writ too large to yield to the microscopic scrutiny to which responsible scholarship is adjusted. Moreover, it would be reductionistic to imply that Augustine's

1. Although Plotinus's only polemical treatise was directed "Against the Gnostics," the quotation at the beginning of this essay indicates that he shared their sense of an intimate relationship among all creatures of the universe; see also *Ennead* 5.2.1: "The higher soul seems to reach as far as plants. . . ."

2. Sorrell, *St. Francis and Nature*, 74.

3. Raitt, ed., *Christian Spirituality*, 340.

theory of human community is solely responsible for these effects. Historical "causes" are too various to be explained by a single idea; neither can an author predict the extent and the practical results of a conceptualization s/he proposes. Nevertheless, the victory of Augustine's argument was the historical moment in which two radically different understandings of nature competed within Christian discourse

The decisive defeat of the Manichaean view has had dramatic effects in the history of the West. In the last decade of the twentieth century, every newscast enumerates the effects of congenital inattentiveness to the suffering of living beings. How the twentieth-century world might have been different if the Manichaean vision of community had carried the day must be conjecture. Yet it is likely that if the Manichaean doctrine of a suffering Jesus, "hanging on every tree," symbol of the struggle and suffering of the whole creation, had woven itself into mainstream Christianity, the exploitive anthropocentrism of Western societies might have been significantly modified.

The attitudes, beliefs, and values represented in Augustine's position against the Manichaeans have been assumed and accepted for almost fifteen hundred years. My primary purpose is not to assess Augustine's construction of "community" in the context of the pressures and problems of his own time. Rather, examination of these two different religious sensibilities and value systems reveals their historical construction and opens dominant Western ideas of nature, the natural world, and living beings to deconstruction and reconstruction. For centuries of hindsight suggest that Augustine's understanding of human community and responsibility does not adequately serve the desperate needs of the present. Twentieth century people need not convert to Manichaeism in order to recognize that fourth-century Manichaeans had a worldview and religious values that may suggest directions for our own reconstruction of community.

Manichaeism in North Africa

Mani, a Persian who called himself the "apostle of Jesus Christ," claimed to offer a revelation that superseded that of Christ's earthly teachings. He taught that the Holy Spirit, promised three centuries before, had finally descended on him. Mani was martyred by crucifixion in C.E. 276 at the instigation of Zoroastrian priests. Manichaeism was a secret religion, but it was also a missionary religion with claims to universality.[4] Within Mani's lifetime it

4. It is important to note that at the end of the fourth century catholicity was still a

had spread beyond Mesopotamia to Iran and adjoining parts of the Roman Empire. Advancing along commercial routes, Manichaean groups were also in Arabia, Armenia, Syria, Asia Minor, Palestine, the Balkans, Italy, Spain, and Gaul. Manichaeism spread from Egypt to North Africa at an early date, nearly twenty years earlier than the first evidence of Manichaeism in Rome.[5]

Manichaeism was syncretistic, incorporating features of Buddhism, Zoroastrianism, Taoism, Confucianism, and Christianity. It was suspect in the Roman Empire, however, not only for its beliefs, but even for its place of origin—Persia, the third century "California" of new religious movements. And this "most persecuted of heresies"[6] was not accepted by the religions with which it sought to affiliate, perhaps largely because Mani claimed to have the only true interpretation of each. Despite claims to possess Truth, the virtual absence of polemical literature in Manichaeism is striking in comparison with the volume of anti-Manichaean literature.

Latin translations of Manichaean texts appeared at the end of the third century, less than a century after the first North African Christian writings in Latin. The aesthetic qualities of the great tomes that contained Mani's teachings were not the least of Manichaeism's attractions; they were inscribed with graceful calligraphy and lavishly illustrated. Tradition has it that Mani himself was a skillful painter. Mani is reported to have said of his teachings: "I have written them in books and pictured them in colors; let him who hears them in words also see them in an image, and let him who is unable to learn them from words learn them from pictures."[7]

Only twenty years or so after Mani's death, sometime between March 31, 297, and the same date in C.E. 302,[8] the Emperor Diocletian dispatched the first prohibition of Manichaeism to Julianus, the proconsul of Africa. The rescript demanded that "Manichees and magicians and their sacred books" be burned. Yet, in the West, the fourth century was the time of the greatest numerical and geographical development—and the greatest persecution—of Manichaeism. Following Diocletian's Edict of C.E. 297 outlaw-

---

contested designation. Universality was a fundamental ingredient of catholicity's definition, so that Manichaeism could legitimately lay claim to catholicity.

5. Frend, "Gnostic-Manichaean Tradition," 16. Decret, *L'Afrique manichéenne*, 1:176.

6. Lieu, *Manichaeism*, 154. In fact, the only Christian heretics to be executed in the first five centuries were Manichaeans.

7. Lieu, *Manichaeism*, 139. Klimkeit, *Manichaean Art and Calligraphy*.

8. Decret, *L'Afrique manichéenne*, 162. Oddly enough the rescript was dated by the day, but not the year.

ing Manichaeism, emperors throughout the fourth century reiterated and attempted to enforce the edict—Constantine in 326, Valentinian in 372, and Theodosius in 381.[9] Yet Manichaeism survived both the Arian Vandal rulers of fifth-century North Africa, and Justinian's sixth-century reconquest of North Africa, which brought a reassertion of Catholic persecutions of Manichaeans. As late as 724, "Pope Gregory II would still warn against the ordination of Africans who had fled to Italy from Islamic invaders because many of them were either still Manichaeans or former heretics who had been rebaptized."[10] Manichaeism existed in North Africa until Christianity itself was extinguished by Islamic invasions.[11]

At the time of Augustine's encounter with the Manichaeans, Manichaeism had been established in North Africa for almost a century.[12] It flourished within Catholic congregations,[13] claiming to be an intellectually sophisticated and rigorously ascetic version of Catholic Christianity,[14] a Christianity of the "inquiring mind."[15] In *Epistula* 236, Augustine acknowledged that one of his sub-deacons had been a Manichaean Hearer for years without being detected by the Catholic congregation to which he ministered. Although historians have emphasized the differences between Catholics and Manichaeans, these differences seem to have been less evident on location. Clearly, Augustine's efforts to reveal and dispute the errors of Manichaeism occurred in a context in which these differences were not evident. Both the popularity of Manichaeism and its compatibility with Catholic Christianity made it especially difficult to extirpate from North Africa.[16]

---

9. Asmussen, *Manichaean Literature*, 18.

10. Lieu, *Manichaeism*, 164.

11. Asmussen, *Manichaean Literature*, 17.

12. Lieu, *Manichaeism*, 85–86.

13. Decret, *L'Afrique manichéenne*, 181. In *Contra Faustum Manichaeum*, Augustine complains of the similarity of Catholic and Manichaean Christianity: "For those whom they [Manichaeans] lead astray are Christians already born of the gospel, whom the Christian profession of the heretics misleads" (13.12).

14. In Augustine's debate with the African Manichaean Faustus, Faustus called Catholic Christianity "semi-Christianity" in contrast with the more detailed and demanding teachings of Mani; Augustine *Contra Faustum Manichaeum* 1.2.

15. Frend, "Gnostic-Manichaean Tradition," 23.

16. Frend, "Manichaeism," 865.

Ironically, Augustine himself was repeatedly and throughout his life ac-cused of Manichaeism.[17] His ordination was delayed while these suspicions were investigated. In his youth, he had been a Manichaean Hearer for nine years; his *Confessions* describe both his attraction to Manichaeism and his subsequent disenchantment. As a Catholic priest and bishop, his commit-ment to ascetic monasticism, and his teaching that marriage and sex are inevitably implicated in the transmission of original sin, repeatedly sparked accusations that he had never completely departed from the religion of his youth.[18] Perhaps his personal vendetta against Manichaeism was motivated at least in part by his eagerness to demonstrate his orthodoxy. His harshness toward the priest who simultaneously discharged his duties as a Catholic priest and participated in a Manichaean cell also witnesses to Augustine's need to demonstrate his lack of sympathy for the Manichaeans.

Manichaean Beliefs

Manichaeans were dualists, positing a kingdom of light and a kingdom of darkness eternally at war with one another. Their primary appeal to the young Augustine lay in their clear and satisfying answer to the problem of the origin of evil.[19] The kingdom of darkness, eternally at odds with the king-dom of light, was the cause of pain and evil; it was also the home of bodies and the natural world. However, Manichaeans' metaphysical dualism was tempered by their recognition that *in experience*, the kingdom of darkness and the kingdom of light—the material and the spiritual worlds—were in-

---

17. Ibid., 859–66.

18. In response to the second charge—that of denigrating marriage—Augustine wrote a treatise, *De bono coniugali* (*The Good of Marriage*), specifically to exonerate himself from these accusations. The treatise failed, understandably, to silence his critics. All states of life, he wrote, are gifts from God, whether celibacy or marriage. As gifts, they are not to be compared with one another as if they were self-trained virtues (8.8; 23.29). Yet his conclusion, namely that nevertheless celibacy is better than marriage, does little to dem-onstrate his respect for "the good of marriage." Similarly, in his old-age controversy with Julian of Eclanum, his harshness toward human sexuality prompted Julian's accusations that Augustine was secretly a Manichaean.

19. Augustine's conversion to Catholic Christianity had been prepared by his discov-ery—in the Platonic doctrine of evil as deprivation of being—of an explanation for the ori-gin and existence of evil alternative to that of the Manichaeans. Nevertheless, it is striking that, in his C.E. 392 debate with Fortunatus, Augustine did not answer when Fortunatus asked him to identify the origin of evil; *Acta contra Fortunatum Manichaeum* 19.

tertwined.[20] This meant that all material things contain particles of spiritual light and thus are sacred.[21] Manichaeans believed that these particles of light are sentient, suffering in their entrapment in the material world of bodies and objects, yearning to breathe free of their prisons and reunite with their spiritual homeland.

The suffering of all things did not, for the Manichaeans, remain an abstract notion; rather it was vivid and concrete. For example, the *Cologne Codex* relates that before Mani organized his own religion, while he was still a member of the Elchasaios sect, he was forced to do agricultural work. As he worked he found that "blood oozed from the places where the plants had been hurt by the blows of the sickle. They also cried out with a human voice because of the blows they received.[22] Manichaean literature resounds with the poignant longing of the light particles to return to the Kingdom of Light, a longing believed to be at its most acute in human beings.[23] "The drama . . . centers on the redemption of the Light Elements which have been swallowed by the archons of Darkness and have thus become mixed and sullied."[24] One Manichaean understanding of Jesus—an understanding documented only in North Africa—was that of "*Jesus patibilis*," Jesus as the prototypical and quintessential living soul (*viva anima*), perennially trapped and suffering in the world of the senses.[25] Augustine quotes Faustus' description of the suffering Jesus:

> The Holy Spirit, by his influence and spiritual infusion, makes the earth conceive and bring forth the mortal Jesus, who, as hanging from every tree, is the life and salvation of humanity.[26]

---

20. The Alexandrian Platonist, Alexander of Lycopolis, in his treatise *Critique of the Doctrines of Manichaeus*, found inconsistency in the Manichaeans' insistence on the absolute incommensurability of divinity and matter: "Why do they speak ill of matter when from the beginning this is blended with the divine power?" (*Alexandrian Platonist*, 81).

21. Faustus, the North African Manichaean, in fact cited the similarity of Catholic belief in the sacredness of the eucharistic elements of bread and wine to Manichaean belief in the sacredness of all things; Augustine *Contra Faustum* 20.2.

22. Lieu, *Manichaeism*, 34.

23. Augustine described the Manichaean theory of transmigration in *De Genesi ad litteram* 7.11.

24. Lieu, *Manichaeism*, 14.

25. Asmussen, *Manichaean Literature*, 47.

26. Augustine *Contra Faustum* 20.11.

From Augustine's perspective, North African Manichaeans displayed an emotional and virtually neurasthenic sensitivity to all suffering—human, animal, plant, and mineral;[27] his observation is supported by Manichaean literature. A Manichaean text, preserved in Sogdian fragments, contains a confession of sin against the five kinds of living beings, "the two-legged human beings, the four-legged living beings, the flying living beings, the living beings in the water, and the living beings creeping on the ground on their belly":

> If we ever, my God, somehow have inspired with fear (or) scared these five kinds of living beings from the biggest to the smallest, if we somehow should have beaten or cut them, somehow have pained and tortured them, somehow should have killed them, we to the same degree owe life to the living beings. (Therefore) we now, my God, pray that we may be liberated from sin. Forgive my sin.[28]

Manichaean Practices

Manichaeism consisted of a body of ideas and doctrines; it was also a "highly regulated way of life."[29] Augustine is the source of a rich store of information about Manichaean practices in North Africa.[30] These must be described under two categories: those required of Hearers, and those expected only of the "Perfect" or Elect. Regulations for both were designed to avoid actions that might harm the light particles or further entrench them in matter. For Manichaeans, nothing short of the redemption of God was at stake: God is Light, trapped in the material world. The release of the light will actively serve to speed the "Future Moment" in which, the liberation of the Light nearly completed, the material world will be abandoned to its native evil and warfare. The faithful will be translated to the kingdom of light, there to participate in and enjoy this blissful reward—Hearers at the right hand of the triumphant Jesus, while the Elect are transformed into angels.[31]

---

27. Augustine wrote: "one of your silly notions is that the tree weeps when the fruit is pulled"; "you maintain that the fruit suffers when it is pulled from the tree, when it is cut, and scraped, and cooked, and eaten"; *Contra Faustum* 6.4.

28. Asmussen, *Manichaean Literature*, 72

29. Lieu, *Manichaeism*, 90.

30. Augustine continued to be accused of Manichaeism throughout his life; Frend describes these accusations in "Manichaeism in the Struggle," 859–66; see also Courcelle, *Recherches*, 238–45.

31. Lieu, *Manichaeism*, 21.

Hearers lived as fully functioning members of secular society. They were permitted to marry, but encouraged not to bear children. Their duties to the sect consisted primarily of a "soul service" in which they cared for the Elect, providing and preparing their daily ritual meal. The *Kephalaia of the Teacher*, a fourth century Egyptian document, describes the connection of food practices to the release of the light particles: "The alms which pass over to the Elect are made like many Icons, and they are purified, and they depart to the Country of the Living."[32] At their death, Hearers could expect to be reincarnated, and the body to which they were reassigned was contingent on the quality and faithfulness of their service to the Elect.

The practices of the Elect were considerably more strenuous. They were contained in the "Three Seals" that Augustine described in *De moribus manichaeorum*: the Seal of the Mouth, the Seal of the Hands, and the Seal of the Breast. What leaves the mouth as well as what enters were governed by the Seal of the Mouth: blasphemous speech was prohibited, as was the eating of meat and drinking of wine. Vegetarianism was prescribed because the bodies of animals contain fewer light particles than those of plants. Animals ingest light by feeding on plants, but a portion of this light was believed to be obliterated in the transfer. Wine was forbidden because it induces intoxication and the forgetfulness of one's real self and home in the kingdom of light, a forgetfulness that Manichaean teachings, doctrines, hymns, and prayers resisted.[33]

The Seal of the Hands stipulates that the faithful must not perform any task that might harm the particles of light. By this Seal, they were "forbidden to till the soil, or to pluck fruit, or to harvest any plant or to kill any animal, no matter how small."[34] Bathing was also forbidden: Manichaeans emphasized the pollution of the water by dirt from the body rather than the cleansing of the body. The Seal of the Breast forbids sexual intercourse in that its result is the propagation of more flesh in which light particles are painfully enslaved.

---

32. Wimbush, *Ascetic Behavior*, 205.

33. Augustine's theological development of the idea of "longing" as that which enlarges the soul, making it sufficiently capacious to receive God, seems to represent the conversion to Catholic Christianity of a method he learned as a Manichaean; see especially his treatise on fasting, *De utilitate jejunii*.

34. Lieu, *Manichaeism*, 20. Frend suggests that the urban location of most Manichaeans should be seen as part of their motivation for eschewing physical labor; "Manichaeism," 860.

In the West, the ritual practices of Manichaeans were conducted in private homes.[35] Once a day Hearers and Elect gathered,[36] the Hearers to prepare and witness the meal—in North Africa it was called "eucharist"—consumed by the Elect. At this solemn ritual, the beautiful and haunting Manichaean hymn cycles and psalms were also sung.[37] A weekly confession of sins—Hearers to Elect, and Elect to Elect—completed Manichaeans' ritual practice. Since the death of both Hearers and Elect represented a liberation from the kingdom of darkness, their deaths were apparently not mourned with funeral rites, though there was a "body and soul" rite, "whose contents and aims are . . . still obscure."[38]

Human Community and Responsibility

Two treatises, both written by Augustine in C.E. 388, shortly after his baptism, are especially helpful for understanding Augustine's conflict with the Manichaeans—*The Practices of the Catholics* (*De moribus ecclesia catholicae*), and *The Practices of the Manichaeans* (*De moribus manichaeorum*). Augustine's rhetorical skills, newly converted to Christianity, are at their peak in these treatises.[39] They demonstrate that some of Augustine's most characteristic and enduring theological tenets were developed in the polemical context of debate with the Manichaeans. I will focus on what they reveal of Augustine's understanding of human community and responsibility.

In *De moribus manichaeorum*, Augustine agrees with the Manichaeans that the body is "man's [*sic*] heaviest bond." The soul loves the body merely from "force of habit," and when the soul has turned completely to God, it will lose its attraction to the body, not only disregarding death, but even

35. Asmussen, *Manichaean Literature*, 61.

36. Manichaeans in North Africa seem to have had no church buildings, but met as house groups, small cells that could readily disappear from sight in times of persecution. This small-group organization contributed to the survival of the Manichaeans.

37. Lieu states that collections of Manichaean hymns are "among the largest and oldest collection of religious songs known to us," predating the hymns of Prudentius and Venantius by more than a century; *Manichaeism*, 134.

38. Asmussen, *Manichaean Literature*, 61.

39. At the end of his life Augustine wrote in *Retractationes*: "When I was at Rome after my baptism, and could not bear in silence the vaunting of the Manichaeans about their pretended and misleading continence or abstinence, in which, to deceive the inexperienced, they claim superiority over true Christians, to whom they are not to be compared, I wrote two books, one on the practices of the Catholic Church, the other on the practices of the Manichaeans" (1.7).

desiring it" (22.40). This minimizing account of the body's integrity to human being supports Augustine's polemical disparagement of the senses: since the Manichaeans claimed to be able to identify different degrees of light in different objects by their color, hue, and saturation, Augustine insists: "We are forbidden to regard things which are seen" (20.37). Similarly, in contrast to Manichaean sensitivity to pain, he minimizes its significance, stating that the mind can "soar above all torture free and glorious" (22.41). He seeks to establish the hegemony of the rational mind over the exigencies of nature and the sufferings of life.

The primary purpose of Augustine's argument, however, is to insist that attention to other human beings is sufficient for fulfilling the Christian's responsibility. He posits love of self and neighbor as fully constitutive of love of God:

> It is impossible for one who loves God not to love himself. . . . We can think of no surer step towards the love of God than the love of human for human. . . . Our love of our neighbor is a sort of cradle of our love to God. . . . While the love of God is first in beginning, love of our neighbor is first in coming to perfection. (26.50–1)

Love of neighbor is characterized by concern for both the body and the soul of the neighbor. The neighbor's physical needs should be cared for, he says, with a sort of emotionless charity—the "calm of a rational serenity" (27.52–3). Doing good to the neighbor's soul entails restraining him from wrongdoing first through fear of God, and secondly, by instruction which generates love for God (28.55–6).

A contextual reading of this, Augustine's first full exposition of the importance of love for the neighbor, reveals that this celebrated focus of his theology was articulated in the context of his refutation of the Manichaeans' claim that the arena of human community and responsibility is nothing less than the whole creation. Augustine wrote in rebuttal: "There is no community of rights between us and brutes and trees," and he listed scriptural warrants for the killing of animals (13.27).

The extension of sympathetic community to plants, rocks, and soil, Augustine claimed, attenuated Manichaeans' empathy for human suffering: "you feel so much more for melons than for men" (17.62). He ridiculed the idea that plants suffer, that "part of God exists in corn, beans, cabbage and flowers and fruits" (15.38). He acknowledged that animals suffer, but denied that their suffering constitutes a moral imperative for humans: "For we see and hear by their cries that animals die with pain, although man disregards this in a beast with which, as not having a rational soul, we have no community of rights" (18.52).

Augustine maintained love of the human neighbor as the centerpiece of his theology throughout his career. He continued to insist that the community of human accountability excludes animals, who exist to serve human beings and to provide food for them:

> When we read "Thou shalt not kill" we assume this does not refer to bushes, which have no feelings, nor to irrational creatures, flying, swimming, walking, or crawling, since they have no rational association with us, not having been endowed with reason as we are, and hence it is by a just arrangement of the Creator that their life and death is subordinated to our needs.[40]

Different religious sensibilities underlie Augustine's theology of "reality" and that of the Manichaeans. In contrast to the Manichaeans' "emotional" view of the suffering universe, Augustine argued that the only "just judgment" results from a mind "composed," rational, and free of emotion.[41] Augustine's idea of God's participation in the universe is interdependent with his view of suffering. Augustine's God is "present by the power of divinity, for administering and ruling all things, undefilably, inviolably, incorruptibly, *without any connection with them*" (my emphasis). According to Augustine, the Manichaeans' God, by contrast, was "everywhere mixed up in heaven, in earth, in all bodies, dry and moist, in all sorts of flesh, in all seeds of trees, herbs, humans and animals . . . fettered, oppressed, polluted."[42] The Manichaeans' God was intimately and integrally engaged in the world and its processes, deeply interior to the universe.

Conclusions

The triumph of Augustine's construction of "human community" as composed solely of "rational beings" presented an influential rationale for the use of animals and plants for human aggrandizement. Along with, and as

---

40. Augustine *De civitate Dei* 1.20.

41. In Augustine *Contra epistolam manichaei quam vocant fundamenti*, Augustine exemplified the difference between an emotional and a rational judgment in his contrast between perceiving a lion in terms of its danger to animals and humans and a "leisurely" appreciation of its beauty; 34.38.

42. Augustine *De natura boni* 46.44.

an interpretation of, the Genesis injunction to "be fruitful and multiply and subdue the earth," Augustine's argument supported—and advocated—what came to be the dominant Western attitude of indifference to animal suffering and to the exploitation of natural resources.

Ironically, Augustine's argument that human beings must attend solely to *human* suffering does not seem to have produced the sensitivity to this suffering that Augustine himself experienced.[43] Thus, while Augustine's argument blocked attention to animal suffering, it did not in practice overcome Western indifference to human suffering, largely because of his views on society. A complex and interlocking structure of dualism based on gender, class, and race privileged "higher" over "lower" and effectively isolated Augustine's "community of rational minds" to ruling class men.

From his earliest description of society—*De moribus ecclesia catholicae* 30.63—to his mature social theory—*De civitate Dei* 19.13–15—Augustine held the same view. In a fallen world, he saw no other social possibility than domination and subordination. Social order, he wrote, begins within human beings in the soul's obedient subordination to God, and the soul's domination over the body.[44] The relationship of ruler and ruled is echoed in all social relationships—in the subordination of wife to husband, subjects to rulers, and slaves to masters. Even when applied solely to human community, then, Augustine's theory of sympathy and responsibility fails to promote the inclusiveness it claims.

The metaphysical dualism of the Manichaeans, while objectionable from many twentieth-century perspectives, was, curiously, not incompatible with a strongly developed sensitivity to the suffering of all living creatures. The "community of rational minds," successfully argued by Augustine, and subsequently institutionalized in Catholic Christianity and Western societies, does not seem justified in its *effects*—effects that were unknowable to Augustine but that are abundantly visible to people who have inherited and lived with them. Can a twentieth-century reconstruction of the arena of human community and responsibility be formulated in which the Manichaean idea of a community of life is incorporated? Socio-biologists, philosophers,

43. Augustine himself felt, in relation to human suffering, something close to Manichaean "neurasthenic sensitivity" to the suffering of animals and plants. In *De civitate Dei* 22, he lists a long catalog of the "ills to which human nature is prey," illustrating his contention that human life cannot be construed otherwise than as "a state of punishment."

44. Michel Foucault once observed that, in contrast to the Platonic axiom, "the soul is the prisonhouse of the body."

science-fiction writers, ecologists, and others are presently describing the essential interdependence of all forms of life, and secular "spiritualities" also advocate loyalty to the earth and its resources. But is it not crucial to formulate specifically *religious* commitments to the natural world? Can such responsibility be seen as a religious commitment?

The Christian tradition certainly contains suggestions for such a mandate. The doctrines of creation, of an incarnate God, and of resurrection of the body imply the religious worth of the sensible world. Yet, for reasons too complex to discuss here, these suggestions have not been effective in bonding Christians' loyalties to the natural world. Judaism and non-Western religions have perhaps emphasized more effectively than Christianity the consummate value of the earth and its creatures.[45] My task here, however, is the evaluation of a claim within a broadly construed "ecumenical" Christianity to provide a more accurate and heuristic account of the community of human responsibility.

Manichaean constructions of the community of all living beings contain a powerful mystical appeal, but they also raise two questions. First, the inclusion of soil and rocks in the "community of life" would seem to attenuate too drastically the moral imperative of responsibility. In fact, in Manichaeism itself, this comprehensive community of life was not sustained in practice. It was technically surmounted by protecting the *perfect* from agricultural work; Hearers, however, provided food for the Elect by their ordinary occupations. Moreover, to think of human community as coextensive with soil and rocks requires an intense, profound, and inclusive mystical vision that is not likely to be achieved by many people.[46]

For most people, some constructions of human community are more intuitively accessible than others. To include inanimate objects in human community may attenuate the idea of community well beyond most people's

45. One recent attempt to imagine and advocate responsibility for the natural world on religious grounds is Drew Leder's *The Absent Body*. His examples of religious rituals that can produce vivid unitive experiences and the awareness of responsibility for all living creatures are the Christian eucharist and Zen meditation.

46. A skilled and experienced contemplative can perhaps see the universe in this way most of the time. Plotinus, the third-century Neoplatonic philosopher/mystic, seems to have had this developed capacity, as evidenced in the quotation at the head of this essay. Such an acute and inclusive consciousness, however, is perhaps as rare as is the ability to contemplate in the subway at rush hour. For example, Plotinus described rocks as living creatures that continue to grow as long as they remain in their native soil, albeit too slowly to be observable in the lifetime of a human being (*Ennead* 5.3.5).

imaginative capacity. Thus, although there may be theoretical and practical warrants for doing so, more is lost than gained by insisting that rocks and soil are part of human beings' community. Self-interest may be a more honest rationale than community for advocating the responsible use of soil and minerals.

Secondly, the notion of "community" may itself need revision before the term can adequately evoke the diversity that must exist in a "community of all living beings." Recently, Iris Young has argued that appeals to "community" are problematic in that they "privilege unity over difference, immediacy over mediation, sympathy over recognition of the limits of one's understanding of others from their point of view."[47] The anthropocentrism of many contemporary ecological groups could be masked and perpetuated by the appeal to a "community of life."

Young's critique of the idea of community, however, assumes that the imagined community is composed solely of human beings, a community closer to Augustine's community of rational minds than to the Manichaeans' community of life. It is precisely the appeal to a "community of rational minds" that has historically entailed exclusionary practices based on hierarchical discriminations. A "community of life," on the other hand, can hardly fail to highlight and delight in difference, in "unassimilated otherness" and "inexhaustible heterogeneity."[48] If the notion of a "community of life" is to correct the abuses fostered by the "community of rational minds," living beings must be understood to be alike in nothing else than their participation in the fragile, evanescent, and exuberant property of life.

Despite the dangers inherent in invocations of "community," responsibility to a community of living beings has a rhetorical persuasiveness that has a broad popular appeal in a world threatened by ecological and nuclear crises. And broad popular appeal is necessary for the political activity needed to address myriad abuses of the natural world. In contrast to fourth-century Manichaeans, twentieth-century ideas of a community of life will need to take into account the power of contemporary human beings to intervene in the conditions of life for humans as well as for other creatures. No fourth-century Manichaean could have imagined a world in which myriad species were rapidly moving toward extinction, natural resources were in danger of exhaustion, a world in which nuclear holocaust is possible. In a world in

47. Young, "Ideal of Community," 300.
48. Ibid., 301.

which the fate of all living beings depends on human responsibility, religious traditions must be critiqued for their particular exclusionary ideas and practices, and searched for resources that can contribute to vivid and compelling appeals for empathy with all living creatures.

CHAPTER 10

Sex and the City (of God): Is Sex Forfeited or Fulfilled in Augustine's Resurrection of Body?

"I don't want to be immortal through my work; I want to be immortal
by not dying. I don't want to live on in the hearts and minds of my
countrymen; I want to live on in my apartment." (WOODY ALLEN)

A perennial complaint of Christian preachers is the incredulity,
of believers and nonbelievers alike, about the doctrine of the resurrection of body.[1] In the fifth century Augustine complained that even though
"the whole world" believed in the resurrection of body, there were still many
who found it dubious. The same refrain appeared repeatedly in medieval
sermons, in spite of efforts to encourage belief by picturing the resurrection in stone and paint. Similarly, twenty-first-century Christians assert their
belief in the resurrection of body whenever they recite the creed, but many
acknowledge the lack of a robust idea of bodily resurrection. Yet the doctrine
that bodies will rise from death at a point beyond present experience is far
from incidental or accidental to Christian faith. "If it is incredible that God
raises the dead," Paul said in Acts 26:8, "then our preaching is vain," a theme
repeated in 1 Cor 15. In the twenty-first, as in the first century, the resurrection of body is, for Christians, an article of faith; in the two thousand years
since the earliest Christians, little or no progress has been made in rendering
bodily resurrection credible.

---

1. I avoid use of the common expression "the body" because it implies a generic (male)
body that has never been seen or touched. Bodies are always sexed (biology) and gendered
(socialization); they are also marked by race, age, social location, and many other factors.

165

Although there may be many reasons for skepticism about this essential Christian doctrine, I will address only one impediment to belief. Augustine (d. 430 C.E.), the most articulate proponent of the resurrection of body, insisted enthusiastically on the presence and integrity of bodies, even of male and female sexes, in the resurrection, but he seems to have excluded sexuality from the perfection and completion of humanity. Yet Christians are, first of all, human beings, most of whom are unable to imagine themselves without sexuality. Indeed, sexuality seems so integral and intimate a part of human life that any account of the perfection and completion of humanity that omits it must be inadequate.

Augustine's influence is widely blamed for negative views of body and sexuality in the dominantly Christian West. Indeed, Augustine was the greatest single influence on Catholic and Protestant theology through such authors as Thomas Aquinas, Luther, and Calvin. Moreover, because Christian values have pervasively influenced western culture beyond religious communities, caricatures and misconceptions of Augustine's teachings have contributed to western societies in which all bodies—human and non-human—are the helpless victims of the joyless pursuit of sex, power, and possessions. A more accurate understanding of Augustine on physicality and sexuality offers the possibility of beginning to dismantle attitudes toward bodies that continue to fund economic injustice, ecological irresponsibility, and oppression based on race, class, and sexual orientation. Because Augustine's values relating to human bodies and their capacities are most transparent in his discussions of the perfection of humanity in the anticipated resurrection of body, these discussions provide the basis for our exploration of his construction of sexuality.

Why did Augustine eliminate what he himself described as the "sharpest joy" (*summa voluptas*) of human experience ("a pleasure surpassing all physical delights"[2]), from his repertoire of resurrection rewards? Augustine's interpreters have too easily invoked Augustine's own sexual experience, famously described in his *Confessions*, as sufficient reason for his distrust of, and apparent distaste for, sex. To approach a more adequate answer to the above question, it will be necessary to go beyond proof-texts to the theological interests that informed his fantasy of resurrection delight.

One of the first questions to be addressed is whether Augustine's conceptual repertoire for thinking about the role of sex in human life was the same as that of twenty-first century people. But surely, someone might respond,

---

2. Augustine *De civitate Dei* 14.16.

if anything is universal it is sex, and "we" know what "we" mean when we speak of it. Wrong. Although sexual acts are presumably as old as the human race, postmodern scholars have shown that "sexuality" is the product of a particular historical discourse, namely, nineteenth-century psychiatry.[3] The word, and the concept, of sexuality as an intimate feature of who a person is, was not part of Augustine's conceptual repertoire.

Augustine recognized sex acts and biological sex. The spiritual bodies of the resurrection, he said, will have biological sex, but there will not be sex acts because "sexual intercourse can only take place between mortal bodies."[4] When he deleted sexual activity from the resurrection, then, Augustine referred to a genitally organized, (potentially) reproductive, "use" of the sexual organs, for which there would be no need in a state in which reproduction is unnecessary because death does not occur.

Lacking the concept, Augustine neither explicitly included nor excluded "sexuality" as a feature of resurrection bodies. His descriptions of beauty and enjoyment, however, provide a foundation for identifying in resurrection bodies an implicit sexuality free from the constraints and damages of present sexuality. Did Augustine think that sex was to be forfeited or fulfilled in the resurrection body? As a simple either-or, the question is unanswerable. I will argue, nonetheless, that Augustine did not deny, and even suggested, that a quality and value we name as "sexuality" will be a feature of resurrected "spiritual" bodies.

Augustine's ideas of sex, like those of anyone else, were historical constructs, both privileged and limited by the discourses in which he participated.[5] Similarly, my discussion of Augustine's views is historically located, made possible by a discourse founded by Freud and expanded and refined by his postmodern students and critics to produce new perspectives on sexuality, sexual pleasure, and sexual relationships. I will first discuss briefly the discourse within which sexuality came to be seen as an irreducible and defin-

---

3. Davidson, *Emergence of Sexuality*, 37.

4. Augustine *De bono coniugali* 2; *Retractationes* 2.22.1.

5. Even more remote from Augustine's conceptual repertoire was the notion, popularized by historian Peter Brown, that sexuality is a "uniquely resonant key" to individual personality, the core "truth" of the person. Brown's interpretation of Augustine anachronistically adopts Freud's account of sexuality as "irremovably at the center of the human person" (*Body and Society*, 403). Augustine's ideas of paradisiacal sex, present sex, and the possibility of sex in the resurrection must be explored with greater precision if his thought is to be freed from the preoccupations of scholars dependent on Freud's construction of "sexuality."

ing aspect of human lives; then I will seek to demonstrate that Augustine's most focused mature writings on the resurrection include something like our notion of sexuality. Although he never explicitly discussed the sexuality of resurrected bodies, he scattered clues in sermons and treatises. These can be collected and composed as a post-Augustinian proposal for an ideal sexuality that is not incompatible with, but that extends, elaborates, and refines Augustine's description of resurrection bodies. Freud and his critics suggested ways to articulate an ideal sexuality that goes beyond Augustine's ability to conceptualize such sexuality.

The Construction of Sexuality: Freud

> "Now we see through a glass, darkly. Then, however, face to face."
> (1 CORINTHIANS 13:12)

No summary can do justice to the nineteenth-century creation of "a new object of medical discourse—sexuality."[6] My aim will not be to provide a summary of Freud's teachings, then, but to gather from it several suggestions that carry forward our understanding of Augustine's construction of resurrection bodies. Freud's most radical innovation was his proposal that "to know a person's sexuality is to know that person, [for] sexuality is the individual shape of the personality," a permanent and irreducible aspect of personhood, whether or not that sexuality is ever acted on.[7]

Beginning in about 1870 psychiatric interest focused on sexual "perversity," which had formerly been addressed primarily in "treatises of moral philosophy, moral theology, and jurisprudence, not in medicine."[8] Freud's discovery of infantile sexuality emerged as he sought the origins of the so-called "perversions," especially sadomasochism, "inversion" (homosexuality), and fetishism.[9] He argued that sexuality is not, in the first instance, characterized by genital organization. Rather, genital organization, which establishes a sexual object and sexual goal, is the *accomplishment* of a process of development. Uncoupling sexuality from a "natural" object (a body of the "opposite" sex) and goal (intercourse) led Freud to identify the origin of "perversions"

---

6. Davidson, *Emergence of Sexuality*, 69.

7. Ibid., 21.

8. Ibid., 23.

9. Freud, "Sexual Life," 11.

as fixation in unconscious processes of earliest childhood, not in physiology or moral flaws.

It was a short step from thinking of "perversions" as rooted in childhood sexuality to "loosening the bond that exists in our thoughts between instinct and object. It seems probable that the sexual instinct is . . . independent of its object; nor is its origin likely to be due to the object's attractions."[10] "Freud's argument, his structure of concepts, leads to the claim that neither the erotogenic zone of the genitals nor the aim of copulation bears any privileged connection to the sexual instinct. . . . deviations from the aim of genital intercourse appear to lose their status as genuine perversions."[11] In short, "perversions" are neither morally reprehensible nor a disease but simply human—*anthropological* rather than pathological. "Sexuality," no longer confused with the genitals, can be understood to encompass far more than the fact of one's sex.

Freud was the first thinker decisively to abandon Augustine's conceptual universe in his thinking on sex/sexuality. Augustine's experience had taught him that he was unable, by the use of *will power*, to subordinate sex to will, the organizing principle of reason and emotion. Freud, instead of attempting to integrate sexual desire, made sexuality itself the organizing principle of the self. Three results, important for our project of understanding Augustine on resurrection bodies, emerged from Freud's reconstruction of sexuality: First, Freud created the possibility of thinking of sex as more than *functional*. Second, Freud suggested (and his followers have clarified) that genital organization, or "normal" sexuality, entails loss, or narrowing, of sexual possibilities. Third, Freud's idea "that the sexual instinct is made up of components, that it . . . combines a multiplicity of erotogenic zones and aims," extends the field of sexuality beyond genital activity.[12] Each of these suggestions will be further considered in the conclusion. Together, they create the possibility of reconstructing an ideal sexuality that even Augustine might recognize as characterizing resurrection bodies.

Freud's Critics

Freud's construction of sexuality was criticized on several grounds in the second half of the twentieth century. Postmodern critics have dismantled Freud's

10. Freud, "Three Essays," 146.

11. Davidson, *Emergence of Sexuality*, 84.

12. Ibid., 85.

insistence on the centrality of sexuality to human personhood. Describing Freud's construction of "sexuality" as a form of power/knowledge that was constructed "so much the better to control the body," Michel Foucault preferred to speak, not of sexuality, but of "bodies and pleasures," "a certain mode of relation to the self in the experience of the flesh."[13] Arnold Davidson questioned nineteenth-century psychiatry's assumption that "sexuality is the externalization of the hidden, inner essence of personality."[14] Similarly, sociologist William Simon wrote, "There is no reason to believe that the sexual is universally a major part of the narrative of the self."[15] Simon argued further that Freud's focus on genital sexuality as the mark of a person's sexual maturity obscured the extent to which "not all sexuality occurs in recognizable sex acts," a suggestion to which I will return.[16]

Feminist psychoanalytically-based critics like Luce Irigaray have demonstrated that Freud's account of sexual development incorporates women into a fundamentally male scenario. "Up to now," Irigaray wrote, "nothing can be clearly articulated but the history of the practice of 'male sexuality' with regard to Sexuality."[17] According to Irigaray, Freud insisted "that the sexual pleasure known as masculine is the paradigm for all sexual pleasure, to which all representations of pleasure can but defer in reference, support, and submission."[18] Feminists Carol Vance and Linda Williams also contested the dominance of a male construction of sexual pleasure. Feminist film critics Carol Clover, Patricia Erens, Jane Gaines, Miriam Hansen, E. Ann Kaplan, Annette Kuhn, Meaghen Morris, Laura Mulvey, B. Ruby Rich, Kaja Silverman, and others explored women's distinctive sexual pleasure as articulated by race, class, and other variables.

Assuming, as did Freud, that sexual identity was central to a sense of self, psychiatrist Jessica Benjamin's 1988 *The Bonds of Love* proposed an alternative account of sexual development. Benjamin suggested that for both boys and girls, the primary task was not to disidentify with the mother, the first love object, but the mutual recognition of two subjectivities, the mother's and the child's. Her later work contrasted "love objects" and "like subjects." Neither

---

13. Foucault, *History of Sexuality*, 157.

14. Davidson, *Emergence of Sexuality*, 63.

15. W. Simon, *Postmodern Sexualities*, 120–21.

16. Ibid., 137.

17. Irigaray, *Speculum*, 22.

18. Ibid., 28.

identificatory love, which "incorporates or assimilates what is other to self," nor "split complementarities" (love objects) can achieve intersubjectivity (like subjects):[19] "the other must be recognized as another subject in order for the self to fully experience his or her subjectivity in the other's presence."[20] The creation of a "space of dialogue potentially outside the mental control of either of the participants" permits a mutuality of exchange "that allows for and presumes separateness."[21]

Social theorists criticized Freud's preference for looking for the origins of sexual behavior in individual development, claiming that heteronormativity and its alternatives are socially constructed. Sex is not a "wild card," a way for individuals to rebel against society and socialization (as Herbert Marcuse, Norman O. Brown, and the gurus of the 1960s taught). Rather, instead of challenging social arrangements, nonconforming sexual behavior ultimately reinforces those arrangements by making people happy "enough" not to rebel in ways more threatening to the social order. Even so-called "perversions" respond to, rather then undermine, social life. For example, William Simon understood sadomasochism as a reaction against the prevailing social consensus that insists on equality.[22]

In addition to its inevitable sociality, sexuality also relates directly to material conditions. Elizabeth Grosz pointed out that the concept of desire as a lack to be satisfied is useful to capitalist acquisition,[23] whereas Rosemary Hennessy argued that "localizing sexuality in the body" places it outside history.[24] Asking why homosexuality, which was illegal in over half of the United States in the mid-1970s, has now become acceptable, John D'Emilio's essay, "Capitalism and Gay Identity," cited two features of late capitalism, wage labor and commodity consumption, as material conditions that permitted the emergence of new sexual identities. The "late nineteenth-century shift to a consumer economy provoked a more widespread acceptance of pleasure, self-gratification, and personal satisfaction that easily transferred to the prov-

---

19. Benjamin, *Like Subjects*, 7.

20. Ibid., 30.

21. Benjamin, *Shadow of the Other*, 28–29.

22. W. Simon, *Postmodern Sexualities*, 133.

23. Grosz, *Volatile Bodies*, 71.

24. Hennessy, *Profit and Pleasure*, 42. Simon added, "There is little truth to be found in the body as such, and even less truth to be found in the body abstracted from life." W. Simon, *Postmodern Sexualities*, 142.

ince of sex."[25] Teresa Ebert and Rosemary Hennessy protested mainstream feminism's neglect of economics, labor, class struggle, and exploitation in its account of pleasure and sexuality. Mary Hunt's "*just* good sex" recognized that the privileges of westerners, including "private" sex, depend on the "increasingly sophisticated injustice" of the global economy.[26]

Maxine Sheets-Johnstone proposed an alternative to Benjamin's language-based concept of intersubjectivity. She argued for *intercorporeality* as the basis of relationships, sexuality, and society. Body, or "animate form," she said, precedes and determines consciousness. Critical of psychoanalytic dependence on language, she claimed that the living body "is a cultural universal . . . the common denominator of cultures."[27] Power and politics are rooted in bodies, and "social relations are always intercorporeal relations, . . . meanings engendered and/or articulated by living bodies."[28] The first task of intercorporeality is "reflecting on what it is like to be that other body . . . educating ourselves in the deepest possible sense on what it is to be a human body."[29]

Together, these followers and critics of Freud contribute a significantly revised version of the concept of "sexuality." Historicizing "sexuality" frees the concept for revision so that sexuality can be pictured as social rather than individual, as *part* rather than essence of the self, as gendered rather than universal, and as embedded in social assumptions and arrangements rather than isolated. After discussing Augustine's idea of resurrected bodies, I return to Freud and his critics in order to construct a post-Augustinian idea of sex and the city (of God).

Heavenly Sex: *facie ad faciem*

> "Take away faith in the resurrection of the dead and the whole of Christian doctrine crumbles." (AUGUSTINE *SERMO* 361. 2)

Although philosophers of the Hellenistic and Roman worlds (with the exception of Epicureans) held a doctrine of immortality of the soul, belief in resurrected bodies seemed to them the worst kind of literalistic naiveté.

---

25. Hennessy, *Profit and Pleasure*, 103.

26. Jung, Hunt, and Balakrishnan, *Good Sex*, 164.

27. Sheets-Johnstone, *Roots of Power*, 4, 70.

28. Ibid., 57.

29. Ibid., 329.

Augustine's defense of Christian belief in the bodily resurrection in the *City of God* was directed at the Platonic philosopher Porphyry, the most recent and respected of the scoffers. Augustine said that Porphyry's advice to "flee all bodies" was intended as a direct rebuttal of the Christian teaching of the resurrection. Augustine's views largely repeat those of his Christian predecessors, but he went beyond scripture and earlier authors to describe a detailed and frankly imaginary picture of the resurrection.[30]

Augustine's speculations on the nature and activities of resurrection bodies spanned the full term of his authorship as a Christian (from *De quantitate animae*, written in 388, two years after his conversion, to the final book of *De civitate Dei*, written about 425, five years before his death). He drew his theology of the resurrection from St. Paul's description of the bodily resurrection in 1 Cor 15. Accepting his patristic forbears' insistence (against pagans and Gnostics) on the substantiality of resurrection bodies, he felt urgency throughout his career to defend the belief.

Several preliminary considerations must be noted before we explore sex in Augustine's account. First, Augustine did not *teach* the details he imagined; he taught only that the mortal body would be resurrected to immortality. He invariably attached disclaimers to his discussions of the bodily resurrection, reminding readers of their tentative and imaginary quality: "rash to offer any description of it . . . yet we cannot keep silence. . . . I do not know. . . . I have never seen it with my physical sight. . . . I cannot say that I see now. . . . do our best to conjecture." Second, although he addressed his discussion in the *City of God* to unbelievers, his acknowledged fantasy of the resurrection in book 22 and in his sermons (especially *Sermons* 240–43),[31] seem to be for the purpose of enabling and encouraging belief, not convincing philosophical opponents.

Third, Augustine's thinking on the resurrection body changed in emphasis from his earliest to his mature writings. In 388 he was content to affirm the resurrection: "We may hold even the resurrection of the body (which some believe too late; others not at all) to be so certain that the rising of the sun, after it has gone down, is not more certain to us."[32] A bit later, in 393, his primary concern was to distinguish mortal and resurrection bodies. He used Paul's statement, "Flesh and blood shall not inherit the kingdom of

---

30. See Miles, *Augustine on the Body.*

31. See Augustine *Sermones* III/6, 7, and 10.

32. Augustine *De quantitate animae* 23.76.

heaven" to assert that resurrection bodies will not be "flesh," but "body."[33] In his *Retractions*, the review of his writings undertaken shortly before his death, he worried that the passage could easily be interpreted as denying that "these members [and] the substance of the flesh" will be incorporated in the resurrected body.[34] After 410, Augustine's interest in resurrected bodies changed.

Authors from Paul forward had emphasized *discontinuities* between present and resurrected bodies, as had Augustine's earlier writings. In his maturity, however, Augustine was eager to identify *continuities* between present and future experience. His mature writings emphasized repeatedly and in detail the continuity—the concrete fleshiness—of women's and men's present and resurrected bodies.[35] Sermons on the topic reiterated and added detail. Throughout his career his most frequently quoted scripture verse was 1 Cor 13:12: "We see now through a glass darkly; then, however, face to face" ("*Videmus nunc per speculum in aenigmate; tunc autem, facie ad faciem*"). *City of God* 22, his most detailed and sustained discussion of resurrection bodies' capacities and activities, was an extended exegesis of this verse, cited throughout his discussion. From this verse he also drew the frequently used syncrisis: "now . . . then" ("*nunc . . . tunc*"), a formula that connects, even while it contrasts, present and future experience.[36]

Fourth, Augustine's famous hypothesis about sex before the Fall,[37] must not be confused or conflated with his idea of resurrection bodies. Even before the Fall, reproduction was necessary, he said, so that human beings could replace the number of fallen angels. Thus, although marriage and procreation existed, there was "use" of the sexual organs, but no lust was involved. Rather, will took the place of lust, arousing the sexual organs "at the appropriate time and in the necessary degree."[38] Contemporary physical experience provided the prototype for his speculation, as Augustine described how various muscles and organs of the body can be managed—set in motion or stilled—by will. In the resurrection, however, the situation will be different, for there will be no need for procreation.

---

33. Augustine *De fide et symbolo* 10.24; but see *Sermo* 362.14 for Augustine's mature (411 C.E.) interpretation of this passage.

34. Augustine *Retractationes* 1.16.

35. Augustine *De civitate Dei* 22.17.

36. Ibid., 22.1.

37. Ibid., 14.23.

38. Ibid., 14.24.

Three methods directed Augustine's reflections on the doctrine of bodily resurrection. First, the mature Augustine based his fantasy of resurrected
bodies firmly on present experience. He imagined resurrection by citing at
length—and then subtracting—the painful and negative features of present
bodily life, retaining its goodness and beauty.[39] Within the multiple agenda
of *City of God*, he repeatedly sorted the dangers and discomforts of physicality
from its goodness and beauty, beginning with the rape of Christian women
during the 410 C.E. sack of Rome[40] and ending with his euphoric conjecture
that "the eyes of the body will see God."[41] He pictured the resurrection of
body as both continuous, and contrasting, with present physical experience.

Augustine discussed his second method in *Confessions* 10.21. In this
passage he identified "the happy life," even though it did not exist in his
memory, by collecting from memory discrete instances of personal joys,
vividly experienced, and using them to construct a composite image of the
longed-for condition. Any joys will do, "base joys and disgraceful things," as
well as "good and worthy" joys. In spite of lacing the text of *City of God* 22
with frequent denials that he knew anything about resurrection bodies, his
attempt to imagine them required that he use memories of his body's greatest
bliss as a guide to his fantasy. The "old animal body" will be changed, he said
(following Paul), to a "new spiritual body,"[42] but the capacities for pleasure
developed in the "old" body will be retained and transformed in the "new"
body.

Augustine's third method was continuous with, and dependent on, the
continuities and distinctions between the old and new bodies. He classified
all features (including the genital organs) of present bodies as either for "use"
or for "beauty." In more detail than was necessary to make his point, he described the "natural creation" as demonstrating both utility and beauty. The
"miraculous loveliness" of the world, he said, causes wonder, astonishment,
and pleasure. The *beauty* presently visible is permanent, whereas utility applies only to the present. Acquisitiveness of all kinds—"use"—will cease.

Augustine's model for resurrection enjoyment was vision. Vision, specifically the ability to see beauty, will be retained in the resurrection: "We now
see a dim reflection in a mirror; but then we shall see face to face," he quoted

39. Ibid., 22.22, 23.

40. Ibid., 1.16–29.

41. Ibid., 22.30.

42. Ibid., 22.21.

repeatedly. Having said in an earlier writing[43] that it is silly to imagine that the bodily eyes will see God, Augustine unabashedly contradicted himself:

> It is possible, it is indeed most probable, that we shall then see the physical bodies of the new heaven and the new earth in such a fashion as to observe God in utter clarity and distinctness, seeing him present everywhere and governing the whole material scheme of things by means of the bodies we shall then inhabit and the bodies we shall see wherever we turn our eyes. . . . It will not be as now, when the invisible realities of God are apprehended and observed through the material things of his creation, and are partially apprehended by means of a puzzling reflection in a mirror. . . . He will be seen in every body by means of bodies, wherever the eyes of the spiritual body are directed with their penetrating gaze.[44]

"The saints will see God in the body": the phrase is ambiguous, but the passage makes it clear that Augustine did not intend to say that God will have an anthropomorphic body, but that the saints' spiritual bodies will see God "wherever we turn our eyes," for "God will be all in all."[45] How does this vision of God "in every body by means of bodies" differ from present vision, by which we "could not observe [another's] life without their bodies; but we see it in them, without any possibility of doubt, through their bodies"?

Presently, we see life by seeing living bodies. Augustine was adamant that we do not *infer* that a person is alive from observation of her breathing and moving body; we actually see life. It was important to him to eliminate the difference between inferring and seeing because present sight was his model for the claim that resurrected eyes will see God. To see God is to see "life itself," Augustine said elsewhere.[46] Although Augustine contrasted present ability to see life with future vision of God, the only difference he can suggest is that resurrection bodies will have a new and powerfully penetrating (*perveniente*) intellectual (*menti*) gaze, extraordinary in its potency (*vis itaque praepollentior oculorum*), a gaze capable of seeing into the structure and operation of bodies. No longer subject to death and decay, the limbs and organs

---

43. Augustine *Epistula* 92.

44. Augustine *De civitate Dei* 22.29.

45. Ibid., 22.30; 1 Cor 15:28. Yet in *Epistula* 92 (408 C.E.), Augustine had said that it is insane to think that the bodily eyes will see God.

46. "And since all those who think of God think of something living, only they can think of him without absurdity who think of him as life itself." Augustine *De doctrina christiana* 1.8.

of the body will reveal their harmony and beauty to this gaze. The internal organs, he said, have a "rational loveliness" more beautiful than "all that gives pleasure to the eyes in the outward form." Acknowledging that no scripture supports this conjecture, Augustine modified his interpretation for "greater ease of understanding," saying that "perhaps God will be known to us and visible to us in the sense that he will be spiritually perceived by each one of us, in each one of us."[47]

Having cited in detail the dangers and sufferings of present experience, Augustine began his account of "the good things of which this life is full" with a two-page discussion of procreation. The new living being created by procreation, he said, is "a work of such wonder and grandeur as to astound the mind that seriously considers it, and to evoke praise to the creator."[48] In sermons as here, he cited the miracle of birth as justification for belief in a bodily resurrection: "The God who was able to thrust you out in proper shape from the womb, himself wishes you . . . to believe that he can also bring you alive from the tomb."[49]

Citing 1 Cor 13:12, Augustine stated that in the resurrection the "thoughts of our minds will lie open to mutual observation." Elaborating on the meaning of "face to face" in Sermon 243, however, he said that, in fact, "those who are there will not recognize each other just because they see faces; mutual recognition will come from a deeper kind of knowledge."

> So now our thoughts are in the light to each one of us because we know our own. But they are in darkness to our neighbors, because they can't see them. Then however, what you know you are thinking, the other person is going to know too. Why be afraid? Now you want to conceal your thoughts, now you are afraid to publish them; perhaps, I mean, you are sometimes thinking something bad, something dirty, maybe something silly. Then, however, when you get there, you will think nothing but what is honorable, nothing but what is true, nothing but what is pure, nothing but what is sincere. Just as now you wish your face to be seen, so then you will want your conscience to be seen too.[50]

47. Augustine *De civitate Dei* 22.24.

48. Ibid.

49. Augustine *Sermo* 242A.2. "It is a greater miracle, so many people being born every day who did not previously exist, than a few having risen again, who did exist"; *Sermo* 242.1.

50. Augustine *Sermo* 243.5.

City of God 22.30 returns to Augustine's classification of present and future experience. What is to be eliminated? Evil, inactivity and idleness, toil, constraint, decay, necessity, and hidden agenda.[51] But "no good will be withheld," he insisted. The "goods" he cited are true glory, true honor, and true peace: "God will be all in all," he repeated: "He will be the goal of all our longings; and we shall see him forever and ever; we shall love him without satiety; we shall praise him without weariness." Freedom of the will, the committed capacity to act in the direction of one's greatest good, will continue in the resurrection. Unable to sin, the will is "immovably fixed in a delight in not sinning. The resurrection will initiate an "eternal vacation" (*vacabimus in aeternum*). "There we shall be still and see; we shall see and we shall love; we shall love and we shall praise."

Augustine's "compressed pile of blessings" of present experience included: sustenance of life, the mind and its capacities, the capacity for a good life and the possibility of eternal happiness, the virtues, the arts, the body, and the natural world. All of these "beauties" (except reproduction) will be retained in the resurrection. He insisted that it was not "the body" that Christians should deplore, but the "*corruptible* body." His sermons employ the same method of sorting the negative from the positive effects of bodies: "What is it about the body that you don't like? . . . the body's liability to decay, its mortality? . . . The things you like will be there, the things you don't like, won't. What you like comes to life again, what you don't like perishes."[52]

Sermon 362 takes as its topic "what sort of bodies the saints will have, and what kind of life the just are going to have in the resurrection." The resurrected body of Jesus provided a prototype for Augustine's suggestions about resurrection activities: "Our Lord rose again in the very same body in which he had been buried. Resurrection is what Christians have been promised. So we should be hoping for the same sort of resurrection as in the case of our Lord has preceded the faith of us all" (10). Like the risen Christ and the angels, resurrection bodies can eat and drink, but they do not need to do so: "It's one thing, after all, to do something because you can, another to do it because you have to" (11). Similarly, sleep will not be necessary because there will be no fatigue. Did Augustine suggest that eating and drinking, no longer prompted by physical need, would be done for pleasure in resurrected bodies? This interpretation is made plausible, if not probable, by the frequency

---

51. *Sermo* 242A adds to this list fear, poverty, weariness, and clumsiness. "None of these things will be there, but the body will be."

52. Augustine *Sermo* 242A.3.

with which Augustine characterized the quality of resurrected life as filled with delight: "Nothing will be lacking for complete satisfaction" (31).

Noticing whether a feature of human experience surfaces in his imagined resurrection body is often a key to Augustine's values. Sex (male and female) appears in Augustine's resurrection of body;[53] sex acts do not. In Augustine's conceptual universe it was possible to affirm bodies in the resurrection (more or less) "as we knew them" and yet to subtract from them all sexual desires and acts.[54] Whatever Augustine omitted from resurrection reward fell into the category of "punishment" (*poena reciproca*) for the disobedience of Adam and Eve.[55] But proof-texts often mislead. The question "is sex part of the punishment or part of the reward?" is too crude; it is both and neither. Augustine sorted the (present) "punishment" of human life from the beauty and pleasure that are part of (resurrection) reward.

Augustine said that there will be no lust (*libido*) or "use" of the reproductive organs in the resurrection, but only "enjoyment of one another's beauty for itself alone."[56] His account of pre-Fall sex in *City of God* 14.23, as well as in his *Confessions*, helps to explain what he found problematic and disturbing about *libido*. For Augustine, the damages of present sex included: rape as a practice of war;[57] domestic vulnerability to unwanted or forced sex;[58] unpredictability and uncontrollability, most evident (to Augustine) in impotence;[59] urgency or compulsiveness that overrides the ability to choose (*Confessions*, passim); and feelings of guilt and shame.[60] *Sermon* 243.8 adds boredom to his list of the negative possibilities of present sexual experience: "Such is the weakness of the flesh, such is the irksome nature of this life, that everything,

---

53. Augustine *De civitate Dei* 22.17.

54. Quoting one of Augustine's earliest extant writings, Peter Brown stated: "Sexual love remained, for him, a leaden echo of true delight . . . [he wanted] to behold God's Wisdom in an 'utterly untroubled gaze, a most clean embrace; to see and to cling to Her naked, with no veil of bodily sensation in between'" (Augustine *Soliloquia* 1.13.22). Yet surely a "leaden echo of true delight" would not provide an adequate analogy for the vision of God! Augustine's image refuses Brown's interpretation and illustrates the inadequacy of interpretations that do not take into account Augustine's developing views; early statements were significantly modified in his maturity. Brown, *Body and Society*, 394.

55. Augustine *De civitate Dei* 14.17.

56. Ibid., 22.24.

57. Ibid., 1.16–19

58. Augustine *Sermones* 9.4; 82.11; 132.4; 224.3; 392.2.

59. Augustine *De civitate Dei* 14.16

60. Ibid., 14.17–18.

however wonderful, ends in boredom." All of these must disappear if resurrection bodies are to "enjoy one another's beauty for itself alone."

Beneath and beyond Augustine's objections to particular features of sex was his primary objection that sex does not seem to bring happiness. According to his later and highly interpretive account of his own sexual experience in the *Confessions*, sexual activity merely "scratch [ed] the itching scab of concupiscence,"[61] bringing little more than the satisfaction of a repetition compulsion. Certainly, Augustine's criteria for happiness were ambitious: intensity and permanence.[62] Sex, he said, notoriously meets one criterion at the expense of the other.

I have largely ignored Augustine's stated agenda in order to focus on his methods for imagining resurrection bodies, their activities and their properties. He introduced his speculations with an admonition to those who say that a material body cannot become a spiritual body. His method of using present physical experience as the basis for imagining resurrection, however, works as well for convincing unbelievers as for encouraging believers. The "present state of things," he said, has been cheapened by familiarity, but it is, in fact "*much more wonderful* than that transition which our philosophers find incredible. Why are we not *more violently amazed* that immaterial souls, superior to celestial bodies, are bound within earthly bodies, than that bodies, although earthly, should be exalted to abodes which are material, albeit heavenly."[63] The rhetorical beauty and poignant longing expressed in his imaginings indicate that much more was at stake for him than a simple refutation of unbelief. His sense of the simultaneous fragility and consummate preciousness of bodies directed his interest in their perfection and completion: "I know you want to keep on living. You do not want to die. And you want to pass from this life to another in such a way that you will not rise again as a dead person, but fully alive and transformed. This is what you desire. This is the deepest human feeling."[64]

The continuity between present and resurrection bodies was based on the astounding miracle of present bodies. The *only* problem of present bodies is sin, by which bodies have become vulnerable to hunger, thirst, sickness, difficulties of all sorts, death and decay. These ills are not native to

---

61. Augustine *Confessiones* 9.1.

62. "Life will only be happy when it is eternal." Augustine *De civitate Dei* 14.25.

63. Ibid., 22.4; emphasis added.

64. Augustine *Sermo* 344.4.

bodies; rather, bodies are the helpless victims of the sin of the first parents of the human race. The "real" condition of bodies will be achieved only in the resurrection: "The flesh will rise imperishable, the flesh will rise without blemish, without deformity, without mortality, without being a burden or a weight."[65]

According to Augustine, intercorporeality (Sheets-Johnstone) as well as intersubjectivity (Benjamin) will characterize resurrection society. Bodies are ubiquitous in Augustine's heaven. God "will be seen in every body by means of bodies, wherever the eyes of the spiritual body are directed with their penetrating gaze."[66] But not a word about sex. Did Augustine think that there would be sex in the City of God? It is time to reconsider Augustine's fantasy of resurrected bodies in the light of a conceptual world—our own—to which Augustine had no access.

Reconstructing Sexuality

> "How poorly sex serves sexuality." (WILLIAM SIMON, *POSTMODERN SEXUALITIES*, 155)

In western cultures, impressions—whether caricatures or accurate descriptions—of Christian negativity toward sex are common. But more fundamental and incontestable than negativity is the unique significance Christianity has placed on sex. Within Christianity, Peter Brown wrote, sex is a "peculiarly resonant symptom of the frailty inherited by mankind from Adam's first act of disobedience."[67] Although Augustine sometimes referred to Aristotle's complaint that it is difficult to think while engaged in sexual activity, this was not his primary objection. Rather, Augustine regretted that will had little jurisdiction over sexual desire.[68] In his experience, as well as in pastoral observation, sexual desire stubbornly eluded integration. Sex received its significance for Augustine not as "an ultimate, if obscure, truth of the human being," but

---

65. Augustine *Sermo* 240.3.

66. Augustine *De civitate Dei* 22.30.

67. Brown, *Body and Society*, 416. In Augustine's conceptual universe, however, it was not sex that defined a human being, but will, the integration of reason and emotion. In its strongest form, Augustine said, will is love (*De trinitate* 15.41); thus, to know a person, one must ask, What does she love? (*Enchiridion* 31).

68. See Brown, *Augustine of Hippo*.

by frustratingly eluding integration. He found it difficult to praise sex, even when, in opposition to ascetic extremists, he deliberately set out to do so.[69]

Centuries later, and in a vastly different conceptual universe, Freud made sexuality the organizing principle, the "externalization of the hidden, inner essence of personality."[70] Freud's critics criticized this attribution of significance, objecting that "sexuality is too easily seen as possessing a quality of importance that may not be descriptive of many individuals or most individuals most of the time." A century after Freud, in western media cultures that invoke sexuality to stimulate and sell, sexuality assumes a cultural centrality that is, in other times and places, odd, if not unknown. "As a culture we take sex seriously, perhaps too seriously; in its appearance, something emblematic of 'true' character is assumed to be revealed."[71] In Freud's critics, "human sexualities [are] destabilized, decentered, de-essentialized; the sexual life is no longer seen as harboring an essential unitary core locatable within a clear framework . . . with an essential truth waiting to be discovered."[72]

Freud's critics also extended Freud's description of sexuality as multi-faceted, operating in persons from infancy forward throughout life. "Much that is sexual, much that is intensely sexual, can be experienced without what is commonly regarded as sexual behavior occurring."[73] The *kind* of sex Augustine eliminated from the resurrection pursuits of the saints was genitally organized sexual acts. His integration and distribution of "the sharpest pleasure" in resurrection bodies is similar to the de-centering of sexuality in Freud's critics. Their account provides a broader palette with which to envision sexuality as more inclusive than that of recognizable sex acts.

References to the somatic quality of resurrection experience: beauty, pleasure, wonder, amazement, and loveliness are woven through Augustine's text. His requirements for happiness—intensity and permanence—are met in what we may see as the *distributed* sexuality of resurrected bodies. The primary "organ" of resurrected sexuality is the eyes: "By use of the bodily eyes everyone possesses all that s/he delights to see."[74] Scopophilia, the "perver-

---

69. See Augustine *Do bono coniugali*.

70. Davidson, *Emergence of Sexuality*, 63.

71. W. Simon, *Postmodern Sexualities*, 133.

72. Ibid., xiv.

73. Ibid., 147–48.

74. Augustine *De trinitate* 14.19.

sion" that *replaces*, rather than acts as preliminary to, genital sex plays a major role in Augustine's account of the resurrection.

Sight, for Augustine, was a kind of touch. Plato's theory of vision, adopted by Augustine, pictured a quasi-physical ray of light projecting from the eyes to *touch* its object: "Rays shine through the eyes and touch whatever we see."[75] Vision connects viewer and object, establishing a two-way street on which, as the viewer sees the object, the object travels back along the visual ray to imprint itself on the memory. The visual ray theory has long been superseded by more accurate accounts of the physics of vision yet, as an account of the experience of vision, it has validity. "The natural power of optics is not strictly a visual lure; whatever attracts us visually or whatever we long to see is not purely a visual datum but something that encompasses or spills over into other sense modalities, most specifically, touch."[76]

Vision involves two different somatic reactions: intensity registers on the skin, and signification registers in modulations in heartbeat and breathing. These somatic reactions give the impression of touch and may explain why Augustine's—and before him, Plotinus's—accounts of the vision of God (the One) culminate in touch. Moreover, the scopophilic vision of resurrection bodies, in Augustine's description, is more like Benjamin's recognition of another subjectivity than like voyeuristic sight. In spite of his adoption and constant use of "face to face" to describe the resurrection's intimate knowledge, Augustine qualified his metaphor. Mutual recognition will occur, he said, "not just because they see faces" but by "a deeper kind of knowledge."[77]

The second characteristic of Augustine's account of resurrection experience is synesthesia, a flooding of the senses in which "perceptual modes come together in unexpected combinations" to create vivid pleasure.[78] As "faintness, weariness, and corruption all disappear," hyperacuity of the senses occurs.[79] Instead of orgasm, with its notoriously transient intensity, resurrection bodies experience a pan-sexuality in which the whole body is pleasurably sensitized, and "God is all in all."[80] Again, present extraordinary experience

75. Augustine *De trinitate* 9.3.3; see chapter 12 below, 206–25.

76. Sheets-Johnstone, *Roots of Power*, 28.

77. *Sermon* 243. Recall Benjamin's definition of intersubjectivity: "the capacity of the mind to directly register the responses of the other, . . . the capacity to recognize the other as an independent subject." *Like Subjects*, 183.

78. Chidester, *Word and Light*, 14.

79. Augustine *Enarrationes en Psalmos* 43.4.

80. Augustine *De civitate Dei* 14.28; 22.30.

provides the template: "You called, you cried out, you shattered my deafness: you flashed, you shone, you scattered my blindness: you breathed perfume, and I drew in my breath and I pant for you: I tasted, and I am hungry and thirsty: you touched me, and I burned for your peace."[81]

A post-Augustinian resurrection sexuality emerges from the insights of Freud and his followers, an extension of Augustine's fantasy, but not incompatible with it. Challenging *both* Augustine's narrow conception of sex (as sexed bodies and acts) and modern usage (despite Freud and his critics) by which "sexuality" is used to refer to genitally organized activity, a sexuality of eternally blissful sensuality can be imagined.[82] But several of Freud's critics will remain unsatisfied by Augustine's account.

Hennessey, Hunt, and Ebert insist that "good sex" can occur only in just societies. Augustine argued that the City of God is a just society in that each is rewarded the appropriate "grade of honor and glory," but his vision of the resurrection did not include a society of equals. He attempted to compensate by saying that in the resurrection, "No inferior will feel envy of his superior . . . . he will have the compensatory gift of contentment with what he has."[83] Although rewards are unequal, however, women and men will be equal; women, equipped with a "new beauty," will no longer be subject to "use"—male lust and childbearing.

What Augustine sought, but did not fully achieve, either in his experience or in his imagined description of the perfection of humanity, was integrated sexuality. Augustine's twenty-first century readers, nourished on elaborate and unrealistic media depictions of the concentrated power of genital urgency, may not be content to picture a resurrection with "distributed sexuality." Yet Freud's critics insist that sex and its multiple expressions is *part* of the continuing process of creating the self, not the centerpiece it became for Augustine due to its intractability, nor the "key" to selfhood identified by Freud. Indeed, as sociologist William Simon acknowledged, "Well-integrated individuals, . . . tend to have relatively uninteresting sex lives."[84] Apparently, now (*nunc*) as "then" (*tunc*) an integrated sexuality distributes pleasure so that it characterizes all experience, yet invites evaluation as "uninteresting"

81. Augustine *Confessiones* 10.27.

82. A media/male perspective that leans heavily on a pre-Freudian definition of sex as defined by "object and goal" might interpret Augustine's description of resurrection sex as infinite "foreplay."

83. Augustine *De civitate Dei* 22.30.

84. W. Simon, *Postmodern Sexualities*, 150.

in relation to the focused excitement of sex acts.[85] If Augustine's resurrection sexuality is not attractive in the context of the hedonism of American culture, we need to consider who has the luxury of thinking of sex as an unambiguous good—who, in terms of social location, gender, and economic status? For many women and men, now as in Augustine's day, sex is problematic, if not disastrous.

Given Augustine's experience as a rape crisis counselor,[86] it is not surprising that he was reluctant to give sex acts a place in resurrection society. Yet he described a pan-sexuality from which the painfully urgent focus on genitally organized sexual object and aim have been eliminated and pleasure has been retained. Augustine tried to imagine the properties and capacities of bodies no longer vulnerable to impotence, disease, or death. Having no concept of "sexuality" with which to work, he nonetheless described what we would call "sexuality" as a property of resurrected bodies in the city of God. As *one* of the beauties and goods of human life, this "sharp joy" of human experience belongs to the calmer bliss of resurrection. Reading sexuality in Augustine's idea of resurrection bodies begins to sketch a model that can function to correct and shape present ideas of sex and its role in human relationships. The value of imagining ideal sexualities is that only then can one begin to make "good sex" *now*.

---

85. Aristotle concurred: "The life of the actively good is inherently pleasant. . . . So their life does not need to have pleasure fastened about it like a necklace, but possesses it as a part of itself." *Nicomachean Ethics* 1.8.

86. Augustine *De civitate Dei* 1.16–20.

CHAPTER 11

Santa Maria Maggiore's Fifth-Century Mosaics: Triumphal Christianity and the Jews

Introduction

The fifth-century mosaics of Santa Maria Maggiore in Rome represent the oldest surviving program of mosaic decoration in a Christian church.[1] Its political context includes the steady drain of political authority and power to the Eastern empire from the early fourth century forward, the proscription of paganism at the end of the fourth century, and the massively disruptive Sack of Rome by Alaric in 410 C.E. In the vacuum of political power in the West, the papacy under Sixtus III made a strong claim for a new basis of Roman power—the religious primacy of the city of Peter and Paul under papal leadership.[2] The building and decoration of Santa Maria Maggiore played an important role in the consolidation and public announcement of papal power.

The first goal of this article is to reconstruct the social world of a work of art that appeared at a pivotal intersection of ecclesiastical and imperial power. The second goal, interwoven with the first, is to demonstrate the value of interdisciplinary methodology for making visible features of history that might not appear if the tools of a single discipline were used. I begin, then, with a work of art and proceed to investigate its role in a complex social, political, legal, and theological discourse.

---

1. Spain, "Promised Blessing," 518.

2. Richard Krautheimer writes, "The Empire in the West had collapsed. The emperor in Ravenna was a mere shadow. The Eastern emperor, powerful though he was, was distant and uninterested. The Roman aristocracy, pagan to the last, was gone as a political force." See Krautheimer, "Architecture of Sixtus III," 301.

In the later Roman Empire, effective power was *visible* power. In 313 C.E., Christianity had emerged from persecuted sect to authorized and imperially funded religion almost overnight. Formerly without trace in the landscape of Roman cities, the building of Christian churches under Constantine altered the appearance of ancient cities. The fourth-century historian Eusebius, an admirer of Constantine, eulogized Constantine's church buildings because they made Christianity's dramatic change in status visible. Just as the incarnation of Christ had made God visible, Eusebius said, the triumph of Christianity was visible, incarnated in the magnificent new cathedrals that were springing up in the empire's major cities during the fourth century. These buildings witnessed silently to the power of the God who had given the victory at the Milvean Bridge to an outnumbered and outmanoeuvered Constantine. Describing the church at Tyre, Eusebius wrote, "The cathedral is a marvel of beauty, utterly breathtaking. . . . The evidence of our eyes makes instruction through the ears unnecessary."[3]

If the city of Rome was to be recognized as the spiritual center of Christianity under the pope's leadership, papal foundations needed to equal or overtake those of the fourth-century emperors. A sermon by Sixtus III's archdeacon, Leo—later Leo I—exults in the new vision of a Christian Rome. No longer to be seen as a major site of imperial power, the city of Peter and Paul "has become a priestly and royal city, the head of the world through this holy see of Peter. Wars, indeed, have made fewer conquests [for the city] than the Christian peace."[4]

It may seem odd, then, that in a Christian church, built and decorated by a pope, the entire length of the nave is covered with scenes from the Hebrew Bible. Why not miracle stories from the New Testament? Why not episodes from the lives of Christian martyrs and saints? Yet Jewish tradition and scriptures would not have received such prominence in an important Christian church had they not been crucial to the articulation of Christian—more specifically, papal—triumphalism. Power newly made visible demonstrated its authority not merely by magnificence, but also by effectively reinterpreting public life. It is neither accidental nor coincidental that Santa Maria Maggiore and its extensive mosaic program were commissioned and executed at the same time and in the same city in which the

---

3. Eusebius *Historia ecclesiastica* 10.44.2; see my discussion of fourth-century Christian architecture and decoration, "Evidence of Our Eyes."

4. Leo I *Sermo* 82; quoted in Krautheimer, "Architecture of Sixtus III," 302.

Jewish people were being dramatically and rapidly "repositioned" within the Roman Empire, marginalized and restricted in their activities.

The mosaic program at Santa Maria Maggiore did not *cause* the marginalization, oppression, and popular violence against Jews that was contemporary with its execution. Nor do social, political, and ecclesiastical events explain or account for the content or style of the mosaics. Rather, both the artworks and the events are related in the public life of a city at a particular historical moment. Although the events and the works of art can be assumed to relate to one another, the nature of the relationship between the mosaics and the social and political realities can be reconstructed only through a careful examination of fifth-century Roman society.

Santa Maria Maggiore and its Legend

Although the legend associated with the building of Santa Maria Maggiore can be traced back no further than the thirteenth century, it is relished to this day by Roman tourist guides.[5] In 358 C.E., in August—the hottest month in Rome—a Roman patrician named John and his wife,

> being childless and wishing to leave their wealth to the Virgin, were visited by her in their sleep and told to build a church in her honour in a spot that would be marked by snow. Approaching Pope Liberius to inform him of their intention, they were surprised to learn that he had had an identical dream.[6]

As predicted, snow appeared on the noble's property on the Esquiline Hill, and Pope Liberius built the basilica with the couple's money. The exact location of this first building has been lost; its replacement, the present Santa Maria Maggiore, was built by Pope Sixtus III (432–40) "who wished to single out for honour the Blessed Virgin, whom the Council of Ephesus (431 C.E.) had recently declared, in opposition to Nestorius, to be the Mother of God."[7]

Santa Maria Maggiore so closely resembles a second-century imperial basilica that it has sometimes been thought to have been adapted from a ba-

---

5. A fifteenth-century painting, Masaccio and Masolino's "Miracle of the Snow," depicts the legend of Santa Maria Maggiore's founding; see Braham, "Emperor Sigismund"; Dunkerton, et al., 252–54; Joannides, "Cotonna Triptych"; Strehlke and Tucker, "Santa Maria Maggiore Altarpiece," 105–24.

6. Spain, "Promised Blessing," 518.

7. Ibid.

silica for use as a Christian church. Its plan was based on Hellenistic principles stated by Vitruvius at the time of Augustus.[8] The exterior dates from much later times: the twelfth-century facade has been masked by an eighteenth-century reconstruction, and its campanile—the highest in Rome—was completed in the fourteenth century.

The interior of the church features a nave divided from the aisles by thirty-six marble and four granite columns (fig. 1). The columns were originally unmatched, but an eighteenth-century architect, Ferdinando Fuga, "boldly transformed the existing heterogeneous collection of columns by paring down those that were too thick, shortening those that were too long, and providing them with identical Ionic capitals and bases."[9] The coffered ceiling of the nave is leafed with Peruvian gold, said to be the first gold brought back from America by Columbus and given to Pope Alexander VI by the Spanish rulers, Ferdinand and Isabella. Five lavishly decorated side chapels enhance the magnificence of the interior.

Upon entering the church, the eye is initially caught by the apse mosaic, a coronation of the Virgin with angels, saints, the contemporary pope, Nicholas IV, and other ecclesiastical and political leaders. As one architectural historian has written,

> In the building designed for worship, the whole building is directed axially to the center of worship, the altar. . . . The whole decoration of the church interior. . . is arranged in such a way as to lead the eye towards the altar. . . . The same principle applies to pictorial decoration. The apogee is reached in the "culminating point" of the axis, in the vault of the apse.[10]

This principle is especially evident in Santa Maria Maggiore. The present apse mosaic dates from 1295 and is signed by Jacapo Torriti; it is purported, however, to be a reproduction of the original fifth-century mosaic.[11]

8. Beny and Gunn, *Churches of Rome*; the "height of the columns is 9 1/2 times their base diameter; spacing between col-umns is five times the diameter" (61, see also 104).

9. Ibid., 106.

10. L'Orange and Nordhagen, *Mosaics*, 18; see also Thébert, "Private Life," 339.

11. Santa Maria Maggiore has been celebrated for having in this mosaic the earliest known representation of the imperialized Mary, Mary Queen of Heaven. Recently, however, Suzanne Spain has questioned this, showing that in the Latin West it was not until the late sixth century that Mary was placed in imperial garments and depicted ruling from a throne. The original apse mosaic was indeed dominated by the figure of Mary, Spain concludes, but a traditionally clothed Mary, "wearing a tunic of dark material, her head covered by a maphorion or shawl, her hair bound in a white cap . . . with youthful fea-

Santa Maria Maggiore's Fifth-Century Mosaics

The fifth-century mosaic program lines the walls of the nave and appears on the triumphal arch. Twenty-seven of the original forty-two panels remain, although some are damaged (fig. 1, nave toward apse).[12] The nave mosaics, set above the Ionic columns and below the clerestory windows are rich and complex. Scenes from the Hebrew Bible feature moments of covenant and promise between God and the Hebrew people: God's promise to Abraham that his progeny would become a great nation and that they would inherit the land of Canaan, for example, and the promise of the Messiah (fig. 2). On the left wall facing the altar are scenes from the lives of Abraham, Isaac, and Jacob; on the right wall are scenes of Moses and Joshua (fig. 3). Many of the scenes are difficult or impossible to identify; they depict obscure stories from the Hebrew Bible featuring God's support and guidance of the Jewish people. Panels on the left wall narrate events in Genesis from the separation of Abraham and Lot to the offspring of Jacob (Genesis 13–34). As the eye passes along the nave and reaches the mosaics of the triumphal arch, Melchizedek, Isaac, Jacob, Moses, and Joshua all become types and foreshadowings of the Christ whose advent appears on the arch (fig. 4).[13]

The mosaics of the triumphal arch insistently connect the events from the Hebrew Bible that are pictured on the nave walls with those associated with the birth of Christ by including figures from the Hebrew Bible in events surrounding Christ's birth. Sarah and Abraham are present at the betrothal of Mary and Joseph,[14] and David and Isaiah greet the infant Christ; these figures act as witnesses to the fulfillment of the prophecies and promises made to the Hebrew people. On the triumphal arch, the long series of nave mosaics

---

tures, wearing red shoes." Like the thirteenth-century mosaic, the original Mary was shown seated on a throne, her child on her lap, surrounded by angels and martyrs, accompanied by Pope Sixtus. See Spain, "Promised Blessing," 534.

12. Half of the clerestory windows were boarded over sometime in the baroque period, reflecting the baroque preference for crepuscular lighting in churches. This adjustment of the lighting of the interior means, among other things, that the nave mosaics are now barely visible by natural light; with the full complement of clerestory windows, they were well lighted.

13. Spain identifies (ibid., 524) figures meeting the infant Christ as David and Isaiah.

14. On iconographical grounds, Spain identifies the figure holding the Christ Child as Sarah. In a scene of Mary and Joseph's betrothal, an angel plays the part of a priest, and they see a vision of the child to be born to Mary. Abraham also appears in this scene; he and Sarah are present as "ancestors of Mary, Joseph, and Christ, as antetypes of Mary and Joseph, and as witnesses to the fulfillment of the promises made to them" (ibid., 535).

showing God's covenanted promises with the Jewish people culminates in and is superceded by Christ's incarnation.

The Mosaics' Theological Agenda

The fifth-century mosaic program of Santa Maria Maggiore has two theological agenda: (1) the glorification of the Virgin as *theotokos*, Godbearer,[15] and (2) a systematic and comprehensive articulation of the relationship of the Hebrew Bible and the Christian scriptures as one in which the Hebrew Bible foreshadows Christianity. These themes were featured in a sermon delivered by Pope Leo I (the former archdeacon of Sixtus III) soon after the completion of Santa Maria Maggiore. The incarnation, he said, was

> promised from the foundation of the world, and had always been prophesied by many intimations of facts and words: but how small a portion of mankind would these types and foreshadowed mysteries have saved had not the coming of Christ fulfilled these long and secret promises, and had not that which then benefitted but a few believers in the prospect, now benefitted myriads of the faithful in its accomplishment. Now no longer are we led to believe through signs and types, but being confirmed by the gospel story we worship that which we believe to have been done; the prophetic lore assisting our knowledge, so that we have no manner of doubt about that which we know to have been predicted by such sure oracles. For hence it is that the Lord says to Abraham: "In thy seed shall all nations be blessed"; hence David, in the spirit of prophecy sings, "the Lord swore truth to David and he shall not frustrate it"; hence the Lord again says through Isaiah: "behold a virgin shall conceive in her womb, and shall bear a son, and his name shall be called Immanuel, God with us."[16]

15. Spain questions the relevance of the Council of Ephesus to the theological concerns of Santa Maria Maggiore's fifth-century mosaics: "In Rome, the decisions of the Council were inconsequential. . . . The christology and mariology of S. Maria Maggiore are orthodox, but it is doubtful that they are so in response to the acts of a distant council" (ibid., 534 n. 69). It is important to remember, however, that the Mediterranean provided an expeditious route for the circulation of ideas as well as commerce: twenty days' sailing was sufficient to traverse the Mediterranean from one end to the other. Also, Krautheimer has pointed out ("Architecture of Sixtus III," 296) that there is evidence of stylistic influence in architecture from Constantinople to Rome; if such influence can be demonstrated, theological influence is also probable.

16. Leo I *Sermo* 24.1 (Feltoe, 12.134); see also Sieger, "Visual Metaphor as Theology."

Fig. 1: Nave toward apse, Santa Maria Maggiore, Rome.

Fig. 2: Abraham and the three heavenly visitors.
Nave mosaic, Santa Maria Maggiore, Rome; fifth century.

Fig. 3: The Red Sea crossing. Nave mosaic,
Santa Maria Maggiore, Rome; fifth century.

Fig. 4: Annunciation. Triumphal arch mosaic,
Santa Maria Maggiore, Rome; fifth century.

I shall consider separately the two themes that are connected in Pope Leo's sermon: (1) glorification of the Virgin and (2) supercessionist theology.

(1) The rebuilding of Santa Maria Maggiore began in 432 C.E., only a year after an ecumenical council met at Ephesus to decide a matter of contemporary debate and schism. The building and decoration has been called "Sixtus III's ex-voto gift to the Virgin."[17] After an intense discussion, the Council of Ephesus had ruled that it was theologically accurate to call the Blessed Virgin Mary "*theotokos.*"[18] The central issue of the debate was Mary's role in the Incarnation. Was she to be thought of as a mere "vessel"[19] through which the incarnated Christ passed, as Nestorius said?[20] Or, was she to be seen as the mother whose flesh provided Christ's flesh and from whom he was born as all human babies are born? The Council decided for the latter interpretation. The "majority leader," Cyril of Alexandria, described what was at stake in the decision:

> For if he had not been born as we according to the flesh, if he had not taken part like us of the same, he would not have freed the nature of humanity from the blame contracted in Adam, nor would he have driven away from our bodies the decay.[21]

(2) In the iconographical program of Santa Maria Maggiore, scenes from the Hebrew Bible receive their contextualization and interpretation as the prologue to the Christian saga. Christians had of course used stories and scenes from the Hebrew Bible—especially those that featured God's miraculous deliverance—in the earliest Christian catacombs. Worship, liturgical ritual, and sacraments, as well as Christian scriptures and prayer, demonstrate Christians' systematic dependence on Jewish rites. Clearly, Christians felt themselves to be in continuity with the Jewish people. It is, however, one thing to picture a community—even a worldwide community—as a shoot recently grafted onto an ancient and powerful trunk; it is another to think of the trunk itself as existing only to support and supply the new branch.

The catacomb paintings of Hebrew Bible stories—Daniel in the den of lions, Jonah and the great fish, Adam and Eve—were executed in times of po-

---

17. Krautheimer, "Architecture of Sixtus III," 295.

18. Holum, *Theodosian Empresses,* chap. 5, 147–74.

19. See Ottley, *Doctrine of the Incarnation,* 391–400.

20. Holum notes (*Theodosian Empresses,* 188) that the Nestorian "heresy" "appeared to contemporaries to be of Jewish origin."

21. Cyril *Epistle of Cyril to Nestorius* 14.203.

tential or actual persecution. They witness to Christians' need for well-known and deeply interiorized images that reassured and comforted. In a society in which Christians were marginalized and powerless, such an appropriation of stories and images from the Hebrew Bible represents an entirely different impulse than that of the triumphal imagery of Santa Maria Maggiore. Moreover, in the catacomb images, there was seldom an attempt to reposition figures and events from the Hebrew Bible within a Christian narrative. Although both catacomb images and mosaics appropriate aspects of Jewish scriptures and history, different social conditions directed the selection of different topics, creating a vastly different representational communication. At Santa Maria Maggiore a powerful social, political, and religious institution reinterpreted Jewish history and the Jewish people as precursors, shadowy adumbrations, types, and signs of the fulfillment of God's promises in Christianity.

Augustine's Interpretation of Jewish Tradition

Forty years before the Santa Maria Maggiore mosaics were designed and executed, one of the most respected and influential theologians of the dominantly Christian West, Augustine, bishop of Hippo in North Africa, wrote a detailed exposition on the culmination of Jewish scriptures and tradition in Christianity. One of his sermons to his congregation contains a striking statement of his assessment of the relationship of Judaism to Christianity:

> The Jew carries the hook from which the Christian takes his faith. They have become our librarians, like slaves who carry books behind their masters; the slaves gain no profit by their carrying, but the masters profit by their reading.[22]

Augustine's most detailed exposition of the role of Jewish tradition in relation to Christianity occurred in the context of his debate with North African Manichaeans. Those who identified themselves as Manichaean Christians did not accept the Hebrew Bible as authoritative for Christians. Thus, in his carefully recorded public debate with the Manichaean Faustus, Augustine reiterated story after story from the Hebrew scriptures in order to demonstrate that each was a foreshadowing of Christianity: "The New Testament lies hidden in the Old; the Old Testament becomes plain in the New."[23]

---

22. Augustine *Enarrationes in psalmos* 56.9.
23. Augustine *Contra adversarium legis et prophetarum* 1.7.35.

The basis of Faustus's rejection of the Hebrew Bible was that since Christians no longer "keep the precepts," they should not lay claim to the documents.[24] Faustus apparently respected the integrity of Jewish scripture and ritual practice. Augustine, however, saw a distinct advantage in reinterpreting Jewish practices and events as "shadows" of Christianity although dispensing with its ritual practices. For example, he cited Jewish circumcision of the flesh as the prefiguration of Christian circumcision of the heart:[25] "What was then a type is now revealed truth."[26]

Augustine identified a parallel—and pernicious—theological logic in Faustus's denial of Christ's incarnation, death, burial, and resurrection and in his rejection of the transformation of the "letter" of Judaism into the "spirit" of Christianity.[27] Unable to accept that matter can be transformed into spirit, Faustus, according to Augustine, simultaneously missed both the significance of the body in Christianity *and* the transformation of the literal practices of Judaism into the spiritual truth of Christianity. Augustine, by contrast, understood Judaism and Christianity to he in essential—not accidental—relationship to one another: just as in the resurrection of the body it is not that "one garment is to be laid aside and a better one taken instead," but "that *the same* body will be changed for the better"—that is, from material to spiritual so Jewish tradition is the same tradition, transformed in Christianity.[28]

Book twelve of Augustine's treatise against Faustus endeavors to demonstrate his claim that "the whole contents of [Jewish] scriptures are either directly or indirectly about Christ";[29] "the whole narrative of Genesis, *in the most minute details*, is a prophecy of Christ and the Church"[30] (my emphasis).

---

24. Augustine quotes Faustus: "Christians have not adopted these observances, and no one keeps them; so that if we will not take the inheritance, we should surrender the documents" (Augustine *Contra Faustum Manichaeum* 4.1); "I reject circumcision as disgusting; and if I mistake not, so do you. I reject the observance of Sabbaths as superfluous: I suppose you do the same. I reject sacrifice as idolatry, as doubtless you also do" (ibid. 6.1).

25. Ibid., 6.3.

26. Ibid., 6.9.

27. Faustus denied, according to Augustine, "that Jesus was born of the seed of David . . . that he was made of a woman. . . . he denies his death, burial, and resurrection . . . [and] he denies, too, that our mortal body will be raised again, changed into a spiritual body" (ibid., 11.3).

28. Ibid.

29. Ibid., 12.7.

30. Ibid., 12.8.

For example, "as a wife was made for Adam from his side while he slept, the Church becomes the property of her dying Savior, by the sacrament of the blood which flowed from his side after his death."[31]

It would be tedious to enumerate the myriad examples Augustine cited as evidence of the intimate relationship of Jewish and Christian scripture and tradition; several will suffice. The story of Noah's ark leads Augustine to give a slightly different metaphor—yet with the same intent—as his depiction of the Jews as Christians' "librarians": "For what else is this nation [Jews] but a desk for the Christians, bearing the law and the prophets, and testifying to the doctrine of the church, so that we honor in the sacrament what they disclose in the letter?"[32] Noah's naked drunkenness prefigures the disclosure– "uncovering" of "the mortality of Christ's flesh."[33] The blessing of Japheth, the promise to Abraham, the near sacrifice of Isaac, the stone placed under Jacob's head, Jacob's dream, Judith's murder of Holofernes,[34] and many other stories demonstrate that the Jewish scriptures "teem" with predictions of Christ's coming.[35] A similar repertoire of scenes appears in the nave mosaics at Santa Maria Maggiore.

Augustine acknowledged the "ingenuity" of his reinterpretation of Jewish tradition: "Will it be said that these things happened in the regular course of things, and that it is a mere fancy to make them typical of Christ?" he asks, in order to preempt such a question. He insists, "Whoever with a candid mind reads all these things that are contained in the Old Testament Scriptures, must feel constrained to acknowledge that they have a meaning"[36] and that this meaning must be "read in the clear light of Christ."[37]

In juxtaposing "Old" and New Testament accounts, Augustine used a strategy repeatedly employed in Christian sermons, prayers, and works of art. His debate with the Manichaeans, conducted at the beginning of the fifth century, however, represents a more systematic treatment of this theme and demonstrates it in more detail than earlier sermonic or artistic references.

31. Ibid.

32. Ibid., 12.23.

33. Ibid.

34. "What is that woman boldly piercing the temples of the enemy with a wooden nail, but the faith of the church casting down the kingdom of the devil by the cross of Christ?" (ibid., 12.2).

35. Ibid., 12.25.

36. Ibid., 12.37.

37. Ibid., 12.42.

Moreover, although by the end of the fourth century his interpretation was conventional, it was reinforced, reiterated, and supported in fifth-century society in newly vivid and detailed ways. Augustine's attention to detail and precise correspondence was matched in the depiction of "the most minute details" of Jewish tradition as incorporated in the Christian story in the mosaics of Santa Maria Maggiore. Even the tiny size of the mosaic tesserae that make up the mosaics can be seen as a stylistic reflection of the thoroughness with which Jewish tradition and scriptures were, in this most public, accessible, and impressive way, located in relation to Christianity.

The two theological agenda of the mosaics of Santa Maria Maggiore each makes a powerful statement; their intersection represents an even more complex, subtle, and skillful communication. The new imperative of honoring the Virgin as the Mother of God created a potential embarrassment: if Christ received his specific humanity and particular flesh from his mother, Christ could not be thought of as racially neuter, but explicitly Jewish. Roman Jews in the mid-fifth century were, however, as we shall see in a moment, publicly labeled "beasts and madmen."[38] How could Jesus' irreducible Jewishness be rationalized in a society that increasingly ostracized Jews?

The answer lay in demonstrating visually—and therefore more powerfully, concretely, and accessibly—what Augustine had argued theologically, namely, that the incarnation of Christ simultaneously appropriated and canceled the independent existence of the Jewish people. Christ's flesh was the concrete medium in which his Jewishness was transmogrified into the church, the "Body of Christ."[39] The church had "inherited," in Christ, the physical and historical "substance"—the flesh—of Judaism. Henceforth, the Christian attitude toward the Jews would be disparaging. In Augustine's words,

> The Church admits and avows the Jewish people to be cursed, because after killing Christ they continue to till the ground of an earthly circumcision, an earthly Sabbath, an earthly passover, while the hidden strength or virtue of making known Christ, which this tilling contains, is not yielded to the Jews while they continue in impiety and unbelief, for it is revealed in the New Testament.[40]

---

38. *Codex Theodosianus* 16.1.2.

39. Augustine *Contra Faustum Manichaeum* 11.7.

40. Ibid., 12.11.

The Social World of Fifth-Century Roman Jews

Fifth-century Roman society, its laws, politics, social arrangements, and current events corroborate the picture of Jewish marginalization suggested by Christian mosaics and theology.[41] How did Santa Maria Maggiore's artistic agenda relate to contemporary Jews in the city in which their scripture, tradition, and ritual practices were being appropriated and reinterpreted by Christians? The Santa Maria Maggiore mosaics must ultimately be understood in the context of an imperial church that actively and effectively sought to eliminate other religious alternatives within the Roman Empire.

What was happening to Jews in the Roman Empire, and especially in Rome itself, at the time of the rebuilding and decoration of Santa Maria Maggiore? The situation can be grasped most readily by comparing it with Jews' earlier position in the Roman Empire, From the first century C.E., Judaism had enjoyed the status of a *religio licita*, a privileged religion in the Roman Empire; such privilege was still in effect at the end of the fourth century. Because fourth-century legislation supports arguments on both sides, scholars disagree about the extent to which Judaism and the activities of Jews were curtailed after the Peace of the Church and throughout the fourth century.[42] Christian emperors seem to have been genuinely ambivalent about the status of Jews: their "policies toward Jews varied as to whether they thought of themselves principally as emperors or as Christians."[43] To the extent that they thought of themselves as emperors, they protected Jews; if they thought

41. Historians often seek to show how societies work; they therefore adopt the perspective of those for whom the society worked. This privileging of privilege accords well with extant historical evidence; the authors, lawmakers, artists, and other spokespersons who wrote descriptions and evaluations of their society were the beneficiaries of educational institutions, and their perspectives were authorized by their participation in dominant political, social, and legal institutions. Evidence of the perspectives and insights of those for whom a society did not work is more difficult both to find and to interpret. Yet the modes and victims of ostracization, marginalization, and oppression can reveal a great deal, not only about the costs and damages, but also about the successes of a society. The values, preoccupations, and loyalties of historical authors and artists that seem mysterious to twentieth-century historians can frequently be clarified by taking into account the exclusionary strategies upon which a triumphal society is built.

42. See Marcel Simon's discussion in chapter four of *Verus Israel*, 98–134, and Robert Wilken's somewhat different evaluation: "It seems that the status of the Jews in the empire was changing rapidly during this period [the fourth century], but, if so, these changes were probably not perceptible to the people living at that time" (see Wilken's *John Chrysostom and the Jews*, 54).

43. M. Simon, *Verus Israel*, 126.

of themselves primarily as Christians, they frequently overlooked illegal and unjust actions against Jews and their property.

In the first decades of the fourth century, Constantine's legislation recognized and sometimes even reinforced the privileges of Jewish communities as long as Jews did not seek to attract Christians to Judaism. He exempted Jewish clergy from compulsory state service of all kinds and, in effect, "made possible a system of Jewish self-government that strengthened Jewish life and identity."[44] At the end of the fourth century, Theodosius—the emperor under whom Christianity became the official religion of the Roman Empire—still reminded anti-Semitic bishops such as Ambrose of Milan that Judaism, as an ancient and honorable religion, was protected by the state.[45] Moreover, public offices were open to Jews until the beginning of the fifth century.

Although Constantine's espousal of Christianity did not immediately lead to dramatic legal changes, Jews nevertheless gradually came to be regarded as second-class citizens, and Jewish privilege began to shrink. For example, Jews were not permitted to circumcize slaves, and marriage between Christians and Jews was prohibited both by ecclesiastical and by imperial law.[46] Moreover, Constantine's edicts already reflect the language of vitriolic sermons and anti-Jewish propaganda. Judaism was, for the first time, referred to as a "shameful" (*secta nefaria*) or "bestial" (*feralia*) sect, as contemptible and perverse (*turpes, perversi*).[47]

Increased imperial hostility toward all non-Christians is evidenced in Theodosius I's edict of February 380, by which Christianity was established as the official religion of the Roman Empire. Although this edict did not single Jews out for opprobrium or punishment, it clearly stipulated official attitudes of intolerance:

> We desire that all peoples who fall beneath the sway of our imperial clemency should profess the faith which we believe to have been communicated by the Apostle Peter to the Romans and maintained in its traditional form until the present day. . . . And we require that those who follow this rule of faith should embrace

---

44. Wilken, *John Chrysostom*, 51.

45. "Judaeorum sectam nulla lege prohibitam satis constat" ("no law prohibits the sect of the Jews"), *Codex Theodosianus* 16.8.9.

46. Canons 17 and 78 of the Council of Elvira; *Codex Theodosianus* 3.7.3 and 9.67.5: "No Jew shall receive a Christian woman in marriage, nor shall a Christian man choose marriage to a Jewish woman."

47. Jacobs, "Rome," 446.

the name of Catholic Christians, adjuring all others madmen and ordering them to be designated as heretics. . . condemned as such, in the first instance, to suffer divine punishment, and therewith, the vengeance of that power which we, by celestial authority, have assumed.[48]

Universal enforcement of this edict was not immediately attempted, but outbreaks of popular violence against Jews indicate that official attitudes were reflected and reinforced by popular anti-Semitism.

Late fourth-century and early fifth-century emperors had, however, often insisted on the rebuilding, at Christian expense, of synagogues that had been destroyed by Christian mobs.[49] This measure was effectively challenged and criticized by Bishop Ambrose of Milan.[50] In the 380s, a Christian mob burned a Jewish synagogue in Rome; the Emperor Maximus ordered it rebuilt at the expense of the state, but he was overthrown and killed by Theodosius I before this was done.[51]

Theodosius's laws relating to Jews continued to demonstrate the ambivalence of earlier fourth-century Christian emperors. He wavered between laws inhibiting and laws protecting Jews. In addition to already existing laws forbidding Jews to proselytize and protecting Jewish converts to Christianity, Jewish parents were forbidden to disinherit children who became Christians. The Theodosian Code also prohibited the building of new synagogues and stipulated that "Christians could escape punishment for violence against synagogues simply by converting them into Christian churches and returning

---

48. *Codex Theodosianus* 26.1.2; compare Constantine's Edict of Toleration which has a very different tone. In the edict of 313 C.E., Constantine proclaimed himself "unwilling to constrain others [religiously] by the fear of punishment"; see Eusebius *Vita Constantinii* 2.56.

49. Imperial attempts to discourage the razing of synagogues can be documented as late as the reign of the Ostrogoth Theodoric.

50. Ambrose *Epistula* 40.23.

51. A progressive weakening of the state's protection of synagogues can be traced in early fifth-century laws. Laws of 397, 412, and 418 restate protection of existing synagogues, but "what had been a crime that must be remitted to the imperial tribunal now became a matter for the jurisdiction of local authorities" (M. Simon, *Verus Israel*, 228). Three laws published in 423 no longer mention restitution; they merely required those responsible for the destruction of a synagogue to return cult objects or to pay for them and to provide land for their rebuilding—at the expense of the Jewish community. Another law of 423 forbade Jews to build new synagogues (except when an existing synagogue had been destroyed) or to repair or improve already existing synagogues.

any treasures which had been confiscated."[52] Many details could be added to supplement this picture of gradual but systematic suppression and curtailment of the activities of the large Jewish population in late fourth-century Rome.[53]

Contradictory laws continued to be promulgated between 398 and 404, but anti-Jewish policy began to dominate in 404 when Honorius declared "Jews and Samaritans" unfit for military service. In 415, Theodosius II issued the first edict that forbade the construction of new synagogues and even suggested that synagogues "in desert places" could be destroyed, "if it can be accomplished without riots." This edict apparently acted as "an invitation to fanatics to go about their work of intimidation and destruction."[54] Furthermore, by August 425, all Jews and pagans were expelled from imperial service. This meant that henceforth Jews could not practice law in imperial courts and thus marks another significant increment in Jewish marginalization from positions of public authority. In sum, by the early fifth century, it was clear that Jews were rapidly losing many of their traditional privileges as they were marginalized from public life, their growth circumscribed, and their authorities disempowered.

The so-called *Novella* of 31 January 438—published as Santa Maria Maggiore was being completed—amounted to a total prohibition on Jews' holding public office of any kind. It also forbade any act of Jewish proselytism under pain of death. In this legislation, Theodosius II declared himself the protector of true religion against "Jews, Samaritans, pagans, and heretics":

> Among the other duties which our love of the common weal indicates to us in an every vigilant consideration, we perceive the search for the true religion as the imperial majesty's foremost care. If we could maintain its cult, we shall open the way of prosperity to human endeavor. . . . The blindly senseless Jews, Samaritans, pagans, and other kinds of monstrous heretics dare to question that Christianity is the true religion. If we endeavor to recall them to sanity . . . by a healing law, they themselves shall bear responsibility for its severity, they who do not leave room for mercy by their obstinate crime of an obdurate front. For this reason we decree in this law—that shall stand forever—that no Jew . . . shall accede to

---

52. Hunt, "St. Stephen in Minorca," 118.

53. M. Simon (*Verus Israel*, 127–32) details these laws.

54. *Codex Theodosianus* 16.812; Holum, *Theodosian Empresses*, 98.

honors and dignities, to none of them shall be opened an admin-
istration with public obedience.[55]

Official attitudes toward Jews, incendiary language, and discriminatory
legislation were supplemented by popular violence against Jews and their
property. Anti-Jewish riots occurred in 388 in Callinicum on the Euphrates.
Similar events, instigated by the local bishop, occurred in Minorca in 415. In
Alexandria, Bishop Cyril led attacks on synagogues, expelled Jews from the city,
and turned synagogues into churches. Edessa, Dertona, and Constantinople
recorded similar anti-Jewish activities. By the second decade of the fifth century, "official utterances were increasingly coming to reflect and acknowledge
the anti-Jewish violence which was taking place locally around the empire."[56]
A law of 420 cautioned Jews against provoking Christian attacks, revealing an
official attitude of blaming the victim.

Synagogues continued to be destroyed by Christian mobs. Even when
emperors attempted to protect Jews, anti-Jewish riots were often instigated
by bishops in apparently deliberate attempts to create acrimony between Jews
and Christians.[57] This pattern of episcopal denunciation of Jews is attested
in many locations within the Roman Empire. In Antioch, for example, John
Chrysostom preached notoriously vitriolic sermons against Judaism, depict-
ing the synagogue as the "haunt of vices of every description."[58]

Christian leaders, moreover, began to assimilate Jews into a growing
pool of "heretics." As a category of intolerable dissidence was constructed,
dissident groups lost their particularity in Christian eyes and were conflated
with one another. Name-calling—perennially indifferent to particularity and
difference—identified Jews with heretics and heretics with Jews. Nestorius,
the opponent of "theotokos" at the Council of Ephesus, was called apparently
without further reason than his unpopular views—"Nestorius the Jew."[59]

---

55. *Codex Theodosianus* 16.1.2.

56. In one of these riots, the Platonic philosopher Hypatia was murdered by a Christian
mob; see Hunt, "St. Stephen in Minorca," 118.

57. Ibid., 115.

58. Chrysostom compared the synagogue to the theater and a brothel, calling it a "den
of robbers," a "lair of wild beasts," and a "place of idolatry"; *Adversus Judaeos* 1.3; quoted in
Hunt, "St. Stephen in Minorca," 115.

59. Holum, *Theodosian Empresses*, 168 n. 111; also 188.

Conclusion

At approximately the same time that the mosaic program of Santa Maria Maggiore was designed and executed, Sozomen, the church historian, reported that in the Eastern empire, the relics of the Hebrew prophets Habakkuk, Micah, and Zechariah were revealed as a sign of God's favor to the Christian rulers, Theodosius I and Valentinian, during whose reigns they were found.[60] These purported discoveries were considered material evidence validating a by-now stabilized method of dealing with the Jewish foundation of Christianity: the bones of the prophets gave concreteness to the claim that Judaism had existed only as a preparation for Christianity and that it was decisively superceded, eviscerated, and fulfilled by the incarnation of Christ.

This chauvinistic interpretation would perhaps never have achieved its long-term effects if it had not been amply and visibly supported in popularly accessible forms. As we have seen, a thorough, complete, and detailed appropriation of Jewish scripture and tradition effectively reinforced this interpretation. A Christian population heard in sermons and liturgies and saw in mosaics their own roots traced from the creation of the world, through the history of the Jewish people's relationship with their God, to the birth, life, death, and resurrection of Jesus. They saw it first at Santa Maria Maggiore in Rome.

The traditional status of Jews within the Roman Empire as members of an ancient and honorable religion was challenged and overturned in the first half of the fifth century. It is safe to conjecture that none of the theological, artistic, and legal Christian revisions of Jewish privilege would have worked in isolation as powerfully and effectively as they did in concert. Together, they reflected and reinforced a massive social marginalization of Judaism as well as Jewish people.

A composite Christian portrait of "the Jew" was gradually constructed. Ironically, it was composed largely by pasting together prophetic denunciations of the Jewish people from their own scriptures. The Hebrew Bible "provided the Christians with a repertoire of offensive and damaging epithets with which they invariably accompanied every mention of the Jews": Jews were regularly characterized as "uncircumcized and stiff-necked people."[61]

---

60. Sozomen *Historia ecclesiastica* 9.16–17: "It seems as if God openly manifested his favor towards the present emperor, not only by disposing of warlike affairs in an unexpected way, but also by revealing the sacred bodies of many persons who were of old most distinguished for piety" (427).

61. M. Simon, *Verus Israel*, 215.

Historians of art and religion often explain representations of Judaism within Christianity by tracing them back to the earliest Christian liturgies, sermons, literature, and images. This historical genetic fallacy, however, will not adequately explain the specific power of such representations in the particular dominantly Christian societies that gave them credence and acted upon them. In the first half of the fifth century, as I have argued, the power of these ideas and images can be reconstructed only in relation to a triumphal Church and in the context of the multiple fronts on which Jews were losing social ground.

Even though Christians appropriated Jewish images throughout the history of Christianity, one cannot assume that the selection and meaning of images were prompted by similar religious needs in different times and places. In changing societies, similar images and ideas occupy different positions, respond to different situations, and are interpreted according to different associations, attitudes, and values.[62] Images from the Hebrew Bible apparently provided comfort for Christians in the times of persecution; figures and events from Jewish tradition carried very different religious and social meaning when represented in the context of a triumphal church. The mosaics at Santa Maria Maggiore represent an important moment in the public representation of supercessionist theology. In fifth-century Roman society, these powerful visualizations of the triumph of Christianity contributed to an attitude toward Judaism and the Jewish people that would persist—acted out variously by different Christian societies—to our own time.

62. Michel Foucault wrote (*Archeology of Knowledge*, 176), "Even if a statement is composed of the same words, bears exactly the same meaning, and preserves the same syntactic identity, it does not constitute the same statement if it is spoken by someone in the course of a conversation, or printed in a novel; if it was written one day centuries ago, and if it now reappears in an oral formulation. A statement must have a substance, a support, a place, and a date. And when these requisites change, it too changes identity."

CHAPTER 12

Vision: The Eye of the Body and the Eye of the Mind in Augustine's *De trinitate* and *Confessions*

"Our whole business in this life is to restore to health the eye of the heart whereby God may be seen." (AUGUSTINE *SERMO* 88.5.5)

The importance of Saint Augustine's use of physical vision as a model for his description of the most satisfying fulfillment of human life, the vision of God, has been noted by many commentators.[1] It is only, however, when we follow Augustine's analysis of physical and spiritual vision—the activity of the "eye of the body" and the "eye of the mind"—that we can understand the extent to which Augustine extrapolates a nuanced account of spiritual vision from his model of physical vision. It is, I will claim, Augustine's understanding of the physics of vision that enables him to describe a process by which one comes to a vision of "That Which Is."[2] Although we must be careful to note dissimilarities as well as similarities between the two types of vision, the pivotal role of physical vision can be demonstrated at precisely the point of Augustine's most intense interest, the understanding of "God and the soul,"[3] the project of his extended effort of understanding in *De trinitate*, the powerful treatise of his maturity. His method, clearly outlined at the beginning of the work and reiterated several times in the body of the work, acknowledges the necessity, for all theological work, of finding the fruitful metaphor:

1. E.g., Nash, *Light of the Mind*, 91: "Augustine depends a great deal on the analogy between physical and mental sight."

2. Augustine *Confessiones* 7.17.23.

3. Augustine *Soliloquiorum* 1.2.

If we at any time try to distinguish internal spiritual things more subtly and describe them more easily, we must take examples from external things to illustrate them. Now the outer person, gifted with the bodily senses, perceives bodies. As is easily noted, this bodily sense is actually five senses: sight, hearing, smell, taste, and touch. But it is difficult and unnecessary to ask all the senses for that for which we are seeking. For what one of them informs us also holds true for the rest. Let us therefore use in particular the testimony of the eyes, because this sense far excels the rest, and although it is a different kind of vision, it is close to spiritual vision.[4]

The metaphor of physical vision constitutes a leitmotiv throughout Augustine's many accounts of spiritual vision. It occurs as early as *De quantitate animae* 23.43 and reappears with emphasis on various aspects of the motif in preaching, in scriptural exegesis, and in the autobiographical writings, and it appears in its most fully articulated form in *De trinitate*. It is a metaphor that enables Augustine "to distinguish internal spiritual things more subtly and to describe them more easily." In identifying and selecting the metaphor of physical vision for exploration, we must acknowledge that its proper location is within Augustine's description of the primacy of divine illumination in any act of human understanding. Yet a long history of interpretive work on Augustine's theory of divine illumination has focused on the meaning and activity of divine illumination and has largely neglected analysis of the role of human beings in understanding. It is not accidental that in discussions of divine illumination the role of human responsibility has not received its proper attention. Augustine's model of physical vision underlines and supports his description of the necessity of human effort, concentration, and training; if this model is not noticed, the initiative of the viewer and the necessity for training "the eye of the mind" are not likely to be given their proper weight. This article will attempt to redress the neglect of attention to the balancing role of human responsibility by exploring the model that emphasizes it.

We will look first, then, at the account of physical vision with which Augustine worked. Second, we will look at his description of "seeing God." Finally, we will ask whether there are, for Augustine, any points of continuity between physical and spiritual vision, that is, whether the training of

4. Augustine *De trinitate* 11.1.1; 1.1.2. Translations are adapted from Augustine, *The Trinity*, translated by Stephen McKenna. I am grateful to Professor James Halporn, Department of Classics, Indiana University (Bloomington), for his help with these emended translations. Further citations in parentheses in text are from *De trinitate* unless otherwise specified.

the physical eye is useful for the training of spiritual vision. The following observations are not intended to provide a "key" to the difficult and complex arguments of *De trinitate* but only to draw a facet of Augustine's teaching on the vision of God that illuminates that teaching.

Contemporary analyses of the visual metaphor to describe an act of human knowledge rely on a long historical development that has come to emphasize the distance between the viewer and the object that is necessary in every act of seeing. The viewer must, it is alleged, stand back, be emotionally separate from, and without prior intellectual commitment to, the object if a genuine act of seeing/knowing is to take place. This emphasis on distance is understandable as a correction of the passionate intellectual subjectivity with which many of our historical predecessors identified "truth." But we have, in general usage, retained the description of knowledge as "seeing" without noticing the physical model that originally informed and supported that description. It is only by ignoring or rejecting the "visual ray" account of vision that we can accept the description of an act of understanding as "seeing" and still insist that the central feature of the metaphor is its emphasis on the distance of the viewer from the object. For the classical people who originated the metaphor, sight was an accurate and fruitful metaphor for knowledge because they relied on the physics of vision, subscribed to by Plato and many others, that a ray of light, energized and projected by the mind toward an object, actually touches its object, thereby connecting viewer and object. By the vehicle of the visual ray, the object is not only "touched" by the viewer, but also the object is "printed" on the soul of the viewer. The ray theory of vision specifically insisted on the connection and essential continuity of viewer and object in the act of vision.

It was this theory of vision which Augustine held and which he used as a model for his account of the possibility of the interaction of God and the human soul. Rays "shine through the eyes and touch whatever we see."[5] Let us begin to explore how Augustine uses this model of physical vision. First, vision must be initiated by the viewer: ". . . Sensation does not proceed from that body which is seen, but from the body of a living being that perceives" (11.2.3). Concentration or focus is required before an object can be seen. Physical vision implies effort and selectivity on the part of the viewer. The

---

5. Augustine *De trinitate* 9.3.3: "Quia radios quia per oes emicant et quidquid cernimus tangunt." See also *De trinitate* 9.6.11: "Ista vero aut praesentia sensu corporis tangimus." See my discussion of similarities and differences in Augustinian, Stoic, and Plotinian accounts of vision in *Augustine on the Body*, 10–11.

attention of the soul must be directed to the object: "Before the vision was produced, there already existed a will which to form the sense attached it to the body to be perceived" (11.5.9).[6]

Second, in the act of vision, viewer and object are momentarily united. "Three things," viewer, object, and the power that unites them, are barely distinguishable, even "to the judgment of reason." In the act of vision itself, "the will possesses such power in uniting these two [viewer and object] that it attaches the sense to be formed to that thing which is seen" (11.2.5). Vision, then, connects or attaches the viewer to the object. Moreover, the soul of the viewer both initially projects the visual ray, and it also "absorbs into itself" the form or image of the object, which is then permanently retained by the memory. Vision is definitely, for Augustine, a two-way street: the soul forms images of sensible things "out of its own substance" (*substantiae suae*), but the result is that the mind itself is formed by the very images it formulates and carries. The soul is "fitted together" with, or "takes the shape of" (10.5.7–8),[7] the objects of its focused attention.

The energy required to initiate vision and to retain the form of its object in the memory is also an investment of the soul's affection. The soul's selection of objects becomes habitual so that the soul does not recognize itself without a constant supply of its objects: "The mind draws in with itself those things upon which it has long reflected with love, and to which it has become attached through its devoted care [*curae glutino inhaeserit*], even when it returns in some way to think of itself" (10.5.7).[8] The mind, when its attention and affection is compulsively directed outward, "binds itself to these images with so strong a love as even to regard itself as something of the same kind . . . it is made like them" (10.6.8).[9]

---

6. Cf. Arnheim, *Art and Visual Perception*, 28: "Vision is not mere passive reception. The world of images does not simply imprint itself on a faithfully sensitive organ. Rather, in looking at an object, we reach out for it. With an invisible finger we move through the space around us, we go out to the distant places where things are found, touch them, catch them, scan their surfaces, trace their borders, explore their texture. It is an eminently active occupation."

7. See also Augustine *De doctrina christiana* 1.20.19: "incipit configurari."

8. See also Augustine *De trinitate* 11.2.2: "conjungit."

9. See also Augustine *De trinitate* 10.8.11: The mind "can no longer separate the images of sensible things from itself, so as to see itself alone. For they have marvelously cohered to it with the glue of love [*glutino amoris*], . . . sensible things leave the footprints [*simulacra*], as it were, in our mind of many attentive actions."

This strong interpretation, both of the initiating role of the viewer and of the powerful effect of the objects of vision on the viewer, is important if we are to grasp Augustine's account of spiritual vision. The soul, to mix metaphors for a moment, votes with its feet; it cannot be passive in vision as, for example, the ear can be passive—to a far greater extent— in hearing. In the act of hearing, the soul neither necessarily selects its objects nor necessarily turns its attention toward them. Rather, hearing is initiated by the object that imposes itself on the ear; the ear is helpless, while it is in the environs, not to hear a sound that strikes it.[10]

But although it is tempting to extend the contrast of vision and hearing, we must be careful to acknowledge Augustine's imprecise use of both senses to indicate activity *and* passivity, reaching out and being drawn by an attractive and powerful object. In *De trinitate* he says he will discuss sight as representative—at a higher power—of all the senses. And in the *Enarrationes in Psalmos* 41, a parallel description of the *Confessions'* vision accounts[11] is given, using an auditory model:

> It is from these eternal, everlasting festivities that the ears of our heart catch a something, a sweet melodious singing. . . . And so, even if, when the clouds disperse, by walking in desire, somehow or other . . . we reach up to this sound at times, so that we by straining our ears catch something from that house of God; yet under the burden of our weakness we fall back again to the humdrum things we are used to.[12]

In the same passage, Augustine weaves visual and verbal metaphors. The person, "led by the joyfulness of that inward and intelligible sound," succeeds "with the eye of the mind" (*acies mentis*), in "catching a glimpse, sudden and momentary as it was. . . ."[13] This weaving of discursive/auditory and presentational/visual models continued from Augustine's earliest to his latest works. In some passages, the hearing model, for which the discursive mode

---

10. Augustine *Confessiones* 6.8.13.

11. Ibid., 7.17.23, 9.10.25.

12. Augustine *Enarrationes in Psalmos* 41.9.10.

13. In an earlier work, *Augustine on the Body*, I claimed that Augustine, in his maturity, came to favor an auditory model for descriptions of the Christian life, emphasizing, as an auditory model does, the discursive or pilgrimage aspect. I now think that this claim overschematizes the textual evidence; *De trinitate*, completed in C.E. 416 or 417, with its extended visual metaphor, is sufficient evidence that there were features emphasized by the visual model that made it indispensable to Augustine.

is an appropriate model, dominates; and in other passages, the visual model. In short, Augustine continued to find it necessary to use the auditory model to emphasize the pilgrimage aspect of the Christian life. He used the visual model to emphasize (1) the necessity for effort and initiative on the part of the viewer, and (2) the inevitable attachment to the object of vision through the soul's investment of energy and the shaping of the soul by its object.

At this point it is important to pause and observe that Augustine's idea of the soul is different from most modern ideas of the soul or self. Augustine's idea of the soul as initiating sensation and in turn being shaped by its objects must not be conflated with popular modern ideas of the self as a self-contained, relatively autonomous and distinct entity. For Augustine, the soul is not primarily a separated entity for whom the problem is the formation of "relationships" with other souls, with the natural environment, and with God; Augustine's "soul" is primarily a partially centered energy, initially barely distinguishable from its cosmic, physical, and spiritual environment, which comes to be cumulatively distinguished and defined by the objects of its attention and affection.[14] For such an object-oriented or intentional entity, the pressing problem of human existence is not relationship, the building of bridges between separate entities, but differentiation, the construction of a center that defines itself and determines the direction of its investment of energy.

The act of vision, in which viewer and object are united, is the perfect model for this understanding of human being, united with, and defined by, the objects of its attention and affection. Even the body of the viewer can be shaped by the object of vision—Augustine cites the chameleon and the fetus, imprinted by its mother's objects—in cases of an exceptionally strong bonding between viewer and object (11.2.5). If even the body can take the shape of the object of the soul's habitual attention and affection, how much more does the soul, with its greater sensitivity and impressionability, come to be differentiated and defined by its passionately cathected objects.[15]

---

14. Cf. Plotinus *Ennead* 4.3.8: "We are what we desire and what we look at."

15. The impressionability of the soul is explicitly rejected by Plotinus as incompatible with the soul's activity (*Ennead* 5.5.7). Despite Augustine's commitment to a description of the soul that features its activity in sensation, he does not avail himself of Plotinus's arguments. While it is possible that Augustine did not know these sections of the *Enneads*, it may also have been significant that he uses the Stoic account that permits him to retain the visual ray theory rejected by Plotinus in *Ennead* 3.6.1.

It is this account of the mechanics and results of physical vision that grounds Augustine's description of the vision of God.[16] We have seen that physical vision involves a viewer and an object that are united in an activity whose energy is provided by the will. In spiritual vision also, the object and the viewer are both essential to an activity in which the attention of the human being has been consciously concentrated and trained. The *possibility* of the vision is given: divine illumination is the sine qua non of spiritual vision, just as the sun must be present if physical vision is to occur. But divine illumination does not impose or guarantee vision. The initiative remains with the viewer, as Augustine's insistent and extended use of the visual ray model emphasizes. While it is certainly true that human beings can know divine truths only as illuminated by God, it is at least as important, and perhaps more heuristic, to underline, as Augustine does by the use of the visual model, the importance of the role of the human being. Divine illumination is necessary; it is the condition of spiritual vision, but it is not sufficient.

On the part of the human being, then, the first prerequisite to spiritual vision is faith, the faith that there is something to see and that it can be seen by human beings: "But even before we are capable of seeing and perceiving God, as he can be seen and perceived, a thing which is granted to the clean of heart: for 'blessed are the clean of heart, for they shall see God,' unless he is loved by faith the heart cannot be cleansed so as to be fit and ready to see him" (8.4.6.). Faith is the initial investment of attention and affection, of love and of longing, in God who is not yet seen "face to face": "We walk by faith and not by sight" (8.4.6; 2 Cor 5:7). And yet, blind faith is not required: "Who loves that which he does not know? . . . And what does it mean, to love God except to see him and to perceive him steadfastly with our mind?" (8.4.6). We will shortly examine Augustine's nuanced claim that a vision of God is possible in this life; for now it is enough to note that Augustine insists that faith is essential; it is the willingness "to prepare the means of seeing what you love before you try to see it."[17]

16. For a more complete discussion of the development of Augustine's idea of sensation, especially his use of the concept of *spiritus* in *De Genesi ad litteram* 12, see my *Augustine on the Body*, chap. 2, passim.

17. Augustine *Enarrationes in Psalmos* 99.5; see also *De trinitate* 14.2.4: "We must walk by faith, and sight will take its place by which we shall see face to face, just as now, although we do not see, yet because we believe, we shall deserve to see [*videre mirebimur*], and shall rejoice that we have been brought to sight through faith."

Just as the bodily eye requires the most strenuous exercise and strengthening before it can see strongly illuminated objects, so the eye of the mind requires intensive exercise and training before it can see—even momentarily—eternal truth. Here a development in Augustine's thought is clearly discernible; in an early work Augustine said:

> There are some eyes so healthy and vigorous [*tam sani et vegeti*], that they can without hesitation turn toward the very sun as soon as they are opened. . . . Others, however, are dazzled by the very luster that they so ardently desire to see. . . . To these . . . it is dangerous to want to show what they are as yet incapable of seeing. . . . They are, therefore, first to be trained and . . . their love is to be trained and nourished.[18]

In the later work, *De trinitate*, however, Augustine acknowledges no automatically "healthy and vigorous" eye. The agenda of *De trinitate* is the careful, steady drawing of a cumulative understanding of the Trinity. Even though, at the beginning of the effort, the Trinity's "own light seemed to be present around us, still, no trinity appeared to us in nature, for in the midst of that splendor we did not keep the eye of our mind fixed steadily upon searching for it . . . because that ineffable light beat back our gaze, and the weakness of our mind was convinced that it could not yet adjust itself to it" (15.6.10).

Preliminary, even to "seeing somewhat," then, are faith and the cleansing and the strengthening of the eye of the mind. At this point, Augustine is explicit about his use of the physical model of the visual ray, indicating both its relevance and the point at which it may not be an accurate model. Augustine questions his model at an important point: he has argued, in *De trinitate* 10 and 11, that a certain kind of self-knowledge is necessary; human beings must be able to see their own minds in such a way as to perceive "the image of God in ourselves" (9.2.2). But in physical vision, Augustine says, the eye would only be distracted by seeing itself at the same time that it tried to see an object: "For we see bodies through the eyes of the body, because we cannot refract the rays which shine through them and touch whatever we see, and reflect them back into the eyes themselves, except when we are looking in a mirror" (9.3.3).[19] At this point, the visual ray model does not

---

18. Augustine *Soliloquiorum* 1.23.

19. "Per oculos enim corporis corpora videmus, quia radios qui per eos emicant et quidquid cernimus tangunt, refringere ac retorquere in ipsos non possumus, nisi cum specula intuemur"; see also *De trintate* 10.3.5.

serve Augustine's argument. Yet even here he is not willing to jettison the model but adds that its explication may simply need more work: "But this is a subject that is discussed very subtly and very privately, until it may be publicly shown whether this is actually so or not so" (9.3.3).

The second step of preparation for spiritual vision and the vision of God is the cleansing of the eye of the mind: "These eyes must be cleansed."[20] What does Augustine mean by this? We should first notice what he does not mean. It would have been easy, even tempting, for him to literalize his use of the theory of the visual ray which reaches out and touches its objects to argue the necessity of ascetical disciplines which deprive the bodily eye of its objects. But it is not the eye of the body but the eye of the mind that must be cleansed, and Augustine does not advocate that the bodily eye be "cleansed" of sensible objects. He contents himself with the observation that the eye of the mind, invested as it is through daily habituation to sensible objects, must self-consciously correct its predilection for searching for God as if God were a body: "We must, of course, take care lest the mind [*animus*], in believing what it does not see, fashion for itself something which it is not, and hope for and love that which is false" (8.4.6).

It is not, then, rejection of visible objects that cleanses the eye of the mind, and the elimination of sensible objects is not preliminary to the gathering of the mind's attention and affection for spiritual vision. Images of sensible objects, either experienced, or retained in the memory, "do no harm *if one does not seek after them passionately* if they cause pleasure, or *flee them like a coward* if they are unpleasant" (11.5.8; emphasis mine).[21] Only fear and love are powerful enough concentrations of psychic energy, the energy of the will, to bond the soul to its objects. Thus it is only when the soul's energy is spent in passionate attention to objects that attract or repel that visible things can be a threat to the soul's integrity. Even then visible objects are not in themselves dangerous; it is the soul's investment of disproportionate amounts of attention to them that must be changed. The cleansing of the eye of the mind urged by Augustine is the collection of the soul's central energy of attention and affection that has been "poured out" onto sensible objects of

---

20. Augustine *Enarrationes in Psalmos* 127.8.21

21. It is not entirely accurate, however, to speak of passionate attachment to visible objects as "love": "For only true love may be called love; otherwise it is desire [*cupiditas*]. Therefore, it is a misuse of terms to say of those who desire love. . . . But this is true love, that while holding fast to the truth we may live justly [*inhaerentes veritate juste vivimus*]" (Augustine *De trinitate* 8.7.10).

fear or love.[22] Again, the model used is that of the visual ray which connects the soul and its objects, both carrying the soul's attention to the object and carrying the object back to the soul as an image.

The cleansing that is preliminary to spiritual vision and the vision of God is the collection of *oneself* from the variety of images that occupy and structure the soul. In the *Confessions* Augustine calls this activity of gathering the soul's energy continence: "It is by continence that we are brought together [*colligimur*], and brought back [*redigimur*] into one."[23] Whatever external form continence takes, its sole purpose and function, according to Augustine, is to break the momentum of the outrush—the hemorrhage of energy from the soul toward sensible objects: "I have been spilled and scattered . . . my thoughts, the innermost bowels of my soul, are torn apart with the crowding tumults of variety," Augustine wrote in telling his own story.[24]

The third stage of preparation for the vision of God, again modeled on the visual ray theory, is exercise and training to strengthen the eye of the mind. The vision will not occur until the mind is "fit and ready." It must be "built up" (8.4.6, 15.27.49); a "better trained mental vision" is necessary. In many passages, Augustine acknowledges "the difficulty of giving health to the eye of the interior person so that it may be able to gaze upon its own sun."[25] Spiritual vision is always hard to achieve, and momentary: "Only a few succeed in arriving at these reasons [*rationes*] with the eye of the mind, and when one does arrive, insofar as is possible, the very one who arrives does not abide in them, but as it were the eye (of the mind) itself is beaten back and repelled" (12.14.23). In physical vision, the visual ray must be focused and trained if it is to touch its object with precision; the parallel strengthening of the eye of the mind is the conscious cultivation of longing, the visual ray of the mind's eye. The vision of God will never be a passive or voyeuristic vision. Quotations from Augustine's works could be multiplied to demonstrate his preoccupation with the exercise of longing; the following quotation is characteristic: "The whole life of the good Christian is a holy longing. . . . That is our life, to be exercised by longing."[26] Augustine also described the psychology of longing: "What you long for as yet you do not see. . . . By with-

---

22. "We flowed downward [*defluximus*]," Augustine wrote in the *Confessiones*, "into the many" (10.29.40).

23. Ibid., 10.29.40.

24. Ibid., 11.29.39.

25. Augustine *Contra epistolam manichaei quam vocant fundamenti* 25.1 (ALW 194); 17–18.

26. Augustine *Tractatus in epistolam Joannis ad Parthos* 4.6.

holding of the vision, God extends the longing; through longing he extends the soul, by extending it he enlarges it. . . . So let us long, because we are to be filled. . . ."[27]

Both in physical vision and in spiritual vision the insufficiently trained eye fatigues rapidly in strong light—the light of the sun, or the "light inapproachable" (15.6.10).[28] Emphasis in Augustine's description of spiritual vision is on the responsibility of the person to exercise and strengthen the capacity for vision by concentrating the energy of longing on the desired object. This longing becomes the visual ray of the eye of the mind that can, Augustine claims, touch its object.

We have seen that in the process of "restoring to health the eye of the heart whereby God can be seen," faith, the initial direction of attention and affection toward God, and the cleansing and training of the mind's eye are necessary. But in what sense does longing, the trained ray of the eye of the mind, "touch" its object? Characteristically, Augustine seeks to describe the dynamics of the process and to identify for his readers the energy that activates it: "One is not only instructed so as to see you, . . . but also so as to grow strong enough to lay hold on you."[29]

In physical vision, the will focuses the energy of the visual ray on a sensible object in the presence of the illumination of the sun. In spiritual vision, the focused and intensified longing of the eye of the mind reaches out, in the divine illumination provided, to touch God "in a trembling glance."[30] The cultivation of the soul's longing is the concentration of its love. Longing, the desire for happiness, leads to an ardent search for an object of fulfillment. And this search already begins to participate in the object for which it reaches out: "Although the desire, that is, this seeking does not seem to be love, by which that which is known is loved, . . . yet it is something of the

27. Ibid.; see also *De utilitate jejunii* 1: "When they are hungry, they stretch out; while they are stretching they are enlarged; while they are enlarged they become capacious, and when they have become capacious they will be filled in due time."

28. "That ineffable light caused us to turn aside our gaze [*reverberabant obtum*], and the weakness of our minds was convinced that it could not yet adjust itself to it."

29. Augustine *Confessiones* 7.21.27.

30. Ibid., 7.17: ". . . In the flash of a trembling glance, my mind arrived at That Which Is" [*Et pervenit ad id quad est, in ictu trepidartis aspectus*); see also *Confessiones* 9.10: ". . . In a flash of thought had made contact . . ." (*et rapida cogitatione attigimus . . .*); cf. Plotinus *Enneads* 5.3.17: "At the moment of touch there is no power whatsoever to make any affirmation; there is no leisure; reasoning upon the vision is for afterwards. We may know we have had the vision when the soul has suddenly taken light."

same kind. . . . This same desire by which one yearns for the knowing of the thing becomes love of the thing when known, while it holds and embraces [*tenet atque amplectitur*], the beloved . . ." (9.12.18).[31] Longing, the visual ray of the soul, contacts its object: "The more ardently we love God, the more certainly and calmly do we see him" (8.9.13). To the extent that the concentrated and strengthened eye of the mind participates in the activity of love, it touches the God who is love: "The God of God [*Deus ex deo*] therefore, is love" (15.17.31).

At this point another dissimilarity appears between physical vision and the vision of the eye of the mind: in physical vision, the soul creates, from its own substance (*substantiae suae*) (10.5.7), the image of a sensible object which then remains in the memory and informs the mind. The vision of God, on the other hand, is the only activity in which the soul does not construct from its own substance the image that is seen and remains in the memory after the moment of vision. Augustine's extended discussion of the love of God as God's very substance (15.17.27–29) precedes his claim that, in the activity of loving, a human being actually participates in God's substance, which then informs the soul through the activity of the Holy Spirit: "When God the Holy Spirit, therefore, who proceeds from God has been given to a human being, he inflames him with the love of God and for his neighbor, and he himself is love. *For human beings do not have whence to love God except from God*" (15.17.31; emphasis mine).

Just as, in physical vision, the will unifies, in the act of vision, two separate entities—the viewer and the object—so in the vision of God, it is love, "a stronger form of will" (15.21.41),[32] that, in the activity of loving, connects and unites human longing with God's activity of love. Augustine is careful to insist on both distinction and unity in his account of the vision of God, just as he had been careful to emphasize both the distinctness of viewer and object and their unity in the act of physical vision.

A further aspect of Augustine's analysis of physical vision is important to Augustine's account of spiritual vision and the vision of God. Again and

---

31. Cf. the following quotation from a contemporary novel: "To crave and to have are as alike as a thing and its shadow. For when does a berry break upon the tongue as sweetly as when one longs to taste it, and when is the taste refracted into so many hues and savors of ripeness and earth; and when do our senses know anything so utterly as when we lack it? And here again is a foreshadowing—the world will be made whole." Robinson, *Housekeeping*, 152–53.

32. "Vel amorem seu dilectionem quae valentior est voluntas."

again he quotes 1 Cor 13:12: "We see now through a darkened mirror; then, however, face to face." How can Augustine hold both that human longing can touch God under the present conditions of human life, *and* that our vision is flawed and not yet "face to face"? He does this by distinguishing two kinds of vision: "glimpse" and "gaze." Now, it is the glance that touches That Which Is, while *then*, the gaze is to be "our highest reward . . . the enjoyment of God and each other in God."[33] As we have seen, even with the trained energy of longing, human beings are presently unable to "see with a steady gaze": "It is impossible . . . to fix your gaze upon this, so as to behold it clearly and distinctly. I know you cannot" (15.27.50). But even the longing glance, brief as it is, has the two-way connecting power of the visual ray so that, as we have seen, while the soul pours its energy into its object, it is simultaneously informed by the vision. The mind is formed by the objects in which the will delights (11.3.6, 5.8).

This analysis of "touch," the moment of vision, into glance and gaze, permits Augustine to maintain the possibility of the vision of God, the ultimate goal of spiritual vision, in the present, while still postponing the permanent fulfillment of the vision beyond the limits of the present life. He can thus integrate the spatially modeled anthropology of Platonic tradition with a temporal anthropology that defines human being as a being that suffers and struggles in time. In the spatial model, the cosmically fluid human soul is differentiated by the direction of its attention and affection, whether upward to the intelligible world and through it, in an ecstatic touch, to the One, or downward, to the physical world that lies furthest from the source of being. Augustine's sense that the milieu of human life is primarily that of time rather than of space has led to his fascination with memory and the way that the individual selects and constructs a life story that can be either crippling or fruitful. Just as the ear, in order to perceive a melody, and not just a succession of unrelated tones, must retain and reformulate the elements of the melody at each moment of hearing, the mind gathers and constructs a life story that, once constructed, will govern future experience. Human being, instead of struggling upward, now struggles onward in a pilgrimage toward the full vision of God. A discursive account of human being is "easier" (*facilior est*) now, Augustine says (9.12.17).

Moreover, Augustine's analysis of the vision into the brief moments of glance and the timeless luxury of gaze allows him to correct the Neoplatonic

---

33. Augustine *De doctrina christiana* 1.32.25.

formulation without rejecting what has been to him both intellectually attractive and experientially powerful. He has reconstructed large chunks of the pilgrimage of his early life in the *Confessions*; he has seen clearly and drawn exquisitely for his readers the journey through time, each moment of which has meaning and significance when seen as part of a journey toward God. And yet, it was not only the cumulative painful learning of his youthful energetic pursuit of sex, power, and possessions that led him to recognize and acknowledge the activity of God—God's love—in his life. It was also those timeless moments of ecstatic vision—those glimpses—that energized his radical reinterpretation of his life story. His formulation of a painful difference between the glance (*vix vidisti*), and the gaze of the eye of the mind ("*non pates ibi aciem figere . . .*"), enabled him to construct a corrected model of the vision of God, a model that we find nowhere in his intellectual predecessors.

And yet, despite his frequent statements about the difference between glimpse and gaze, Augustine refers repeatedly to the "gaze of the mind" (*acies animi*: 11.7.11, 9.16, 10.17) as a present possibility. Is the momentary dazzling glimpse not the only human activity in which "God may be seen?" Augustine does describe another activity in which God may be seen in the present, that of "loving one's neighbor." At no point of his teaching has Augustine been more misunderstood and resented than in his description of the love of one's neighbor as a training and preparation for love of God. We must look more closely at Augustine's claim that "enjoyment of one's neighbor without reference to God" should not be an end in itself.

In the process of discussing what is meant by "love," Augustine gives his clearest exposition of his idea of loving the neighbor in God. He remarks first on the appropriateness of scriptural passages that "place one for both" in enjoining either love of God or love of neighbor:

> At times it mentions only the love of God as in this passage: "We know that for those who love God all things work together unto good," . . . and so on in many other texts. For one who loves God must logically do what God commanded, and loves God just so much as he does so; therefore he must also love his neighbor since God has commanded this.
>
> At other times, Scripture mentions only the love of our neighbor . . . we find many passages in the sacred Scriptures where love of our neighbor alone seems to be commanded for perfection, and the love of God is passed over in silence. . . . But this also follows

logically, for he who loves his neighbor must also love love above everything else. But "God is love, and he who abides in love abides in God." Therefore, he must needs love God above everything else. [8.7.10]

The one who loves, "knowingly or unknowingly,"[34]— as opposed to one who grasps possessively at other human beings in relationship—participates in the very activity that *is* God, for "God is love and the one who abides in love abides in God." It is, according to Augustine's description, impossible to love without such participation. The only other possibility of relationship with other human beings is that of *cupiditas*, the anxious desire to manipulate the "neighbor" into the position of supporting and reinforcing one's fantasies of sex, power, and possession. But: "Let a person love his brother, and he will love the same love, i.e. God-who-is-love" (8.8.12).

In all love that is not possessive, the "love by which one loves" is more immediately knowable to the loving person than is the person loved, because the person loved must necessarily be loved as she or he is seen, namely, "through a darkened mirror." It is, therefore, in one's activity of loving relationship that God becomes accessible, concrete, and "visible": "How, then, can he who does not love his brother whom he sees, love God, whom he does not see, since God is love, and this is wanting to him who does not love his brother" (8.8.12). This argument lays the foundation that Augustine will develop in later books of *De trinitate*, for the claim that in loving human relationships—admittedly a rarity in proportion to exploitive relationships and the inevitable aspect of possessiveness in all human relationship —God is directly experienced. Augustine emphasizes that only this kind of love preserves the consummate value of the neighbor; it is clearly possible to "desire" another human being too much, but it is not possible to love, in the proper sense of the word, too much: "Neither should we let this other question disturb us, how much love we ought to spend upon our brother, how much upon God. . . We love God and our neighbor from one and the same love" (8.8.12).[35]

---

34. Augustine *Soliloquiorum* 1.1; cf. Saint Thomas Aquinas *Summa theologica* 2a-2ae, 23,1: "Not every love has the quality of friendship. In the first place it is reserved to that love for another that wills his well-being. When what we will is not the other's good for his own sake, but the desire of it as it affects us, that is not friendship but self-regarding love, and some form of concupiscence."

35. "Ex una igitur eademque caritate Deum proximumque diligimus."

One further effect of Augustine's use of the visual ray theory of vision as a model for the vision of God should be noticed. The model of the visual ray, requiring exercise, strengthening, and training before it can touch its object, allows Augustine to balance—although not to integrate—two theological statements both of which he is committed to maintaining in full strength. On the one hand, Augustine fully affirms the exclusive prerogative of God to determine the course of a human life, the necessity of divine illumination, and of predestination to salvation. On the other hand, Augustine was acutely aware of the necessary effort involved in preparing oneself for participation in the love, service, and vision of God. Augustine's careful statement of the sine qua non of both God's grace and human effort appears in *De trinitate* 14.17.23:

> Whoever, then, is being renewed in the knowledge of God, and in justice and holiness of truth, by making progress day by day, transfers his love from temporal to eternal things, from visible to intelligible things, from carnal to spiritual things, and constantly endeavors to restrain and turn desire from the former and to align himself in love to the latter. He does so, however, to the extent that he receives divine help [*Tantum autem facit, quantum divinitus adiuvatur*].

The remaining task of this paper is to explore the relationship between physical and spiritual vision. Does physical vision act only as a metaphor for spiritual vision? We have already seen that physical and spiritual vision are contiguous,[36] but is there any sense in which they are continuous? Is there, for Augustine, any sense in which the training of the physical eye is useful for the training of spiritual vision? I think we must find that there is, and the remainder of the paper will attempt to unravel Augustine's claim that, on the one hand, the accurate "seeing" of visible objects irreducibly involves the exercise of spiritual vision, while, on the other hand, spiritual vision ultimately includes seeing with the eyes of the body.

The mechanics of physical vision, according to Augustine's analysis, require that the viewer exercise an essentially spiritual capacity. Because physical vision takes place "in the sense," that is, in the uniting of viewer and object in the connecting visual ray, there is irreducibly in physical vision "something spiritual, because it cannot take place without the soul." The will that energizes and focuses the visual ray is a spiritual energy. Therefore,

36. See note 4 above.

physical vision that fails to recognize the spiritual aspect of its own functioning fails also to "see" its object accurately in that it fails to take into account
an essential feature of the object—its life, that is, the spiritual quality that
informs or creates it.[37]

Augustine's description of the inference of the life of another human
being from the perception of the person's body is the paradigm for all perception of spiritual qualities in visible things; one never *sees* life or the soul, but
one learns to recognize this from one's self-knowledge (8.6.9):

> For we recognize the movement of bodies also from their resem-
> blance to ourselves, and from this fact we perceive that others live
> besides ourselves. . . . For even when a living body is moved, there
> is no way opened for our eyes to see the soul, a thing which can-
> not be seen with the eyes; but we notice that something is present
> within that bulk, such as is present in us, so that we are able to
> move our bulk in a similar way, and this is the life and the soul.

The perception of visible objects "in their life" is the perception of these
objects as created, implying, requiring, and pointing to their creator. The natural world, like other human beings, can only be accurately perceived when
they are contemplated in such a way that they give evidence that "God made
us." "My question," Augustine wrote in the *Confessions*, "was in my contemplation of them, and their answer was in their beauty."[38] To the trained eye,
the contemplative eye, objects of the sensible world are direct evidence of the
beauty and goodness of the creator. Augustine describes the way in which this
evidence is gathered in a passage in *De trinitate* 8.3.4:

> Behold again, and see if you can. Certainly you do not love anything
> but good, because the earth is good by the height of its mountains,
> the moderate elevation of its hills, and the flat surface of its fields;
> and good is the farm that is pleasant and fertile; and good is the
> house that is arranged throughout in symmetrical proportions and
> is spacious and bright; and good are the animals, animate bodies;
> and good is the mild and salubrious air; and good is the food that
> is pleasant and conducive to health; and good is health without
> pains and weariness; and good is the countenance of a person with
> regular features, a cheerful expression, and a glowing color; and

---

37. Cf. Goethe, quoted in Friedländer, *Plato*, 1:21: "The eyes of the mind must constantly cooperate with the eyes of the body in a loving bond, because otherwise there is a
danger that we will see and still miss seeing."

38. Augustine *Confessiones* 10.6.9.

good is the soul of a friend with the sweetness of concord and the fidelity of love; and good is the just man; and good are riches because they readily assist us; and good is the heaven with its own sun, moon and stars; and good are the angels by their holy obedience; and good is the lesson that graciously instructs and suitably arouses the listener; and good is the poem with its harmonious rhythm and the seriousness of its thoughts.

But why should I add still more? This good and that good; take away this and that, and see good itself if you can; *thus you will see God* who is good not by another good, but is *the good of every good*. . . . Thus, God is to be loved, not as this or that good, but as good itself. For the good of the soul that is sought is not that over which one flees by judging, but that to which one adheres by loving, and what is this but God? [Emphasis mine]

To look with the trained eye more deeply into visible things, and not to be preoccupied with possessing them, however, is a difficult and slippery task: "Let no one wonder, then, that we labor to see anything at all, even in this manner of seeing, which has been granted this life, namely through a mirror in an enigma. For the word enigma would not be used here if this seeing were something easy" (15.9.16). One can easily slide either into devaluation of these objects, which effectively if implicitly "scorns the Creator," or into fascination with their surface beauty, and "to love this is to be estranged."[39]

Since the integration of physical and spiritual vision is such a difficult venture, visible objects—the beauty of creation (15.2.3), and especially other human beings—are also "seen" in their life only in what must be described as glimpses or glances, *per speculum in aenigmate*. But it is the glance that provides the stimulus for longing and the training that prepares human beings for the full enjoyment of one another is continuous with the training for the full vision of God (8.6.9, 7.8.12). The present activity of loving other persons and the present training of the eye of the mind for the vision of God are an identical activity: "If, however, he loved his brother whom he sees by human sight by a spiritual love, he would see God, who is love itself, with that inner sight by which God can be seen" (8.8.12). Likewise, the full enjoyment of other persons and the full vision of God are understood by Augustine

---

39. Augustine is careful to explain this statement in the *Retractiones* 2.15 so that he cannot be interpreted as denigrating physical objects. His statement of method is in 12.5.5: "Assuescat in corporalibus ita spiritualium reperire vestigia, ut cum inde sursum versus duce ratione ascendere coeperit, ut ad ipsam incommutabilem veritatem per quam sunt facta ista perveniat. . . ."

as interwoven: "Now this is our highest reward that we should fully enjoy God, and that all who enjoy God should enjoy one another in him."[40] The continuity of physical and spiritual vision is frequently and strongly affirmed by Augustine.

But Augustine will go further to claim that spiritual and physical vision will be, in the fulfillment of the resurrection, not only continuous but identical. Predictably, his description of the role of the "eyes of the body" in the resurrection lacks clarity and is admittedly speculative.[41] But the claims made by Augustine are important for our purposes, that is, for understanding the significance of physical vision in Augustine's thought and teaching. As always in the study of Augustine, one needs to look to his description of human perfection and fulfillment in order accurately to grasp his analysis of the present human condition. In the last chapters of *De civitate Dei*, Augustine affirms a settled integration of physical and spiritual vision in the resurrection in which the vision of God will "possibly and indeed most probably" be with the eyes of the body. With an "extraordinary power of sight," Augustine says, the blessed will be able "to see the immaterial."[42] A long development of Augustine's idea of the question of whether the eyes of the body will see God[43] culminates in this passage, his final word on the subject. The significance of his claim is attested by Augustine's admission that there are no scriptural warrants for his idea. But, even though it is difficult, if not impossible, to support his idea from Scripture,

> it is possible, indeed most probable, that we shall then see the physical bodies of the new heaven and the new earth in such fashion as to observe God in utter clarity and distinctness, seeing him present everywhere and governing the whole material scheme of things by means of the bodies we shall then inhabit and the bodies we shall see whenever we turn our eyes.[44]

Moreover, in the resurrection vision of God, the glimpse of the present time will be fulfilled by a gaze that is "face to face." This gaze, the settled

---

40. Augustine *De doctrina christiana* 1.32.35.

41. Augustine *De civitate Dei* 22.21.

42. Ibid., 22.29.

43. See my *Augustine on the Body*, 110–11.

44. Augustine *De civitate Dei* 22.29: "Quam ob rem fieri potest valdeque credibile est sic nos visuros mundana tunc corpora caeli novi et terrae novae, ut Deum ubique praesentem et universa etiam corporalia gubernantem, per corpora quae gestabimus et quae conspiciemus quaqua versum oculos duxerimus, clarissima perspecuitate videamus."

touch of the visual ray of the eye of the mind, will so powerfully inform the soul that the human mind, heretofore an imperfect, but progressing, image of God will be perfected "by the vision itself": "But the image which is being renewed day by day in the spirit of the mind and in the knowledge of God . . . will be perfected by the very vision which will then be . . . face to face, but it is making progress towards it now through a mirror in an enigma" (14.19.25). The present glimpse gives human beings an appetite (*appetitus*) for the time-less gaze (15.26.45);[45] the same longing "which had been its desire in seek-ing, now becomes its love in enjoying" (15.26.47).[46] In the resurrection, the enjoyment of God will take the form of contemplation, the satisfaction of longing, the permanent embrace of the visual ray of the eye of the mind. "We shall see the truth there without any difficulty and shall enjoy it to the full since it is most clear and most certain. Nor shall we seek anything by the reasoning of the mind, but by contemplating we shall perceive. . . . In that light there shall no longer be any inquiry" (15.25.45).

The full significance of Augustine's teaching on the vision of God can only be recognized when we have examined the model he used to understand and describe spiritual vision. The visual ray of the physical eye that unites the soul to the objects of its habitual attention provided Augustine with a powerful description of the vision of God, a coordination of physics and metaphysics that grounded his "vision" of the process and goal of life.

45. "Imago vero quae renovatur in spiritu mentis in agitione Dei, non exterius, sed in-terius de die in diem, ipsa perficietur visione, quae tunc erit post judicium facie ad faciem, nunc autem proficit per speculum in aenigmate."

46. "Voluntas . . . qui fuerat appetitus quaerentis, sit amor fruentis."

PART III

Augustine's Successors

CHAPTER 13

A Sea of Love: Marguerite Porete's
A Mirror for Simple Souls

Marguerite Porete's devotional book *A Mirror for Simple Souls* provides an example of the fruitfulness of paying attention to a book deemed heretical by ecclesiastical authorities in its own time. On June 1, 1310, Porete was burned as a heretic at the Place de Grève in Paris. A decade before, her book had been condemned as containing fifteen erroneous theological beliefs. Porete was fully aware that her book might be misunderstood. Before its publication she had sent it to three theologians for their approval—a Franciscan friar, a Cistercian monk, and a lay theologian. None of them found fault with the manuscript, though the theologian advised that its readership be limited to those advanced in the spiritual life. Its powerful advocacy for mysticism might, he felt, make that path seem the only viable spiritual life. At her trial Porete, confident of the legitimacy of her writings, refused either to negotiate with authorities or further explain her teachings.

Despite the condemnation by what Porete called the "Little Church," the book had a life of its own. Circulating as an anonymous devotional text in the centuries following her death, it was widely recognized and treasured by adepts of Christian spirituality. Five medieval translations—two in Latin, two in Italian and one in English—of the original Middle French attest to its popularity. The book was not reconnected with its author until 1946 when the Italian scholar Romana Guarnieri identified it as Porete's work.

Historian Peter Dronke has called Porete "the most neglected of the great writers of the 13th century."[1] Her social and religious context was the passionate and volatile lay religiosity of late medieval northern Europe. Though suspect to church leaders, vernacular treatises on Christian devotion and

1. Dronke, *Women Writers*, 202.

mysticism were fascinating to a broad popular audience—they were the best sellers of their time. Porete's particular ambiance was the groups of laywomen known as "beguines" who banded together to live lives of poverty, chastity, manual labor, charitable service, and worship. These groups were active in northern Europe, France, the low countries, the Rhineland, and Switzerland. Without vows, organization, officials, wealthy founders or leaders, beguine associations were a "new and attractive alternative" to the cloistered life, notes historian Caroline Walker Bynum.[2] Beguines were drawn largely from the new bourgeoisie and lower nobility of late medieval towns.

The line between heresy and orthodox religious intensity had never been less clearly defined than in these groups of laywomen and men. On the radical edge of the spectrum were the so-called "Free Spirits" whose claims to immediate and permanent union with God supported their assertions of freedom from both ecclesiastical and civic laws. At one time or another, most mystics of this period were forced to defend themselves against accusations of association with Free Spirit teachings, among them Jan van Ruysbroeck, Heinrich Suso, and Meister Eckhart. For some mystics, priesthood or affiliation with a monastery often—though not invariably—supplied authorization and legitimation. Porete had neither ecclesiastical office nor monastic affiliation to protect her, and some of her claims for divinization and for freedom from liturgical duties and devotional practices seemed to her accusers and judges identical to those of the Free Spirits.

The late medieval interest in *A Mirror for Simple Souls* was based neither on the recognized authority of its author nor on the book's validation by the Catholic Church. Rather, its powerful attraction was founded on its spiritual insights and on the strength and beauty of its vivid language. An example:

> [The simple soul] swims in the sea of joy—that is, in the sea of delights flowing and streaming down from the godhead. She feels no joy, for she herself is joy, and swims and floats in joy without feeling any joy, for she inhabits joy and joy inhabits her.[3]

The text testifies to a mystical ecstasy that was difficult to attain. It also reconceptualizes theological knowledge itself, placing at its center the overwhelming, mind-boggling experience of God as love; her purpose in the work, Porete writes, was "to show the way love works." The experience of God as love, she asserts, is foundational to theological understanding.

2. Bynum, "Religious Women," 126.

3. See the bibliography entry for Porete for information on the Latin, French, and English versions of Porete's writings.

The book's theology is systematic; it is both comprehensive and graded or mapped. Though not founded on discursive reason, it employs the tools of reason to demonstrate the route to God. Repeatedly, however, Porete cautions against attempting to understand her theology with the head alone, without a corresponding change of life:

> I beg you, those who read these words, try to understand them inwardly, in the innermost depths of your understanding, with all the subtle powers at your command, or else you run the risk of failing to understand them at all.

Although they are peppered throughout the book, these admonitions fell largely on deaf ears in Porete's own time, as did her caution that "the same word can have different meanings." Her doctrine of mystical annihilation, expressed so vividly in water metaphors—especially the metaphor of drowning—emphasizes that absorption in God can replace an intentional practice of virtue. She contrasts the "slavery" that results from founding one's spiritual life on "reason and fear" with the effortless spontaneity that comes from acting out of love.

The "perfect soul" experiences herself as "less than nothing" and simultaneously sees "not herself in God, but God in herself." The freedom of the perfect soul depends entirely on a state of nonwilling or "deadness to the world" in which God's will replaces human will and "you bathe in the flood waters of God's love." In this state "she needs no masses or sermons or fastings or prayers," and all desires, "even holy desires," are suspended: "Everything she has is from God, and she is what God is, and was, and what she was before God made her, in union with him."

Porete's description of the experience of God's love suggests the inadequacy of religious training based "book learning." Destabilizing habits and dissolving securities is, she argues, fundamental to "knowing nothing, being able to do nothing by herself, and willing nothing"—requirements for experiencing "the nothingness [that] brings her everything." She testifies to a quality of life that cannot be described in the language of reason. The language of love is allusive and easily misinterpreted: "What Love says can only be said in condensed images":

> Being completely free, and in command on her sea of peace, the soul is nonetheless drowned and loses herself through God, and with him and in him. She loses her identity, as does the water from a river . . . when it flows into the sea. It has done its work and can relax in the arms of the sea, and the same is true of the soul. Her

work is over and she can lose herself in what she has become: Love. Love is the bridegroom of her happiness enveloping her wholly in his love and making her part of that which is. This is a wonder to her and she has become a wonder. Love is her only delight and pleasure.

In addition to its positive agenda—a theology of love—Porete's book presents two critiques, at least one of which proved fatal to her. She questions the validity of relying on reason alone for theological knowledge, and she criticizes the institutionalization and routinization of religion in the church. Reason, she writes, is "stupid and blind"; it has ears and cannot hear. Reason looks for God "in creatures and in nature, striving to find him with [the] senses." What is inadequate is the method, not the visible objects.

> People who look for God in hills and woods and valleys see him as bound by his sacraments and works, and are silent and miserable for not finding him. But those who find him everywhere, not just in forests and mountaintops, through uniting their will to his, have a happy and enjoyable life.

The problem with reason is twofold: it is too laborious—too "deliberate and complex"—to provide a fluent vehicle for the Spirit, and its self-conscious operation actually stands in the way of the "inner impulse to love." People "become so wrapped up in conscious reasoning that they cannot hear the spirit when it prompts them." In short, those whose religion is based on reason try to "do everything by [their] own efforts."

Porete accused the church of following the "law" of reason rather than that of love. She contrasted the "lesser Church," ruled by reason and populated by reason's "insect-brained followers," with the "greater Church," populated by perfect souls ruled by love. The interrelatedness of Porete's two critiques is evident in her description of the shortsightedness of the lesser church, reliant on book learning and the hard work of practicing the virtues.

Porete's claims are dramatic. They are stated, moreover, in language that seems designed to shock and provoke. They must, however, be "carefully" understood. For example, although the perfect soul bids "good-bye to the virtues," because of her attunement with God's will, she nevertheless "has more virtues than anybody else." Porete's language must also be understood as a reaction to and compensation for her lack of social and institutional power. The same words, as she pointed out, can have different meanings; triumphal language means different things depending on whether it is ut-tered by the spokesmen of powerful institutions or by the politically and socially powerless. Moreover, Porete's language of mystical experience was particularly threatening to church leaders, who recognized the Free Spirit movement's subversive potential.

• • •

Why should we consider Porete's book a Christian classic? What can a book with such countercultural concepts as the annihilation of the self offer to Christians in the final decade of the twentieth century? Consider first several of the book's more obvious contributions.

As the product of a particular historical situation, the book has conspicuous value: Dronke has called it "a text of fundamental importance in relation to the movement . . . known as the 'Free Spirit.'" It is also valuable as a literary document; its lyrical poetry, occurring at climactic moments of prose narration, make it, according to Kurt Ruh, "a religious testimony of incomparable originality." Moreover, its theological insights elevate it to classic status: Porete's systematic critique of reason as the primary access to knowledge of God challenges academic theology of her time and of ours. Her understanding of a *via negativa* in which "all knowing leads to loss of understanding" is consonant with Eastern Orthodox theology. She also anticipates by two centuries Martin Luther's emphasis on salvation by faith alone. And her insistence on personal appropriation of Christ's death on the cross ("You have undergone all your sufferings just for me alone! All this, just for me!") anticipates the devotional passion of eighteenth-century Pietism.

There are, however, other reasons to consider the book a classic. Porete should be heard in the twentieth century because, while she represented in her own time a marginalized and alternative form of Christianity, she may also have been, despite the judgment of her contemporaries, a profound orthodox thinker. Porete's orthodoxy could be argued either by demonstrating the similarity of her spirituality to that of orthodox contemporaries, or—anachronistically—by comparing her theology to that of later Protestant theologians. On the other hand, her teachings do contain the claims to divinization of which she was accused, and her insistence on the freedom of the "perfect soul" certainly could suggest to a careless reader that virtues and pious practices were expendable. However, Porete's orthodoxy—or heresy, for that matter—are not the most significant aspect of her work for us.

For twentieth-century Christians, familiarity with a history that includes the diversity of Christian identities can help us acknowledge and support our own diversity. Historical theologians have often contributed to a narrow sense of Christian identity by presenting a past that consists solely of the orthodox and the heretics, rather than multiple—and continuously contested—interpretations of Christian ideas and practices. Martin Luther, John Calvin, Huldreich Zwingli and other reformers criticized the beliefs and practices of Catholic Christianity far more drastically than did Porete. Yet we recognize the religious genius of authors whose insights are subsequently institutionalized; the "heretics" of the sixteenth century were the founders of alternative Christianities.

Porete's book helps us reconstruct a more inclusive history of Christianity, a history that includes individuals and groups that have insistently identified themselves as Christians even when they were condemned by the church. Heterodox views represent not merely alternative interpretations of faith and practice but corrections of mainstream or orthodox views.

In their strongest moments, Christian churches have been attentive to internal criticism, recognizing critique as crucial to the process of responsiveness and self-correction that maintains the church's life. The church of Porete's time—the "lesser church"—revealed its weakness by its use of force to exterminate threatening criticisms.

Finally, it is Porete's passionate spirituality that argues most strongly for including her volume among Christian classics. The book evokes a profound religious experience that perennially eludes the church's best efforts to reproduce it through teaching, worship, or piety. She describes union with God as more like relaxing than intensified labor, more like floating than determined effort. She taught that the experience of God's love does not supersede but simultaneously incorporates and transcends virtues and practices. If the soul, at the "highest stage of her perfection," is "beyond noticing the rules of the church," "beyond the works of virtue," and immune to feelings, it is because "she has assimilated [each of these] to the point where they are part of her and obey her intrinsically."

Instead of a spirituality that elects either the path of intellect or the path of feeling, Porete advocates spirituality that incorporates all human functions and attributes. The resulting religious identity is not simply the sum of its human parts. Nor is it predicated upon the idiosyncrasies of a person's historical and social location. Rather, it is rooted in "what she was before God made her, in union with him." God alone guarantees the existence and identity of the Christian and "she swims in the sea of God's love."

CHAPTER 14

The Mystical Method of Meister Eckhart

Meister Eckhart, fourteenth-century mystic, teacher, and Dominican priest, was considered in his own time to be very difficult to understand both by the "folks" to whom he preached and by the theological authorities of the Catholic Church.

> Someone complained to Meister Eckhardt that no one could understand his sermons. Whereupon he said: "To understand my preaching, five things are needed. The hearer must have conquered strife; he must be contemplating his highest good; he must be satisfied to do God's bidding; he must be a beginner among beginners; and, denying himself, he must be so a master of himself as to be incapable of anger."[1]

Apparently Eckhart's clues to understanding his sermons were not greatly helpful; he was misunderstood—or understood correctly and rejected—by the theological authorities of his time. On 27 March 1329, a bull of Pope John XXII declared that Eckhart, deceived "by the father of lies who often appears as an angel of light," had sown "thorns and thistles amongst the faithful and even the simple folk." Since the fourteenth century, scholars have attempted to understand and analyze Eckhart's ideas; the amazing richness and beauty of his description of self-knowledge and knowledge of God makes study of Eckhart delightful and fruitful for the aphorisms it yields. Yet puzzling inconsistencies and contradictions remain when one tries to demonstrate the unity of Eckhart's ideas.

Part of the difficulty of understanding Meister Eckhart is attributable to the necessarily esoteric nature of the normative experience of the union

---

1. Translations are from Blakney, *Meister Eckhart*, 93.

of God and the soul that he describes. But a second reason for this difficulty is that many of his instructions and descriptions seem to be in direct
contradiction. From some of his writings we gather that the body, intellect,
and "works" are to be totally rejected; in others, all these aspects or activities
of human being seem to be affirmed. It is only, I think, when we examine
Meister Eckhart's teaching as a *method* of mystical apprehension of God and
self, a process that begins with a particular understanding or world view and
moves from that fundamental understanding, through a discursive process,
to a corrected understanding of the self, the world, and God, that we can see
the unity of Eckhart's thought.

The understanding—at the same time an experience—from which
Eckhart begins is that of a separation between God and the soul. Western
Christian thinkers since Augustine had placed emphasis on the essential separateness of Creator and creature, rejecting the deification talk of the Eastern
Church. Eckhart had been thoroughly initiated in this experience of painful
separateness; his mystical method is the result of his longing to overcome this
separation and to discover a sense—a place—in which an experience of union
replaces the original experience of disjunction. Rather than simply describing
the experience of union, though, Eckhart has taken the trouble to take apart,
or describe discursively, the method by which the Christian can arrive at a
union "more intimate with him than a drop of water put into a vat of wine,
for that would still be water and wine; but here one is changed into the other
so that no creature could ever again detect a difference between them."[2]

This language was highly alarming to Eckhart's contemporaries, and it
may suggest to us an inflation or megalomania if we are not careful to place
the talk about union with God precisely at the stage of Eckhart's method
at which he placed it. But before we begin to explore Eckhart's method, we
should ask two preliminary questions: first, why does Eckhart advocate the
actualizing of union with God? Because, he writes in the *Aristocrat*, "the seed
of God is in us,"—a capacity is a need. The union with God is implicit in
human beings and forms the core of human being: "Creatures receive their
being directly from God and that is why, in their true essence, creatures love
God more than they love themselves."[3]

Why, then, is the union not actualized more frequently by human beings, if it is, in fact, the most central aspect of human being? Because "so

2. *Talks of Instruction*, 20.
3. *Sermon* 25, "Get beyond time."

much is required to that end. The principle requirement is that one shall get beyond phenomenal nature and in this process he begins soon to be weary."[4] The "weariness" that comes from the attempt to "get beyond" the limitations of one's conditioned customary consciousness results in an uneven development of the soul's "two eyes"; one of these eyes looks inward and the other outward. "It is the inner eye of the soul that looks into essence and takes its being directly from God." This eye is slenderly developed. The developed outward eye, the eye that is directed toward the external world is, on the other hand, highly trained and minutely developed. The undeveloped muscles of the inner eye fatigue quickly when this eye is used. Not everyone will withstand the effort and discomfort of developing the inner eye.

Secondly, given this condition of the arrested development of the inner eye, we must ask where the impetus and the energy come from for those who do set out to actualize the implicit "seed of God." Eckhart's answer is that God's love attracts and draws the soul to itself. The love of God is itself the grace whose function is to "transform and reconvey the soul to God." The activity of grace translates the love of God into the experience of the individual: "Grace is not a stationary thing; it is always found in a becoming."[5] The powerful drawing activity of God's love is described by Eckhart in the metaphor of the fishhook:

> . . . God lies in wait for us with nothing so much as love. Love is like a fisherman's hook. Without the hook he could never catch a fish, but once the hook is taken the fisherman is sure of the fish. Even though the fish twists hither and yon, still the fisherman is sure of him. And so, too, I speak of love: he who is caught by it is held by the sweetest of bonds and yet the stress is pleasant. He who takes this sweet burden on himself gets further, and comes nearer to what he aims at than he would by means of any harsh ordinance ever devised by man. Moreover, he can sweetly bear all that happens to him; all that God inflicts he can take cheerfully. Nothing makes you God's own, or God yours, as much as this sweet bond. When one has found this way, he looks for no other. To hang on this hook is to be so completely captured that feet and hands, and mouth and eyes, the heart, and all a person is and has, become God's own.[6]

4. Ibid.
5. Fragment 12.
6. *Sermon* 4, "Eternal birth."

Let us begin, then, to unravel Eckhart's method for the transcending of separateness in the mystical experience. His method is one of methodically stripping oneself of everything that protects or conceals that "core of the soul," and that makes inaccessible to a person's experience and knowledge this "void" that God is "obliged" to fill when a human being has stripped himself of everything that is not this "place." Moving from the "outer" to the "inner," Eckhart says: "begin, therefore, with yourself, and forget yourself."[7] But: "the truth is that the more ourselves we are, the less self there is in us."[8] "Self" is used ambiguously: how are we both to "begin with" and "forget" ourselves? And how can we be "more ourselves" by having "less self?" Surely this language is used for the purpose of provoking, of stopping, the ordinary intellectual process by which we think we have understood a concept when we understand the meaning of all the words used to express that concept. What is the "self" that is being rejected, and what is the "self" that we need more of?

We must notice, first of all, that Eckhart's definition of "inner" and "outer" do not correspond to soul and body. Eckhart includes in the definition of "outer" every aspect of human being which is determined and ordered by the accidents of one's birth and social conditioning.[9] The "inner," although the tiniest "kernel" of human being, is the only aspect of human being that is untouched by the conditions of a particular life with all its inevitable idiosyncrasies. The first aspect of the self to be "forgotten" is the socially conditioned and programmed phenomenal self. The self that is constituted by the accidents of birth in a particular time and place and by one's formative experiences—as well as the self that participates in a social consensus of values—is not the self that can experience God. The phenomenal self is rather a defense from the "simple stillness" of the core of the soul, a "covering" that conceals the very existence of this core. "Feeling" is a part of this socially-conditioned phenomenal self and should be understood as such so that we do not take it with inappropriate seriousness. "Attach significance, not to what you feel like, but rather to what you are to receive . . ."[10] It is, Eckhart says, an enormous mistake to identify with the aspect of the self that feels, and to require a strong emotion as a vindication of one's "condition."

7. *Talks*, 3.

8. *Talks*, 11.

9. *The Aristocrat*.

10. *Talks*, 20.

Likewise, "practices" are to be rejected as part of the phenomenal self.

> Any devotion to any practice that limits your freedom to wait
> upon God in this present moment and to follow him into the
> light, by which he may show you what to do and what not to
> do—how to be as new and free with each moment as if you had
> never had—or wanted, or could have another—any such commit-
> ment or premeditated practice which limits your freedom, I call
> voluntary bondage.[11]

Even ritual is a "practice" of the outer self: "To seek God by ritual is to get the
ritual and lose God in the process."[12] This advice must have sounded quite
startling and dangerous to Eckhart's contemporaries, both those within his
order and lay people.

Secondly, and still moving from "outer" to "inner," the body must be
"forgotten." The soul must, Eckhart tells us, "break away from the body and
seek God." Since the body stores the soul's conditioned agendas, ascetic practices are sometimes useful in that they are instrumental in releasing the soul
from its own conditionedness as this limitation is faithfully and accurately
reflected in the body:

> The whole of a life of penitence is only one among a number of
> things such as fasting, watching, praying, kneeling, being disci-
> plined, wearing hair shirts, lying on hard surfaces, and so on. They
> were all devised because of the constant opposition of the body
> and flesh to the spirit. The body is too strong for the spirit and so
> there is always a struggle between them . . . The body is bold and
> brave here, for it is at home and the world helps it. The earth is
> its fatherland and all its kindred are on its side: food, drink, and
> comforts are all against the spirit. Here the spirit is alien. Its race
> and kin are all in heaven. It has many friends there. They assist the
> spirit in its distress, to weaken the flesh for its part in the struggle
> so that it cannot conquer the spirit, penances are put upon the
> flesh like a bridle to curb it, so that the spirit may control it. This
> is done to bring it to subjection, but if you wish to make it a thou-
> sand times more subject, put the bridle of love on it.[13]

The trouble with the body, then, is its habituation to the material world with
its comforts and pleasures, an habituation that "outweighs" the soul's longing

11. *Sermon* 24, "God enters a free soul."
12. *Sermon* 5, "The love of God."
13. *Sermon* 4.

to experience its proper home, "heaven." Eckhart is not careful to distinguish, at this point, between "flesh," the aspect of human being under sin, and "body," the good creation of God. This is because he is referring precisely to the aspect of body that serves "flesh" and thus participates in the addiction that attempts to compensate increments of deadness.

Thirdly, both will and knowledge are included in the acitivity of the soul that Eckhart calls "the soul's agents." The "agents" or activity of the soul operate in two directions: in external activity and in ideation. External activity, the result of the will, is rejected as one moves toward the "inner": "There is no way of making a person real unless he gives up his own will. In fact, apart from complete surrender of the will, there is no traffic with God."[14]

> As long as a person keeps his own will and thinks it his will to fulfill the all-loving will of God, he has not that poverty of which we were talking, for this person has a will with which he wants to satisfy the will of God, and that is not right. For if one wants to be truly poor, he must be as free from his creature will as when he had not yet been born.[15]

The mechanics of the soul's investment in external activity are described by Eckhart:

> If the soul goes out to attend to external activities, it will necessarily be the weaker in its inward efforts and for this birth in the soul God will and must have a pure, free, and unencumbered soul, in which there is nothing but him alone, a soul that waits for nothing and nobody but him.[16]

But a similar outflowing of the soul's energies is required for ideation, which Eckhart defines as the construction of ideas "by abstraction from external things through the senses":

> When the agents of the soul contact creatures, they take and make ideas and likenesses of them and bear them back again into the self. It is by means of these ideas that the soul knows about external creatures. Creatures cannot approach the soul except in this way, and the soul cannot get at creatures, except, on its own initiative, it first conceive ideas of them. Thus the soul gets at things by means of ideas and the idea is an entity created by the soul's agents. Be it

14. *Talks*, 11.

15. *Sermon* 28, "Blessed are the poor."

16. Ibid.

a stone, or a rose, or a person, or whatever it is that is to be known, first an idea is taken and then absorbed, and in this way the soul connects with the phenomenal world.[17]

Since, then, the soul gets all its ideas "in from outside, through the senses," and in itself is "free, innocent of all instrumentalities and ideas," the soul can have no self-knowledge: "Of nothing does the soul know so little as it knows of itself, for lack of means . . . the soul knows about everything but itself."[18] It is precisely this condition of non-objectivity that makes it possible for the soul to receive God, who is also "pure, and without idea or likeness."

Finally, the part of human being that lies closest to the "inner" but which still belongs to the "outer" is the intellect. Yet the contiguity of intellect to the "core" of the soul does not automatically enable intellect to grasp the experience of God that happens in the core of the soul:

> Thus it is true that you cannot know God by means of any creature science nor by means of your own wisdom. If you are to know God divinely your own knowledge must become as pure ignorance, in which you forget yourself and every other creature.
>
> But perhaps you will say, "Alas, sir, what is the point of my mind existing if it is to be quite empty and without functioning? Is it best for me to screw up my courage to this unknown knowledge which cannot really be anything at all? For if I know anything in any way, I shall not be ignorant, nor would I be either empty or innocent. Is it my place to be in darkness?"
>
> Yes, truly. You could not do better than to go where it is dark, that is unknowing (*unwissen*).[19]

Three aspects of intellect inhibit knowledge of God. First, Eckhart in his sermon, "God enters a free soul," after saying that Jesus must necessarily be received by a virgin, defines a virgin as "a person who is free of irrelevant ideas, as free as he was before he existed." The journey to the interior stops at the point at which the intellect's attachment to the ideas it has constructed stop the movement to the "core." Also, intellect's claim to have insight into one's condition—to have constructed a "case history"—is an impediment. We have said that, in the strict sense, no self-knowledge is possible, but there is a knowledge of "self that is necessarily preliminary to knowledge of God:

17. *Sermon* 1, "This is Meister Eckhart from whom God hid nothing."

18. Ibid.

19. *Sermon* 4.

> To get at the core of God at his greatest, one must first get into the core of himself at his least, for no one can know God who has not first known himself. Go to the depths of the soul, the secret place of the Most High, to the roots, to the heights; for all that God can do is focused there.[20]

Further, the movement from outer to inner involves the "forgetting" of the soul's most fundamental constructions of space, time, and self-consciousness: "As long as one clings to time, space, number, and quantity, he is on the wrong track and God is strange and far away."[21] And: "I am as sure as I am that I live and God lives, that if the soul is to know God it must know him above space and time . . ."[22]

> Further, I say that if the soul is to know God, it must forget itself and lose itself, for as long as it is self-aware and self-conscious, it will not see or be conscious of God. But when, for God's sake, it becomes unself-conscious, and *lets go of everything*, it finds itself again in God, for knowing God it therefore knows itself and everything else from which it has been cut asunder, in the divine perfection.[23]

It is only at *this* point of being stripped of "all phenomenal nature" that the "self" that takes its being from God is located and Eckhart can speak of the indistinguishability of God and the soul. This is the "self" that must gather energy and strength by diverting this energy from the phenomenal "self: "the more ourselves we are the less self there is in us."

At this point Eckhart has completed the description of the methodical divestiture of all impediments or "coverings" that obscure the "place" in the soul in which God may be known. Eckhart calls this place "a simple stillness,"[24] in which, in the "Now-moment," "the Father begets his only begotten son and in that birth the soul is born again." This event in the soul is only possible at the point at which the soul has achieved a stillness that is "more like God than anything in all creation."[25] When the soul's activities are stilled, a "void" is created that God is "obliged" to fill:

20. Fragment 37; see also *Sermon* 28.

21. *Sermon* 25.

22. *Sermon* 6, "the kingdom of God is at hand."

23. Ibid., italics mine; see also Fragment 39.

24. Fragment 39.

25. Fragment 29: "If a person withdraws into himself with all his powers, mental and

> Do not imagine that God is like a carpenter who works or not, just
> as he pleases, suiting his own convenience. It is not so with God,
> for when he finds you ready, he must act, and pour into you, just
> as when the air is clear and pure the sun must pour into it and may
> not hold back. . . . God may not leave anything empty or void.
> That is not God's nature. He could not bear it.[26]

At that instant the soul becomes a perfect void so that it is not thinking
even on God's goodness, wisdom, or power;[27] "even one single thought or
consideration will cover it up," because the spark or light that is God refuses
to "take precedence over the least and coarsest of my faculties, such as hearing or vision, or any other that can be influenced by heat or cold, hunger or
thirst."[28] The activity, then, in which the human person can "co-operate with
God," the "single act that remains to him (the person), justly and properly
his own . . . is, of course, to reduce the self to nothingness."[29] Even this act is
not entirely attributable to the human being; it is only "sufficiently perfect"
when God effects it.

> Such is the divine order of things, and when God finds this order
> in a soul he begets his Son, and the soul bursts into light with all
> its energy and from that energy, that light, there leaps a flame.
> That is love; and the soul, with all its energy, has penetrated to the
> divine order.[30]

Eckhart does not speak of deification, the realization of an implicit connection, but of union, the transcendence of distinctness. He insists, in the
Defense, that the union with God must be carefully interpreted in the same
awareness in which he describes it:

> All that has been said is false and ridiculous, according to the imag-
> ination of my opponents, but it is true according to the true mean-
> ing. . . . For in the sacrament on the altar the whole is changed into
> the whole, but it is not so in us. Whence it does not follow that
> we are God, as in Christ the firstborn man is God, begotten the

---

physical, he comes at last to a condition in which he has no ideas and no limitations and
in which he exists without activity of inner or outward life."

26. *Sermon* 4.
27. Fragment 28.
28. Fragment 39.
29. *Talks*, 23.
30. Fragment 30.

> idea and likeness of the Father-God, for we are after the idea and
> likeness, and created.[31]

Moreover, only at the point at which the soul is stripped to its core of being—without any attachment to its "phenomenal nature—does it participate
in the God who gives being: "contemplating the creature, God gives it being, and contemplating God, the creature receives its being."[32] This capacity
of the soul to receive being is the "place" of the birth of God in the soul.
When "God is born in the soul," the soul "bursts into light," and the union
is achieved of which Eckhart writes:

> Here the core of God is also my core; and the core of my soul the
> core of God's, and here I am independent as God himself is inde-
> pendent. Ah, beloved people, *why don't you let God be God in you?*
> . . . in this unity the Father begets his Son in the secret springs of
> your nature. [33]

In this union with God, "in the inmost core of the soul, where God begets his
Son (and) human nature also takes root,"[34] the soul is unified:

> When the soul so lives in its own secret place that it is the image of
> God, then it has true unity that no creature can divide . . . nothing
> can separate the soul from the image of God. This is true unity and
> true blessedness depends upon it.[35]

We will look further at the implications of this aspect of the union with God.
But we should notice first that as soon as one becomes aware of union with
God, it is over; the consciousness of oneself as experiencing is the consciousness of separation: "When a person is happy, happy to the core and root
of beatitude, he is no longer conscious of himself or anything else. He is
conscious only of God."[36]

The soul is organized into a unity in the same moment in which it
comes into union with God. Life is then spontaneously reorganized around
this normative center. The person has moved to the overcoming of the separ-

---

31. *Defense* IX, 39.

32. *Sermon* 25.

33. *Sermon* 5, italics mine.

34. Ibid.

35. Fragment 40.

36. Aristocrat; see also *Sermon* 26, "Like a morning star God shines": "I am happy only
by the fact that God can be known and that I can know him."

ateness of God and the soul by the methodical elimination of every aspect of the self that is not "the seed of God," but when the union is actualized, the unity of all aspects of the soul is an inevitable result. Now Eckhart moves to inclusions that are fully as dramatic as the exclusions he has specified at the earlier stage: "The person who has let go of things here on this lowest plane where all is mortal shall receive them again in God where they are truth."[37] What can now be gathered into the unified soul? Everything, Eckhart says:

> I am often asked if it is possible, within time, that a person should not be hindered either by multiplicity or by matter. Indeed it is. When this birth really happens no creature in all the world will stand in your way, and what is more, they will all point you to God and to this birth. . . . Indeed what was formerly a hindrance becomes now a help. Your face is turned so squarely toward it (the eternal birth), that whatever you see or hear, you get only the birth out of it. Everything stands for God and you see only God in all the world . . . if you are not looking for God and expecting him everywhere, and in everything, you lack the birth.[38]

First, and not —it is important to note—in order, because all inclusions occur simultaneously in the unified soul, the body can be gathered into the soul's unity. Eckhart's insistence on the full participation of the body in the union is very explicit: ". . . our hearts and his are to be one heart; our body and his, one body. So it shall be with our senses, wills, thoughts, faculties, and members: they are all to be transported into him, so that we feel with him and are made aware of him in every part of the body and soul."[39] Eckhart says that the soul's care for the body should not be threatened even by the soul's absorption in the union with God. "Our Lord hides himself from time to time," he writes, "for the soul is an elemental form of the body, so that what once gains its attention holds it. If the soul were to know the goodness of God, as it is and without interruption, it would never turn away and therefore would never direct the body." The importance of the body is indicated by Eckhart's remark, "No soul can really do anything except through the body to which it is attached."[40] The ordering of the human being that occurs in the union with God changes the relation of soul and body: while

37. *Talks*, 20.
38. *Sermon* 4.
39. *Talks*, 20.
40. *Legends*, 4.

before the union the soul had been a tiny kernel or core in the body, after the union, the body is experienced as in the soul: "My body is more in my soul than my soul is in my body but both body and soul are more in God than they are in themselves and that is justice, righteousness, and the prime cause of everything."[41] Further, the body can be so thoroughly integrated in the unified soul that "The light in the soul's core overflows into the body, which becomes radiant with it."[42]

Secondly, "activities" can be gathered into the unity of the soul. The spontaneity of good works is the evidence that the birth of God in the soul has taken place so that a person is not still "doing his own work," but that "God is doing it":

> One may test the degree to which he has attained to virtue by observing how often one is inclined to act virtuously rather than otherwise. When one can do the works of virtue without preparing, by willing to do them, and bring to completion some great and righteous matter *without giving it a thought*—when the deed of virtue seems to happen by itself, simply because one loved goodness and for no other reason, then one is perfectly virtuous and not before.[43]

Thirdly, the intellect, freed from "irrelevant ideas" and the hegemony of its own "inventions," and integrated in the unified soul, can attain "pure, clear knowledge of divine truth."[44] It was not intellect itself, but the presumptuous hegemony of intellect, and intellect's claim to order human being, that Eckhart has rejected in the process of moving toward the union with God. Once the intellect has been integrated by the union with God, Eckhart makes very strong claims for its capacity: "Intellect is the temple of God and nowhere does he shine more holy than there . . . intelligence draws aside the veil and perceives God naked, stripped of goodness, or of being, or of any name."[45]

But there is also an aspect of "effort," "cultivation," and "watchful, honest, active oversight of all one's mental attitudes toward things and people"[46]

41. *Sermon 25.*

42. *Sermon 2.*

43. *Talks* 21, italics mine; see also *Sermon 1,* "This is Meister Eckhart from whom God hid nothing."

44. *Sermon 25.*

45. *Sermon 26.*

46. *Talks,* 6.

involved in overcoming conditioned activity and ideation. The understanding of God that the intellect receives in the union with God must be translated into the daily world of practical concerns:

> We ought to keep a free mind in all we do, but it is rare that an untrained person can do this, so that neither circumstances nor jobs bother him. It requires great diligence. Expert attention is necessary. . . .You may say: "But when a person has a job to do, he must give attention to it and thus concentrate on external things, for it takes an idea to make a job possible." And that is quite true, but the reference of ideas to things does not belong to the objective world as far as the spiritual person is concerned, for all things are to him simply channels of the divine and spiritual. And this viewpoint is possible only through discipline and the training of the intellect to the ways of God . . . [47]

This trained attitude in which "everything will taste like God and reflect him," is not to be achieved by "world-flight, running away from things, turning solitary and going apart from the world." Eckhart uses the metaphor of a person learning to write to describe the careful training and practice that is necessary in order to make easy and spontaneous what had at first required diligent effort:

> It is like learning to write. To acquire this art, one must practice much, however disagreeable or difficult it may be, however impossible it may seem. Practicing earnestly and often, one learns to write, acquires the art. To be sure, each letter must first be considered separately and accurately, reproduced over and over again; but once having acquired skill, one need not pay any attention to the reproduction of the letters or even think of them. He will write fluently and freely. . . . So a person should shine with the divine presence *without having to work at it.* . . . So one must be permeated with divine Presence, informed with the form of beloved God who is within him, so that he may radiate that presence *without working at it.*[48]

Finally, the intellect will achieve self-knowledge of a different order than that of the self-conscious "insight" that Eckhart has rejected on the way to the union with God. Even temptation and sin are, from the perspective of the unified soul, seen as useful: "Know that the impulse to wrong is never with-

---

47. *Talks*, 21.
48. *Talks*, 6, italics mine.

out use and benefit to the just person."[49] The struggle to overcome one's own destructive predilections is not the same as the struggle to "stop sinning," but it is the struggle to transform the "excitement" and energy of the "impulse to evil" into "the exercise of virtue": "The impulse to do wrong makes us more diligent in the exercise of virtue, driving us to it with a strong hand, like a hard taskmaster, forcing us to take shelter in doing well." The "evil urge" is seen as supplying energy that can then be used for good. There is no suggestion here of simply "repressing" evil urges or even "sins":

> If you have faults, then pray often to God to remove them from you, if that should please him, because you can't get rid of them yourself. If he does remove them, then thank him; but if he does not, then bear them for him, not thinking of them as faults or sins, but rather as great disciplines, and thus you shall merit reward and exercise your patience; but be satisfied whether he gives you what you want or not. For he does give to each according to what is best for him and what best fits the need. If a coat is to fit, it must be cut to measure, for what fits one will not fit another; each person must be measured if his coat is to fit.[50]

Only from the perspective of the unified soul can one begin to understand his faults and sins as spiritual discipline because they are the occasion of strengthened and renewed love for God, and therefore one can affirm even these apparently negative and destructive energies as fruitful:

> . . . once justly set in the will of God, a person will not wish that the sin he committed had never happened. To be sure, it was contrary to God, but by it he is committed to greater love, being abased and humbled because he did act contrary to the will of God. You may, however, fully trust God not to have put this sin upon you, except to bring out the best that is in you. . . . Thus, God bears the brunt of sin gladly and puts up with a lot of it . . . he causes people to sin when he foresees that by sinning they will move up to higher things. . . . New repentance makes new love and increases it.[51]

Eckhart's location of the "self," not in the activities that comprise a person's social existence, and not even in the structuring and ordering activities of intellect, but in the aspect of self that listens and speaks to God, was of major

---

49. *Talks*, 9.

50. *Talks*, 23.

51. *Talks*, 12.

importance as an influence on a new sense of the individual's responsibility and privilege of an absolute inner authority that would, two centuries after Eckhart, appear in Martin Luther. Meister Eckhart never described his teachings as parts of a method for achieving union with God and the unity of the soul in all its aspects and functions. But understanding his statements, gleaned from the contexts of sermons and treatises, in this light makes statements understandable and consistent, which on any other reading appear bewilderingly contradictory. Understanding Eckhart's teachings as a method also helps us to interpret accurately his statements about the transcending of distinction in the union of God and the soul, and makes understandable the puzzling statement: "The more ourselves we are the less self there is in us."

CHAPTER 15

"The Rope Breaks When it is Tightest": Luther on the Body, Consciousness, and the Word

Martin Luther's revolutionary insight concerning the location of the event of justification in the "bottom of the heart" contained, as is well known, some ancillary results toward the displacing of external activities—"works"—from a central position in the quest for salvation. One effect of his theology was a radical redistribution of weight in his anthropological understanding, a shifting of focus away from a person's active participation in liturgy and the sacraments, asceticism and good works, and toward the event of justification in the "consciousness," "depths of the heart," or "the inmost heart."[1] Moreover, a new understanding of the psychological situation in which the Gospel can operate involved Luther in new methods for preparing and reinforcing the justification event. This article will examine Luther's description of the psychological situation in which justification occurs; his

---

1. Luther's *sententia* has been read as *conscientia* by the Erlangen edition of the 1525 Latin text of the *Lectures on Jonah*, and has been translated accordingly "conscience" by Charles D. Froehlich in Luther's *Works* (= LW) 19. The 1526 German text of the *Lectures on Jonah* gives the word *Gewissen*, which is also translated as "conscience" by Martin H. Bertram (ibid.). I prefer to translate both the Latin and German words as "consciousness" in most contexts in this article. "Consciousness" is, in my judgment, more accurate in denoting Luther's meaning in contemporary usage. "Conscience" carries connotations that emphasize a socially conditioned sense of guilt, while "consciousness" designates a subjective activity in which thinking and feeling are coordinated in the construction of a world view and self-image that govern, in turn, the formation of one's perceptions, values, and behavior. Luther's description of the capacity of the justification event to constellate altered and more accurate reality-oriented values, perceptions, and emotions is better described by "consciousness" than by "conscience."

Throughout the article I have slightly altered quotations for the sake of gender inclusiveness.

revised anthropology, especially as it affected his view of the human body; his identification of the ear as the direct access to the "bottom of the heart"; and, finally, the consequences of Luther's anthropology for the understanding of asceticism, death, and the sacraments.

Luther's theological work, especially as it pertains to a revised anthropological understanding, is most fruitfully approached from a biographical angle. Luther himself gives this context for his idea of justification in his preface to the first volume of the Wittenberg edition of the *Collected Works* (1545). Already word oriented to a degree that frequently irritated his fellow monks—he sometimes confessed for six hours at a time—Luther described his obsession with the word "justice" in Rom 1:17:

> For I hated this word "the justice of God" which according to the use and custom of all the teachers I was taught to understand philosophically in terms of that so-called formal or active justice with which God is just and punishes the sinners and unrighteous.
>
> For however irreproachably I lived as a monk, I felt myself before God to be a sinner with a most disturbed conscience, nor could I be confident that I had pleased him with my satisfaction. I did not love, yes, rather I hated this righteous God who punishes sinners, and if not with blasphemy, certainly with huge murmurings I was angry with God, saying, "As though it really were not enough that miserable sinners should be eternally damned with original sin and have all kinds of calamities laid on them by the law of the Ten Commandments, God must go and add sorrow upon sorrow and even through the gospel itself bring justice and wrath to bear!" I raged in this way with a wildly aroused and disturbed conscience. . . . I thought about it day and night.[2]

The "wildly aroused and disturbed conscience" of the young Luther was exacerbated by monastic ascetic practices in which the body was harshly disciplined for the alleviation of spiritual distress. "If ever a monk got to heaven by monkery," Luther reports, "I can safely say I would have made it. All who were my fellows in the cloister will vouch for it that had I gone on so I should have killed myself with pious exercises."[3] This asceticism, a preoccupation with the heavy undertow of the recalcitrant body, appeared to Luther in retrospect as entirely useless.

2. Translation adapted from *Martin Luther: Selections*, 11.
3. Quoted in E. Simon, *Luther Alive*, 32.

Nevertheless, he came to the end of his rope ("the rope breaks when it is tightest")[4] and at last understood the word "justice"—the Word "justification by faith alone." This breakdown and breakthrough must have been hastened and intensified by his ascetic disciplines.

> At long last, God being merciful, as I thought about it night and day, I noticed the context of the words, namely, "The justice of God is revealed in it; as it is written, the just shall live by faith." Then and there I began to understand the justice of God as that by which the righteous man lives by the gift of God, namely, by faith. . . . This straightaway made me feel as though reborn and as though I had entered through open gates into Paradise itself. From then on the whole face of Scripture appeared different. I ran through the Scriptures then as memory served, and found that other words had the same meaning. . . . This passage in Paul was to me a real gate to Paradise.[5]

Consciousness and the Word

The personal experience of the young monk determined the reforming agenda of Luther's theological work. The Word, powerful in its capacity for the reorganization of consciousness and the reconstellation of values and perceptions, came to be the center of Luther's theology. Luther received his "key" to the understanding of Scripture and human life from this understanding. The justification consciousness was formulated by the activity of the Word of God that simultaneously exposed the moral bankruptcy of human effort and, to the terror that accompanies this recognition, speaks the salvific word.

Even Scripture becomes the "Word of God" only when it communicates both dimensions of awareness—the less-than-nothingness of one's efforts that are, in reality, nothing but the sublimest form of self-intending—and the saving efficacy of the Word. The Word of God is not a general communication; it is the word that confronts a particular individual in her/his life, the Word of God "for you."

The Word exposes the system of hideouts that the person has constructed as shelter from the awareness of her/his own helplessness. The pitiful and touching inadequacy of these hideouts, like the blankets under which a child huddles when it is afraid of the dark, can be recognized only in the presence

---

4. *Lectures on Jonah* 2:7 (*LW* 19.79).
5. *Preface to the Latin Writings*, in *Martin Luther: Selections*, 11.

of the confronting Word. Scripture, Luther demonstrates, again and again tells the story of the Word that simultaneously destroys the covering shelter and redeems with the "covering" of Christ's righteousness.

The story of Jonah provides one of Luther's most powerful expositions of this paradigm, which, he says, is the "key" to Scripture, the key without which we comprehend none of the meaning of Scripture. The story of Jonah, Luther remarks, is about "how powerful, active, and effective God's Word is. . . . Otherwise, it seems an insignificant story."[6] The story of Jonah is typical of the structure of scriptural designations of crises in which the protagonists, not knowing the outcome, were called to acts of faith for which the reward was unprepared and unguaranteed:

> Because we are only spectators of tragedies of this sort, they do not appear so great and so terrible to us as they really are. But if we were experiencing them ourselves in our consciousness, we would understand what it is to feel God's wrath against oneself and what that faith is which even in the middle of wrath holds on to God as merciful and kind.[7]

Real understanding of the story requires that the hearer supply from his/her own life an experience resembling the form of the story. Jonah's story, recounted by Luther, bears a striking resemblance to Luther's story, the universal story, as Luther understood it from within his own experience, of the simultaneity of despair and faith in the justification event. *Only* in this psychological condition does God act to redeem. Luther writes:

> At this point Jonah thought he was done for both in body and soul. It is as if he were saying: "All these things that You were doing to me were driving me to despair. Terrified by these signs of Your wrath I saw nothing except that I was done for, that I was hurled forth from Your presence." This is the common factor in indescribable groanings. This is the deepest sighing and the supreme death in temptation. These are not empty words, but the only people who can understand them are those who have at some time been in this kind of trouble. Such people will know what it is to feel their consciousness against them and to be truly thrown out by God.[8]

---

6. "Preface to the Prophet Jonah," *Lectures on Jonah* (Latin text; *LW* 19.4).

7. Ibid., 10.

8. Ibid., 18.

"All of this," Luther insists repetitiously, "takes place in the heart and the consciousness, where there is no work and where no work can enter."[9] It is a subjective crisis, and only in this crisis does God act:

> He is a God who looks into the depths and helps only the poor, despised, afflicted, miserable, forsaken, and those who are nothing; there a hearty love for Him is born. The heart overflows with gladness, and goes leaping and dancing for the great pleasure it has found in God.[10]

The psychological situation in which God will act to redeem is that of a highly intensified and concentrated experience of unbearable tension:

> It is impossible for nature to act or conduct itself contrary to what it feels. And now that it feels God's anger and punishment, it cannot view God otherwise than as an angry tyrant. Nature cannot surmount the obstacle posed by this wrath, it cannot subdue this feeling and make its way to God against God and pray to Him, while regarding Him its enemy. . . . The second lesson that we derive from this is that we must feel that our crying to God is of a nature that God will answer, . . . That means nothing else but to cry to God with the heart's true voice of faith; for the head cannot be comforted, nor can we raise our hands in prayer, until the heart is consoled. And as I have already said, the heart finds solace when it hastens to the angry God with the aid of the Holy Spirit and seeks mercy amid the wrath, lets God punish and at the same time dares to find comfort in His goodness. Take note what sharp eyes the heart must have, for it is surrounded by nothing but tokens of God's anger and punishment and yet beholds and feels no punishment and anger but only kindness and grace; that is, the heart must be so disposed that it does not want to see and feel punishment and anger, though in reality it does see and feel them, and it must be determined to see and feel grace and goodness, even though these are completely hidden from view. Oh, what a difficult task it is to come to God. Penetrating to Him through His wrath, His punishment, and His displeasure is like making your way through a wall of thorns, yes, through nothing but spears and swords. The crying of faith must feel in its heart that it is making contact with God.[11]

---

9. Ibid., 48 (German text).

10. "Introduction" to *Magnificat* (*LW* 21.300).

11. *Lectures on Jonah* 2:2 (LW 19.72–74).

Luther's Anthropology

The identification of consciousness as the location of the justification event resulted, in Luther's theological work, in a revised anthropology, an anthropology adopted for its capacity to support his focus on consciousness. Luther rejected the metaphysical nuances of medieval theological anthropology in order to formulate the primal situation of human being, the confrontation of Adam by God. Luther's interest in anthropology was strikingly different from that of classical and medieval theology in that he did not begin, as did classical theologians like Augustine, by insisting on the integrity and permanence of the human body as given in creation, modeled in the Incarnation, and consummated in the resurrection of the body. Nor was Luther theologically concerned with protecting the body and the sensible world from being swallowed by the stronger being of metaphysical realities as was Thomas Aquinas. Luther neglected to draw the careful articulations of earlier thinkers of the exact metaphysical status of the human body and its integration with the human personality because of his strong interest in a simplified anthropology that reinforced his interpretation of the justification event.[12] Theology was not, for Luther, primarily philosophically or metaphysically oriented; rather it was insistently existential.[13]

Three aspects of Luther's anthropology are important for our understanding of his innovative focus on consciousness. We will look briefly at his metaphysical and developmental anthropology, and their influence on his sacramental theology. In the *Magnificat*, Luther describes the Pauline anthropology of spirit, soul, and body, all of which, he says, may be "spirit or flesh." Spirit he describes as "the highest, deepest, and noblest part of human being.

---

12. It has been remarked by several modern expositors of Luther (among them Kerr, *Compend of Luther's Theology*, ix) that Luther's "positive theology" is "extremely simple," consisting of the "elaboration of a few simple themes." In spite of the long list of "subjects with which it is necessary to deal in the true Christian Church," in *An Exhortation to the Clergy Assembled at the Diet of Augsburg*, Luther himself did not follow his own program. Again and again he expounds the themes of law, sin, grace, and faith that comprise his idea of the consciousness in which simultaneously shelters melt and the "righteousness of God" as formulated in God's promise becomes the trustworthy shelter of the person.

13. See, e.g., Luther's accusation that Erasmus did not take seriously the debate concerning free will due to his feeling "no personal interest; he never has his heart in it and finds it wearisome, chilling, or nauseating, (thus) how can he help saying absurd, inept, and contradictory things all the time since he conducts the case like one drunk or asleep . . . theology requires such feeling as will make a person vigilant, penetrating, intent, astute, and determined." *On the Bondage of the Will*, 179.

. . . It is, in brief, the dwelling place of faith and the Word of God."[14] The soul coincides with the spirit in "nature," but differs in function, "giving life to the body and working through the body . . . The soul may live without the body, but the body has no life apart from the soul." The task of the body is "to carry out and apply that which the soul knows and the spirit believes."[15] It is important to notice Luther's use of "flesh" and his insistence that any of the "parts" of human being can be either flesh or spirit. In the Preface to the *Epistle to the Romans*, Luther says we must beware of a misleading distinction that would call "flesh" anything to do with outward practices and "spirit" anything to do with what is inward. He uses the term "flesh" as does Paul, for "everything that is born of the flesh," that is, the whole human being as oriented to the flesh:

> Thus you should learn to call "fleshly" whoever thinks, teaches, and talks a great deal about high spiritual matters, but without grace ("flesh") does not refer to unchastity, but to all sins, above all to unbelief, which is the most spiritual of all vices. . . . Thus "the flesh" is a person who lives and works, inwardly and outwardly, in the service of the flesh's profit and of this temporal life.[16]

Spirit, on the other hand, is the whole person as oriented to God and acting in the Spirit's grace. Flesh is, by definition, that aspect of human being which "is not able to believe the Word of God and entrust itself to God,"[17] while spirit "is the person who lives and works, inwardly and outwardly, in the service of the Spirit and the future life."[18] Spirit and flesh, in Luther's description, compete for possession of both soul and body. When the soul identifies with spirit, the body is integrated as the instrument of the Spirit of God that vivifies the human spirit. This part of the description is similar to that of earlier authors. But when Luther applies his metaphysical description in practical instruction, he does it in a way that no longer, as in medieval theology, understands the body as an access to the soul and spirit, through ascetic practices, but rather as *reflection* of what has taken place already in the spirit:

14. *Magnificat* (*LW* 21.303) on Luke 1:46.

15. Ibid., 303–4.

16. Translation from *Works of Martin Luther*, 6.453.

17. *Lectures on Jonah* 1:3 (Latin text; *LW* 19.8).

18. Preface, *Epistle to the Romans*, in *Works of Martin Luther* (Jacobs translation), 6.453.

> When this spirit that possesses the whole inheritance is preserved, both soul and body are able to remain without error and evil works. On the other hand, when the spirit is without faith, the soul together with the whole life cannot but fall into wickedness and error. . . . As a consequence of this error and false opinion of the soul, all the works of the body also become evil and damnable, even though a person killed himself with fasting and performed the works of all the saints. In order, therefore, . . . that we may become truly holy, it is necessary that God preserve, first, our spirit, and then our soul and body, not only from overt sins but much more from false and apparent good works.[19]

It is the spirit that must be ordered toward God: "If the law were for the body, it could be satisfied with works; but since it is spiritual, no one can satisfy it, unless all that you do is done from the bottom of the heart. But such a heart is given only by God's Spirit."[20]

The conflict of flesh and spirit for possession of the whole human being formulates, on the metaphysical level, the dynamics of the justification event. Luther's famous insistence that a Christian is *"simul justus et peccator"* is the result of his description of the experience of justification as normative for the Christian life. Throughout earthly life, the Christian will be aware of a psychic war between spirit and flesh for hegemony, a reenactment of the original impasse that provided the setting for justification.

Secondly, Luther's account of the process of the human race formulates strengthened versions of the human condition before and after the fall in order to present the dynamics of justification. His description of Adam's capacities before the fall emphasizes and heightens Adam's perfection for purposes of contrast with his postlapsarian condition:

> Therefore the image of God, according to which Adam was created, was something far more distinguished and excellent, since obviously no leprosy of sin adhered either to his reason or to his will. Both his inner and his outer sensations were all of the purest kind. His intellect was the clearest, his memory was the best, and his will was the most straightforward—all in the most beautiful tranquility of mind, without any fear of death and without any anxiety. To these inner qualities came also those most beautiful and superb qualities of body and of all the limbs, qualities in which he

19. *Magnificat* (*LW* 21.305–6) on Luke 1:46.

20. Preface, *Epistle to the Romans*, in *Works of Martin Luther* (Jacobs translation), 6.449.

surpassed all the remaining living creatures. I am fully convinced
that before Adam's sin his eyes were so sharp and clear that they
surpassed those of the lynx and the eagle. He was stronger than the
lions and the bears, whose strength is very great; and he handled
them the way we handle puppies.[21]

In order to demonstrate a marked contrast between this state and the
present state in which human beings are "corrupt in body and reason and
will," Luther is determined not to "minimize this evil which human nature
has contracted as a result of the sin of our first parents."[22] Only a strong description of the contrast between present human experience and the original
condition of perfect integration will reveal the deficit condition of present
experience and precipitate the "turn to Christ": "Let us emphasize it [evil].
Then we shall both regret deeply this state of ours and have a profound longing for Christ our Physician."[23]

The integrated anthropology of the prelapsarian condition, organized
around Adam's creation in the image of God in "moral substance or nature,"
was so radically lost by the first sin that human beings do not even have access
to knowledge of what it was:

> Therefore when we speak about that image, we are speaking about
> something unknown. Not only have we had no experience of it,
> but we continually experience the opposite; and so we hear noth-
> ing except bare words.[24]

Because of the nonexperiential character of the state of human perfection, the
longing for the fulfillment of human being in the resurrection—not of the
flesh, but of the body—is generated by faith in the promises of God:

> However, a right faith goes right on with its eyes closed; it clings
> to God's Word; it follows that Word; it believes the Word even
> when all creatures are against it, even if it should seem to the flesh
> that nothing is less likely to happen than what the Word wants

---

21. *Lectures on Genesis* 1:26 (*LW* 1.62).

22. Ibid., 143.

23. Ibid., 143–44.

24. Ibid., 63. See also 65: "Although we utter the words, who is there who could understand what it means to be in a life free from fear, without terrors and dangers, and to be
wise, upright, good, and free from all disasters, spiritual as well as physical?"

believed, and to happen even if heaven and earth should first seem to be destined to pass away.[25]

The Ear and the "Bottom of the Heart"

Denial that present experience is normative for human beings is a result of Luther's polarized description of the process of the human race. He expresses this denial of present experience in the juxtaposition of sight and hearing in the quotation above: "A right faith goes right on with its eyes closed; it clings to God's Word."[26] Far from being a casual formula, this identification of the ear as the most direct access to the "bottom of the heart" is a pivotal feature of Luther's theological anthropology. The importance of Luther's rejection of the medieval identification of the eye as the most intimate avenue to the heart cannot be overestimated. Augustine used a physics of spiritual vision that relied on a classical model of physical vision. This description of vision featured the activity of the viewer and his/her contact, in the act of vision, with the object of vision. The visual ray, a quasi-material beam, generated by a fire within the eye, was projected onto its object and created a two-way street along which the viewer's attention and affection attached to the object. The object, in turn, passed back along the visual ray to imprint itself on the psyche of the viewer.[27]

Luther's rejection of vision as the physical sense most capable of apprehending religious insight is instructive, for by transferring the normative human sense to hearing,[28] Luther rejects, among other things, the necessity of concentrated activity on the part of the hearer of the Word. The appropriate posture of the human being before God is passivity; the Word is active, confronting and accosting the hearer and creating the justification event:

25. *Lectures on Jonah* 1:1 (Latin text; *LW* 19.8).

26. Cf. Calvin's statement: "Place must be given to faith alone, whose nature it is to prick up the ear and shut the eye." *Institutes* 3.12.4 (Battles, 767).

27. See chapter 12 above, "Vision: The Eye of the Body and the Eye of the Mind in St. Augustine's *De Trinitate* and the *Confessions.*"

28. The first specific identification of passivity/hearing as the appropriate mode of human access to God of which I am aware is that of Meister Eckhart: "Hearing brings more into a man, but seeing he gives out more, even in the very act of looking. And therefore we shall all be blessed more in eternal life by our power to hear than by our power to see. For the power to hear the eternal word is within me, and the power to see will leave me; for hearing I am passive, and seeing I am active. Our blessedness does not depend on the deeds we do but rather in our passiveness to God . . . God has set our blessedness in passivity." Eckhart, *Meister Eckhart*, 108.

> Therefore the afflicted consciousness has no remedy against despair
> and eternal death except to take hold of the promise of grace of-
> fered in Christ, that is, this righteousness of faith, this passive or
> Christian righteousness. . . . I put myself beyond all active righ-
> teousness, all righteousness of my own or of the divine Law, and I
> embrace only that passive righteousness which is the righteousness
> of grace, mercy, and the forgiveness of sins.[29]

Luther's distinction between written and spoken words, and his identification of the Word with the spoken or proclaimed word, reinforces his insistence on the passivity of the hearer. The written text lacks the power of direct address that is a feature of the spoken word. The Word is made immediate and pressing in vocal presentation in a way that parallels and models the inner activity of the Word on a passive recipient. The greater passivity of the auditor over that of the viewer was often contrasted in medieval literature; the ear requires no focusing in order for sound to be heard—anyone in the vicinity of a sound of a certain loudness will hear it. Unlike vision, which originates with the viewer, hearing occurs when the ear is "struck" by a sound originating with the object. The written word, although it can certainly become Word to the reader, does not so aptly model the justification event as the spoken word. The reader is more active relative to the written text than is the hearer of the spoken word.

Ideally, Luther says, the Scriptures should not have been written: "Christ did not command the apostles to write, but only to preach."[30] "The Gospel should not be written but screamed."[31] The function of preaching is precisely this translation of the written word of Scripture into the living Word that transforms the existential situation of the hearer into the presence of God, a confrontation that questions, convicts, and redeems. Luther's description of the generation of the kind of human speech that reflects and communicates the inner activity of the Word appears, appropriately, in the *Magnificat*:

> But when one ponders well His divine works in the depths of the
> heart and regards them with wonder and gratitude so that one
> breaks out from very ardor into sighs and groanings rather than
> into speech; when the words, not nicely chosen nor prescribed,
> flow forth in such a way that the spirit comes seething with them,
> and the words live and have hands and feet, in fact, the whole body

29. "The Argument," *Lectures on Galatians* (LW 26.5–6).

30. Pelikan, *Luther the Expositor* (companion volume to LW) 63.

31. Ibid., 63–64.

and life with all its members strives and strains for utterance—that is indeed a worship of God in spirit and truth, and such words are all fire, light, and life.[32]

Although Luther himself never advocated the violent destruction of the images that were such an important feature of late medieval worship, he was not unaware of the logic of the iconoclastic activity that followed reformation ideas in Germany.[33] Characteristically, Luther's interest in the "bottom of the heart" to the point of indifference to externals was decisive in his attitude toward images:

> I approached the task of destroying images by first tearing them out of the heart through God's Word and making them worthless and despised. . . . For when they are no longer in the heart, they can do no harm when seen with the eyes.[34]

His senior colleague at the University of Wittenberg, Andreas Bodenstein von Karlstadt, had another view of the "harmlessness" of images. Karlstadt's essentially medieval understanding of the ease with which a person can think himself unattached to a particular practice until he attempts to relinquish it is the opposite of Luther's sense of the external as reflection or expression of the inward consciousness. Karlstadt, Luther wrote, "reversed the order by removing them [images] from sight and leaving them in the heart."[35]

In his statement about religious images, Luther was certainly concerned with the excessively visual nature of late medieval worship and devotional practice. Ulrich Zwingli, the reformer of Zurich, gives a catalogue of objectionable devotional practices that might well have been sufficient to sour Luther on images.[36] Yet it is Luther's apparent nonchalance about religious

---

32. *Magnificat* (*LW* 21.326) on Luke 1:49.

33. As Carl C. Christensen states: "Iconoclastic disturbances can be useful as an index of the degree of public support for the reform." *Art and the Reformation in Germany*, 23.

34. *Against the Heavenly Prophets in the Matter of Images and Sacraments* (*LW* 40.84).

35. Ibid. Karlstadt's statement is quoted by Christensen, *Art and the Reformation*, 25: "My heart since childhood has been brought up in the veneration of images, and a harmful fear has entered me which I would gladly rid myself of, and cannot. When one pulls someone by the hair, then one notices how firmly his hair is rooted. If I had not heard the spirit of God crying out against the idols, and read his word, I would have thought thus: 'I do not love images.' 'I do not fear images.' But now I know how I stand in this matter in relation to God and the images, and how firmly and deeply images are rooted in my heart."

36. "Men kneel, bow, and remove their hats before them; men name them after the saints whom they represent; men kiss them; men adorn them with gold and jewels; men

images that is striking. In the light of abundant information from the six-teenth century concerning the mania for images in popular devotion, Luther's mild attitude toward images, his willingness to maintain their usefulness for devotion and instruction, and his refusal to advocate their violent removal from churches seem all the more moderate. Again, his interest in conscious-ness preceding and governing all external activity is determinative.

Asceticism

We have already mentioned Luther's attitude toward a similarly "external" and highly valued religious activity of late medieval people—asceticism. Luther's standard formula for "practices" appears in the third of his ninety-five theses in his description of ascetic practices as "outward signs" of the ac-tivity of the Word in producing penitence.[37] He understands all influence to move from consciousness to external manifestation. He gives no evidence of understanding the capacity of ascetic practices to alter the habitual behavior that shields one from awareness of one's sins. Augustine's view of asceticism as working by external practices to effect true repentance is reversed in Luther's understanding of asceticism. Luther's "bodily mortifications" had not led to the dismantling of protecting habits that kept his soul invulnerable to feel-ing effective repentance, to seeing itself in an altered perspective, as corrupt and broken. Rather, for Luther, it was the Word that effected the intensifi-cation of consciousness in which he experienced simultaneously terror and assurance, nothingness and salvation. Thus in Luther's teaching, asceticism is the result of repentance, not a method of achieving it. Luther's emphasis on consciousness simultaneously turned attention away from the body and subordinated the human body to the status of a reflection of the spirit and soul. This metaphysical subordination of body to soul was surely not new, but it had been balanced, in medieval authors, with a practical understanding of bodily disciplines as method, as access to the soul.[38]

designate them with the appellation merciful or gracious; men seek consolation merely from touching them, or even hope to acquire remission of sins thereby" (ibid., 22).

37. "Such penitence is null unless it produces outward signs in various mortifications of the flesh." *Writings*, 490.

38. Cf. *The Freedom of a Christian*: "We must, however, realize that these works reduce the body to subjection and *purify it of its evil lusts*, and our whole purpose is to be directed only to the driving out of lusts. Since by faith the soul is cleansed and made to love God, it desires that all things, and especially its own body, shall be purified so that all things may join with it in loving and praising God. . . . In this way everyone will easily be able to learn for himself the limit and discretion, as they say, of his bodily castigations, for he will fast,

Luther's instructions concerning ascetic practice thus give no general rules nor even guidelines but allow for two kinds of asceticism. First, he advocates that each human being regard the external conditions of her/his life as precisely the condition in which one can "exercise oneself and suffer" productively. Marriage, the life of a clergyman, temporal rule, even, in the 1519 treatise, "The Holy and Blessed Sacrament of Baptism," religious orders, are to be understood as conditions, "instituted by God," in which a person may begin to fulfill his/her baptism in "toil and labor to kill the flesh and accustom it to death."[39] The ordinary daily disciplines that follow from one's "estate," rightly regarded as conditions for spiritual growth, thus become an invaluable ascetic practice. In marriage, for example,

> He who binds himself to the estate of matrimony, walks in the toils and sufferings which belong to that estate and lays upon himself its burdens, in order that he may grow used to pleasure and sorrow, avoid sin, and prepare himself for death better than he could do outside of that estate.[40]

Secondly, Luther describes an individualized asceticism designed to address the particular compulsions that damage a person's spiritual growth by sub-ordinating it to pursuit of "all that is pleasing for this life."[41] Both of these forms of asceticism follow from one's baptismal vows in which "the dying or drowning of sin" is undertaken. Baptism, in turn, renders all the ordinary sufferings of life, "especially death, profitable and helpful; they simply have to serve baptism in the doing of its work, the slaying of sin."[42]

---

watch, and labor as much as he finds sufficient to repress the lasciviousness and lust of his body" (ibid., 68). Two suggestions are made in this passage: first the suggestion that bodily disciplines are effective in addressing what is essentially a bodily problem—lust. This is in striking contrast to medieval authors who, taking their clue from Augustine, understand lust as a disorderly energy of the soul that imposed itself on the body and used the body as its tool and expression. See my *Augustine on the Body*, chapter 3 and passim. Secondly, Luther here, as elsewhere, describes the purification of the body to follow as the result of the soul's cleansing.

39. *LW* 35.39.
40. Ibid., 41.
41. Ibid., 39–40.
42. Luther, *Writings*, 65.

"Taste Death as if It Were Present"

Luther's references to present embodied experience range widely, as is well known, from the trivialization of the body in some of his scatological remarks to profoundly loving statements about the care of the body as a "Christian work."[43] He did not understand the body's role in religious practice as earlier theologians had, but there is one aspect of physical existence that interested Luther as a theologian of consciousness directly. That aspect is the death of the body. Luther had two different ways of speaking about the death of the body, depending on whether he was concerned to correct a nonproductive terror, or whether he wanted to intensify the terror of death in order to force consciousness to the point of collapsing into trust in the mercy of God.

At first consideration these texts seem contradictory: is death a bonus and a blessing, a "short and sweet sleep," entirely natural and "pictured to us in the day and night, and in the change and alteration of the seasons"? Is death already destroyed by "Christ, the destroyer of death"?[44] Or is it an evil, the evidence and experience, even for the Christian, of God's wrath against the "flesh"?[45] Should the Christian be unmoved by the terror of death, since "for the believer death is thus already dead and behind its cloak and mask it holds no terrors."[46] And what are we to make of his enigmatic statement: "Fear of death is death itself and nothing else. Anybody who has torn death from deep down in his heart does not have death or taste it"?[47] Is his occasionally matter-of-fact acceptance of death to be understood as his "real" view of death?

> Although we are otherwise mortal on account of our sins, if we die in behalf of the Word of God our death will be very costly. We'll all be saints, and our hide will be sold dearly enough.[48]

43. Ibid.

44. *LW* 54.296.

45. Ibid., 65; *Table Talk*, recorded by Veit Deitrich, 1531–33: "I don't like to see examples of joyful death. On the other hand, I like to see those who tremble and shake and grow pale when they face death and yet get through. It was so with the great saints; they were not glad to die. Fear is something natural because death is a punishment." See also *Fourteen Consolations* (*LW* 42.129): "There is no one who would not choose to submit to all other evils if thereby he could avoid the evil of death. Even the saints dreaded it, and Christ submitted to it with trembling fear and bloody sweat."

46. "The Future Blessing," *Fourteen Consolations* (*LW* 42.150).

47. *Table Talk* (*LW* 54.429), recorded by Caspar Heyenreich; see also *LW* 42.142: "For us death is dead."

48. Ibid., 336; *Table Talk*, recorded by Anthony Lauterbach.

Luther's first interest in death seems to minimize or even deny the reality of death for the Christian. Death ends not only the pains and evils of this life, but the sins and vices that perpetually beset the Christian. From the perspective of this viewpoint, death is a blessing, "if we but realized it." "Thus death," Luther writes, ". . . delivers us from these perils, and cuts sin fully away from us."[49] But the death of a Christian has an irreducible ambiguity: the simultaneity of the death of the "flesh" and the death of the body makes death ambiguous. It is at once the final victory and the final defeat of the devil:

> So many members as we have, so many deaths have we. Death peeps out at every limb. The devil, a causer and lord of death, is our adversary, and hunts after our life; he has sworn our death and we have deserved it; but the devil will not gain much by strangling the godly; he will crack a hollow nut. Let us die, that so the devil may be at rest.[50]

Luther found, even in the midst of the pains and evils to which the body is vulnerable, sufficient reason to anticipate the resurrection—not of the "flesh" but of the body; he writes, in a 1528 sermon on the Catechism:

> When we Germans hear the word "flesh" (*Fleisch*), we immediately think that what is being spoken of is flesh in a meat market. What the Hebrews call flesh we call "body"; hence I believe that our body will rise from death and thus live eternally.[51]

Luther's selection for his own epitaph was his translation of Job 19:25–26: "I know that my Redeemer lives, and he will waken me out of the earth, and I will go about in my body and in my flesh will I see God."[52]

Luther's second interest in death, however, finds in the terror of death the paradigm of the justification event in which the Christian, totally devoid of schemes for self-help, cries out for deliverance. Luther repeatedly instructs his hearers to contemplate their own death in order to gather the concentration of consciousness necessary for the realization of their plight before God.

---

49. *Fourteen Consolations* (LW 42.150).

50. *Table Talk of Martin Luther*, 320.

51. Luther, *Writings*, 213.

52. *Christian Songs, Latin and German for Use at Funerals*; *Works* (Jacobs translation) 6.290.

"I say die," Luther wrote, "taste death as if it were present." "How will it be with you in the hour of death?"[53]

The *Commentary on Jonah* presents Jonah's expectation of imminent death as the paradigm of the situation in which God acts to rescue. Jonah, "unaware of his delivery, . . . did not think any other way than that his death was certain and imminent. Thus he felt and tasted death."[54] In addition, Jonah knew himself to be experiencing the anger of God. Jonah's situation, however, is only an intensified version of the inevitable aspect of God's wrath in the death of every Christian. Luther makes the curious statement that the death experience is more difficult for Christians than for "heathens" because the Christian recognizes the wrath of God in the experience of death and is in terror of God's anger.[55] It is in the face of this wrath that Jonah must throw himself upon God's mercy, and it is often, as with both the Ninevites and Jonah, only the terror of death that brings human beings to this point ("That dread of death was good for them, for they were turned to the true God").[56] "In order that the terror of death might be all the greater, not only was Jonah thrown into the sea, where there was no hope for help either from God or man, but when he thought that he must surely die, he was also swallowed alive by a fish."[57] Jonah's consciousness in this situation of imminent death is painstakingly described by Luther:

> God takes on a glowering mien. It seems that His anger is not appeased by the death and the penalty . . . and that He cannot avenge Himself fiercely enough on him. It must have been a horrifying sight to poor, lost, and dying Jonah when the whale opened its mouth wide and he beheld sharp teeth that stood upright all round like pointed pillars or beams and he peered down the wide cellar entrance to the belly.[58]

It is at this point, when Jonah is grappling with "nothing but thoughts of death," that "different thoughts come to mind"; Jonah says, according to Luther:

53. *Magnificat* (*LW* 21.306) on Luke 1:46.

54. *Lectures on Jonah* 2:1 (German text; *LW* 19.70).

55. *Table Talk* (*LW* 54.190).

56. *Lectures on Jonah* 3:9 (German text; *LW* 19.89).

57. Ibid., 15 (Latin text).

58. Ibid., 67 (German text).

> Just when I lay in the depth of death, when hope was at its lowest ebb, yes, when it seemed impossible that I should live, then You appeared on the scene with Your might and miracle and led my life away from death and perdition.

Luther comments, "The rope breaks when it is at its tightest."

> First God grants grace and spirit to cheer the heart, He reminds it of God's mercy, dismissing thoughts touching on God's wrath, turning the heart from God the Judge to God the Father. But this does not lie in the power of man; for Jonah says here that his soul fainted within him and that faintheartedness was the strength and power of his soul. But the fact that he thinks about himself and begins to have faith is not the work of his soul. The Spirit, and no one else can bring the Lord to mind.[59]

Jonah's experience of redemption in the midst of death illustrates the experience of justification of every Christian.

The Sacraments: "Practice for Dying"

Thus, the Christian is not without preparation for the inevitably harsh experience of physical death; it has become a learned and reinforced response for Christians constantly to turn to the merciful God out of the depths of misery. The keen insight of the heart—"Take note what sharp eyes the heart must have"—has learned to perceive even in its present sinful state the continuing "consolation" of forgiveness: "A Christian is not one who has no sin, or feels no sin, but one to whom God imputes not sin because of his faith in Christ. This doctrine brings strong consolation to afflicted consciences in serious and inward terrors."[60]

But there is also a more specific "practice for dying." In the sacraments, the Christian has been trained to orient him/herself entirely to the *promise* of God that informs the sacrament.[61] Baptism, the sacrament of death and rebirth, begins the "drowning of sin" that will be completed only at death.[62]

---

59. Ibid., 79.

60. *Commentary on Galatians* (1531); Luther, *Writings*, 112.

61. "These promises of God are holy, true, righteous, free, and peaceful words; the soul which clings to them with a firm faith will be so closely united with them and altogether absorbed by them that it will not only share in all their power, but will be saturated and intoxicated by them." *The Freedom of a Christian*, in *Writings*, 58. See also Luther's "A Sermon on Preparing to Die" (1519) in *LW* 1 passim.

62. *A Treatise on Baptism* (1519), in *Works* (Jacobs translation) 1.57.

Baptism and death are similar in structure: both recaptiulate the justification event in which the Christian calls to God in faith in the midst of death—symbolic or literal. The whole of the Christian life, Luther says, is nothing but an extension of baptism:

> This life is nothing else than a spiritual baptism which does not cease till death, and whoever is baptised is condemned to die; as though the priest, when he baptises, were to say, "Lo, thou art sinful flesh; therefore I drown thee in God's Name, and in God's Name condemn thee to thy death, that with thee all thy sins may die and be destroyed." . . . The sooner after baptism a person dies, the sooner is that person's baptism completed; for sin never entirely ceases while this body lives, which is so wholly conceived in sin that sin is its very nature. . . . So, then, the life of a Christian, from baptism to the grave, is nothing else than the beginning of a blessed death, for at the Last Day God will make the Christian altogether new.[63]

Both baptism and the Lord's Supper are, for Luther, exercises in learning "to pay more heed to the word than to the sign."[64] The complicated arguments of the reformers concerning the status of the elements of the Lord's Supper were not as interesting to Luther as was his idea of the sacrament as a training for death:

> We see now how necessary this sacrament is for those who must face death. . . . Therefore it is also profitable and necessary that the love and fellowship of Christ and all saints be hidden, invisible and spiritual, and that only a bodily, visible and outward sign of it be given to us. For were this love, fellowship and help known to all, like the temporal fellowship of human beings, we should not be strengthened nor trained thereby to put our trust in the invisible or eternal things, or to desire them, but should much rather be trained to put our trust only in the temporal, visible things and to become so accustomed to them as to be unwilling to let them go and to follow God onward; we should thus be prevented from ever coming to Him, if we followed God only so far as visible and tangible things led us. For everything of time and sense must fall away, and we must learn to do without them, if we are to come to God.[65]

63. Ibid., 57–58.

64. *The Babylonian Captivity of the Church* (*LW* 36, passim).

65. *A Treatise Concerning the Blessed Sacrament* (1519), in *Works* (Jacobs translation) 2.24–25.

The training Christians receive in participation in the sacrament, then, makes the Lord's Supper "for us a ford, a bridge, a door, a ship, and a litter, in which and by which we pass from this world into eternal life."[66]

We began with a discussion of Luther's central insight and the starting point of his theology, that is, his identification of the individual subjective consciousness as the location of the justification event. From this perspective it has been possible to understand his anthropology as profoundly affected by his concern to demonstrate the exclusive centrality of consciousness in salvation. For Luther, the ambiguity of the human body is never fully overcome in this life. Nevertheless, the body reflects and participates in the justification event:

> The Holy Spirit gives people faith in Christ . . . , that is, he renews heart, soul, body, works, and conduct, inscribing the commandments of God not on tables of stone, but in hearts of flesh. . . That is the work of the Holy Spirit, who sanctifies and also *awakens the body to such a new life* until it is perfected in the life beyond.[67]

66. Ibid.

67. *On the Councils and the Church* (*LW* 41.145–46). Emphasis added.

CHAPTER 16

Theology, Anthropology, and the Human Body in Calvin's *Institutes of the Christian Religion*

Shines

in the mind of heaven   God
who made it
more than the sun
in our eye
(POUND, *CANTO* 51)

One of the most important questions to ask when one is beginning to reformulate the views of a historic author on the human body is the question of what role his discussion of the body plays in his theology. Does his theology require and depend on his evaluation of the meaning and value of the body? Do pressing polemical or cultural discussions demand the author's interest in describing the role of the body in human life?[1] These questions are consistently useful in illuminating the author's intent in writing about the body. Placing ideas of the body in the theological and anthropological context in which they appear is essential if we are to avoid the inevitable distortion of an author's ideas, which is the result of "proof-texting" the author's statements about the body. In approaching John Calvin's ideas of the human body, then, we will first ask what his central theological agenda is, that is, what it is that has energized and organized Calvin's theological work. We will discuss next Calvin's anthropology, the nature of soul and body and

---

1. As, e.g., Augustine of Hippo, challenged by Manichaean views of the body as well as a cultural strain of "body-hatred" (Dodds, *Pagan and Christian*, 29), had pressing psychological and polemical reasons for philosophical/theological integration and rehabilitation of the human body; see my *Augustine on the Body*.

270

their relationship to one another. Finally, we will explore the relationship of Calvin's view of the human body to his theology, asking whether there are aspects of this theology that we can understand more adequately after exploring his anthropology and idea of the body.

Calvin had one central interest that strongly organized his theological work: demonstrating, maintaining, and heightening the "glory of God," the pervasiveness and finality of God's ubiquitous will and work in the universe and in human affairs. God alone "fills"—in the sense of being interior to—the universe. In order to dramatize and display this vision of the glory of God, Calvin used the human race as a foil: all human faculties are vitiated and corrupted, all human works less than useless toward salvation. Calvin is explicit about his use of the human race as a foil: "Our insignificance is his exaltation." By definition, anything "our own" (*proprium*) is "naturally averse to God."[2] This is Calvin's vision, the impetus for his theology; it is also the foundation of some of his most difficult teachings. If we lose sight of Calvin's central interest in the "glory of God" and approach his statements about human being without this context, we will not adequately understand his anthropology, his idea of the human body, or his theology.

Calvin's theological agenda is the description of a *method* of achieving the consciousness of God's glory, for seeing what Calvin has seen. Calvin repeatedly characterizes the consciousness of the glory of God as "quickening" (*vivificatio*) a consciousness that has been trained and focused—as was Calvin's consciousness—on the glory of God that fills the universe. "Quickening," as Calvin describes it, is an intensely concentrated consciousness that cannot be equated simply with intellectual understanding.[3] "Quickening" is the result of the intimate connection of the believer with Christ by which "his life passes into ours and becomes ours, just as bread when taken for food gives vigor to the body."[4] "Quickening" is necessary if the Christian is to be able to see particular events and individual lives as a concrete form of God's glory. Only a supernaturally-heightened consciousness can achieve the requisite

2. Calvin, *Institutes* 3.3.8; see also 2.2.11: "Nostra humilitas eius est altitude." I have used the translation of the *Institutes* in the Library of Christian Classics by Ford Lewis Battles, except when otherwise indicated. All references are to the *Institutes*.

3. In a passage, e.g., in which Calvin discusses the significance of the Lord's Supper, he finds one important meaning of the sacrament to be the intention of Christ to teach that "we are quickened by the true partaking of him, which he designated by the terms eating and drinking, lest anyone should suppose that the life which we obtain from him is obtained by simple knowledge" (4.17.5).

4. Ibid.; see also 3.1.2.

speed and agility to perceive as "the glory of God" the kaleidoscope of rushing lifefulness that everywhere meets the eye. Calvin uses many images of change speeded up to a terrifying rate; for him the glory of God is, in the words of the poet Rainer Maria Rilke, "nothing but beginning of Terror that we're still just able to bear." Everything "rushes headlong," although "everything longs for permanent existence . . . that fixed condition which nowhere appears on the earth."[5] The world of human experience is a "slippery place,"[6] not only externally, but in every human being's most intimate experience: the human body is "unstable, defective, corruptible, fading, putrid, and pining," and the mind is equally untrustworthy in its "boiling restlessness . . . the fickleness with which it is borne hither and thither, [and in its] eagerness to hold op- posites at one time in its grasp, its ambition."[7]

Calvin proposes no political or social solutions for the slippery condi- tion of human life; in external things, he counsels only a status quo. He uses the idea of "calling" to absolutize the condition in which a person finds himself:

> Therefore, lest through our stupidity and rashness everything be turned topsy-turvy, he has appointed duties for each man in his particular place in life. And that no one may thoughtlessly trans- gress his limits, he has named these various kinds of living "call- ings." Therefore each individual has his own kind of living assigned to him by the Lord as a sort of sentry post so that he may not heedlessly wander about throughout life. . . . no one, impelled by his own rashness, will attempt more than his calling will permit, because he will know that it is not lawful to exceed its bounds.[8]

Calvin effectively blocks every impulse to social or political reform. The natural world, human events and conditions are to be accepted as given, as- signed, or imposed by God. This reduction to "duty" of all external activities has the effect of diverting the instinct to rectify, adjust, or reform to subjec- tive activity.[9] But a person's subjective condition is equally "assigned" by God, and work on one's own psyche is entirely within the Providence of God so that, for example, an individual will learn to turn toward the light—or will

5. Ibid., 3.9.5.

6. Ibid., 3.10.1.

7. Ibid., 3.10.6.

8. Ibid.

9. Ibid., 1.16.6.

not, and will not even want to—just as God gives. Just as a person busily endeavored to construct a new ground of inner activity on which to take his stand on the very abyss on which he finds himself when the total governance of the external world is recognized, Calvin effectively whisks away this pitiful piece of threadbare carpet on which the person had been balancing so that there is nothing, nothing to do, nothing to own, nothing to be, but all suddenly—if the legerdemain works—appears in its true form as the glory of God. It is only from this perspective that self-knowledge and knowledge of God is possible. Both appear simultaneously,[10] and it is this simultaneous understanding of self and God that Calvin called "quickening." It is invariably preceded by the apprehension and experience of terror of the nothingness of all human endeavor. Quickening occurs when a person responds to this terror with faith:

> When a man is laid low by the consciousness of sin and stricken by the fear of God, and afterwards looks to the goodness of God—to his mercy, grace, salvation, which is through Christ—he raises himself up, he takes heart, he recovers courage, and as it were, returns from death to life.[11]

That which keeps human beings from seeing this in-side of events, their "order, method, and necessity,"[12] is "sluggishness," a term Calvin uses again and again, along with synonyms: torpor, lethargy, intoxication,[13] dullness of apprehension.[14] It is this inertia that is overcome by "quickening." Just as the natural world and the world of human affairs are only rightly seen from the perspective of the quickened consciousness, even Christian doctrine is only perceived accurately—so that it collapses from abstraction into immediacy—from this perspective:

> For it is a doctrine not of the tongue but of life. It is not apprehended by the understanding and memory alone, as other disciplines are, but it is received only when it possesses the whole soul, and finds a seat and resting place in the inmost affection of the

---

10. Ibid., 1.1.1–3; see also 115.1: "We cannot clearly and properly [*liquido et solide*] know God unless the knowledge of ourselves be added."

11. Ibid., 3.3.3; "respiciens, sese erigit respirat [literally, begins to breathe] animum colligit, et velut e morte in vitam redit."

12. Ibid., 1.16.9.

13. Ibid., 3.12.8.

14. Ibid., 1.15.3.

> heart. . . . it must enter our heart and pass into our daily living, and
> so transform us into itself that it may not be unfruitful for us. . . .
> its efficacy ought to penetrate the inmost affections of the heart,
> take its seat in the soul, and affect the whole man a hundred times
> more deeply than the cold exhortations of the philosophers.[15]

But quickening, the intensification of consciousness by which the
Christian understands the whole energy of the universe to be the glory of
God, does not provide a *method* of incorporating this vision into a whole
human life. Quickening only becomes "sanctification"—the lifestyle that
continuously appropriates the quickened consciousness—when the Christian
finds a method of weaving together "holiness" and this intensified and concentrated consciousness.[16] It is this process that interests Calvin most when
he describes the quickened consciousness.[17] And it is this process/progress in
the Christian life that is more important than any yardstick of achievement:

> I do not insist that the moral life of the Christian breathes nothing
> but the very gospel, yet this ought to be desired, and we must strive
> toward it. . . . But no one in this earthly prison of the body has
> sufficient strength to press on with due eagerness, and weakness so
> weighs down the greater number that, wavering and limping and
> even creeping along the ground, they move at a feeble rate. Let
> each one of us, then, proceed according to the measure of his puny
> capacity and set out upon the journey we have begun. No one
> shall set out so inauspiciously as not daily to make some headway,
> though it be slight. Therefore, let us not cease so to act that we
> may make some unceasing progress in the way of the Lord. And
> let us not despair at the slightness of our success for even though
> attainment may not correspond to desire, when today outstrips
> yesterday the effort is not lost. Only let us look toward our mark

---

15. Ibid., 3.6.4.

16. Surely this is an enormously important insight of Calvin's, which cannot receive
adequate treatment in terms of a contemporary application in this essay. The contemporary
cultural location of "intensity" in erratic/erotic activity makes it difficult for us to recognize
in Calvin's theology precisely the rejection of this identification—a rejection of the "spicy
by-taste"—and a method for integrating intensity and integrity. Calvin's testimony that
this identity of the "heightened consciousness" and "holiness" is a human possibility must
be taken seriously before we can understand the method he recommends for achieving it.
If we remain unable or unwilling to "vision" this possibility, Calvin's method will never
achieve greater significance in our minds than anachronistic interest in a quaint historical
devotional exercise.

17. Ibid., 3.6.5.

with sincere simplicity and aspire to our goal; not fondly flattering ourselves, nor excusing our own evil deeds, but with continuous effort striving toward this end: that we may surpass ourselves in goodness until we attain to goodness itself.[18]

How, then, is the Christian to effect this steady working of the quickening of Christ into his life? This renovation, which Calvin insists is "not accomplished in a moment, a day, or a year, but by interrupted, sometimes even slow progress,"[19] is to be accomplished by a careful and continuous balancing of "repentance" and "gratitude." His objection to "certain learned men who lived long before the present day" and divided the doctrine of repentance into a temporal succession of "mortification" and "quickening" is that repentance and gratitude cannot be distinguished temporally; both must be held in suspension in a cyclic oscillation that corrects the preponderance of either. The Christian must learn to balance repentance with gratitude lest an overdose of repentance bring discouragement; he must learn how to balance gratitude with repentance lest an overdose of gratitude bring that slackening of attentiveness that Calvin calls "sluggishness." The Christian life is, for Calvin, exactly this process of translating "quickening" into the method of repentance and gratitude that both generates and stabilizes the Spirit-given energy:

> The Spirit is called the Spirit of sanctification, because he quickens and cherishes us, not merely by the general energy which is seen in the human race, as well as other animals, but because he is the seed and root of heavenly life in us.[20]

The method, then, of repentance and gratitude is the lifestyle by which the Christian translates "quickening" into a Christian life that retains both intensity and "holiness."

What role does the human body play in "quickening"? Before we can answer this question we must examine Calvin's anthropology, which begins with a familiar statement of the differentiation of body and soul: "There can

18. Ibid.

19. Ibid., 3.3.9.

20. Ibid., 3.1.2; Calvin puts more emphasis on urging that repentance should "in every Christian, last as long as life," than that gratitude should be continually interwoven as method because repentance had not been seen as method but only as part of a temporal penitential sequence (3.3.3), whereas, from the earliest Christian pre-theological descriptions of the content of Christian faith, gratitude was seen as a continuous component of the Christian life.

be no question that human being consists of a body and soul, meaning by soul an immortal but created essence, which is its nobler part."[21] The term "spirit" is also important to Calvin and is used, he says, ambiguously: when used alone, it is equivalent to soul, but when used in addition to soul, it becomes the awareness of good and evil, or conscience.[22] But the relationship of the parts of human beings differs at different moments of the experience of the human race. Calvin, who is against the "nice" distinctions of "the philosophers and Thomas,"[23] finds it irreducibly necessary to talk about human being in three different moments of experience. Congruent with his theological project of describing the glory of God, Calvin gives a before-and-after picture of the human being; a third condition, the future resurrection of the body, although not yet experienced, completes Calvin's anthropological discussion. Not to make these distinctions would be to give a reductionistically foreshortened version of human being, which would not provide the context in which Calvin's vision of God's glory can be apprehended. Again, Calvin's literary method "heightens" the original condition of human being as the good creation of God and its "miserable condition" as fallen. The resurrection of the body, which completes and complements the soul's immortality, is also used as a foil to display the present fallen condition of human being. We will follow Calvin's lead by discussing his anthropology in these three stages.

Calvin begins to discuss the state of "original integrity."[24] by discussing the creation of the first human being as image and likeness of God. After rejecting the traditional distinction between these terms, he defines the image and likeness of God as extending "to everything in which the nature of human being surpasses that of all other species of animals."[25] The picture he paints is one of spontaneous and effortless integration:

---

21. Ibid., 1.15.2; translation mine.

22. There is still a question in my mind as to whether *conscientia* is more adequately translated "conscience" or "consciousness." Although the latter word appears broader—and hence, perhaps, vaguer—some modern definitions of consciousness place the irreducible valuing function of conscious activity as central to its definition. This may be quite close to Calvin's understanding of *conscientia*—as awareness of good and evil—and therefore closer to our use of "consciousness" than to our understanding of the traditional term "conscience" which now connotes for us a self-judging and usually self-condemning psychic activity.

23. Ibid., 1.15.7–8.

24. Ibid., 1.15.1.

25. Ibid., 1.15.3.

> By the term "image of God" is denoted the integrity with which
> Adam was endued when his intellect was clear, his affections sub-
> ordinated to reason, all his senses duly regulated, and when he
> truly ascribed all his excellence to the admirable gifts of his maker.
> And though the primary seat of the divine image was in the mind
> and the heart, or in the soul and its powers, there was no part even
> of the body in which some rays of glory did not shine. . . . At the
> beginning the image of God was manifested by light of intellect,
> rectitude of heart, and soundness of every part.[26]

In this integrity, human being was accurately regarded as "a mirror of the
divine glory." Locating the image of God in the soul, Calvin finds the most
intimate evidence and experience of the fall in the soul's dramatically weakened capacity to maintain the integrity of body and soul. God's likeness in
the human soul is, quite literally, "the internal good of the soul,"[27] not something adventitious or external to human being. Thus, the results of the fall are
experienced in one's "inmost heart." When the image and likeness of God in
the human soul is "vitiated, almost destroyed, nothing remaining but a ruin,
confused, mutilated, and tainted with impurity," the intimate repercussions
"almost destroy" the integrity of human being.[28]

Thus the soul, as the "highest part" of human being is both the place
of the image and likeness of God in the state of original integrity, and the
location of the crippling effects of the corruption of the image through the
sin of the first human beings. In the present state, then, instead of a clear mirror that accurately reflects God, human being is rather the crazily distorting
glass of the funny house. To the question—variously answered by traditional
Christian authors—as to whether the image of God referred to woman as
well as to man, Calvin explicitly says yes; he corrects the apparent misogyny
of 1 Cor 11:17 "in which the man alone, to the express exclusion of the
woman, is called the image and glory of God." It is evident, Calvin says, "that
it merely refers to the civil order," and that woman, because of being capable,
as is man, of "spiritual and eternal life" shares in creation in the image and
likeness of God. The civil order that subordinates woman is symptomatic of
the fallen condition of human being.[29] A summary of the entire saga of the

26. Ibid., 1.15.3–4; Beveridge translation.

27. Ibid., 1.15.5.

28. Ibid., 1.15.4; the result of the fall is the "fearful deformity" (*horrenda sit deformitas*)
of human being.

29. Ibid.

experience of the one human psyche in which all human beings participate is given in Calvin's summary of the permutations of the image of God in the soul:

> Therefore, as the image of God constitutes the entire excellence of human nature, as it shone in Adam before his fall, but was afterwards vitiated and almost destroyed, nothing remaining but a ruin, confused, mutilated, and tainted with impurity, so it is now partly seen in the elect, in so far as they are regenerated by the Spirit. Its full lustre, however, will be displayed in heaven.[30]

Calvin chooses to keep to a simple schema in describing "parts" of the soul. He distinguishes only for the purpose of describing an anthropology that reinforces and supports his vision of the glory of God. Therefore, he distinguishes only intellect and will: "The intellect is to us, as it were, the guide and ruler of the soul; [and] the will always follows its beck and waits for its decision in matters of desire."[31] In the original state, "human being excelled in these noble endowments . . . when reason, intelligence, wisdom, and justice sufficed, not only for the organization of this life on earth, but also for coming to God and eternal happiness."[32]

But the soul cannot exist without a "habitation." The body is, for Calvin, quite simply the habitation of the soul; it depends on the soul for life:

> [Although] the substance of the soul is incorporeal, we must now add that though it is not properly enclosed by space, it however occupies the body as a kind of habitation, not only animating all its parts, and rendering the organs fit and useful for all their actions, but also holding the first place in regulating their conduct.[33]

The soul *does* everything. But the condition of the body accurately and intimately reflects the state of the soul; in original integrity, as we have seen, there was "no part of the body in which some rays of glory did not shine." In the fallen state, the body, still the perfectly accurate reflection of the dynamics of the soul, becomes problematic. But this we will look into more in a moment.

Calvin is eager to underline the distinction of body and soul. His assignment of all activity to the soul and his emphasis on the passivity of the

30. Ibid.; "Plenum vero fulgorem obtinebit in coelo."

31. 1.15.7.

32. 1.15.8; translation mine.

33. 1.15.6; Beveridge translation.

body are both consonant with traditional Christian authors and congruent with his own theological agenda.[34] It is immediately apparent in his discussion that the reason for exaggerating the difference of soul and body is for the purpose of firmly ensconcing the soul in immortality. Calvin wants to be careful not to "attach the powers and faculties [of the soul] so much to the present life that nothing is left external to the body."[35] This is a crucial point; we will not understand Calvin until we have realized its importance to him.[36] There lurks in humanity, Calvin writes, "something separated from the body":

> The body is not affected by the fear of spiritual punishment, which falls upon the soul only; from this it follows that the soul is endowed with essence. Now the very knowledge of God sufficiently proves that souls, which transcend the world, are immortal, for *no transient energy could penetrate to the fountain of life* [ad vitae fontem non pervenerit vigor evanidus]. . . . For sense perception inhering in brute animals does not go beyond the body, or at least extends no farther than to material things presented to it. But the nimbleness of the human mind in searching out heaven and earth and the secrets of nature, and when all ages have been compassed by its understanding and memory, in arranging each thing in its proper order, and in inferring future events from the past, clearly shows that there lies hidden in human being something separate from the body. With our intelligence we conceive the invisible God and the angels, something the body can by no means do. We grasp things that are right, just, and honorable, which are hidden to the bodily senses. . . . unless the soul were something essential, separate from the body, Scripture would not teach that we dwell in houses of clay and at death leave the tabernacle of the flesh.[37]

Body, in itself, then, for Calvin, is that part of a human being that is without affectivity, without psychological predicates, without animation, that is, the part buried at death.

34. Ibid., 1.15.2; see also 1.15.5.

35. Ibid., 1.15.6.

36. Again, we should acknowledge that at least a part of the contemporary interest in the human body, and the feeling that historical theologians have not described the physical aspect of human being in an adequate way, comes from a lack of interest in immortality—the very center of Calvin's concern. Many of us want the "powers and faculties of the soul" firmly attached to "this present life." Calvin emphatically did not.

37. Ibid., 1.15.2; emphasis mine.

In speaking of the body in the present condition of human being, Calvin shows a rather curious ambivalence about the body that can only be understood in the context of his identification of the purpose of the body as the habitation of the soul. "When the soul is freed," he writes, "from the prison-house of the body, God becomes its perpetual keeper."[38] Since the soul's present condition is ambiguous, both reflecting and in daily struggle with corruption and "taint," the body demonstrates—bodies forth—an analogous struggle. On the one hand, Calvin frequently uses such descriptions of the body as prison-house,[39] fetters, and infirmity.[40] Each of these metaphors relates to the quotation above that while the soul is housed in the body, it is not housed with God, but must participate in the struggle of the soul. Quoting Paul's "so long as we are present in the body, we are absent from the Lord" as a leitmotif throughout the *Institutes*,[41] Calvin speaks metaphorically of the body as "tabernacle," which is his favorite expression to describe the ambiguity of the "habitation" that keeps the soul occupied with its care and maintenance and reminds it of its alienation from God, its true home. On the other hand, however, Calvin makes the surprising statement that the body needs no earthly conversion, and that is why the rebirth of the soul will not affect the body until the resurrection. Calvin clustered all the faculties and energies of human being in the soul; yet his interest—even in terms of which aspect of human being to blame for sin—remains with the soul.

"A person must be born again because he is flesh. He requires not to be born again with reference to the body."[42] Here we face a most important distinction in Calvin's thought between "flesh" and "body." Curiously, the soul participates in "flesh" more than the body does. Using Paul's synecdoche, "flesh," to designate the whole human being in the fallen condition of sinfulness, Calvin reduces human being to two organized activities, both located in the soul: flesh and spirit. Spirit has direct access to the Spirit of God, as evidenced in the sense of immortality and the capacity for distinguishing between good and evil:

---

38. Ibid.

39. Ibid., 1.15.2; 3.9.4; 3.6.5, etc.

40. Ibid., 3.6.5.

41. Ibid., 1.15.2; 3.25.1; 3.9.5, etc.

42. Ibid., 2.3.1; ". . . oportere hominem renasci, quia caro est. Non secundum corpus renasci praecipit."

> Conscience, which, distinguishing between good and evil, re-
> sponds to the judgment of God is an undoubted sign of an im-
> mortal spirit. How could motion devoid of essence penetrate to
> the judgment seat of God, and under a sense of guilt strike itself
> with terror?[43]

We will have occasion to look again at this quotation when we have seen
Calvin's care to characterize "flesh" in a way that clears the body of responsibility for sinful activity.

As we have seen, Calvin uses "spirit" *either* to designate the soul, when
human being is analyzed into two categories, or to refer to conscience or
consciousness of good and evil, when human being is analyzed as body, soul,
and spirit. In the former usage, Calvin can say that there are "two parts in
which the taint of sin resides," in the flesh and the spirit.[44] Everything not
informed by the Spirit of God is "flesh"—whether it be human flesh or human spirit, Calvin tells us; both are synecdoches for human being under
different aspects:

> In the contrast between spirit and flesh, there is nothing left of an
> intermediate nature. In this way everything in humanity which is
> not spiritual falls under the denomination of carnal. But we have
> nothing of the Spirit except through regeneration. Everything,
> therefore, which we have from nature is flesh. . . . Grant that there
> is nothing in human nature but flesh, and then extract something
> good out of it if you can. But it will be said that the word *flesh*
> applies only to the sensual, and not to the higher part of the soul.
> This, however, is completely refuted by the words both of Christ
> and his apostle. . . . a person must be born again because he is
> flesh. He requires not to be born again with reference to the body.
> . . . he places depraved and unlawful desires not in the sensual
> part merely, but in the mind itself. . . . The human mind receives
> a humbling blow when all the thoughts which proceed from it are
> derided as foolish, frivolous, perverse, and insane.[45]

"Flesh," then, is an attitude of mind in alienation from God that uses
and abuses the body *and* the soul in its compulsive grasping at sensory ob-

43. Ibid., 1.15.2; see n. 22 on *conscientia*.

44. We must be careful here, though, not to equate "flesh" and "body" (as the argument
of this section has shown), as we are explicitly invited to equate soul and spirit.

45. Ibid., 2.3.1: "Sic enim carni comparatur spiritus, ut nihil relinquatur medium.
Ergo quidquid non est spirituale in homine, secundum eam rationem dicitur carneum.
Nihil autem habemus spiritus, nisi per regenerationem"; see also 3.14.1.

jects. The whole human being in its present condition can be identified by Calvin with "flesh": "A person must be born again because he is flesh."[46] And: "As we are formed by nature, sooner shall oil be extracted from a stone than good works from us."[47] Apparently, "flesh" is the governing aspect of human nature.

Calvin uses the term "nature" with considerable ambiguity. Often, as in the quotation above, he uses "nature" as the origin of "flesh": "Everything which we have from nature is flesh."[48] But in other places he insists that human beings, despite their fallen condition, have a "natural" access to the knowledge of God *through their own nature*:

> Let each of us, therefore, in contemplating his own nature, re-member that there is one God who governs all natures, and, in governing, wishes us to have respect to himself, to make him the object of our faith, worship, and devotion. Nothing, indeed, can be more preposterous than to enjoy those noble endowments which bespeak the divine presence within us, and to neglect him who, of his own good pleasure, bestows them upon us.[49]

Even the central duty of human being—the knowledge of God—is contained in human nature itself:

> Though the stupid hardness in their minds, which the impious eagerly conjure up to reject God, wastes away, yet the sense of divinity, which they greatly wish to have extinguished, thrives and presently burgeons. From this we conclude that it is not a doctrine that must first be learned in school, but one of which each of us is master from his mother's womb and which nature itself permits no one to forget, although many strive with every nerve to this end.[50]

Calvin's tortuous use of "nature" in the following quotation also betrays the ambiguity that the word has for him:

---

46. Ibid., 2.3.1: "Est igitur caro quidquid habemus a natura."

47. Ibid., 3.14.5.

48. We must note, however, that even the term "flesh" has a range of uses and does not always designate a sinful agenda for Calvin; see, e.g., 3.7.6: the stranger as "your own flesh"; 3.25.7 the "resurrection of the flesh."

49. Ibid., 1.5.5.

50. 1.3.3: "Cuius neminem oblivisci natura ipsa patitur."

> Humanity is corrupted by a natural viciousness, but not from one which proceeded from nature. In saying that it proceeded from nature, we meant that it was rather an adventitious event, which befell humanity, than a substantial property assigned to us from the beginning.[51]

When Calvin is referring to nature as ordered by God—either the natural world, or human nature—both creation and creatures mirror the activity of God and are accessible testimony of God's glory. The human race is "a bright mirror of the Creator's works,"[52] and creation, as mirror of God's works, is not a "book" to be lightly skimmed:

> There can be no doubt that the Lord would have us constantly occupied with such holy meditation, in order that, while we contemplate the immense treasures of wisdom and goodness exhibited in the creatures, as in so many mirrors, we may not only run our eye over them with a hasty, and, as it were, evenescent glance, but dwell upon them long and seriously and faithfully turn them in our minds, and every now and then bring them to recollection.[53]

Yet, consonant with his theological project of exaggerating the helpless inadequacy of human being in order to heighten the glory of God, Calvin most frequently finds "our own nature" (*proprium*) the source of all wickedness, the helpless pawn of "flesh":

> For when they [the prophets] recall man from evil, they demand the destruction of the whole flesh, which is full of evil and of perversity. It is a very hard and difficult thing to put off ourselves and to depart from our inborn disposition. Nor can we think of the flesh as completely destroyed unless we have wiped out whatever we have from ourselves. . . . the first step toward obeying his law is to deny our own nature.[54]

Calvin's description of "flesh" as the repository of all evil is related to his central vision of the glory of God and his agenda of describing the "quickening" of the Spirit that allows one to grasp this vision. It is the flesh that is responsible for the sluggishness, lethargy, torpor, dullness, and stupefied condition that is the opposite of quickening. The debility of inertia that prevents

51. Ibid., 2.2.11; Beveridge translation.
52. Ibid., 1.5.3.
53. Ibid., 1.14.21.
54. Ibid., 3.3.8: "Illa naturae nostrae abnegatio."

even saints from advancing with "quickened pace" toward God is explicitly identified with "flesh" in *Institutes* 3.19.4:

> [Even the saints,] although they love God with their mind, and with a sincere affection of the heart, yet both are still in a great measure occupied with the lusts of the flesh, by which they are retarded and prevented from proceeding with quickened pace towards God. They indeed make many efforts, but the flesh partly enfeebles their strength, partly binds them to itself.[55]

Clearly, it is "flesh," and not the body that is the location of the "sluggishness" that opposes the quickening of the Spirit of God. Is the body, then, totally exonerated from responsibility for human sinfulness? In the fallen condition of human being, the body shares with the rest of creation in bearing "part of the punishment" by its participation in a world in which the whole order of nature has been confused,[56] but Calvin is careful to emphasize that "the offense is not with the work itself but with the corruption of the work."[57] The body plays no role, for Calvin, either in the corruption of the soul or in its own corruption, but is the helpless victim, along with the soul, of the destructive hegemony of "flesh."

Yet, while the regenerate soul, by making Christ the object of its attention and affection, can be rehabilitated in part to its original condition as the image of God, so the body can also begin, even under the conditions of this life, to participate in the soul's quickening. It is in Calvin's teaching on the sacraments that we can see most clearly the present possibility he finds for the human body. The quickening, which is his great concern, operates in the Christian's body and is mediated through participation in the body of Christ in the sacraments of the church:

> For how little assurance would you grasp if you heard that the Word of God . . . contains in itself fullness of life, but in and round about yourself nothing but death meets you and moves before your eyes? But when the Source of life begins to abide in our flesh, he no longer lies hidden far from us, but shows us that we are to

---

55. See also 3.14.1: "Flesh, under which name are comprehended all those works which are enumerated by Paul; adultery, fornication, uncleanness, lasciviousness, idolatry, witchcraft, hatred, variance, emulation, wrath, strife, seditions, heresies, envyings, murders, drunkenness, revellings, and all kinds of pollutions and abominations which it is possible to imagine."

56. Ibid., 2.1.5.

57. Ibid., 2.1.11.

partake of him. *But he also quickens our very flesh in which he abides,*
that by partaking of him we may be fed unto immortality. . . .
he teaches not only that he is life since he is the eternal Word of
God, who came down from heaven to us, but also that by coming
down he poured that power upon the flesh which he took in order
that from it participation in life might flow into us.[58]

The sacrament of baptism is informed by the same concrete connection of
Christ's body with the Christian's body:

For he consecrated and sanctified baptism in his own body, that he
might have it in common with us as the firmest bond of union and
fellowship which he deigned to form with us.[59]

This communication of quickening life depends on the premise that "our
bodies are the 'members of Christ.' . . . We perceive that all these things cannot take place unless he adheres to us wholly in body and spirit."[60] We cannot
analyze thoroughly Calvin's Eucharistic teaching here, but at the center of
this teaching is his insistently concrete view of the intimate connection of the
"symbol" of the breaking of bread with the "thing itself," the body of Christ
that mediates life to the Christian: "The flesh of Christ is like a rich and
inexhaustible fountain that pours into us the life springing forth from the
Godhead into itself."[61] It is the Spirit of Christ that forms "the bond of connection," and not that Christ is "annexed to the element of bread."[62] Because
Christ's body—like human bodies—continues to share limitedness in time
and place, "according to the invariable rule in the human body, and is contained in heaven, where it was once received, and will remain till it returns to
judgment," Calvin cannot accept the view that "the body of Christ, locally
present, [is] taken into the hand, and chewed by the teeth, and swallowed
by the throat."[63] Nevertheless, faith must conceive what "seems an incredible
thing, that the flesh of Christ, while at such a distance from us in respect of

58. Ibid., 4.18.8: "Sed descendendo vim istam in carnem quam induit, diffudisse, ut
inde ad nos vitae communicato promanaret." Emphasis mine.

59. Ibid., 4.15.6: "Ideo enim baptismum in suo corpore dedicavit et sanctificavit, ut
communeum eum nobiscum haberet, ceu firmissimum unionis ac societatis quam nobiscum inire dignatur est vinculum."

60. Ibid., 4.7.9.

61. Ibid.

62. Ibid., 4.17.12: "Vinculum ergo istius coniunctionis est Spiritus Christi, cuius nexu
copulamur."

63. Ibid.

place, should be food to us. . . . what our mind does not comprehend let faith conceive—that the Spirit truly unites things separated by space."[64] Because of the operation of the Spirit of Christ within the human spirit and body, not only is the human mind quickened, but the body is also vivified. Becoming "one body with him," the Christian, being made a partaker in his substance, "feels the result of this fact in the participation of all his blessings"[65]—an *embodied* experience.

We have yet to examine Calvin's description of the human body in resurrection, but before we do, we must ask again whether Calvin's esteem of the Christian body—which, as we have seen, can participate in the present life in the quickening of the soul by the Spirit of Christ—is without qualification. We will attempt to answer this question by looking at two aspects of Calvin's treatment of the present embodied condition. Both of these topics, death and the role of the body in consciousness (*conscientia*), uncover significant nuances of Calvin's view.

Death, like "flesh," is adventitious to human being for Calvin and is not a necessary or intrinsic feature of embodiment.[66] Like sexual lust, death is not located in the body but in "flesh," as the outcome and symptom of the fallen condition of humanity. Calvin's strong "denial of death" depends on the connection of death with "flesh," and the dissociation of death from the human body. The Christian should, Calvin says, "ardently long for death." Yet immediately following this statement he admits: "But everything longs for permanent existence." The Christian sheds both the "flesh" and the slippery fragility of life in the present world at death: "I therefore contend that we ought to look to future immortality, where we may attain that fixed condition which nowhere appears on the earth."[67] Calvin has dissociated "life" from biological life in order to locate it in perfect and permanent supply after the death of the "flesh."

Precisely because "life" is so consummately valuable, "if departure from the world is entrance into life, what is the world but a grave, and what is existence in it but immersion in death?"[68] But even in the midst of urging "greater alacrity and less hindrance in aspiring to the future and eternal life,"

64. Ibid., 4.17.10.
65. Ibid., 4.17.11.
66. Ibid., 3.25.7.
67. Ibid., 3.9.5.
68. Ibid., 3.9.4.

Calvin is careful to caution that it *is only* by comparison with the heavenly life that earthly life appears properly "disdained and contemned":

> Thus, when the earthly is compared with the heavenly life, it may undoubtedly be despised and trampled under foot. We ought never, of course, to regard it with hatred except in so far as it holds us subject to sin, and *even this hatred ought not to be directed against life itself.* . . . Still, let us ardently long for death and constantly meditate on it, and in comparison with future immortality, let us despise life.[69]

Seen in this light, Calvin labels "monstrous" the "blind and stupid longing of the flesh" to maintain itself in earthly existence:

> Surely it is no wonder if the natural awareness in us bristles with dread at the mention of our dissolution. But it is wholly unbearable that there is not in Christian hearts any light of piety to overcome and suppress that fear.[70]

Calvin's exhortations to long for death, however, even though he describes this longing as a longing for more life, are a denial of death in the sense that he does not entertain the fact that death touches the human being quite a bit more closely than his description acknowledges. The "flesh," the adventitious aspect of human being and the only aspect that merits death, is not the only part to experience it. The body also experiences death harshly and painfully.[71] In attempting to see why Calvin might have been committed to ignoring the body's experience of death, the quotation from the *Institutes* 1.15.2 given above (note 37) and the following quotation, also from 1.15.2, give a clue:

> Consciousness [*conscientia*], which, distinguishing between good and evil, responds to the judgment of God, is an undoubted sign of an immortal spirit. . . . The body cannot be affected by any fear of spiritual punishment. How could motion devoid of essence penetrate to the judgment seat of God, and under a sense of guilt strike itself with terror?

---

69. Ibid.; emphasis mine.

70. Ibid., 3.9.5.

71. See my *Augustine on the Body*, 120ff., for a discussion of Augustine's very different treatment of death as a "separation of body and soul," two aspects of human being that are joined by a "natural appetite" so that 'their separation is a "harsh and unnatural" experience (asperum sensum et contra naturam).

It is the mind and its potential for consciousness of the glory of God that interests Calvin and organizes his theological work. The body has no potential for consciousness and no role to play in the soul's quickening even though it participates, as we have seen, in the results of this powerful increment of concentrated attention by which the world is seen as God's glory. The body, for Calvin, is "motion devoid of essence"; the soul is "endowed with essence" precisely because it is capable of the terror that precedes and prepares the soul for quickening.

An interesting result of Calvin's lack of interest in the role of the body in consciousness is his discussion of ascetic practices. A long tradition of medieval thought on ascetic practice, which culminated in the work of Calvin's contemporary, Ignatius Loyola, had recognized that carefully designed ascetic practices became a method of gathering and focusing psychic energy, of breaking the habits of ordinary living, and of intensifying consciousness of the self and God.[72] These goals of asceticism might have attracted Calvin as valuable methods of achieving precisely the conscious focus that he prized. But his short discussion of private ascetic practice in the *Institutes* 4.12 gives no indication that Calvin recognized the value of "exercises" involving the body to collect psychic energy. Even the insight of Augustine—with which Calvin was familiar—that physical asceticisms directly transfer to the preparation of a particular state of soul[73]—has not outweighed in his mind the more immediate antagonism he felt toward the traditional ascetic practices advocated by the Roman church. The only value he acknowledges in the two practices he mentions—fasting and sexual abstinence—is their usefulness for aiding public and private prayer by a "disencumbered" mind. Predictably, Calvin emphasizes that public repentance requires and depends on "a feeling of the mind" that precedes and naturally results in "external manifestations."[74] There is none of Augustine's awareness that an exaggerated state of physical hunger can effect a correspondingly intensified longing in the soul in Calvin's mild acknowledgment of the usefulness of fasting:

> We certainly experience that after a full meal our mind is not so lifted up to God that it can be drawn to prayer with a serious and ardent affection and persevere in it.[75]

72. See my *Fullness of Life* for a discussion of Ignatian ascetic methods and goals.

73. *Augustine on the Body*, 62ff.; Augustine *De utilitate jejunii* 1.

74. Calvin, *Institutes*, 4.12.15: "in animi affectu."

75. Ibid., 4.12.16.

For Calvin the capacity of the soul to affect the body is not matched by any capacity of the body to affect the soul. The body remains "motion devoid of essence."

Nor can we reduce Calvin's disregard of traditional asceticism to his reformist antagonism to "Romish" practices. If he had not had an anthropology that permitted and supported his practical neglect of asceticism and a theological problem with the body as the unconscious "side-kick" of the soul, he might have had incentive to place more attention on an attempt to discern the value of asceticism, even though rejecting its development in the Roman church. Both Calvin's cavalier treatment of physical death and his relative disinterest in ascetic practices demonstrate a judgment that the real significance of the human body is its capacity to reflect the dynamics of the soul, whether in "original integrity," in the present embodied condition, or in the resurrection.

We have examined Calvin's description of the human body in the first two stages of human experience. We have seen that the body in the original created state was spontaneously integrated in the whole human being and shared in the glory of God; in the present experience, the body shares in the onus on the whole created world caused by the fall, but also shares in the quickening and sanctification process of the Christian. Just as the created world is not to be scorned or devalued except by comparison to the next world, the human body, in its capacity as "tabernacle" performs a necessary and valuable function that will only become unnecessary when the soul is "tabernacled in God." What, then, will be the condition of the body when it is no longer needed to house the soul?

Calvin's discussion of the resurrection begins with a consideration of current errors that he undertakes to refute. One group holds, Calvin says, that the soul will be given a new body in the resurrection. The "unworthiness" of the present body to share in the perfection of the resurrection is no argument that compels, however, because this is as if "there were no uncleanness in the soul; and yet this does not exclude it from the hope of heavenly life. . . . whatever now exists in us that is unworthy of heaven does not hinder the resurrection."[76] Quoting Paul's "I pray God your whole spirit, soul, and body to be preserved blameless unto the coming of our Lord Jesus Christ," Calvin adds his exegesis:

---

76. Ibid., 3.25.7.

He says "body" as well as "spirit and soul," and no wonder; for it were most absurd that bodies which God has dedicated to himself as temples should fall into corruption without hope of resurrection. What? *Are they not also members of Christ?* Does he not pray that God would sanctify every part of them, and enjoin them to celebrate his name with their tongues, lift up pure hands, and offer sacrifices? That part of human being which the heavenly judge so highly honors, what madness is it for any mortal to reduce to dust without hope of revival? . . . Nor, indeed, on any subject does Scripture furnish clearer explanation than on the resurrection of our flesh.[77]

Calvin also quotes Tertullian with evident relish: "Nay, as Tertullian says, 'he could not have spoken more expressly if he had held his skin in his hands.'"[78] It is because death is not a natural property of the body that the body is altered but not discarded at death: "For if death, which originated in the fall of human being, is adventitious, the renewal produced by Christ must be in the same body which began to be mortal."[79] The body, then, is not adventitious to human being, but an integral and permanent aspect. It is "flesh" that is responsible for the painful insubordination of the immortality of the soul represented by death; again, the body is in the role of helpless victim.

An indication of the significance of the resurrection of the flesh to Calvin's theology is contained in the statement: "He alone has made solid progress in the gospel who has acquired the habit of meditating continually on the blessed resurrection."[80] The immortal soul needs no resurrection; it is the resurrection of the body that should organize the Christian's consciousness. Calvin's instructions as to the place to which one's attention should be focused are crucially important if we are to understand his theology. Only from the perspective of the ultimate validation of all that naturally belongs to human being in the resurrection of the body can Calvin's difficult teaching concerning human experience as we know it be understood.

The Christian must put the energy and attention of contemplation on the resurrection. From this perspective, we can see the present life in the light in which Calvin presents it: "As shapeless ruins, all things in heaven

---

77. Ibid.; Beveridge translation; emphasis mine.

78. Ibid.; Tertullian *De resurrectione carnis* 51.

79. Ibid.

80. Ibid., 3.25.1.

and earth struggle for renovation."[81] From this perspective of perfection and permanence we can understand the pervasive weakness and helplessness of the world of our present experience. But how to achieve this admittedly non-experiential perspective? Calvin was not unaware that any attempt to contemplate the resurrection will bear the characteristic inadequacy of all human effort and will be colored by the vitiation and weakness of the mind in its fallen condition; it is plainly "too difficult for human apprehension to reach it."[82] All the Christian can do, with humility and longing, is to contemplate what is known from Scripture of Christ's resurrection body, "free from all corruption . . . a spotless body." "In this mirror," Calvin writes, "we behold a living mirror of the resurrection."[83] The only other idea needed in order fruitfully "to be perpetually occupied with this pursuit" is the awareness of the immense power of God to effect the resurrection: "It is difficult to believe," Calvin admits, "that after our bodies have been consumed with rottenness, they will rise again at their appointed time."[84] Only the combined scriptural "proof" of the "likeness of Christ's resurrection" and the omnipotence of God can generate and sustain the Christian's faith in the resurrection.

It is not, then, the immortality of the soul that is difficult to believe but the resurrection of the body. Calvin is most explicit concerning the aspect of human being that is the subject of the resurrection:

> Shall we say that the soul rests in the grave, that it may there hear the voice of Christ, and not rather that the body shall at his command resume the vigor which it had lost? . . . For what would avail to apply hands, feet, eyes, and tongues to the service of God did not these afterwards participate in the benefit and reward?[85]

Warning against "licentious indulgence in free and subtle speculation" on these matters, Calvin has Scripture to substantiate his affirmation that "the body in which we will rise will be the same as at present, but the quality will be different. . . . If Scripture has any authority with us, we cannot desire a clearer or stronger proof of any doctrine."[86]

---

81. Ibid., 3.25.2.
82. Ibid., 3.25.3.
83. Ibid.
84. Ibid.
85. Ibid., 3.25.7–8.
86. Ibid., 3.25.8.

Let us keep in mind Calvin's insistent instructions that the Christian concentrate his attention and affection on the consummation of human being in the resurrection of the body as we proceed to examine briefly whether we can understand Calvin's theology more adequately from this perspective.

> If our Lord will share his glory, power, and righteousness with the elect, nay, will give himself to be enjoyed by them; and what is better still, will, in a manner, become one with them, let us remember that every kind of happiness is herein included. . . . In short, as Christ, by the variety of his gifts, begins the glory of his body in this world, and gradually increases it, so he will complete it in heaven.[87]

If we have seen the conditions and events of the present life in relation to the fulfillment of the resurrection, Calvin says, it will be only a short step to recognizing the operation of the omnipotence and informing glory of God in the world of our experience. The difficult doctrine of predestination can only be perceived adequately with the quickened consciousness that the Spirit grants as the Christian focuses on the resurrection glory. Only this perspective—already a consciousness of election—apprehends what Calvin emphasizes as the inevitable sense of absolute safety that accompanies this understanding: "Nothing, therefore, which pertains to our safety will ever be wanting."[88]

Calvin would have been horrified, I think, by the casual ignoring of these instructions concerning the admittedly non-ordinary consciousness necessary for the understanding of the glory of God that informs the doctrine of predestination by generations following him who are fascinated and repelled by this teaching. If all the attention is on this doctrine rather than on the "faithful protection" of God, one of the pivotal elements of the quickened consciousness will be missing—gratitude:

> How great ingratitude would it be now to doubt whether this most gracious Father had us in his care, who we see was concerned for us even before we were born! How impious would it be to tremble for fear that his kindness might at any time fail us in our need, when we see that it was shown, with the greatest abundance of every good thing, when we were yet unborn! . . . we are indeed his faithful children, whom he has received into his faithful protection

87. Ibid., 3.25.10.

88. Ibid., 1.14.22: "Ergo nihil unquam nobis defutuum est quoad salutis nostrae referet."

to nourish and educate. We are therefore to await the fulfillment of all good things from him alone and to trust completely that he will never leave us destitute of what we need for salvation, and to hang our hopes on none but him![89]

Even the emphasis of Scripture, Calvin says, is on the resurrection to blessedness, "for Christ came properly not for the destruction of the world, but for its salvation." Although the resurrection to damnation is a necessary corollary to which we "must hold," still, "Scripture more often sets forth resurrection, along with heavenly glory. . . . in the creed also, there is mention solely of the blessed life."[90]

How does Calvin's view of the human body affect his larger theological agenda, that is, making explicit the implicit and pervasive glory of God and providing a method for achieving a state of consciousness that invites "quickening"? In particular we must focus on Calvin's repeated description of the doctrine of predestination as a "comforting doctrine." Unless we are willing to examine *both* our own governing assumptions *and* the texts in which Calvin describes his doctrine, we will not approach an understanding of these ideas. We have difficulty with understanding anything but the harshness of Calvin's view of predestination, I think, because we hold a very different view of the body than did Calvin. We might begin to describe this difference by asking in what anthropological context Calvin's teachings might be reasonable, intelligible, and attractive. This question shelves, for the moment, questions concerning the authority of scriptural or traditional Christian teaching, but it immediately illuminates our question concerning the relationship of Calvin's view of the body to his theology of the glory of God. If, we might answer, one thought of the human body as incapable of biological, affective, or conscious existence apart from the animating presence of the soul, it would not be so difficult conceptually to disconnect the life of the soul from the biological life. If, in addition, we were to grant that, if "life" is not identical with biological life, the enemy of human life might be no longer death, but deadness (sluggishness, torpor, inertia, lethargy, etc.), then the appropriate and natural human longing for "life" would not be fulfilled by the mere sustenance of biological life. If we then posited that even though the body is a lowly aspect of human being, since it is the soul that must sup-

---

89. Ibid.
90. Ibid., 3.25.9.

ply it with life,[91] it is still an integral and intimate aspect which continually demonstrates its affinity for the soul by accurately reflecting every nuance of the soul's life, we might conclude that the good of the whole human being was best attended to by focusing the entire attention and affection of the soul on the Source of its life. Finally, if we saw that the eventual fulfillment of human being would be the validation and glorification of the humblest aspect of human being—the body—we might have in place all the anthropological assumptions that would make Calvin's theology collapse into immediacy and become knowable to us.

But this is almost an impossible conceptual exercise for us. It is well-nigh impossible for modern people to organize consciousness around a center that is the resurrection of the body. We have lost Calvin's orienting point, and so we, who think of the human body in its present condition as containing our life, find it difficult to reconstruct the consciousness that is necessary for understanding Calvin's teaching on predestination and the omnipotent glory of God. The nuances of Calvin's distinctions between "body" and "flesh," between biological life and "life," are difficult to maintain for modern people who *want* our life "tied to the body," and who do not automatically make the distinction between "flesh" and body that Calvin found in Paul and continued to use.

Calvin's discussion of human being in the *Institutes* matches and supports his vision of the glory of God which is perceived by the quickened consciousness and worked into one's whole life—present life and the life to come—by the method of gratitude and repentance. The principle "parts" of human being, body and soul/mind, both have their roles to play in coming to God. The mind, as image of God, begins now to receive the "quickening Spirit of Christ"[92] and to become conscious of the glory of God; the body, as "member of Christ," receives, through the sacraments of the church, the "quickening of our very flesh in which Christ abides."[93] The effect of Calvin's idea of the passivity of the body and the activity of the soul is to relieve the body of responsibility for the sinful agenda of the "flesh," and to demonstrate the permanent integrity of the body in each of the stages of human experience.

91. Ibid., 1.15.6: "The soul occupies the body . . . not only animating all its parts, and rendering the organs fit and useful for their actions . . ."

92. Ibid., 1.15.4.

93. Ibid., 3.25.7; "Quid quod etiam membra stint Christi?"

Bibliography

Abbreviations

ACW   *Ancient Christian Writers: The Works of the Fathers in Translation*. Edited by J. Quasten, J. C. Plumpe, W. J. Burghart, J. Dillon, and D. D. McManus. New York: Newman, 1946–.

ALW   *Augustine, Later Works*. Library of Christian Classics 8. Tranlsated by John Burnaby. Philadelphia: Westminster, 1955.

ANF   *The Ante-Nicene Fathers: Translations of the Writings of the Fathers Down to A. D. 325*. Edited by Alexander Roberts and James Donaldson. Buffalo: Christian Literature, 1885–96.

FC   *Fathers of the Church*. Edited by L. Schopp, R. J. Deferrari, H. Dresler and T. P. Halton. Washington D. C., 1947–.

LW   Martin Luther's *Works*. Edited by Jaroslav Pelikan. 55 vols. St. Louis, MO: Concordia, 1955–86.

NPNF   *A Select Library of the Nicene and Post-Nicene Fathers of the Christian Church*. Edited by Philip Schaff. New York: The Christian Literature Company, 1880–.

PG   *Patrologiae Cursus Completus, Series Graeca*. Edited by J.-P. Migne. Paris: Migne, 1857–66.

PL   *Patrologiae Cursus Completus, Series Latina*. Edited by J.-P. Migne. Paris: Migne, 1844–65.

WSA   *The Works of Saint Augustine: A Translation for the 21st Century*. Translation and notes by Edmund Hill. Edited by John Rotelle. Brooklyn: New City, 1990–

Works cited

Alexander of Lycopolis. *An Alexandrian Platonist against Dualism: Alexander of Lycopolis' Treatise "Critique of the Doctrines of Manichaeus"*. Translated with an introduction and notes by P. W. van der Horst and J. Mansfield. Leiden: Brill, 1974.

Ambrose. *Epistulae*. FC 26.

Aquinas, Saint Thomas. *Summa Theologica*. Blackfriars edition. New York: McGraw-Hill, 1969.

Aristotle. *Nicomachean Ethics*. Translated by J. A. K. Thomson. Baltimore: Penguin, 1953. Also *The Nichomachean Ethics of Aristotle*. Translated and introduced by W. D. Ross. New York: Oxford University Press, 1954.

Arnheim, Rudolph. *Art and Visual Perception: A Psychology of the Creative Eye.* Berkeley and
     Los Angeles: University of California Press, 1965.
Ash, James L., Jr. "The Decline of Prophecy in the Early Church." *Theological Studies* 37,
     no. 2 (1976), 227-252.
Asmussen, Jes Peter. *Manichaean Literature.* Delmar, NY: Scholars' Facsimiles and Reprints,
     1975.
Athanasius. *Vita Antonii.* NPNF second series 4.
Augustine. *Acta contra Fortunatum Manichaeum.* NPNF first series 4.
————. *De baptismo.* NPNF first series 4.
————. *De bono coniugali.* In *Augustine: De bono coniugali, De sancta virginitate.* Edited
     and translated by P. G. Walsh. Oxford: Clarendon, 2001.
————. *De catechizandis rudibus.* NPNF first series 3.
————. *De civitate Dei.* In *De Civitate Dei: Concerning the City of God Against the Pagans.*
     Translated by Henry Bettenson. Harmondsworth, Middlesex: Penguin, 1984. Also
     in *The City of God Against the Pagans.* Translated by R. W. Dyson. Cambridge:
     Cambridge University Press, 1998.
————. *Confessiones.* In *The Confessions of Augustine.* Edited by John Gibb and William
     Montgomery. Cambridge: Cambridge University Press, 1908. Also in *Confessions.*
     Translated by Rex Warner. New American Library. New York: Mentor-Omega,
     1963.
————. *De continentia.* NPNF first series 3.
————. *Contra adversarium legis et prophetarum.* PL 42. CCL 49.
————. *Contra epistolam manichaei quam vocant fundamenti.* NPNF first series 4.
————. *Contra Faustum Manichaeum.* NPNF first series 4.
————. *Contra litteras Petiliani.* NPNF first series 4.
————. *De doctrina christiana.* Translated by D. W. Robertson, Jr. New York: Library of
     Liberal Arts, 1958. PL 3.
————. *Enarrationes in Psalmos.* NPNF 8. ACW 29–39.
————. *Enchiridion ad Laurentium de fide et spe et caritate.* FC 4.
————. *Epistulae.* FC 12, 13, 18, 20, 30, 32. NPNF 1.
————. *De fide et operibus.* In *Seventeen Short Treatises of S. Augustine, Bishop of Hippo.*
     Oxford: Parker, 1847.
————. *De fide et symbolo.* NPNF first series 3.
————. *De Genesi ad litteram.* ACW 41–42.
————. *De moribus ecclesiae catholicae.* NPNF first series 4.
————. *De moribus Manichaeorum.* NPNF first series 4.
————. *De musica.* FC 4.
————. *De natura boni.* NPNF first series 4.
————. *De nuptiis et concupiscentia.* NPNF first series 5.
————. *De quantitate animae.* FC 4.
————. *Retractationes.* FC 60.
————. *De sancta virginitate.* NPNF first series 3.
————. *Sermo 7.* "Ten Homilies on the First Epistle General of St. John." ALW.
————. *Sermones.* In *Sermons.* WSA III/6, III/7, III/10.
————. *Soliloquia.* In *Soliloquies.* FC 5. PL 32.
————. *De spiritu et littera.* In *The Spirit and the Letter.* ALW.
————. *Tractatus in epistolam Joannis ad Parthos.* ALW.
————. *De trinitate.* FC 45.
————. *De utilitate jejunii.* FC 30.

Bailie, Gil. *Violence Unveiled: Humanity at the Crossroads*. New York: Crossroad, 2001.

Barnes, Timothy D. *Tertullian: A Historical and Literary Survey*. Oxford: Clarendon, 1971.

Benjamin, Jessica. *The Bonds of Love*. New York: Pantheon, 1988.

————. *Like Subjects, Love Objects: Essays on Recognition and Sexual Difference*. New Haven: Yale University Press, 1995.

————. *Shadow of the Other: Intersubjectivity and Gender in Psychoanalysis*. New York: Routledge, 1998.

Beny, Roloff, and Peter Gunn. *The Churches of Rome*. New York: Simon & Schuster, 1981.

Bergman, Martin S. *In the Shadow of Moloch*. New York: Columbia University Press, 1992.

Blakney, Raymond Bernard. *Meister Eckhart: A Modern Translation*. New York: Harper, 1941.

Bowersock, G.W., Peter Brown, and Oleg Grabar, eds. *Late Antiquity: A Guide to the Postclassical World*. Cambridge: Harvard University Press, 1999.

Braham, Allan. "The Emperor Sigismund and the Santa Maria Maggiore Altarpiece." *The Burlington Magazine* 122 (1980) 106–12.

Brown, Peter. "Augustine and Sexuality." *Colloquy* 45. Berkeley: The Center for Hermeneutical Study, 1983.

————. *Augustine of Hippo*. New edition with epilogue. Berkeley: University of California Press, 2000.

————. *The Body and Society: Men, Women, and Sexual Renunciation in Early Christianity*. New York: Columbia University Press, 1988.

Butler, Judith. "The Lesbian Phallus and the Morphological Imaginary." *Differences* 4:1 (1992).

Bynum, Caroline Walker. "Religious Women in the Later Middle Ages." In *Christian Spirituality: High Middle Ages and Reformation*, edited by Jill Raitt. New York: Crossroad, 1987.

Calvin, John. *Institutes of the Christian Religion*. Translated by Ford Lewis Battles. Edited by John T. McNeil. The Library of Christian Classics 20–21. Philadelphia: Westminster, 1960.

————. *Institutes of the Christian Religion*. Translated by Henry Beveridge. Grand Rapids: Eerdmans, 1975.

Capps, Donald. "The Scourge of Shame and the Silencing of Adeodatus." In *The Hunger of the Heart: Reflections on the Confessions of Augustine*, edited by Donald Capps and James E. Dittes, 69–92. Society for the Scientific Study of Religion Monograph Series 8. West Lafayette, IN: Society for the Scientific Study of Religion, 1990.

Cary, Philip. *Augustine's Invention of the Inner Self: The Legacy of a Christian Platonist*. New York: Oxford University Press, 2000.

Chadwick, Henry. *Augustine*. New York: Oxford University Press, 2000, 1986.

Charles-Picard, G. *Les religions de l'Afrique antique*. Paris: Plon, c1954.

Chidester, David. *Word and Light: Seeing, Hearing, and Religious Discourse*. Chicago: University of Chicago Press, 1992.

Christensen, Carl C. *Art and the Reformation in Germany*. Boulder, CO: Ohio University Press, 1969.

Chrysostom. *Adversus Judaeos*. FC 68. PG 48.847.

Clark, Gillian. *Women in Late Antiquity: Pagan and Christian Lifestyles*. Oxford: Oxford University Press, 1993.

Clark, Elizabeth A. "'Adam's Only Companion:' Augustine and the Early Church Debate on Marriage." *Recherches Augustiniennes* 21 (1986) 139–62.

———. *Ascetic Piety and Women's Faith: Essays on Late Ancient Christianity*. Studies in Women and Religion 3. Lewiston, NY: Edwin Mellen, 1986.

Cochrane, Charles Norris. *Christianity and Classical Culture*. Oxford: Oxford University Press, 1940.

Codex Theodosianus. In *The Theodosian Code*, edited by Jill Harries and Ian Wood. Ithaca, NY: Cornell University Press, 1993.

Cooper, Kate. *The Virgin and the Bride: Idealized Womanhood in Late Antiquity*. Cambridge: Harvard University Press, 1996.

Courcelle, Pierre. *Recherches sur Les Confessions de Saint Augustine*. Paris, 1950.

Cushman, Robert. *Therapeia, Plato's Conception of Philosophy*. Westport, CT: Greenwood, 1958.

Cyprian. *Epistula*. ANF 3.

———. *De habitu virginum*. FC 36.

Cyril of Alexandria. *Epistle of Cyril to Nestorius*. Translated by Henry R. Percival. NPNF second series 14.

Darnton, Robert. *The Great Cat Massacre and Other Episodes in French Cultural History*. New York: Random House, 1985.

Davidson, Arnold I. *The Emergence of Sexuality*. Cambridge, MA: Harvard University Press, 2001.

Decret, Francois. *L'Afrique manichéenne, etude historique et doctrinale*. 2 vols. Paris: Études Augustiniennes, 1978.

D'Emilio, John. "Capitalism and Gay Identity." In *Powers of Desire: The Politics of Sexuality*, edited by Ann Snitow, Christine Stansell, and Sharon Thompson, 100–116. New York: Monthly Review, 1983.

Dodds, E. R. *Pagan and Christian in an Age of Anxiety*. New York: Norton, 1965.

Dronke, Peter. *Women Writers of the Middle Ages*. Cambridge: Cambridge University Press, 1984.

Dunkerton, Jill, Susan Foister, Dillian Gordon, and Nicholas Penny. *Giotto to Darer, Early Renaissance Painting in the National Gallery*. New Haven: Yale University Press, 1991.

Ebert, Teresa L. *Ludic Feminism and After: Postmodernism, Desire, and Labor in Late Capitalism*. Ann Arbor: University of Michigan Press, 1996.

Eckhart, Meister. *Meister Eckhart*. Translated by Raymond B. Blakney. New York: Harper and Row, 1941.

———. "This is another sermon." In *Meister Eckhart*, translated by Raymond B. Blakney, 103–8. New York: Harper and Row, 1941.

Elm, Susanna. *Virgins of God: The Making of Asceticism in Late Antiquity*. Oxford: Clarendon, 1994.

Erens, Patricia, ed. *Issues in Feminist Film Criticism*. Bloomington: Indiana University Press, 1990.

Euseubius. *Historia ecclesiastica*. NPNF second series 1.

———. *Vita Constantinii*. Translated by Ernest Cushing Richardson. NPNF second series 1.

Fingarette, Herbert. *Self Deception*. New York: Humanities Press, 1969.

Foucault, Michel. *The Archeology of Knowledge*. San Francisco: Harper Torchbooks, 1972.

———. *The Care of the Self*. New York: Pantheon, 1986.

———. *The History of Sexuality, Volume I: An Introduction.* Translated by Robert Hurley. New York: Vintage, 1980.

———. *Power/Knowledge.* Edited by Colin Gordon. New York: Pantheon, 1972.

———. *The Uses of Pleasure.* New York: Pantheon, 1985.

Fox, Robin Lane. *Pagans and Christians.* New York: Knopf, 1987.

Frend, W. H. C. "The End of Byzantine North Africa: Some Evidence of Transitions," 387–97. In *Archeology and History in the Study of Early Christianity.* London: Variorum Reprints, 1988.

———. "The Gnostic-Manichaean Tradition in Roman North Africa." *Journal of Ecclesiastical History* 4 (1953), 25–37.

———. "Manichaeism in the Struggle between Saint Augustine and Petilian of Constantine." *Augustinus Magister* 2 (1954), 859–66.

Freud, Sigmund. "Three Essays on the Theory of Sexuality." In *The Standard Edition,* Vol. 7, 130–243. London: Hogarth, 1953.

———. "The Sexual Life of Human Beings." In *The Complete Introductory Lectures in Psychoanalysis,* trans. by James Strachey, 303–19. London: Allen and Unwin, 1956.

Friedländer, Paul. *Plato.* Translated by Hans Meyerhoff. New York: Pantheon, 1958.

Futrell, Alison. *Blood in the Arena: The Spectacle of Roman Power.* Austin, TX: The University of Texas Press, 1997.

Gay, Volney P. "Against Wholeness." *Journal of the American Academy of Religion* 48, no. 4 (1979) 539–55.

Girard, Réné. *I See Satan Fall Like Lightning.* Translated by James G. Williams. Maryknoll, NY: Orbis, 2001.

———. *La Violence et le sacré.* Paris: Grasset, 1972.

———. *The Scapegoat.* Baltimore: Johns Hopkins University Press, 1986.

Goldhill, Simon. "The Erotic Experience of Looking: Cultural Conflict and the Gaze in Empire Culture." In *The Sleep of Reason: Erotic Experience and Sexual Ethics in Ancient Greece and Rome,* edited by Martha C. Nussbaum and Juha Sihvola, 374–99. Chicago: University of Chicago Press, 2002.

Grosz, Elizabeth. *Volatile Bodies: Toward a Corporeal Feminism.* Bloomington: Indiania University Press, 1994.

Harré, Rom. *Personal Being: A Theory for Individual Psychology.* Cambridge, MA: Harvard University Press, 1984.

Hennessy, Rosemary. *Profit and Pleasure: Sexual Identities in Late Capitalism.* New York: Routledge, 2000.

Holum, Kenneth G. *Theodosian Empresses, Women and Imperial Domination in Late Antiquity.* Berkeley: University of California Press, 1986.

Hopkins, Keith. Chapter 1, "Murderous Games," 1–30. In *Death and Renewal.* Cambridge: Cambridge University Press, 1983.

Hunt, E. D. "St. Stephen in Minorca, An Episode in Jewish-Christian Relations in the Early 5th Century AD," *Journal of Theological Studies* 33 (1982) 106–23.

Hunter, David G. "Resistance to the Virginal Ideal in Late-Fourth-Century Rome: The Case of Jovinian." *Theological Studies* 48 (1987).

Irigaray, Luce. "Sorcerer Speech: A Reading of Plato's *Symposium,* Diotima's Speech." In *Feminist Interpretations of Plato,* edited by Nancy Tuana, 181–96. University Park, PA: State University of Pennsylvania Press, 1994.

———. *Speculum of the Other Woman.* Translated by Gillian C. Gill. Ithaca, NY: Cornell University Press, 1985.

———. *This Sex Which Is Not One*. Translated by Catherine Porter. Ithaca, NY: Cornell University Press, 1985.

———. *To Be Two*. Translated by Monique M. Rhodes and Marco F. Cocito-Monoc. New Brunswick, NJ: Athlone, 1999.

Jacobs, Joseph. "Rome." *The Jewish Encyclopedia* 10 (1906) 444–68.

Jerome. *Adversus Jovinianum*. ANF 3.

Joannides, Paul. "The Cotonna Triptych by Masolino and Masaccio." *Arte Cristiana* 728 (1988) 339–46.

Jung, Patricia Beattie, Mary E. Hunt, and Radhika Balakrishnan, eds. *Good Sex: Feminist Perspectives from the World's Religions*. New Brunswick, NJ: Rutgers University Press, 2001.

Kader, Aicha Ben Abed, and David Soren. *Carthage: A Mosaic of Ancient Tunesia*. New York: American Museum of Natural History, 1987.

Kaplan, E. Ann. "Madonna Politics: Perversion, Repression, or Subversion? Or Masks and /as Mastery." In *The Madonna Connection*, edited by Cathy Schwichtenberg. San Francisco: Westview, 1993.

Kerr, Hugh T. *A Compend of Luther's Theology*. Philadelphia: Westminster, 1943.

Kingston, Maxine Hong. *China Men*. New York: Knopf, 1980.

Klein, Melanie. "A Study of Envy and Gratitude," in *The Selected Melanie Klein*, edited by Juliet Mitchell, 211–12. New York: The Free Press, 1987.

Klimkeit, Hans-Joachim. *Manichaean Art and Calligraphy*. Leiden: Brill, 1982.

Krautheimer, Richard. "The Architecture of Sixtus III: A Fifth-Century Renascence?" In *Essays in Honor of Erwin Panofsky*, edited by Millard Meiss. New York: New York University Press, 1961.

Langer, Susanne. *Philosophy in a New Key: A Study in the Symbolism of Reason, Rite, and Art*. Cambridge, MA: Harvard University Press, 1960.

Leder, Drew. *The Absent Body*. Chicago: University of Chicago Press, 1990.

Leo I, *Sermo* 24. In *Letters and Sermons of Leo the Great*, translated by Charles Lee Feltoe. NPNF second series 12.

———. *Sermo* 82. PL 54.422–28.

Levinas, Emmanuel. *Totality and Infinity*. Translated by Alphonso Lingis. The Hague: Martinus Nijhoff, 1961.

Lieu, Samuel N. C. *Manichaeism in the Later Roman Empire and Medieval China: A Historical Survey*. Manchester: Manchester University Press, 1985.

L'Orange, H. P., and P. J. Nordhagen. *Mosaics*. Translated by Ann E. Keep. London: Methuen, 1958.

Luther, Martin. *Martin Luther: Selections from His Writings*. Edited by John Dillenberger. New York: Anchor, 1961.

———. *On the Bondage of the Will*. Translated by Philip S. Watson. In *Luther and Erasmus: Free Will and Salvation*, edited by E. Gordon Rupp and Philip S. Watson. Philadelphia: Westminster.

———. *The Table Talk of Martin Luther*. Translated by William Hazlitt. London: G. Bell, 1875.

———. *Works*. American ed., edited by Jaroslav Pelikan. St. Louis: Concordia, 1955–86. Volume 19, edited by Hilton C. Oswald, 1974.

———. *Works of Martin Luther*. Translated by C. M. Jacobs. Philadelphia: Holman, 1932.

Manchester, Peter. "'As long as that song could be heard': Eternal Time in the *Trinity* of Augustine." In *The Subjective Eye: Essays in Culture, Religion, and Gender*, edited by Richard Valantasis, 59–70. Eugene, OR: Pickwick Publications, 2006.

Marion, Jean-Luc. *Being Given: Toward a Phenomenology of Givenness*. Translated by Jeffrey L. Kosky. Stanford, CA: Stanford University Press, 2002.

———. *God Without Being*. Chicago: University of Chicago Press, 1991.

Meer, Frederik van der. *Augustine the Bishop: The Life and work of a Father of the Church*. London: Sheed and Ward, 1961.

Migne, J. P., ed. *Patrologia Latine*. (*Confessionum; De civitate Dei; De doctrina Christiania; Epistula* 140; *Epistula* 133; *Enarrationes in Psalmos* 26; *Enarrationes in Psalmos* 130; *Sermo* 23; *Sermo* 216). Paris. Translations from *De civitate Dei* are adapted from Bettenson's translation.

Miles, Margaret R. *Augustine on the Body*. Missoula, MT: Scholars, 1979.

———. *Carnal Knowing: Female Nakedness and Religious Meaning in the Christian West*. Boston: Beacon, 1989.

———. *Desire and Delight: A New Reading of Augustine's "Confessions."* Reprint. Eugene, OR: Wipf and Stock, 2006.

———. "The Evidence of Our Eyes: Fourth-Century Roman Churches." In *Image as Insight: Visual Understanding in Western Christianity and Secular Culture*, by Margaret R. Miles, 41–62. Reprint. Eugene, OR: Wipf and Stock, 2006.

———. *Fullness of Life: Historical Foundations for a New Asceticism*. Reprint. Eugene, OR: Wipf and Stock, 2006.

———. *Image as Insight: Visual Understanding in Western Christianity and Secular Culture*. Reprint. Eugene, OR: Wipf and Stock, 2006.

———. *Plotinus on Body and Beauty: Society, Philosophy, and Religion in Third-Century Rome*. Oxford: Blackwell, 1999.

———. *Practicing Christianity: Critical Perspectives for an Embodied Spirituality*. Reprint. Eugene, OR: Wipf and Stock, 2006.

———. "Santa Maria Maggiore's Fifth-century Mosaics: Triumphal Christianity and the Jews." *Harvard Theological Review* 86, no. 2 (1993) 155–75.

———. "Vision: The Eye of the Body and the Eye of the Mind in Saint Augustine's *De Trinitate* and *Confessions*." *Journal of Religion* 63, no. 2 (1983) 125–42.

Miller, David L. "Orestes: Myth and Dream as Catharsis." In *Myths, Dreams, and Religion*, edited by J. Campbell. New York: E. P. Dutton, 1970.

Musurillo, Herbert Anthony, ed. *The Acts of the Christian Martyrs*. Oxford: Clarendon, 1972.

Nash, R. *The Light of the Mind: St. Augustine's Theory of Knowledge*. Lexington, KY: University of Kentucky Press, 1969.

Noonan, John T. *Contraception: A History of its Treatment by the Catholic Theologians and Canonists*. Cambridge, MA: Beknap, 1986.

Nussbaum, Martha C. *The Fragility of Goodness: Luck and Ethics in Creek Tragedy and Philosophy*. Cambridge: Cambridge University Press, 1986.

Nye, Andrea. "Irigaray and Diotima at Plato's Symposium." In *Feminist Interpretations of Plato,* edited by Nancy Tuana, 197–216. University Park, PA: State University of Pennsylvania Press, 1994.

O'Connell, Robert J. *St. Augustine's Confessions: The Odyssey of the Soul*. Cambridge, MA: Harvard University Press, 1969.

———. *St. Augustine's Early Theory of Man, 386–391*. Cambridge, MA: Harvard University Press, 1968.

Ottley, Robert L. *The Doctrine of the Incarnation.* London: Methuen, 1919.

Pedley, John Griffiths. *New Light on Ancient Carthage.* Ann Arbor: University of Michigan Press, 1980.

Piaget, Jean. *The Construction of Reality in the Child.* New York: Ballantine, 1954.

Plato. *Greater Hippias.* Translated by David R. Sweet. In *The Roots of Political Philosophy: Ten Forgotten Socratic Dialogues,* edited by Thomas L. Pangle, 314–39. Ithaca, NY: Cornell University Press, 1987.

————. *Phaedrus.* Translated by Harold North Fowler. Loeb Classical Library. Cambridge, MA: Harvard University Press, 1977.

————. *Philebus.* In *Collected Dialogues,* edited by Edith Hamilton and Huntington Cairns, 1086–1150. Bollingen Series 71. Princeton: Princeton University Press, 1978.

————. *Republic.* In *Collected Dialogues,* edited by Edith Hamilton and Huntington Cairns, 574–844. Bollingen Series 71. Princeton: Princeton University Press, 1978.

————. *Symposium.* Translated by Michael Joyce. In *The Collected Dialogues of Plato,* edited by Edith Hamilton and Huntington Cairns, 526–74. Princeton: Princeton University Press, 1961. Also in *The Dialogues of Plato,* vol. 2. Translated by Benjamin Jowett. London: Sphere, 1970.

————. *Timaeus.* In *Collected Dialogues,* edited by Edith Hamilton and Huntington Cairns, 1151–1211. Bollingen Series 71. Princeton: Princeton University Press, 1978.

Plotinus. *Enneads.* In *Plotinus,* translated by A. H. Armstrong, vols. 1–7. Loeb Classical Library. Cambridge, MA: Harvard University Press, 1966–1988.

————. *Plotinus.* Greek text with English translation by A. H. Armstrong. 7 vols. Loeb Classical Library. Cambridge, MA: Harvard University Press, 1966–1988.

Porete, Marguerite. *Speculum Simplicium Animarum.* In *Corpus Christianorum Continuatio Medievalis LXIX: Marguerite Porete, Speculum Simplicium Animarum,* edited by Paul Verdeyen, SJ. Turnholti, Belgium: Brepols, 1986. English translation: *A Mirror for Simple Souls: The Mystical Work of Marguerite Porete.* Edited and translated by Charles Crawford. New York: Crossroad, 1990.

Power, Kim. "*Sed unam tamen*: Augustine and His Concubine." *Augustinian Studies* 24 (1993) 49–76.

————. *Veiled Desire: Augustine on Women.* New York: Continuum, 1996.

Price, A. W. "Plato, Zeno, and the Object of Love." In *The Sleep of Reason: Erotic Experience and Sexual Ethics in Ancient Greece and Rome,* edited by Martha C. Nussbaum and Juha Sihvola, 170–99. Chicago: University of Chicago Press, 2002.

Raitt, Jill, ed. *Christian Spirituality: High Middle Ages and Reformation.* New York: Crossroad, 1987.

Ramirez, J. Roland E. "Demythologizing Augustine as a Great Sinner." *Augustinian Studies* 12 (1981) 61–88.

Rawson, Beryl. "Roman Concubinage." In *Transactions of the American Philological Association* 104 (1974) 279–305.

Reinach, S. "Le rire rituel." *Revue de l'Université de Bruxelles,* 1911.

Robinson, Marilynne. *Housekeeping.* New York: Farrar, Strauss & Giroux, 1980.

Rogoff, Irit. "Tiny Anguishes: Reflections on Nagging, Scholastic Embarrassment, and Feminist Art History." *Differences* 4, no. 3 (1992) 38–66.

Rousselle, Aline. *Porneia, Desire and the Body in Antiquity.* Oxford: Blackwell, 1988.

Renov, Michael. *The Subject of Documentary.* Minneapolis: University of Minnesota Press, 2004.

Rilke, Rainer Maria. *Duino Elegies.* Translated by J. B. Leishman and Stephen Spender. New York: Norton, 1963.

Ruether, Rosemary Radford. *Religion and Sexism: Images of Woman in the Jewish and Christian Traditions.* New York: Simon and Schuster, 1974.

Saxer, Victor. *Morts, martyrs, reliques en Afrique chrètienne aux premiers siècles.* Paris: Beauchesne, 1980.

———. *Vie liturgique et quotidienne à Carthage vers milieu du IIIe siècle.* Vatican City: Pontificio Instituto di Archeologia Cristiana, 1969.

Schüssler Fiorenza, Elizabeth, *In Memory of Her.* New York: Crossroads, 1983.

Shaw, Teresa M. *The Burden of the Flesh: Fasting and Sexuality in Early Christianity.* Minneapolis: Fortress, 1998.

Sheets-Johnstone, Maxine. *The Roots of Power: Animate Form and Gendered Bodies.* Chicago: Open Court, 1994.

Sieger, Joanne Deane. "Visual Metaphor as Theology: Leo the Great's Sermons on the Incarnation and the Arch Mosaics at Santa Maria Maggiore." *Gesta* 26 (1987) 83–91.

Simon, Marcel. *Verus Israel.* New York: Oxford University Press, 1986.

Simon, William. *Postmodern Sexualities.* New York: Routledge, 1996.

Skutella, Martinus, ed. S. Aureli Augustini, *Confessionum.* Stutgardiae in Aedibus: B. G. Teubneri. Translations from the *Confessionum* are adapted from Warner's translation.

Sorrell, Roger D. *St. Francis and Nature.* New York: Oxford, 1988.

Sozomen. *Historia ecclesiastica.* NPNF second series 2.

Spain, Suzanne. "'The Promised Blessing': The Iconography of the Mosaics of Santa Maria Maggiore." *Art Bulletin* 61 (1979) 518.

Stager, Lawrence W. "The Rite of Child Sacrifice at Carthage." In *New Light on Ancient Carthage*, edited by John Griffiths Pedley, 1–12. Ann Arbor: University of Michigan Press, 1980.

Stevens, Wallace. "Sunday Morning." In *The Collected Poems of Wallace Stevens*, 66–70. New York: Alfred A. Knopf, 1978.

Strehlke, Brandon, and Mark Tucker. "The Santa Maria Maggiore Altarpiece: New Observations." *Arte Cristiana* 719 (1987) 105–24.

Tertullian. *De baptismo.* ANF 3.

———. *De carne Christi.* ANF 3.

———. *De cultu feminarum.* ANF 4.

———. *De monogamia.* ANF 4.

———. *De pudicitia.* ANF 4.

———. *De virginibus velandis.* ANF 4.

———. *De resurrectione carnis.* ANF 3.

Thébert, Yvon. "Private Life and Domestic Architecture in Roman Africa." In *A History of Private Life*, vol. 1: *From Pagan Rome to Byzantium Paul*, edited by Paul Veyne, translated by Arthur Goldhammer. Cambridge, MA: Harvard University Press, 1987.

Thomas à Kempis. *The Imitation of Christ.* Translated by Betty I. Knott. London: Fontana, 1963.

Toner, J. P. *Leisure and Ancient Rome.* Cambridge: Polity, 1995.

Treggiari, Susan. "Concubinage." *Papers of the British School at Rome* 49 (1981) 59–81.

Vance, Carole S. *Pleasure and Danger: Exploring Female Sexuality.* Boston: Routledge and Kegan Paul, 1984.

Whitehead, Alfred North. *Adventures of Ideas.* New York: Macmillan, 1933.

Wiedemann, Thomas. *Emperors and Gladiators.* New York: Routledge, 1991.

Wilken, Robert. *John Chrysostom and the Jews: Rhetoric and Reality in the Late Fourth Century.* Berkeley: University of California Press, 1983.

Williams, J. G., ed. *The Girard Reader.* New York: Crossroad, 1996.

Williams, Linda. *Hard Core: Power, Pleasure, and the "Frenzy of the Visible."* Berkeley: University of California Press, 1989.

Wills, Gary. *Saint Augustine.* New York: Lipper/Viking, 1999.

Wimbush, Vincent L., ed. *Ascetic Behavior in Greco-Roman Antiquity: A Sourcebook.* Minneapolis: Fortress, 1990.

———, and Richard Valantasis, eds. *Asceticism.* New York: Oxford University Press, 1995.

Wittgenstein, Ludwig. *Philosophical Investigations.* Translated by G. E. M. Anscombe. New York: Macmillan, 1953.

Young, Iris Marion. "The Ideal of Community and the Politics of Difference." In *Feminism/Postmodernism*, edited by Linda J. Nicholson, 300–323. New York: Routledge, 1990.

Index

The Index that follows is selective, indicating major themes and subjects when they are discussed in the text, not merely mentioned in passing. It includes only authors whose arguments are discussed in the text; it does not include all authors quoted in footnotes and listed in the bibliography.